Yacht
RATING

also by Peter Johnson

Passage Racing
Ocean Racing and Offshore Yachts
Yachtsman's Guide to the Rating Rule
Boating Britain
The Guinness Book of Yachting Facts and Feats
The Guinness Guide to Sailing
Yachting World Handbook
Offshore Manual International
This is Fast Cruising
The Encyclopedia of Yachting
Whitbread Round the World 1973-93
Yacht Clubs of the World

Yacht RATING

170 years of speed, success and failure against competitors — and the clock

Peter Johnson

Bucksea Guides

First published in Great Britain 1997
by Bucksea Guides
Lymington, Hampshire SO41 9DT

A CIP catalogue record for this book is available from the
British Library.

ISBN 0 9529478 0 3

Typeset by Pardy and Son (Printers) Ltd, Ringwood,
Hampshire
Printed and bound by Hartnolls Ltd, Bodmin, Cornwall

Contents

Author's PREFACE   7
Author's INTRODUCTION   9
DEFINITIONS   12

1 CUTTER CRANKS AND TONNAGE
   TYRANNY   15
2 SKIMMING DISHES OF THE BELLE
   ÉPOQUE   38
3 RATINGS CROSS THE NARROW SEAS   66
4 THE COMING OF OCEAN RACING   94
5 GIVING AND GETTING TIME   123
6 KEEN RACING BUT NO RATING   141
7 FOR TWO DECADES: A WORLD RULE   166
8 SCATTER   214
9 WHAT SAILORS DID   248
10 TAKE YOUR PICK   284
11 RATING FOLLY IN THE PAST: SAILING
   FUN FOR THE FUTURE?   307

NOTES AND REFERENCES   319

APPENDIX I   THE INTERNATIONAL RATING
              CONFERENCE 1906   338
APPENDIX II   KEY OFFICIALS   339
APPENDIX III SUCCESSIVE RATING RULES
              USED FOR THE AMERICA'S CUP
              AND THE ADMIRAL'S CUP   340

SOURCES AND BIBLIOGRAPHY   341
ACKNOWLEDGEMENTS   345
INDEX   346

Photographs, pages i to xvi, are between pages 96 and 97

All line drawings and graphics by
Ray Harvey BSc CEng MRINA MIMarE MCSD

Author's Preface

'Why do holders of office so often act contrary to the way reason points and enlightened self-interest suggests? Why does intelligent mental process seem so often not to function?' – Barbara W. Tuchman in The March of Folly, 1984.

THIS BOOK is about how racing yachts and dinghies (sailboats or just boats, if you like) are enabled to race against each other so that such a contest means something and gives first class sport. To do this boats must be physically measured and then 'rated', or declared identical. If this was not done racing would be pointless. This need was swiftly found out early in the nineteenth century: ever since then sailors have created, maintained and often destroyed rules of measurement and what is known as 'rating'.

The process has been historical with lessons learned, and unfortunately also forgotten, in season after season. So in these pages will be found the succession of attempts over some 170 years to organize an effective rating rule. These efforts were most conspicuous in the USA and in England, but there always were and still are rating systems run for one country or another, or a group of countries (Scandinavia, for instance).

Today tennis rackets and golf balls have their own developing technology. It is hardly surprising that competition between machinery like cars, aeroplanes and boats, power, rowing and sail are very technical, complex – and enthralling. Surely it must be possible to simplify these matters, at least for sailing boats, blown along by the same wind. Yet attempts at simplification often lead to more difficulties.

In 1994, a local class on the south coast of England, the wooden day racing keel boat, the X-class, which had been racing every peacetime summer since 1909 and whose owners are essentially amateur and often middle-aged, was plunged into a measurement dispute which was fairly described as vicious. When newly built boats were found to have advantageous dimensions and the interpretation of the rules was disputed, there were writs flying around and owners and measurers of modest

means found even their houses and personal property
with the possibility of sequestration. A contributing
reason to all this feeling may have been that the rules
were a shade too simple.[1]

This recent squabble demonstrates that the history of
yacht rating is not merely technical, nor even a succession of pictures of attractive race boats. It is a micro-
cosm of the human ability to make laws which produce
the opposite effect to that intended, to fail to act in time,
to pursue self-interest, to ignore obvious evidence, to
believe against the facts one's own previous pronouncements – the list could continue. But as all this involves a
voluntary sport and on the whole fairly prosperous and
educated people in advanced countries, there is a moral.
They are not up against some of the hazards of life such
as crime, poverty or ambition. Yet in this privileged
world on the water still there is folly, be as it may in sport
rather than in world events, as referred to in the quote
above from Tuchman.[2]

For myself, I have been a user, sufferer and organizer
of, and writer about yacht rating since I sailed a little
boat, nearly forty years ago, to the head of an estuary
where an official measurer had his waterfront cottage.
There he measured my mini cruiser racer, lying afloat.
We rowed ashore to his house, where he worked out the
rating, using four figure logarithm tables on the rule
proforma on which he wrote with a fountain pen. This
was then folded into a gold embossed card wallet, which
he handed me in return for five guineas ($8.90 or £5.25).

Since then I have owned and sailed numerous rated
offshore yachts, one-designs and racing dinghies. As
time passed I found myself in positions of responsibility
in formulating and maintaining the rules. This in turn
led to lecturing about them and writing articles, then
books in which they appeared.

Now I have pulled together the resulting lessons, the
stories, the controversies and, if you will permit, opinions. The rating of yachts is a continuing topic among
sailors. These pages may help today's discussions and, I
sincerely hope, tomorrow's decisions.

Peter Johnson
Buckland Dene, Lymington, Hampshire,
SO41 9DT, England, 1997

Introduction
SOME AIMS OF YACHT RATING

'*While some attempt has been made to get a common rating rule with the British, and with the Royal Ocean Racing Club in particular, this has been, so far, impossible*'. – Herbert L. Stone on the CCA Rule 1946.[1]

A T THE HEIGHT of the season the harbour at Marblehead, Massachusetts, is packed with yachts on line after line of moorings. The very sight typifies American east coast yachting and particularly racing – traditional, wealthy, expert.

But April is early in this continental climate. Only a few boats are usually out and the yacht clubs are not fully open. However in April 1974, there was exceptional activity, albeit very much indoors. In the Eastern Yacht Club, one of America's most senior, the front rows of a conference in progress are occupied by influential sailors and owners.[2] Most are members of the Cruising Club of America, the New York Yacht Club, or the Eastern itself. These gentlemen, the world's top offshore yachtsmen, have opinions about the current ratings of their boats and are about to express these forcibly.

When I close my eyes I have a nightmare, but actually it is true memory though at the time I was not perturbed. Thinking back I am amazed how I took this in my stride. For on the podium facing the assembly I am about to reply to their comments, declare my rule philosophy and announce any changes to the International Offshore Rule with its 10,000 certified yachts around the world. Many of these are in the USA.

Of course I am not alone, indeed I am flanked by the chairman of the authority which controls the rule, though I am in charge of its technical committee. One or two other technical supporters are with us.

Then the questions begin: some are more like accusations. It was all some time ago now and the words have long since faded, but since then I have never underestimated the controversy and feeling that can be aroused by yacht rating rules. There are at least two kinds of person making complaints in this kind of gathering: those who object to supposed features of the rule and those whose own yacht has a too high a relative rating against its competitors. They are impossible to tell apart.

What we do not forget are those sailors who are not at the meeting! They are the ones who have gone away quietly, leaving the objectors to struggle with the authorities while they engage designers to devise yachts which will fare well under the rule of rating.

Not for the first time, there is a question, among others, about whether to adjust the rule to make it fair for existing yachts, or if it is better to allow the rule to run until designs to its formulae converge to give good sailing among similar types of boat. This is a recurrent difficulty with rules of rating.

In the pages which follow
There will be accounts of the politics of yachting (today newspapers run regular columns entitled 'sports politics') and particularly of rating rules, for human nature has made these inseparable from their administration. Closely connected to such a topic will be frank descriptions of the rating authorities. Do they keep in touch with sailors, or are they a closed circle of eternal committee men? With hindsight the ability of past authorities can be fairly quickly judged; present ones may be assessed towards the end of the book!

One way of calming all parties (owners, designers, rule makers and others who will appear on stage) in rating disputes is to recount that parallel conflicts have arisen in the past. This does not mean that the arguments over rating are insoluble; on the contrary it means 'there have been such proposals before. They have been solved (or proved wrong as the case may be) in the past; they have been solved more than once. Do not labour to reinvent the wheel'.

Here too will be found the life cycle of a rule of measurement, starting with high hopes, then ... but, no, you must read of the preordained desertion or decadence or ... what? Remember history often sees the same mistakes made a number of times, then quite suddenly be avoided, causing endemic problems to dissolve. Considered too is whether there is a typical period of time over which a rule will last.

Designers of cruising yachts never intended for racing have over the years copied some racing fashion in their design. As the racing boats are subject to rule influence, so the leading rules have determined in many aspects the design of all yachts. Some would dispute this, but we will be seeing how individual features and overall concepts owe much to rules. The results may be beneficial or otherwise. In other words all those interested or involved with the naval architecture of sailing yachts may enjoy some acquaintance with the progress of rating and measurement. Sometimes it is a rating rule long discontinued which is the cause of some design conventions of today.

As for the kind of rating rules that this story will unfold, they will encompass those which measure all the main configurations of sailing yacht: ocean racers, keel boats (the conventional name for open day boats), multihulls and unballasted craft which include racing dinghies (centreboarders). These and other types will be defined.

There will be talk about one-designs (again, to be defined), for this is one avenue of escape from rating rules ... or is it? Its relationship to rating and measurement will be examined.

Topicality, references
This book is being completed in 1996-1997. There is for some a rating rule crisis: maybe, at any moment, there always was! Inevitably the most recent scene receives the author's comments; one hopes any remarks are not out of line with what might be said a few years on. As we discovered at the Marblehead meeting, opinions on rating rules get strong expression; so it will not be surprising if the author comes to firm conclusions. The reader can if he wishes form alternative views from the uniquely collected information in all these pages.

Already we have been scattering around some technical terms and in these preliminaries an early opportunity is taken (below) to make quite sure we all understand the same things by words such as 'rating', 'handicap', 'one-design' 'measurement', even 'fast' and 'slow'.

Lastly, this work is also provided as a reference for sailors, owners, designers and general readers: superscript figures in the text will be found to refer to notes whose purpose is mentioned just below.

ITALICS
When type appears in italics (except for boat names, book names etc), the italics are the author's unless otherwise stated as 'original italics'. The emphasis has been used to highlight decisions, results or opinions in the argument on yacht rating rules.

It is hoped that the reader does not find this technique distracting.

NOTES AND REFERENCES

Superscript numbers in the text like this[2] refer to quite extensive notes, chapter by chapter, starting immediately after Chapter 11. These are full of facts and anecdotes, as well as sources of authority for statements and quotes. They are part of the narrative; worth a book mark or a marline spike, left in there while reading the ordinary text.

DEFINITIONS

The following are some terms used in the world of yacht rating.[3] It seems advisable to state exactly what these ones mean when used in this book. Many other technical words and phrases are simply explained in the text as they occur, as are some of these more fully.

Federation Francaise de Voile (FFV)   National authority for yacht racing in France, previously *Federation Francaise de Yachting au Voile (FFYV)*. There are yachting authorities for all countries mentioned in this book and some others will occur in text.

Fleet   American term for all the boats in a given race, or all the boats measured to a particular rating rule. In USA there are *fleet* positions or placing in race results; in Europe there is less emphasis on this, but there may be reference to 'overall placings'.

Handicap   General term for variation in time allowances, or rating given to a yacht, hence *handicap racing, handicap class(es)*. More common in America; in Europe the class would more likely be referred to as 'IOR class' or 'class 2' (if '2' was the division).

   The word originated in the 17th century from 'hand in the cap', a game in which the competitors deposited forfeit money in a cap and the parties drew out full or empty hands. This developed into a term for a sporting challenge in which one person challenged for some article of another, while offering something of his own in exchange.[4] The concept of an unequal game extended to horse racing, where a disadvantage to one horse and jockey was (and is) administered by adding weight. A number of early yacht racing terms came from the turf; so early yachts had time added (subtracted) to their result as a *handicap*.

International class Strictly a term for those classes recognized as such by the ISAF. Obviously it gets used loosely for classes which are found in several countries.

International Sailing Federation (ISAF) See IYRU.

International Yacht Racing Union (IYRU) The world authority for yacht racing founded in 1906; essentially consists of the national authorities for yacht racing in each country. The name was changed on 1 August 1996 to *International Sailing Federation*. In this book the contemporary name is used, which for 90 years was IYRU; thus ISAF only appears when describing the present or at least 1996 and later.

Measurement The process of taking numerous dimensions of hull and rig to calculate a *rating* or confirm as a *one-design* or *restricted class.*

One-design Racing boats confirmed as exactly the same design, so first boat home is the winner (Chapter 6).

Production class Batches of similar boats from the same manufacturer. They may race together, but are not strictly controlled as is a *one-design*.

Time allowance A time allowed between one yacht and another in a race, which adjusts the time taken over the course to produce a result (full discussion in Chapter 5 and elsewhere). As a term, *time allowance* is preferred here to *handicap*, whenever applicable.

Tonnage Cargo capacity, used in early 19th century rules for arriving at a time allowance (Chapter 1).

Rating Figure allotted to a yacht which will determine her time allowance, under the system in use. If the ratings are equal the respective boats are racing level without time allowance.

Rating rule A complete system to supply ratings to each yacht.

Restricted class Boat regulated by maximum or minimum or exact dimensions for numerous aspects of the design. Within such restrictions and others on construction and so on, each boat can be separately designed. The boats then race without a time allowance.

Royal Yachting Association (RYA) National authority for all boating, including yacht racing, in the United Kingdom. Previously *Yacht Racing Association (YRA)*.

Scoring Term which in America can mean the application of *time allowances* to results. But not used in this book: instead see descriptions or discussions of *time allowance* methods.

US Sailing Association (USSA), abbreviated to *US Sailing (USS)* National authority for all yacht racing in the United States of America. Previously *US Yacht Racing Union (USYRU)* and before that *North American Yacht Racing Union (NAYRU)*, which then included Canada and Mexico.

Distances in miles refer to nautical miles (1 nautical mile = 6080 feet or 1853.2 metres). The length of yacht is the length overall (LOA) unless otherwise stated.

FORMULAE FOR RATING AND MEASUREMENT RULES. The mathematical notation is used like this: a/b means a divided by b, or 'a over b'. $(a)^{1/2}$ means the square root of a. $(a)^2$ means a squared, or a multiplied by a. $a \times b$ means a multiplied by b. For those familiar with other notation,

$(a)^{1/2}$ means $\sqrt{a}$

$(a)^{1/3}$ means $\sqrt[3]{a}$

$(a + L)/2.5$ means

$$\frac{a + L}{2.5}$$

Symbols used in rules and formulae are explained with them, but if not it means that the factor represented by the letter or letters is not of any interest!

1 Cutter cranks and tonnage tyranny

'It is to be hoped that the yachting historian of the twentieth century may reap a like benefit from our controversialists of today and that those mathematicians who now brandish their tonnage formulae to the terror of all quietly disposed yachtsmen will find a reader in the searcher after facts in 1994' – G.L.Watson[1] in *Yachting: the* Badminton Library, 1894.

CONTROVERSY dogged the earliest days of yachting. It immediately became evident that if different sizes of boat were to race together, there must be some form of allowance or the smaller vessel would not bother to sail again. But wait! If you spent the money and effort in building the biggest possible boat to go faster than all others, why should you not reap the reward on regatta day?

So this first chapter tells of the often frustrating attempts to devise forms of time allowance for yachts which went racing in the years before about 1880. It would be tedious to say over and over again that time allowances and handicapping invariably caused heated debate, but they certainly did!

Tonnage origins

There was a precedent for a higher rating for a bigger boat and that was in taxation. Benjamin Franklin said that nothing was certain except death and taxes. From earliest times ships were taxed by their cargo capacity, this often being measured by the number of barrels that could be carried. In fourteenth century England one standard barrel which was used to import wine was called a 'tun', 'containing not less than 252 gallons'. The number of tuns which a ship could carry was called her tunnage.

It seems the word over the centuries acquired various meanings and spellings. A tun or ton involved weight, space and even cost of construction. According to W.P.Stephens, the American yachtsman, designer and historian[2], in 1302 in the reign of King Edward I in England, there was a duty of two shillings per tun on wines imported. Later in the reign of Richard II (1377-1399), a tax of six pence per tun was imposed on all vessels of any nationality passing along the east coast to and from the mouth of London river. In 1587, tonnage is found used as the charge for the temporary charter of a ship, by the Royal Navy of Queen Elizabeth I, of so much per ton (or burden) per week or per month. The formula for this (*you have arrived at the sixteenth century and the first formula in this book!*) was the length times breadth times depth of hold divided by 100: simply

$$(L \times B \times D)/100.$$

One hundred years later in 1694, in the reign of William III and Mary, comes the first record of legal tonnage measurement. The length and breadth of a hold could be measured for tax purposes, but the depth became awkward to find if the hold was full of cargo. The solution to this was a formula, which assumed the depth was half the width of hold: this was, in fact, the case in common coasting vessels of the time. Where L was length of hold and B the width, tonnage was

$$L \times B \times B/2.$$

As a practical step, the measurements began to be taken on the exterior of the built hull (length, for instance, along the keel, which in the distant future will create problems in yachting) with factors and exceptions to arrive at the taxable capacity and so the Act of Parliament was soon amended to:

$$\text{tonnage} = (L \times B \times D)/94.$$

In a further law of 1720, the dimension D was taken as B/2, but the tonnage laws became gradually complex as they were hedged about with rules on where exactly lengths and breadths were taken on the surface of the hull, decks, rubbing bands and so on. Then came developments of deductions for crew and living space (in other words what could never be used for cargo (payload, to use a modern term)). Anticipating the arrival of steam, deductions in later years would be made for machinery and this is the basis of tonnage rules for commercial shipping today, where the resulting figure is used for harbour and canal dues and for enforcing various international regulations.

These general systems of tonnage were in force not only in Britain, but also in the British Empire. (**Fig 1.1**). In 1792 the current tonnage rule known as Builder's Old Measurement, introduced in England in 1773, was also adopted in the United States of America. The rest of the world would not have used anything much different to this system of the English speaking world.

Rewriting it, as explained above:

$$\text{B.O.M.} = (L \times B \times B/2)/94$$

To allow for the rake of the stem, 3/5ths of the breadth (we would say beam today) was subtracted from the length. This innocent refinement would have rating implications in the future.[3]

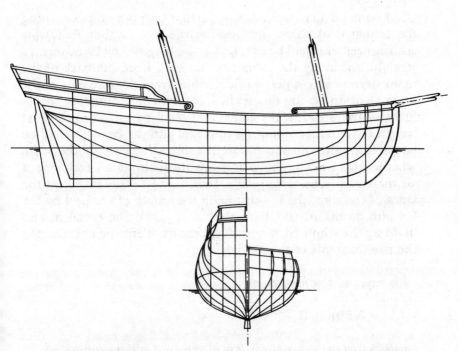

Fig 1.1 *Tonnage figures gave a practical method of measurement to disclose capacity and speed in the 18th century, as in this fast schooner,* Marblehead *(about 65ft, 19.8m), built in colonial New York in 1767 and sold to the Royal Navy.*

Tonnage for yachts

Shortly it will be seen that early attempts at time allowances based them on tonnage. That is precisely why the tonnage figure is going to grow in importance and become a form of rating (the word came a little later) until nearly the end of the nineteenth century. The 'Laws and Regulations, 1845' of the Royal Thames Yacht Club[4] said

'that the maximum tonnage of yachts eligible to sail in matches for cups and prizes given by the club, be 25 tons and that the measurement for the purpose of ascertaining such tonnage shall be taken in the manner prescribed by the Act of the 3rd and 4th Gul. IV, cap 55'

This is a formal way of describing an Act of Parliament (i.e. the law of England) by years of the monarch's reign, 'Gul' being the Latin for William IV; the years mentioned are 1834-5.

The law on tonnage said

'And be it further enacted, that for the purpose of ascertaining the tonnage[5] of ships and vessels; the *rule* (author italic) for admeasurement shall be as follows..the length shall be taken on a straight line along the rabbet of the keel, from the back of the main stern post to a perpendicular line from the fore part of the main stem under the bowsprit, from which, subtracting three-fifths of the breadth, the remainder shall be esteemed the just length of the keel to find the tonnage; and the breadth shall be taken from the outside plank, the broadest part of the ship, whether that shall be above or below the main wales, exclusive of all manner of doubling planks that may be wrought upon the sides of the ship, then multiplying the length of the keel by the breadth so taken, and that produce by half the breadth, and dividing the whole by ninety-four, the quotient shall be deemed the true contents of the tonnage.'

So this says, as already shown:

$$((L - 3/5B) \times B \times B/2)/94$$

In 1845 this quote from the law of the land and its application to yachts was not used for time allowances by the Royal Thames Yacht Club. That year, and probably for some time after, once the tonnage of each yacht had been established, the club raced for two divisions, one for yachts not exceeding 25 tons and the other for yachts not exceeding 12 tons. In each of these the first boat home was the winner.

Even earlier, soon after the inauguration of racing for a cup purchased by the Royal Yacht Club (later the Squadron) at Cowes in 1826 for yachts of 'any rig or tonnage', it was immediately seen that there must be some way of rewarding vessels other than the very biggest. In August 1827 there were three cups, one presented by King George IV and

'a primitive system of handicapping was introduced, when the club restricted its two smaller cups to entries of vessels or yachts not exceeding 75 or 45 tons respectively.'[6]

All other races were 'open' events and racing over the next few years resolved itself into a contest between a few of the larger vessels. Among these few were the Earl of Belfast's *Louisa*, 139 ton cutter, Mr Joseph Weld's *Lulworth*, 127 ton cutter and Mr James Maxse's *Miranda*, 147 ton cutter.

Such was the rivalry for a cup each year presented by the King[7], that after the 1828 race, Lord Belfast sent *Louisa* to be lengthened for extra speed and in 1829, there was the following incident,

'when *Louisa* on starboard luffed [she] caught the after cloth of *Lulworth*'s mainsail, the latter vessel heaving *Louisa* round with her. *Louisa*'s crew from the bowsprit cut the earing of *Lulworth* from the boom as well as her reef pendant. The latter consequently, being disabled, finished a few minutes after *Louisa*.'

The stewards (the rough equivalent to a protest committee) decided that *Lulworth* had tacked too close on the lee bow and 'the cup is awarded to *Louisa*, but we are of [the] opinion that the use of axes was unjustifiable and unnecessary.'

Very earliest time allowances
In the Cowes regatta (in other words what is now Cowes Week) of 1830, a trial was made to divide the starters into six classes, the first being over 140 tons and the sixth being boats of under 40 tons. The first class 'was to concede the rest a certain distance on a 40-mile course. The first gave the second half a mile, the third one and a quarter and so on with the sixth getting seven miles.'[8]

Note that there was no individual allowance; nor does there exist any report on the result of this cryptic scheme. In 1832 at Cowes,

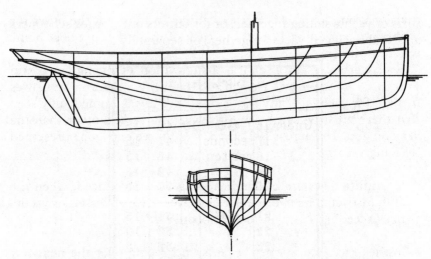

Fig 1.2 *The cutter* Arrow *as lengthened by her owner Thomas Chamberlayne in 1852 to improve her performance in Royal Yacht Squadron regattas. LWL 79ft (24m), draft 11ft 6in (3.5m), tonnage 142. In the wide absence of time allowances, lengthening a yacht would increase her chance of winning. Previous owners included George Ackers (who devised a time scale) and Lord Godolphin. She enjoyed a long and successful racing career.*

there were again six classes divided by tonnage. In the decade which follows various handicapping schemes were tried; these usually grouped vessels by tonnage and even some times by rig (cutters versus schooners) and then allocated arbitrary time allowances for a given race (**Fig 1.2**).

1843 is something of memorable date in the rating of yachts. That season the Royal Yacht Squadron (as it had been called since 1833) introduced for the Queen's Cup, a time allowance for each yacht. This allowance was derived from *The Graduated Time Tables by G.H.Ackers Esq*. George Holland Ackers, a member of the Squadron[9], invented this first consistent system of time allowances, which listed what should be applied to the elapsed time in seconds per ton per mile. It was the basis of scales in later years including those of the YRA. The figures were obtained in a simple manner from Mr Ackers's observations over a long period on the performance of vessels of differing tonnage (**Fig 1.3**). There was adjustment between the main rigs of the day (though nothing for the actual dimensions of the rig) so that 'The scale is suitable for all sorts of yachts sailing together, or for cutters only, or for schooners and square rigged yachts together, or separately'.[10]

Tons.	Diff of Time	h.	m.	s.
Under 16	**60**	10	46	15
17	seconds	...	47	15
18	per ton	...	48	15
19		...	49	15
20		...	50	15
21	**55**	...	51	15
22		...	52	10
23		...	53	5
24		...	54	0
25		...	54	55
26	**50**	...	55	50
27		...	56	40
28		...	57	30
29		...	58	20
30		...	59	10

Fig 1.3 *Extract from the time allowance system devised by George Ackers for the 1843 season. The last three columns might confuse the modern sailor, as they represented the time of start as yachts might be sent away in accordance with tonnage. The important step forward was that the difference in seconds per rating (tonnage) per mile varied in groups; in other words there was a scale of short straight lines of different gradients: nearly a curve, as was always the case (with one or two exceptions) in the future and remains so today. (see pages 125–126)*

1843 was the first year that yachts from royal clubs throughout the kingdom were invited to sail at Cowes, rather than merely those of the RYS. The boats of the Royal Thames came down to Cowes and liked the improvement on their own rule, mentioned above. The result was reported as the best regatta so far; time allowances were endorsed and thereafter persisted.

Fundamentals discovered

What these pioneering sailors had established was that if diverse competitors are to continue to come from different ports (coasts, countries), they must be offered a previously announced and reasonably respected handicap system.

'Under the new dispensation of classes and time allowance, it was difficult for any yacht of this period to declare her superiority, but it is probable that Mr Congreve's *Corsair* was the most notable cutter of the times. *Corsair*, first appeared in the [RYS] list of 1842, was of *middling* size at 84 tons and was regarded as the latest and finest production of Michael Ratsey's famous establishment.'[11]

These were innocent days, demonstrating another principle unknown to the users. There was not yet any attempt to exploit time allowance or tonnage. The system, such as it was, had worked to prevent the largest yachts winning all the prizes and encourage differing sizes to race.

Yet the seeds of decadence were sown. With a time allowance tied to tonnage, however crudely, there will be an incentive to reduce the tonnage figure to improve the time allowance and thus the chance of a better place in the race. That realization has not come yet: it is the 1840s, the new Queen has come to the throne, the Royal Navy rules the waves, Britain has some very rich men, more yachts are building and such boats and their men exceed in number and size the rest of the world put together.

Tonnage starts to bite
The development of time allowances will be looked at very fully later; it is enough to remember that from 1843 they become linked to the tonnage of each yacht to make lower tonnage a racing advantage.

Look at the last formula above, the law of tonnage, the law of 1834-35, known loosely as Builder's Measurement. It was, as we have seen, not much different from the tonnage laws of two hundred years before. The subtraction of 3/5 beam[12] from L was to allow for the usual slope of the stem. L was, as established in earlier times the length of *keel, or the length which 'treads the ground'*. See there is no tax on waterline length, freeboard, displacement or sail area. Now you and I know what is going to happen and it will be seen what did happen! It will turn the relative boom days of yacht racing in England, to frustration, anger and near collapse – until rescued. But this is going to take some years.

There was some control, firstly by the conservatism of the day (though it is easy to fault lack of movement with hindsight);

secondly by the limitation of material: wood, leather, ropes of natural fibre, canvas and some steel. To some extent this prevented extremes; though the Victorians were not held back for long! What happened is described in the words of George Watson,

'... gradually builders discovered that, by increasing draft and amount of ballast, beam could be pared down and a boat of *nominally the same tonnage* made longer and to carry more sail than her predecessor. Lead ballast was slowly introduced, despite all sorts of adverse prophecies from old salts that it would strain the ship and would cause her to plunge so heavily as to go under; and, presently, when some unknown genius first put lead outside, and from a timid hundredweight or two, this increased to tons, the veterans gave the new type up altogether as past praying for and left them to their well merited fate.'[13]

Reducing beam to lower the tonnage rating was one weapon, but

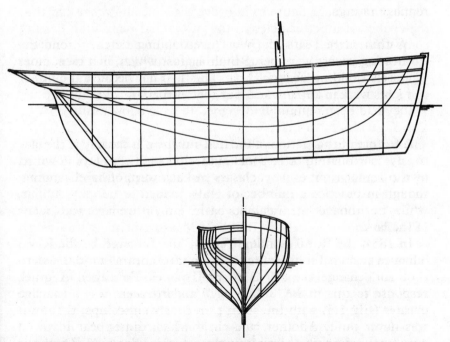

Fig 1.4 *Early rule cheating of a moderate nature. In the 35-ton* Cygnet, *1846, the keel length measurement was shortened by sloping the stem and stern post; the section shows displacement was reduced and draft was large, both of which were unmeasured. LOA was about 67ft (20.4m).*

the rule that length was along the keel was also attacked. In 1846, Mr Wanhill, a builder at Poole, built the 35-ton cutter *Cygnet* (**Fig 1.4**). He sloped the stern post at a modest angle. This gave the normal length on the waterline for less L measurement. (The terms 'builder' and 'designer' were fairly interchangeable in this period).

When the schooner *America* came to Cowes and on 22 August 1851 raced around the Isle of Wight for the One Hundred Guinea Cup, the British yachts which she beat were not extreme, indeed they were conservative. The attempt to exploit the tonnage rules had not yet spread beyond some experimental boats. Note also that this race for what became the America's Cup did not use any time allowance and the boats started from anchor.

John Irving writing in 1937[14], gives the years immediately following 1853 as the start of intense search for lower tonnage. He says this was following the (now) little known visit of the American schooner *Sylvie* to Cowes to repeat *America*'s feat. Apparently she was soundly beaten and this gave a major fillip to British racing yacht construction, which included serious efforts to minimize tonnage ratings.

'Within three years of *Sylvie*'s resounding defeat[15], tonnage-cheating yachts were being built against which, in a race, older vessels stood no chance at all. This was not because the newer yachts were in any marked way, better than the old, but because they had been cunningly designed to have a low rating'.

A feature of this period of the mid-nineteenth century is the lack of any coordinating or national authority; each club lays down its own rules for right of way, classes and any form of handicapping, though in practice a number of clubs tended to be very similar, while the tonnage rule was in its basic form, as we have seen, a law of the land.

In 1854, the Royal London Yacht Club, followed by the Royal Thames arranged to measure L on deck from the stem to the stern post and change the 3/5 B to B (Thames Tonnage). A quick response to this in *Bell's Life* by 'Vanderdecken' was a tonnage cheater (**Fig 1.5**) with the stern post nearly amidships, though it was never built. Another rule cheat which did appear involved curving the stern post away from the actual rudder head. Truly our ancestors were catching on fast!

Up to now the rule was a law and had to be suffered, but now for the first time, yachtsman began to think about changing the rule itself. Dixon Kemp[16] quotes a tonnage rule invented at the New

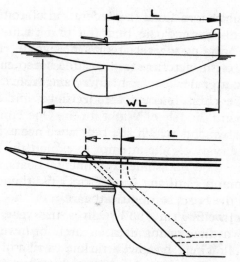

Fig 1.5 *Vanderdecken's famous rule cheater which reduced L by moving the stern post amidships; published as a warning to rule makers, but never built. Another suggestion (lower) was to bring the 'stern post' in from the line of the rudder.*

Thames, Corinthian and Queenstown Model Yacht Clubs. This simply changes the constant and includes D (in this case draft):

$$(L \times B \times D)/200.$$

It did not attract wide support; a few unsatisfactory yachts were said to have been designed to this '200 rule'. Thames Tonnage (or Measurement) prevailed and the formula was:

$$\text{Thames Measurement (TM)} = ((L - B) \times B \times B/2)/94$$

This tonnage measurement was used to describe yachts in the United Kingdom for many years after its disuse as a rating rule, to the bafflement of foreigners. Yachts were certainly described as 10-tonners, 15-tonners and so on until about the 1970s! In the now discontinued *Lloyd's Register of Yachts*, for 1978 there is a column for the TM of each entry. Thames Measurement may even be found occasionally today attached to the description of an older vessel.

To find an accord

There had been attempts to form a kind of sailing Jockey Club (which controlled English horse racing and still does) as early as

1852 with a suggestion for a 'confederation of commodores'. In 1864, the idea re-emerged, the Royal Victoria Yacht Club of Ryde, Isle of Wight, bringing together representatives of eighteen clubs, then a big part of the active racing world. This so-called 'yachting congress' drew up rules for right of way and related subjects, but virtually all the clubs rejected the decisions and the 'congress' never met again.

Julius Gabe writing in 1902[17], described what happened ten years later:

'Count Edmund Batthany (now Prince Batthany-Strattmann) headed a movement to oppose the rule of the New Thames Yacht Club [the 200 rule] and yacht owners gave effect to it by hauling down their racing flags on the Thames in a regatta of May 1875 ... There had been various 'strikes' about tonnage rules at Cowes previous to this, the only result being to spoil a regatta of the Royal Yacht Squadron when the strike occurred. The revolt, however, of 1875 was of very different dimensions.'

As a result three men drew up a set of rules for a body to unify matters. Count Batthany, Captain J.W.Hughes and Dixon Kemp made these known and then held a meeting, which was attended by many yachtsmen, at Willis's Rooms, St James's, London, on 17 November 1875. Thus was formed the Yacht Racing Association.

'Yacht measurement was the principal reason for the YRA's formation', says its official history[18]. The Association consisted of 'former and present owners of racing yachts..and of representative members appointed by royal or recognized yacht clubs.' At first, as in 1864, some leading clubs including the Squadron and Thames refused to be governed by the YRA. But Cowes regatta of 1881 'was practically confined to three or four old schooners and a couple of cutters'[19] because of the rule problems.

Now the Prince of Wales had by this time accepted the post of president of the YRA. In early spring 1882, he was also elected Commodore of the Royal Yacht Squadron and his influence speedily ensured that the senior clubs all came to support the YRA.

The YRA and in particular its permanent secretary, Dixon Kemp, immediately tackled the deteriorating measurement scene. This approach was two-pronged: first, scantlings, in other words, strength of construction of racing yachts and, second, the tonnage formula, which was Thames Measurement, as inherited by the YRA. Poor scantlings were a worry for owners and builders, the only possible beneficiary being the designer of the latest racer and his owner for one season. Some members of the YRA drew up some construction rules; then Lloyds Register of Shipping, an institution founded in the seventeenth century which laid down rules for the strength of commercial ships, took over the work by arrangement and began rules for the construction of yachts. It has been classifying yachts ever since.

As for Thames Tonnage, the YRA in 1881 declared that in future L should be measured on the waterline, rather than on the previous limits along the deck.

Plank-on-edge

It may be early in the long story of rule makers chasing rule cheaters – or more politely, beaters – but this had the effect of encouraging overhangs to give extra unmeasured length (**Fig 1.6**)!

Fig 1.6 *Most rating rules have seen boats get 'bigger', certainly longer, for the same rating. Profiles of two 5-tonners. Between 1873 and 1885, draft (unmeasured) had deepened to extremes, while the change of length measurement on to waterline saw the start of previously unheard-of bow overhang.*

Gentlemen may have begun worthy and informed discussions, but meanwhile yachts were becoming narrower (less beamy) and deeper by the season. They also were being rigged with more and more sail, which, of course, was not rated at all. The plank on edge had little form stability, so more and more lead was added to the keel. The day of the notorious 'plank-on-edge' cutter had arrived. When such boats or their design were exported to America, their supporters, as will be seen, were called 'cutter cranks'.

Fig 1.7 shows the progress of design for a yacht rating 5 tons between 1873 and 1885. That the YRA announced a new tonnage rule in 1882 may not be apparent; in other words it solved nothing. This rule attempted to make the redesign pay more for B, but designers were out for length at any price and it actually made matters worse. This YRA tonnage rule was:

$$Tonnage = ((L + B)^2 \times B)/1730.$$

George Watson pointed out that 'below about $5\frac{1}{4}$ beams to length, the new rule was easier on beam, but the adoption of extreme proportions was hastened rather than averted ... length and displacement went merrily on.'[20]

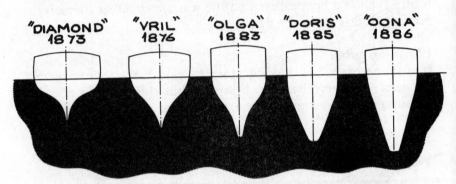

Fig 1.7 *Collapse of the British tonnage rules. Despite attempts to adjust these tonnage rules, year by year beam narrowed and draft increased until the most extreme plank-on-edge of all, Oona, which was lost with all hands. Each yacht shown here was 5 tons.*

It is no coincidence that 1882 was the first year in which the senior clubs (above) were members of the YRA. Though Dixon Kemp probably knew that the tonnage rules were wrong in conception, he was only able to engage in 'tinkering' within his new governing council. The Thames club was not in a hurry to see its own kind of rule disappear.

John Irving[21] wrote of this period in British yacht racing,

'Each year's new yachts were built to a more extreme design than those of the previous season. The newer yachts were heavier, narrower and deeper, but, by reason of the growing cleverness of their designers, rated lower than their predecessors and therefore stood an infinitely greater chance of victory. Each year's new yachts carried all before them for a season or until a newer and more extreme type of ship replaced them at the head of their class. Even a winning yacht was hopelessly outclassed in a very short space of time: *owners, losing heart and patience, ceased to build new craft.* Some owners remaining faithful turned their attention to the small racing classes; others transferred their attention to steam yachting. These were thus lost to first class racing for ever. Gone were the halcyon days, destroyed by the monsters the Frankenstein measurement rules had created.' (**Fig 1.8**)

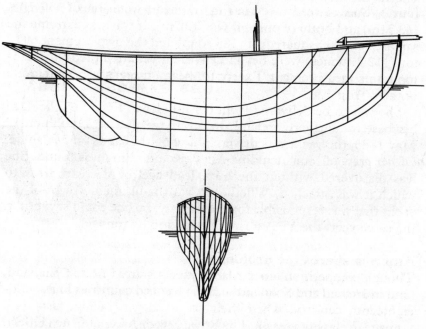

Fig 1.8 *Plank-on-edge in its extreme form. 'The Frankenstein measurement rules created monsters' said John Irving, yet there were reports of fine passages in tough weather by such yachts.*

Nearer the time there were defenders, maybe subjective, of the plank-on-edge[22]:

'*Alouette*, notwithstanding her small amount of beam, was a grand sea-boat..it has become customary to run down the seaworthiness of yachts built under the old rule, but numbers could be produced of comfort and safety carried about by the old boats of five to six beams to their length ... [later] both yachts were reefed down with topmasts housed ..in the thrash to windward quite a third part of the trip was made under water'.

The plank-on-edge did indeed, with its considerable lump of lead, sail to windward. *The argument surely raged as to whether such boats were 'good', 'bad', 'desirable', 'seaworthy' or not: but, as today, these are opinions and are not the decisive criteria. What counts is whether owners will build racing yachts to the class.*

The end of tonnage rating in Great Britain was marked by a famous disaster. A Scottish designer Mr Payton, built a series of 5-tonners between 1880 and 1886; they were very narrow. The fourth, *Oona*, already seen in **Fig 1.7**, had a waterline of 33ft 10in (10.31m) and beam of only 5ft 6in (1.67m). If this was extreme the sail area of 2000 square feet (185 sq m) and the displacement of 12 tons (12.2 tonnes) were beyond anything yet attempted for the 5-ton rating measurement. Except for beam, these factors were quite unrated (**Fig 1.9**).

She was to be delivered from her builder in Essex, England, to her base in Northern Ireland. In severe weather off Dublin on 12 May 1886, the yacht was driven ashore on the sands off Malahide. Of her crew of four including Mr Payton nothing was found. She was discovered without the huge lead keel or the garboards to which it was attached. Whether it was the ultimate design of the yacht that was responsible for the tragedy, no one could say, but in the same year, the YRA abandoned rating by tonnage.

America shares the problems

Though competition among large yachts started first in England, (and in Ireland and Scotland) other advanced countries in the mid-eighteenth century, when their sailors began racing, also used tonnage to classify vessels. The Royal Swedish Yacht Club (KSSS) was formed in 1830, the Société des Régates du Havre in 1838, the New York Yacht Club in 1844 and the Royal Netherlands Yacht and Rowing Club (KNZRV) in 1847.

Because of the big distances in the United States of America, clubs were even more independent in these early days than in Britain. Records are scattered and from this distance the big east coast clubs, especially the New York Yacht Club, tend to fill the story[23]. Jumping ahead, it will be seen that the United States has no unifying authority for racing until 1926 and will not join the international body (IYRU) until 1952.

In the very first full season of the NYYC in 1845, in the very first race, believed to have started from Robbins Reef, and won by the schooner *Cygnet*, the nine starters were given a time allowance of 45 seconds per ton per mile on their Custom House Tonnage. In 1847 the same system was used with a larger fleet being divided at a break point of 50 tons. As at Cowes, there are reports of boats being lengthened to improve performance, but details are not known.

American tonnage of the period, like the British mentioned earlier, did not involve displacement nor sail area. Old Custom

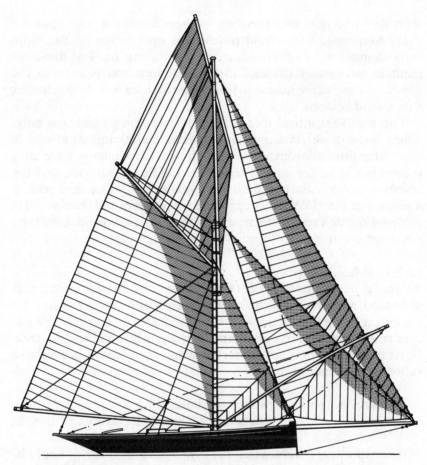

Fig 1.9 *Hull design was not the only extreme in plank-on-edge cutters. The tonnage rules did not measure sail area at all and many commentators were against such a step. So the cutter sail plan extended beyond reach at both ends and huge topsails were set in light weather.*

Measurement, as used in New York, took actual depth of hold and so was less hard on beam than the British. This was probably the same as Custom House Measurement with minor differences.

As in the early days of the leading clubs in England, the handicap system was changed from time to time, no doubt following complaints from competitors, especially as the yachts were large and few and the owners rich and influential. In 1853 the NYYC decided to run races on actual displacement tonnage, in other words, the weight of each vessel. It is interesting that this coincides with the first recorded mention of *crew limitation*: one man for every four tons. This could have been quite clever, as the more crew claimed to be on board, the higher the rating. But displacement is notoriously difficult to measure in practice, even in the 1990s; it is therefore not surprising that this idea was dropped after a couple of seasons.

The next idea introduced in 1856 was to rate by sail area only. There were three classes with divisions at 3300 and 2300 square feet. The time allowance varied with the class: the biggest at 1 second per mile per square foot, the middle, $1\frac{1}{4}$ seconds and the smallest $1\frac{1}{2}$ seconds per mile per square foot. The first official measurer of the NYYC was appointed, Mr Charles H. Haswell. He received ten dollars for the first measurement and five dollars for a remeasurement.

Original handicapping

At the general meeting of 1859, before the handicapping was discussed, a member and his yacht were expelled from the club for importing three hundred slaves from Africa into Georgia. The sail area rule was then scrapped after long argument and a close vote. In its place was put a new waterline area rule: today this would be called waterplane

$$\text{Rating} = \text{length of waterline times}$$
$$\text{maximum beam at waterline, or } L \times B.$$

'The newspapers commented that it was obvious this rule could be beaten almost as soon as it was announced.'[24] Yet the press was wrong for this rule survived until 1870; it was used for the America's Cup race of 1870 in New York harbour in which the 84ft (25.60m) *Magic*, a centreboarder (**Fig 1.10**) beat the British 108ft (32.92m) *Cambria*. The America's Cup race of 1871 used displacement as a rule. This was only voted by the NYYC in May of that year, so neither challenger nor defender were actually built to the rule. If one looks at the magnificent models in the club today, it will be seen that the American and British boats of this period are of quite different shape. No attempt was made to design to these rating rules and anyway time allowances were always applied *right up until 1920*.

In passing, it is seen that the American and British approaches were different and reflected their temperaments. The NYYC scrapped a rating rule which did not appear to work and democratically voted in a new one. The British, who anyway left such matters to the establishment, tinkered (at least until 1886), as already described, with the existing and ancient law.[25]

The new displacement rule was as follows: the sum of three cross sections of the yacht underbody multiplied by one quarter of waterline length; the cube root of the result is multiplied by 100. Sail area was not considered; it was said 'A tax on sail is a tax on skill'.

$$\text{Rating by displacement} = 100 \times (A \times L/4)^{1/3}$$

From this formula one would expect large sail area, low freeboard, long overhangs and a flat rather than deep hull. The boats developed for the races of the NYYC did indeed have these features: they were often shoal draft centreboarders with wide beam in total contrast to the British cutter. As mentioned samples of the cutter imported to America were the work of 'cutter cranks'.

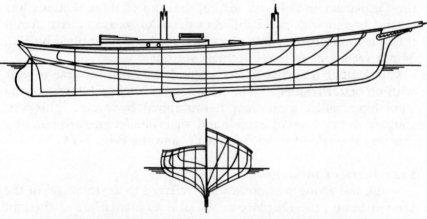

Fig 1.10 Magic, *built 1857, rebuilt 1869, LOA 90ft (27.4m), first defender of the America's Cup (New York harbor 1870). Typical American design with large beam, shallow draft, centreboard and schooner rig: antithesis of the English cutter. She raced to the little known waterline area rule.*

Less widely known is their riposte that the native yachts were 'centreboard bugs'. The latter will develop their own dangerous characteristics. This was accentuated in 1872 when the displacement rule was amended so that measurement was changed from the waterline to the lowest point of the sheer plank (approximately deck level in wooden construction).

This change was for the worst, encouraging even lower free-

board and 'flatter' boats. Sail area remained unchecked. In the
American *Yachting Annual*, the editor wrote

> 'Classification hinges on measurement and this has been a
> constant source of trouble; as nearly every club has its own rule
> and system of time allowance. We want a uniform rule: a rule
> which shall as far as possible, leave owners and builders unfet-
> tered and untrammelled and yet which shall give a fair idea of
> the size of the vessel . . .'

This is an early mention using the subjective word, *fair*. With
the sentiments, one cannot quarrel!

The America's Cups of 1876 and 1881 were Canadian challenges
by relatively light displacement centreboard vessels developed on
the Great Lakes. The rule in use was yet a further new rule adopted
by the defending club, the NYYC. It was called the Cubic
Contents rule. It appears to be little different in most respects to
the Displacement rule. As before, the sum of three sections was
taken, though with some different detail of measurement. Again
this was multiplied by LWL/4, cube rooted and multiplied by 100.
Minor variations followed in most seasons.

Clubs other than the NYYC 'blundered on from year to year
with no better results'.[26] The Seawanhaka Yacht Club was trying
something called mean length multiplied by beam. This was
roughly the average of overall and waterline lengths. Apparently
this was also tried by the Atlanta YC and the Boston YC.[27]

Last years of tonnage
Though the rating was not always referred to as 'tonnage' in the
United States, the Displacement/Cubic Contents line of thought
was similar because with limited hull features it sought to extract a
rating figure for time allowance. In both America and Britain
tonnage will end for ever a few years either side of 1885 and
W.P.Stephens's opinion[28] was

> 'The decade from 1875 to 1885 was the most important period in
> American yachting; early in the 70s a few yachtsmen inaugur-
> ated a crusade against the national type, the broad, shoal, easily
> capsizable centreboard sloop, with inside ballast. As this crusade
> progressed, it assumed a more extreme form in the advocacy of
> the British cutter, a keel yacht with outside ballast, then of
> moderate breadth, but growing more narrow and deep each
> year. A fierce controversy ensued, breaking up friendships and

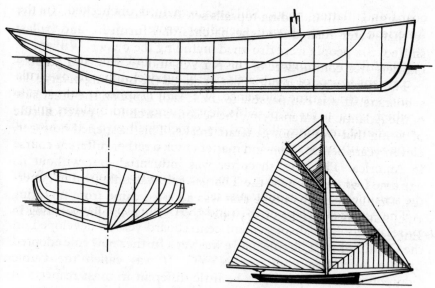

Fig 1.11 *Small American sloop, LOA 24ft (7.3m), typically of the 1870s; stability to cope with the large sail area came from the beam.*

dividing clubs. The end came in 1885 with the construction for the defence [of the America's cup of a compromise design] with a centreboard working through an outside keel and a cutter rig.'

Another commentator said of the wide, flat, overcanvassed centre-boarder:

'The truth is that we are consumed by a madness for speed and everything is sacrificed to that ... The ideal model is in the future, the English yacht is narrow and deep, the American wide and flat. It is not impossible to combine the best qualities of both styles and then we shall take to deep water..'[29] (**Fig 1.11**)

In 1875 the 87ft schooner *Josephine* capsized at anchor while watching a race; the crew was saved. Another schooner of 53ft, *Agnes*, also capsized when anchored at night and three of the crew were drowned. The most famous of these centreboard bugs simply to roll over was the schooner *Mohawk*. On her length of 150ft (45.7m), she had a beam of 30ft 4in (9.2m), a draft of only 6ft (1.8m) and a huge rig. On 20 July 1876 off Stapleton, Staten Island, New York, she was on her anchor chain about to get under way with all sail, including topsails set. A sudden squall heeled her so that water rushed into the hatches and furniture and ballast shifted. Six people were drowned including the owner, William T. Garner, vice commodore of the NYYC, and his wife and guests.

The disaster had a major effect. It ended the building of large flat schooners. It was comparable to the loss of *Oona* on the other side of the Atlantic in intensifying the serious search for a practical rule of rating that would not generate freaks. This happened however, eleven years before *Oona* and matters took a rather different course in America. The English cutter was influential, but without its extreme features because the Thames rule was unknown in America. One local English type that was adopted came from no rating rule, but was the Itchen ferry boat[30], often adapted for yachting in England.

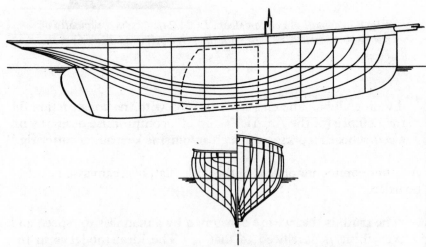

Fig 1.12 *A compromise cutter. Despite being termed 'cutter cranks', the proponents of this type are seen to have avoided the 'centre board bug' and the 'plank-on-edge' extremes. East coast designers including A. Cary Smith, Robert Center and Edward Burgess recommended this reasonable type (sometimes with centre-board) which appeared for a few years (about 1876-1881), but was to be overtaken by a new rating rule in 1883.*

The leading American designer A. Cary Smith was one of those who designed cutters with outside ballast, no centreboard, but with moderate beam (about 4 times ratio or less) to length. Excessive draft was thus unnecessary (**Fig 1.12**). A limited number of

American owners embraced the moderate cutter. A few went for narrow beam in the English fashion, but there was no rating rule to take this to the disastrous English conclusion. To our eyes the American cutters look reasonable. Measurement by tonnage and displacement in America simply wilted on the desire of owners for good boats and, in the early 1880s, on agreement about rating rules of a completely different concept.

2 Skimming dishes of the Belle Époque

'Myself when young did eagerly frequent
Doctor and Saint and heard great argument
About it and about: but evermore
Came out by the same Door wherein I went'
– The Rubaiyat of Omar Khayyam (1859) by Hon. Edward
Fitzgerald (1809-1883), poet and amateur North Sea sailor.

'With shame I confess that the problems and calculations, the combi-
nations of straight and crooked lines, with large and small numbers and
Latin and Greek letters, the mathematical contortions and algebraic
hieroglyphics, are meaningless to my uncultured eyes. They are
fascination; I admire their beauty and can well understand that
inventing rules for rating must be a most charming pursuit for
intellectual yachtsmen' – The Earl of Dunraven in *The Field*, 1892.[1]

IN THE 1880s the yachting scene was expanding, but it must
be remembered that any competition was without ocean
racing and without dinghy racing. The boats with fixed keels
(and in the USA often with additional centreboards) were manned
by paid hands, the owner occasionally being allowed to steer. Many
yachts were very large, but smaller vessels gave plenty of sport.
However the big vessels reaped the publicity and are in the race
reports which historians quote.

In 1812, seven years after the Battle of Trafalgar, 'there were
probably 50 yachts afloat [in Great Britain], owned exclusively by
nobleman and country gentlemen'[2]. By 1851, when the schooner
America came to Cowes, there were 500. British sailing yachts in
1864 numbered 862; in 1878, 1601. Of these yachts those between
10 and 20 tons were in 1850, 127; 1864, 207 and 1878, 403. *Lloyds*
Register of Yachts of 1891 gave as then owned in the United
Kingdom 2428 sailing yachts and 1413 in other countries; probably

the USA was not fully accounted. (Steam yachts were additional to these figures).

Now we are in 1883 in Britain: the Yacht Racing Association has been established for eight years. In America, the clubs are as independent as ever. In both countries the search is on for a rating system for 'modern' yachting. We are going to see the results and practical applications of this search cause even more argument, throw-away boats and controversy than under the old tonnage rules. Yet there will be unprecedented first class racing and unforeseen benefits. The latter will include the coming together of yacht racing nations, the arrival of the biggest racing yachts ever regularly raced, serious consideration of scantlings and the creation of the one-design racer.

Dixon Kemp's rule

The British YRA's first secretary was a powerhouse of energy, keeping in touch with his members and clubs, writing books and articles, wrestling with rules for both racing (right of way and administration) and rating and corresponding with and meeting leading American sailors.

Thus it was that Kemp's proposal for a new rule was effected in the United States before his own country. In 1880 Kemp suggested his rating rule which at a stroke removed everything that was wrong with the plank-on-edge cutter. The rule took in waterline length (L) and sail area (S); they were in feet and square feet respectively.

$$\text{Rating} = (L \times S)/6000$$

The constant of 6000 was merely chosen to make the rating for existing yachts come out at a figure close to its old tonnage rating. In England the YRA was not immediately convinced about this proposed radical change. Enter the Seawanhaka Corinthian Yacht Club, today out at Oyster Bay, Long Island Sound, but in 1882 with a station at Edgewater, Staten Island, where some of the most prominent yachts raced. That year it had added the word 'Corinthian' into its name, 'thereby subjecting itself to much ridicule on the grounds of snobbery and aping English ideas'.[3]

On the rating rule argument ran. Edward Burgess who had returned from a summer on the south coast of England, where he had extensive meetings with Dixon Kemp, wrote in *Forest and Stream*, 'Let me announce myself as a "cutter man" and so no fondness for skimming dishes influences my belief that length on the load waterline is the fairest standard for racing measurement. Of all systems, except perhaps a displacement one, a bulk rule seems to me the very worst'. On 3 March 1882, the Seawanhaka Yacht Club adopted a slightly modified form of the rule of Dixon Kemp.

$$\text{Seawanhaka YC Tons} = (L \times S)/4000$$

There were details of how L and S were measured. The sails of the time, including topsails were defined for measurement and L was at first nine-tenths of the waterline length plus one fifth of the total overhang.

There were dire predictions about the introduction of this rule, but it worked well in its first seasons. Rules invariably work without trouble before yachts are built to them. One year after the 1882 decision, after a satisfactory season at the Seawanhaka, a club committee met again. As well as the operation of the rule, it approached the New York YC and some other clubs in order to try and obtain uniformity of rating and classification (i.e. division by classes).[4]

The Seawanhaka Rule
The result of these meetings was to change the rule, though not in principle, by agreement with the New York YC. Joining in also were the Eastern YC, which was and is the senior Boston club, the Knickerbocker YC and the Toronto YC in Canada. Thus came about the famous Seawanhaka Rule, on which yachts of the United States were rated for twenty years.

$$\text{Rating} = (L + S^{1/2})/2$$

The sail area now appeared as a square root, which made a linear figure (unlike the Kemp amount) and the main factors were added rather than multiplied. One innovation was to measure the sail area by using the spars (masts, booms etc), a system which still exists in today's rules. Length was back to waterline. Instead of 'sail tons' or Kemp's British use of 'tons', the rating was in 'feet', which resulted from the units in the formula. This is a concept which has remained in use until today, with feet or metres of rating.[5] The NYYC declared the Cubic Contents Rule to be dead.

Typical of larger yachts built to the Seawanhaka rule in the 1880s was *Katrina*, designed by A. Cary Smith and built at City Island, NY, in 1888 (**Fig 2.1**). Among her dimensions were LOA

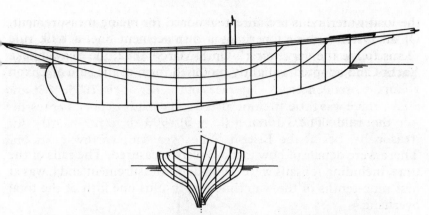

Fig 2.1 Katrina *was an example of a large yacht designed to the Seawanhaka rule. The section had more depth than the early flat centreboarders, but there was a board, as so often in American yachts of the period.*

91ft 3in (27.81m), LWL 69ft 2in (21.06m), draft with (a big) centreboard up 9ft 3in (2.82m), least freeboard 3ft (0.91m), measured sail area 7082 square ft (658 sq m). The underlying weaknesses of the rule are thus seen in what was, however, a fine racing vessel. The overhangs are long at 32 per cent of LWL; freeboard is unduly low and sail area is big, despite it being in the formula.

An important reason for big sail area was that time allowances were until 1890 based on only 40 per cent of rating. This meant there was advantage in plenty of sail in relation to the given waterline. From 1909 time allowances (Chapter 5) were about 60 per cent in relation to rating rules in use and that continued in America into the 1980s.

If time allowances, even after the rating question was settled for a time, were continued sources of debate, then so was *classification*. Today we would talk about 'class divisions'. Different American clubs used varying systems. In 1887, for instance, the New York YC divided by LWL, while the Larchmont YC used the rating. The latter is, of course, the logical division (as used today) because it appears on the rating certificate and is surely meant to reflect the speed! To our eyes quite a meal was made of all this. One way it was expressed by the Atlantic YC in the 1888 season was '4ft divisions from the lower limit from 26 to 30ft, increasing to 10ft bands at the top from 65 to 70ft'.[6] Do not enquire for more detail!

The Seawanhaka Rule gave excellent racing in the United States for at least ten years and for a few years after that[7], but by the later 1890s it was running into trouble with extreme features in design. These were seen most clearly in the America's Cup for the largest yachts and the Seawanhaka Cup for the smallest keel boats.

In the first America's Cup races of the period, in 1885, 1886 and 1887, there was little attempt by the contestants to put any pressure on the rule. The Americans stuck to their centreboards and reasonable beam; the British came over with narrow boats and

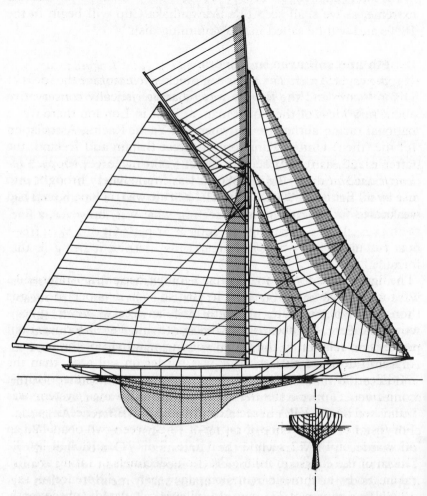

Fig 2.2 Defender *(123ft, 37.5ft), designed by Nathanael Herreshoff and built in 1895 for the America's Cup in the same year. She beat the Earl of Dunraven's Valkyrie III. Under the Seawanhaka rule, there were fairly long overhangs with 'U' sections, deep draft and evidently large sail area.*

fairly deep keels (no longer actually plank-on-edge). Each boat was measured under the Seawanhaka Rule and some peripheral regulations set up for each challenge. They then sailed on time allowance. Lord Dunraven's notorious challenges with *Valkyrie II* and *III* in 1893 and 1895 saw both the defender, which was called *Defender*, and challenger, for the first time in history, designed very much alike to the rule and to restrictions for the cup boats laid down by the NYYC (**Fig 2.2**).

In later challenges (1899, 1901, 1903) boats will become extreme, as we shall see. The Seawanhaka Cup will begin in the 1890s and will be sailed in the skimming dish.

Length and sail area in Europe

If some eager Americans had been quicker to embrace the ideas of Dixon Kemp and the British were characteristically conservative about new ideas of their own man, at least in London there was a national racing authority. So when the Yacht Racing Association [of the (then) United Kingdom of Great Britain and Ireland; the latter island, as today, being a major yachting force] adopted *the length and sail area rule* in 1886, it was immediately brought into use by all British and Irish clubs.[8] The rule was the one Kemp had advocated for several years.

$$\text{Rating} = (L \times S)/6000$$

The figures meant that an existing 5-tonner became a 5-rater and a 20-tonner became a 20 rater. The British soon dropped the words 'tons' in favour of 'rater'. Length times an area, however, gives a cubic measure, so theoretically this was cubic feet or tonnage; but there is no relation to the actual volume or weight of the boat.

Kemp declared that the rule was harder on sail area, than the modification made at Seawanhaka; this no doubt suited British conditions. To operate the rule, a time allowance system was published by the YRA in seconds per mile for difference in rating.[9] For instance a difference of rating of 12 between two boats had an allowance of 141.12 seconds per mile. This is multiplied by the length of the course in miles. Fractions/decimals of rating are also taken. So by arithmetic (sums on paper then) a difference of, say, 12.6 over a course of $33\frac{1}{4}$ nautical miles is calculated; subsequently it is applied to the elapsed time.

Unlike today where there are separate (and thick) publications for racing, rating, safety and other regulations, the rules were all mixed up in one short document entitled 'The Rules of the Yacht

Racing Association'. For instance in 1888, rule 19 dealt with rounding marks, rule 9 with centreboards, rule 11 with distinguishing flags (carried at the main topmast head; if the topmast is housed, the flag must be rehoisted in a conspicuous position). Rule 3 was rating.

This gave the rating rule in words and added, following some rule beating/cheating on previous waterline rules, '. . . the pieces of any form cut out of the stem, stern post, or fair line of the ridge of the counter, with the intentioning of shortening the LWL, shall not be allowed for in measurement . . .'[10] There were other familiar (to today's measurers) echos from this early rule '. . . the crew and other persons [!], who may be on board are amidships, whilst measuring . . . moveable ballast on board . . . note its position . .'

Days of the skimming dish
It took five years before there was widespread alarm about the effects of the length and sail area rule. Up to then existing yachts were measured and when new ones were designed, designers were slow to exploit the formulae. Indeed their creations did not look too much different from boats designed to the tonnage rules. Strangely this is a phenomenon with new rules. Even if some designers know what they ought to do to maximize a rule, the owners are not immediately ready for the new shape.

By 1891-92, in the smaller classes especially, the skimming dish had arrived. The uncontrolled elements in the rule were exploited: light displacement, which worryingly went with light scantlings,[11] very low freeboard and long U-shaped ends to obtain extra unmeasured waterline length when heeled (**Fig 2.3**).

Such small inshore boats were fun, but in the larger sizes boats did sail in more open water, or went on passage between races, or might be needed also for cruising (as mentioned, there was no ocean racing, but day races might be along exposed coasts). The small boats had fin keels, something quite new.

Again in the smaller classes, owners tended to build to fixed ratings: published results of the period show classes including ½-raters, 1-raters, 2½-raters, 5-raters, 20-raters, 40-raters. *In America the fixed rating class was not known; indeed the concept has never been widely supported in US racing.*

The YRA length and sail area rule was to last until 1896. Anticipating changes then, it will not be the end of the skimming dish. Up to this date there will be some five years of intense controversy on 'the rating rule'. It is no exaggeration to say that it was arguably the most bitter period of rating rule bickering in

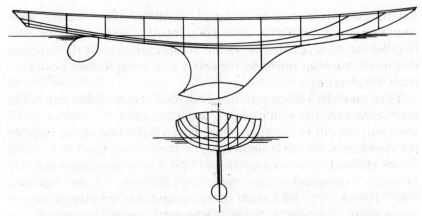

Fig 2.3 *The skimming dish, 1892: a 1-rater under the length and sail area rule, designed by J.M.Soper. Flat sections, long ends, fin and bulb keel. LOA 31ft 6in (9.6m), but LWL only 20ft 6in (6.25m), the result of using LWL as the only length measurement.*

history, though this must be judged by the reader when reaching the end of the book! One reason was that these late Victorians assumed that a rating rule must only show two or three factors. The rule must be a 'displacement rule', or a 'sail area rule' and so on. Then it must be remembered that this was *la belle époque*, that age before the world wars, when the rich got richer and when not hunting or shooting or socializing in the annual season, could indulge in intellectual sporting pursuits such as perfecting the laws of cricket or debating measurement systems for racing yachts.[12] It is no coincidence that the magazine *The Yachting World* began as a weekly in April 1894.[13]

In 1894 'Thalassa' was able to say of the length and sail area rule[14]

'the results have on the whole been highly satisfactory, fine seaworthy vessels, driven by a small sail area at great speed . . . in the large classes. The evolution in the small classes has been more rapid and in 1892 some rather undesirable types were prize winners. A committee under Sir George Lampson . . . obtained the opinions of leading designers' and met twice. It recommended the adoption of the *Seawanhaka Rule and changes in classification*. It also wanted some measurement changes including more tax on overhang and "cut away keels". When these proposals came before the YRA council, they were thrown out, "some of the committee voting against their own report" '.

Designers including Watson and Nathanael Herreshoff[15] began
to urge extra dimensions into a rule, but this was not understood
by the users. Herreshoff's proposal using length, sail area and
displacement was known in 1892, but it will not make any impact
until the next chapter (the twentieth century). 'Thalassa' listed
existing rules and rule proposals such as: the Seawanhaka rule, the
New York rule (very slightly different), the YRA rule, Herreshoff's
rule, Watson's rule (length, beam, depth, sail added using suitable
constants) and his own suggested modifications to some of these!
Additionally there were some strongly expressed 'no-nonsense'
sailors with calls for length only (good business for sail and spar
makers) and 'Mr Richardson' wanted sail area only: the latter not
really quite so intemperate as it appeared, as will be seen in the
'square-metre' classes of the 1930s.

Fig 2.4 demonstrates the dimensions of English raters in the

NAME OF YACHT		RIG	DATE	RATING	L.W.L ft.	SAIL AREA ft²
5 RATERS	ALWIDA	CUTTER	1890	4.95	29.66	1,002
	WINDFALL	LUG CUTT.	1891	4.97	32.89	909
	DACIA	LUG SLOOP	1892	5.00	33.83	888
2½ RATERS	THALASSA	SLOOP	1887	2.46	20.94	706
	MLISS	SLOOP	1890	2.50	24.97	603
	AVADAVAT	LUG SLOOP	1891	2.49	28.00	536
	GARETH	LUG SLOOP	1892	2.48	28.02	533
1 RATERS	PUP	LUG SLOOP	1890	0.99	18.21	328
	DOUSHKA	LUG SLOOP	1892	0.98	21.07	281
½ RATERS	SPRUCE	YAWL	1891	0.41	16.20	154
	DAISY	LUG SLOOP	1892	0.50	17.10	176

Fig 2.4 *An extract from a table of raters which were racing on the
Solent in the early 1890s. It will be seen that LWLs grew and sail
areas reduced as designers gained experience in the length and sail
area rule. The ratings are seen often to be just under the fixed
level. The 'lug rig' was actually a tall efficient mainsail looking
not unlike the later (from about 1925) Bermudian, but with a
separate spar for the top part of the sail.*

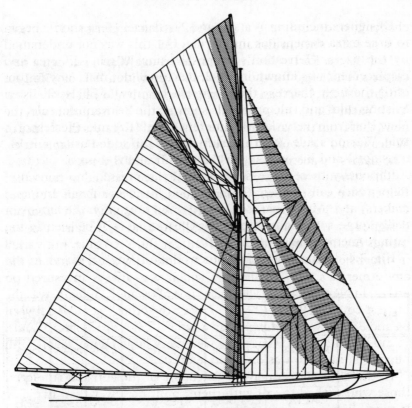

Fig 2.5 *The gigantic* Satanita *(owner, A.D.Clarke), LOA 131ft 6in (40.0m), designed by J.M.Soper, one of the nine great cutters built in Britain and the USA in 1893, an outstanding year in the history of yacht racing. She sailed at 17 knots when reaching. She was rated under the length and sail area rule as a 161.5 rater. The cutters all had slightly different ratings and time allowances were applied; for instance* Britannia *was 151 rating and* Valkyrie *was 147.7.*

Solent (as the area where the most advanced designs were and are seen) in about 1891-93.[16]

The biggest cutters

It is to the credit of the length and sail area rules, the American Seawanhaka and the British YRA, that, within these formulae, the largest racing yachts ever to compete regularly were created. These were the inshore cutters of the big class. The stimulus was the America's Cup which used the Seawanhaka rule in eight cup series between 1885 and 1903. Not all the cutters were built solely to

challenge or defend, several were built to race against such contestants or each other in Britain and the USA.

In 1892 the Earl of Dunraven ordered to a Watson design a new
cutter to challenge for the America's Cup with a WL of 85ft 10in
(26.2m) 4ft 2in less than the maximum length allowed by the New
York Yacht Club. But what really excited the British public was the
news that from the same designer His Royal Highness the Prince of
Wales would also build a vessel for competition to the same rules.
The names respectively were *Valkyrie II* and *Britannia*.

The stimulus of racing against the Prince resulted in two other
British owners ordering similar cutters. Mr Peter Donaldson had
Calluna designed by Fife and Mr A.D. Clarke had *Satanita*
designed by J.M.Soper (**Fig 2.5**). All the boats were fairly close in
rating. *Britannia* measured at 151 under the YRA rule, but varied
in dimensions; so they had to race on time allowance, as indeed did
any America's Cup challenger, which was always measured on
arrival in New York and allotted a time allowance. *Satanita* was the
biggest cutter at 97.7ft (29.8m) LWL; the others were all between
84 and 88ft LWL. *Britannia* had a typical LOA of 121.5ft (37.0m).
It can be understood that these were very large racing yachts with
huge rigs, for each was on a single mast.

In the USA, the American defenders of the cup and similarly,
those who wished to sail with them, built no fewer than five new
cutters all of size close to the British ones. They were *Navahoe*,
Colonia, *Jubilee*, *Pilgrim* and *Vigilant*; the last named was to defend
the cup successfully in 1893 against *Valkyrie II*. There has never
been, before or since, such a sensational arrival on the racing scene
of boats of this size.

It appears that the sheer size and resulting stresses kept extreme
tendencies away from these biggest length and sail area raters.
Britannia's overhangs were considerable (as were those of the other
cutters) and on appearance there was criticism of the concave bow
(**Fig 2.6**). Yet this general shape remained the 'look' of racing
yachts for some sixty years, including those built under later rules.
They were a handful to sail, but they were manned by large
professional crews, who were paid low wages and from time to time
suffered casualties, including falling from the rigging or injury on
deck. The most notable disaster was in Scotland on 5 July 1894,
when the 131ft 6in (40.0m) *Satanita* failed to bear away astern of
Valkyrie II before the start of a race, smashing through her just
abaft the mast. She sank in nine minutes, killing one of her crew.
Lord Dunraven, at the helm, and others escaped on to other
vessels.

The 1893 season, the first for the cutters, which were also joined by one or two older boats, was a superb one in England. Even better, the American *Navahoe* came to Cowes Week and other regattas, her first race against *Britannia* and the British in the Solent, out to Spithead, twice round, 50 miles, being watched by 'many thousand onlookers'.[17] *Britannia* beat *Navahoe*, which was third, by 1 minute 16 seconds. *Valkyrie II* which was second, left to sail the Atlantic after Cowes Week to race in the America's Cup, which she duly lost by three straight races.

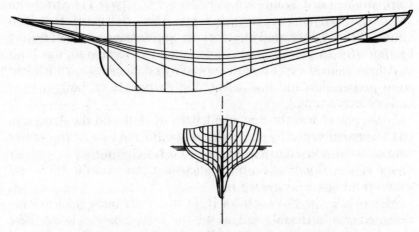

Fig 2.6 *The lines of* Britannia, *the racing cutter built for HRH The Prince of Wales (later Edward VII). The length and sail area rule contributed to the concave bow and long stern. At launch these features were considered odd and ugly, against the existing straight stems and clipper bows, but designers came to regard them as conventional long after the rating rules changed. Not for nearly fifty years was the shape questioned, until* Myth of Malham *appeared; however the concave bow continued until about 1975! Today it has gone in favour of 'cruiser bows' or even straight stems. Contrary to belief, designers are not always quick to respond to rules.* Britannia *was measured and converted during her life to several rules, the last one being the American Universal rule. Today she lies on the seabed near the waters of her many successes.*

The next year, the American winner *Vigilant* came to Britain to race the English cutters, starting her season on the Clyde. Results were mixed; in other words there was good sport. Rules and fixtures had moved a very long way since the visit of *America*, forty-three years earlier!

As for rating, *Vigilant* was slightly larger than *Britannia* and had to give the latter 3 minutes on a 50-mile course.[18] It will be noted that the American yacht was simply measured to the British rule on arrival (as was *Valkyrie II* measured to the American rule when she appeared at New York).

This 1894 visit was the last by a big American length and sail area rule cutter to Britain. For equivalent visits one will have to project forward to the 1930s when other classes, of lesser size, but big for their time, appear.

In America the emphasis was upon the defence of the America's Cup, where Lord Dunraven's challenger *Valkyrie III* arrived in 1895. Her sail area was much larger than the existing British cutters. She was defeated in notorious circumstances of bad feeling by *Defender*. In 1899, *Columbia*, designed by Herreshoff, was built to defend against Sir Thomas Lipton's first *Shamrock*, which had scant preparation and was defeated in every race on both elapsed and corrected time.

Shamrock II was the next challenger in 1901 and the American trials were enlivened by the rivalry of the Boston boat *Independence* whose owner refused to join the New York YC. Another new cutter this year was *Constitution*, but *Columbia* again won the trials and went on to defeat *Shamrock II*.

Meanwhile the Seawanhaka Rule to which these yachts were designed was in trouble and, as will be seen, smaller classes were already moving away from it. But the America's Cup was still thought to demand tradition and less regulation. So in 1903 when *Shamrock III* challenged *Reliance*, they were both extreme. *Reliance* had the same waterline (90ft, 27.4m) as *Columbia* (because this was the cup maximum), but her overhangs ran out to 143ft 8in (43.7m), still the longest America's Cup boat in history and she had 3000 square ft (278 sq m) more sail than the latter: 16,160 sq ft (1501 sq m).

Herreshoff understood that this was an extreme boat, widely known as a skimming dish and a racing machine, with her low freeboard, 54 feet (16.46m) of overhang, minimal displacement and flimsy scantlings. She was an electrolytic mixture of steel, aluminium and bronze: two months after defeating the British challenger in every race, she was broken up for scrap (**Fig 2.7**). It was even said that Herreshoff designed the boat as a lesson that the rule was finished; however he surely designed to the extreme to win the cup, in an age when owners often held back from pushing the rules.

All this was too much for the New York YC and the challenging British. Both sides set about negotiating some better rating rule for the

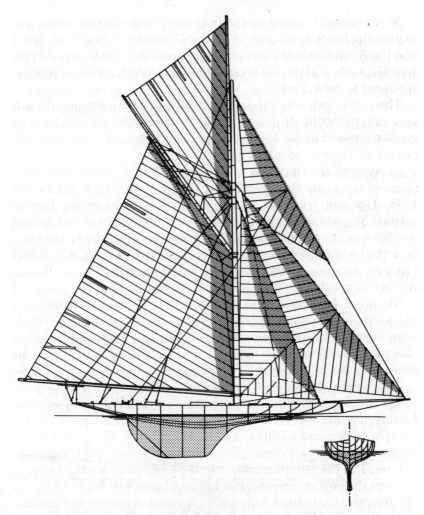

Fig 2.7 Reliance, *the Herreshoff Cup defender of 1903. Huge sail area (16,160 square feet), light displacement, very long ends (LOA 143ft 8in, 43.7m), 'U' or even 'dish' sections, she represented the extremes allowed under the Seawanhaka rule. Herreshoff wanted nothing more to do with this rule and the Universal rule followed quickly.*

big cutters of the America's Cup. In the event there was not another match for 17 years.

Meanwhile in England, the foreign challenge in the big class came now from H.I.M. the German Emperor in his *Meteor* (previously the British Watson-designed *Thistle*) and another new boat *Ailsa* was launched in 1895. A rating crisis had not arrived in the big class, but it arose from the smaller boats. The YRA therefore published a new rule (below) for the 1896 season. This had little effect on the big cutters now also joined by a new *Meteor*, designed by Watson for the Kaiser. Their ratings moved numerically[19] but together in proportion: size and cost mitigated against new vessels. With small adjustments they continued to race. The story for the small skimming dishes was different.

Fins, machines, skimmers
Among the raters from $\frac{1}{2}$ rating to 40 rating, the YRA rule looked more sick each year. As explained, designers were at first slow to take advantages of rating, but from about 1890, the most successful racers were being outdated each new season. A 5-rater of 1883 had an LWL of 20ft (6m), but a top 5-rater of 1892 had an LWL of 36ft (10.4m). $2\frac{1}{2}$-raters LWL grew by about 25 per cent. Some British owners ordered designs from Nat Herreshoff and in the season of 1891, the $\frac{1}{2}$-rater *Wee Win* and the $2\frac{1}{2}$-rater *Wenonah* swept all before them in Solent racing (**Fig 2.8**). Photographs show them with moderate beam, very low freeboard, long ends and large sail area. Displacement was light with a fin keel which had to be secured to the thinly planked hull with the fastenings and caulking of the period. Races in the Solent in 1892 for $\frac{1}{2}$, 1, $2\frac{1}{2}$, 5 and 10-raters totalled 251, given by 12 clubs, most all of whose names are still with us.[20]

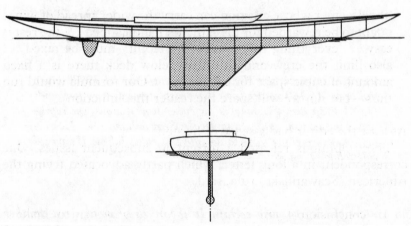

Fig 2.8 *Hull of* Wee Winn, *very successful sloop rigged $\frac{1}{2}$-rater designed by Nathanael Herreshoff for an English owner, Miss W. Sutton, in 1892. This skimming dish raced in the Solent with a crew of three; LOA 23ft 10in (7.28m), LWL 15ft 6in (4.72m).*

An English 1-rater designed by Linton Hope in 1894 had a
centreplate. With this down, draft was 6ft 5in (2.0m); LOA was
28ft (8.5m), LWL 18ft 9in (5.7m), displacement 1470lb (667kg). A
10-rater might have an LWL of 38ft (11.6m) and LOA of 57ft
(17.4m).

Photographs in *Yachting World* 1894, and elsewhere, show quite
attractive groups of these racing craft: whether the type was liked
or not was up to individual yachtsmen, but there were two
substantive complaints. The leading boats were outclassed each
season and the scantlings were very poor.

Towards the end of the 1894 season (21 September), an editorial
in *Yachting World* said,

'In 1892 the principal designers met at the Langham Hotel and
drew up a circular addressed to the YRA. This document urged
the advisability of passing a rating rule which would have the
effect of eliminating the machine and rendering the racer of
today suitable to become the cruiser of tomorrow ... It is absurd
to encourage a type of craft which is outclassed in a year or so
and then is useless for the purpose of cruising. [As a result]
racing is becoming confined to [small] boats, while in the larger
classes, competition is lessening.'

The editor complained that now there were numerous opinions.
He was to throw out sail area because

'the designer whose creation can carry the wider spread of wings
ought to be rewarded for his skill, not handicapped ... the rest is
easy ... everything that makes for stability must be taxed ...
also limit the crew and rule that below deck there is a fixed
amount of cubic space for each man ... Our formula would run
thus – but no, we will spare the reader this infliction'.

At least the editor had a sense of humour.

These opinions released a torrent in subsequent issues. One
correspondent in a long letter, which partly advocated trying the
American (Seawanhaka) rule, said,[21]

'In conclusion I am *certain it is an easy matter* to make a
measurement rule that will produce good vessels as yachts, but I
do not know if the public or the YRA want a yacht or a machine.
Heaven only knows what Dixon Kemp wants and that is the first
thing to find out ... '

Another letter is ahead of its time:[22]

> 'Sir, With regard to the international rule, I think that any rule
> agreed to by England and America would, in all probability,
> meet the views of our club, the Imperial and Royal Yacht
> Squadron of Austria. I am, Sir, etc,
> Batthany-Strattmann, Vienna'.[23]

It was to be 75 years before the UK and USA combined to agree
on a rating rule. In the same issue there was a note of no less than
two rating rules in use in France under different authorities.[24]

Possibly this letter was something to do with a committee which
had been appointed by the YRA to recommend action on the rating
rule, but had slid out from a decision by recommending that first
contact should be made with the USA, or rather the New York YC.
Meanwhile there should be no change until 1896.

Said Thalassa of this,

> 'As for the English and American rating rules, they have been
> examined and discussed so often and so fully, that yachtsmen
> must be rather tired of the subject.'

There was a widely held opinion in England that the Seawanhaka
(USA) rule was better than the YRA rule. It is difficult (for this
author) to find any rationale for this and contemporary argument is
mixed up with methods of measurement, 'classification' (see
Chapter 1) and limits of rating and LWL for the big (including
America's Cup class).

On 12 October 1894, *Yachting World* ran an extensive piece by
Thalassa on possible rating rules discussing such advanced concepts as girth, immersed depth, hull volume, as well as length (of
various kinds), beam and displacement. Towards the end of this
exhaustive essay he argued that displacement was already at a near
minimum owing to the weight of essential materials and that draft
was checked by 'sandbanks', while boats must be strong enough
'not to leak *badly* (!) when pushed in heavy weather.' Fins and bulb
keels were acceptable for classes of 10-rater and below, as they were
too small for cruising anyway.

> 'Our object should be to tax the saucer section, without encour-
> aging the plank-on-edge, or doing anything to assist the further
> development of length. By adopting the American rule for
> rating, we can check length development . . .' He vaguely sug-

gested a tax on 'shallow hulls'. 'As for the date of such change, if change there be, the sooner it comes the better'.

It is evident that despite there being much sailing fun, rating and measurement in the United Kingdom were in trouble.

Towards a new linear rule

As British yachtsmen grappled with the problem of the skimming dish, some of their number hit on a radical solution. In the words of one group, there was

'concern at the ever increasing expenditure attendant on small class racing in the Solent . . . the sport should be conducted in a manner suitable to the means of the majority and not merely with a view to the encouragement of the few, who can afford year after year to build a new boat'.

The result of this statement at a meeting of owners was the concept of a one-design. Away with rating rules, said these sailors and in the winter of 1895-96, ten of these 33ft (10.0m) gaff cutters were built in Southampton. They were called the Solent One-Design and were the first one-design in England.

Some years earlier (1887) in Kingstown (now Dun Laoghaire), Ireland, a dinghy class had formed as a one-design: the Water Wag of 13ft (4.0m). Several other classes followed from 1896 onward; in fact the creation of one-design classes has never ceased (Chapter 6). The point here is that the concept arose as a direct result of frustration with the rating rule in the 1890s.[25]

Meanwhile for the vast majority of existing owners a workable measurement and time allowance system was needed.

Thus it was that at a special meeting of the Yacht Racing Association held at the Langham Hotel in June 1895 the proposal to 'amend the rule of rating', after a long discussion (of course!) was carried by 27 votes to 6.[26] The formula, devised mainly by R.E. Froude, was

$$\text{Rating} = (L + B + .75G + .5(S)^{1/2})/2$$

L was LWL, B maximum beam wherever found, S sail area. G was a new idea, girth. This was the actual outline of the section at 0.6 of the LWL from the forward end (**Fig 2.9**). If there was a centreboard, the depth of the board below the keel multiplied by 1.5 was added to G. This is often called 'the first linear rule'; it being in

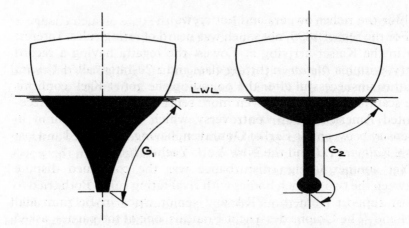

Fig 2.9 *First attempts (in Britain; the French had tried similar methods) to tax light displacement and the skimming dish by the concept of* skin girth measurement. *As shown here the shorter girth, G1, implied a fuller section. The skimming dish attracted a high number, G2, which, in the top line of a formula as G, increased the rating. Girths have been used in various forms in yacht measurement ever since.*

practice a new rule, effective from the 1896 season. It will be seen that it looked somewhat like the Seawanahaka rule with bits added, for the result was now a figure in feet, as the Americans already had, not just a rating number to give a 'rater'. However it was still essentially a length and sail area rule.

G was intended to make a saucer shape with a deep fin keel pay more than a less extreme section and B was taxed for the first time since the tonnage rules.

Controversy was not long in coming: one week to be exact. There was an outcry that the clubs and members of the RYA had not been consulted and that the rule had been announced suddenly.

'A coach and horses will be driven through the new rule' said Thalassa[27] 'The new rule is a thoroughly bad one; it will produce a very costly type, requiring much lead, much sail and much crew power. It will not encourage moderate dimensions, but precisely the reverse'.

He produced examples of winning 5-, 20- and 40-raters of the time. His argument was that by adding lead, cutting down the keel depth a bit and adding sail area, the rule would be circumvented and the boats remain with all their present faults (albeit still fun to sail for the richer owners and hot crews).

For the rest of 1895, not much was heard of rating rules. Interest lay in the Kaiser arriving at Cowes, the regatta having a record entry, with his *Meteor* in the big class and a 20-rater called *Venetta* ('rather unsuccessful after the pounding she got at Kiel' confirms the scantling problems). Even more sensational was the unprecedented America's Cup controversy which grew all autumn in intensity between the Earl of Dunraven, having challenged and lost with *Valkyrie III* and the New York Yacht Club.[28]

Yet another foreign disturbance was the continued dispute between the two French bodies with rival rating rules. Both tried to enlist support from the YRA and senior clubs in Belgium and Holland. The Unions des Yacht Français, one of the parties, asked 'Why has the Congress of Naval Architects (English) (*sic*) not proposed an international rule?'[29] The UYF rule was said to resemble the new YRA rule.

This line of thought will be found more than once over the years as local/regional organizations call for an 'international rule' to solve their own disputes.

It is difficult to judge the success of the new YRA rule in its first season in England of 1896. The voices that were against it from its inception immediately pointed to design changes (more sail area, expensive alterations and so on) for the worse. The complaint was the classic one that if further changes were made, the building of the 1896 boat would have been wasted, but if they were not then it would mark the final eclipse of all the boats that had gone before. The new owners were all new: the previous ones had moved into one-designs, it was alleged.[30]

In October the YRA held a general meeting to consider an alteration to the linear rule for yachts of 36ft rating and below. The proposal was

$$\text{Rating} = (L + 1.2B + G + 0.5(S)^{1/2})/2.2$$

What exactly these small adjustments of constants were meant to achieve is not clear, but the proposal was rejected by a large majority.[31]

So what is often known as the first linear rule went on and with it the skimming dishes, albeit with different proportions between sail, weight on the fin keel and draft. There was still nothing in the rule about displacement, freeboard, control of the overhangs, or scantlings.

In the big class however there now developed difficulties.

Britannia was laid up at the end of the 1897 season, partly because of her change of rating, which had proved difficult to adjust against the new *Meteor II* designed by George Watson for the Kaiser, who achieved his aim of beating 'Uncle Bertie' (the Prince of Wales) on the water.

> 'The new linear rating rule ensured that *Meteor II* would not only be larger than *Britannia*, but would be of lighter construction, more easily driven, much more heavily canvassed [meaning more sail area] and all without commensurate penalty on the rating'[32]

Another royal owner, the Duke of York (later King George V) was actually able to take advantage of the new rule by having a 1-rater, *White Rose*, designed by Sibbick and built in eight days, ensuring it was the latest design at Cowes regatta.

In addition to the change of rule, the YRA made alterations in the bigger classes to the time allowance (the detail is unimportant) and the old chestnut 'classification' also reappeared, when a few ex-40 raters with new linear ratings were allowed to race with the big cutters and beat them on corrected time. One leading authority wrote,

> 'In 1897, as a result of these changes, the great class, founded by *Britannia* and her contemporaries in 1893, deteriorated and broke up . . . The result of the YRA's legislation was a positive disaster. The YRA destroyed first class yacht racing.'[33]

The second linear rule

Late in 1897 a new secretary was sought for the YRA. There were a number of applications, but appointed was Major Brooke Heckstall-Smith. Under new terms of engagement, the secretary could not act as a yacht designer. It will be seen that 'Bookstall' had, over the forty-six years for which he will eventually hold this position, a vast influence on British and European yacht racing and rating.[34]

In the same year in America, there was a meeting in the Fifth Avenue Hotel, New York. Present were representatives from associations already formed by groups of clubs along the American east coast and the Great Lakes. It was agreed that a national association must be formed. In October the same people came together again representing no fewer than 106 clubs in the United States. They resolved to form the North American Yacht Racing Union (NAYRU). Two yachtsmen, who were already scheduled to

go to England on business on the SS *St Louis*, were deputed to
make contact with the British YRA and designers to discuss a
solution to the rating rule difficulties of both countries.

One year later they returned with details of the YRA rule (first
linear) and in 1899 it was used on the Lakes. In October 1900, the
Lakes clubs abandoned it and resolved to use whatever rules each
club wished until an agreed rule could be found.[35]

As for NAYRU, it had never had the approval of the New York
YC, Eastern YC and other important clubs and it quietly faded.[36]
One effect of this failure was that there was no authority in the
United States which could even discuss with the British YRA the
possibility of an agreed and improved rating rule.

At the same time the British were interested in the American
attempts to improve their rating rule, the main contender being the
Herreshoff proposal that put displacement in the bottom line of a
formula. One objection was that the use of displacement would
produce a 'slow' boat, whatever that might have meant, for slow is
relative. Typical of the discussion in 1898 was

'Surely since the tonnage rules, rating has not aimed at measurement of size, but simply at a measure of *racing efficiency* [original
italics], a very different thing; and we have done this by taxing
inefficiency viz., by taxing the well known speed producing
elements – hull length and sail area. So that when a yacht
possessing these elements is not correspondingly fast, she must
be regarded as a racing failure ... Another argument is that
small [light] displacement is speed producing; therefore we will
tax it. But the simplest way to tax [light] displacement is to put a
premium on large [heavy] displacement on the size of immersed
mid-section'[37]

Amazingly at the end of the 19th century, there is still a leading
rule exponent, R.E. Froude, writing that

'It seems to me absurd for racing purposes that boats should not
be allowed to take as much sail as they can utilize to advantage;
therefore I am against all sail tax on principle'[38]

1898 saw more international exchanges than hitherto, when the
Baltic rating rule was thrown into disarray by a 32 footer (9.75m)
(**Fig 2.10**) sailing on Berlin lakes, which made a mockery of the rule
which measured girth round the underwater body only and a
bigger boat was said to be building. It is obvious it could only race

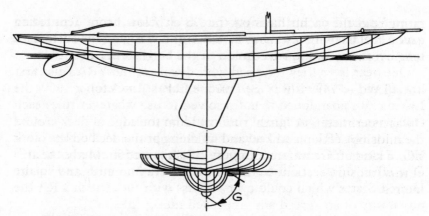

Fig 2.10 '*A hurried assembly of the Northern sailing and yachting clubs in Copenhagen [in April 1898] followed the appearance in Berlin of the this little abnormity* (sic) *called Trirumph. She walks quite through the Benzon rule!' As the rule measured girth to the waterline, G was small on the section. The designer was a Herr Otto Krüger.*

in flat water. The Danish rule guru, a Copenhagen chemist called Alfred Benzon, came up with various solutions for discussion in autumn 1898 at a Baltic conference. 'But why not adopt the English system of measurement, rather than drive yourselves silly by having to select one of the eleven little alternatives offered by Herr Benzon', wrote an Englishman living in Copenhagen[39]

Alfred Benzon actually had an excellent new idea and it appeared in his finalized proposal for a new Baltic rule,

$$\text{Rating} = (L + B + G + d + 0.25(S)^{1/2})/2$$

The small 'd' was the innovation. It was the difference between section girth and chain girth (**Fig 2.11**), measured right up to the deck (to overcome simply the Berlin rule cheater). What it did was detect light displacement and deep fin keels; indeed it directly attacked the skimming dish, which had not been brought to heel despite the efforts over dozen years.

The rating attempts of France
A sign of increased activity between nations was the first One Ton Cup at Meulan on the River Seine, near Paris, between England and France. The host club, Cercle de la Voile de Paris, used its own

rating rule, the yachts having to rate at or below 1 ton. This rating gave a keel boat of only about 17ft (5.2m) LWL with the customary long overhang and low freeboard of the English linear boats.[40]

$$((LWL - P/4) \times (P \times S)/(1000 \times (M^2)^{1/3}) = 1 \text{ ton}$$

P was a perimeter, or 'girth' running from the edge of deck around the midship section and keel and finishing at the deck on the other side, a kind of circumference of the midship section. M was the area of this midship section. Measurements were in metres and square metres.

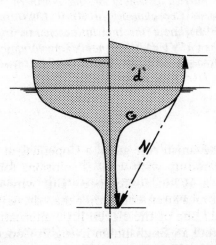

Fig 2.11 *The solution to* **Fig 2.10** *was to take up to the covering board (deck edge), both a skin girth (G) and a chain girth (Z), the difference being d, devised by the Dane, Alfred Benzon. Again it attacked the skimming dish, though it gave an incentive to low freeboard, which would have to be corrected later.*

There had been as much controversy in previous years in France, as in Britain, the USA and Scandinavia on a suitable rating rule. While the Americans were searching for displacement, the concept of P was an enlightened one, not adopted by the British as girth measurement until 1895. The first French attempt after collapse of their own tonnage rule was to use LWL and perimeter only. The Cercle de la Voile rule of 1882 (about the same time as the arrival of the Seawanhaka) was

$$\text{Rating in metres} = (L \times P (2L + P))/300$$

It is seen that there was no sail area, no beam: result – narrow skimming dish.

The Yacht Club de France did not think much of this and was urged by a particularly talented member to use its own rating rule. He was Gustave Caillebotte (1849-94), the impressionist painter whose large collection including many yachting studies is today in the Louvre. An architect, gardener, rower and stamp collector, he was also a keen racing man with the YCF at Argenteuil; he also had views on suitable rating formulae. The result was the YCF rule of 1886, the Caillebotte rule:

Rating in metres $= 1/2\{(P/4)^2 \times (LWL - B/2)\}$

There was still no sail area, though beam was in and still perimeter. Six years later (1896), the French clubs settled their differences and under the banner of UYF (Union des Yachts Français), developed the rule by adding sail area (S); known as the 'formule Godinet', this was

Rating in metres $= (LWL \text{ -}P/4) \times P \times (S)^2/130$

This was revised in 1899 in time for the first ever One Ton Cup, by adding the midship section on the bottom line (the nearest indication of displacement) then adjusting the squares and cubes of the latter and the sail area to end up with a linear figure of around 1. It was then called One Ton which might have been near the actual weight of the size of yacht. The formula (formule Muran) was as shown on the previous page as equal to 1 ton.

A short lived British linear rule
The seasons of 1900 and 1901 were not sparkling in Britain. 'Perhaps the flattest on record'.[41] The South African War broke out; the Queen died in 1901 having been on the throne since 1837; *Shamrock II*, ill prepared some said for a cup attempt, was defeated off New York in three straight matches (see above). However J. Orr-Ewing was still taunting the rule makers and for 1900 he had Sibbick design him a 36 footer (10.97m) with 'flat floor, light displacement, extremely lightly built and bulb keel of about 5cwt (254kg) . . . She was by far the fastest boat of her class, was of little use save that of racing in sheltered waters and went far to indicate the necessity of altering the measurement rule'. In desperation the YRA grabbed at the German/Scandinavian rule (see Appendix I) and incorporated 'd' in a rule that looked like the Baltic one,

but with the alteration of a few constants, one of which made 'd' stronger.[42] G, the girth measurement, was also there. For the 1901 season in the United Kingdom, the following was promulgated,

Rating in feet = $(L + B + 0.75G + 0.5(S)^{1/2}) + d$

With the coming of the 20th century, Brooke Heckstall-Smith, Alfred Benzon and others now began to work, by correspondence, cable and occasional meetings, towards something that would be worthy of the sport of yacht racing. By this was still meant the sailing of keel boats by day in relatively sheltered waters, though the largest yachts might use a rating to complete a rare race along the coast, across the Channel or even for the Kaiser's prize from the Thames to Heligoland. But it was the smaller vessels which were the annual rule beaters. Indeed Orr-Ewing built two 36 footers to the 1901 rule that very season! The first was unsuccessful, so he had a further design constructed. Did she sparkle? Records do not reveal. But, as has been said, it was not that sort of year in England; there was, among other problems, a weariness about new rating rules.

Farewell the Seawanhaka rule

Reliance, the 1903 defender, has already been mentioned as the biggest ever America's Cup yacht and the representatative of unacceptable extremes to the Seawanhaka rule. She carried a racing crew of 64, mostly to sit along the weather rail. It was also pointed out that the smaller classes in clubs of the USA were moving away from the rule prior to 1903.

The foremost international trophy for match racing in small yachts, the Seawanhaka Cup, contested by Britain and Canada against the Seawanhaka Corinthian YC of Long Island Sound in very sheltered water, was towards the end of the century being sailed in the flattest of scows or even catamarans which developed under the Seawanhaka rule. Unlike the America's Cup, all three countries won it at different times.

The original Seawanhaka rule of 1883, $(L + (S)^{1/2})/2$, had been hedged about with various dimensional limits and measurement requirements. For instance the British defenders in 1897 agreed on the basic formula, but the rating (which was then often called 'rated length') was limited to 20ft (6.09m), draft 5ft or 6ft with centreboard, sail area limited to 500 square feet and mainsail to 80 per cent of total. Crew to be amateurs.

Readers will see that these kind of conditions virtually turned

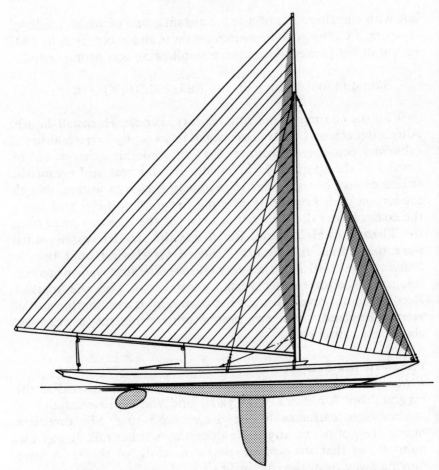

Fig 2.12 Ethelwynn, *two man centreboard sloop, actual Seawan-haka Cup defender in 1895. Designed to the eponymous rule, she was not at all what the rule makers envisaged. The rule was scrapped for such racing, even before its last use in the 1903 America's Cup (see* **Fig 2.7***)*.

the class into a 'restricted class' (which will be examined fully later), though the term was then unknown.

However these were not enough for the use of the rule around the USA and by 1898 a committee of the Seawanhaka Corinthian YC was reporting that, as was well known for some time, the basic formula was inadequate. At the close of the Victorian era, not only in Britain but in America and on the continent, the rule makers took to apologising for the *length of the new proposals* – to us no length at all! The rule committee came up in 1898 with

$$\text{Rating in feet} = (L + S^{1/2} + 2(B + D) - 6.6\ (MS)^{1/2})/2$$

So they were to incorporate B, beam, D draft and MS which was the midship section, a close relation of the displacement. 'In regard to the correction of the evil of too light construction, there would appear to be no simple or very practical way of dealing with the matter ... *It may be well to call to mind the high favour with which one-design classes have recently been received. Their success may justly be regarded as a strong and general protest against extreme features and against the inequalities and uncertainties of racing under present conditions'.*[43]

This proposal, which was not without merit, came to nothing for it was outflanked by the New York Yacht Club which was also busy with rule committees in 1902. Letters were written under the direction of ex-commodore S. Nicholson Kane canvassing views from around the USA, the United Kingdom and the continent. As the club history says,

'The Seawanhaka rule, based on waterline length and sail area, had proved increasingly unsatisfactory, because it produced unseaworthy winners, that were flat long ended scows with little displacement (**Fig 2.12**). The Canadian yachts that were winning ... were disgraceful examples of naval architecture.'[44]

At a December 1902 meeting of the New York YC, the Seawanhaka rule was, after 19 years, dispensed with and a proposal long urged by Herreshoff adopted. As we know, the Seawanhaka remained in use in the America's Cup for 1903 only. The Seawanhaka Corinthian YC itself welcomed the rule change, as did, in the absence of any American national authority, the majority of clubs on the east coast and Great Lakes. In the next chapter, where the rule is reproduced, it will be seen that, with such rapid adoption, the Herreshoff rule became called in 1904 the Universal rule. Nathanael Herreshoff was elected an honorary member of the New York YC, apparently the only untitled one for some years, in the company of HM King Edward VII, HRH The Prince of Wales, HIM Kaiser Wilhelm II and Sir Thomas Lipton Bt.

3 Ratings cross the narrow seas

'Despising, the city, thus I turn my back: there is a world elsewhere.' –
Coriolanus (1623) by William Shakespeare.

*'The rules of yacht racing are now the same in all the countries of
Europe. A few years ago a state of hopeless chaos reigned everywhere.
Different systems of measurement and classification and different codes
of sailing rules prevailed and the yachtsman was quite unable to master
them all. Now this has been rectified . . .'* – Brooke Heckstall-Smith
in 1908.

A RULE of measurement and rating fit for the 20th century
came first in America, used by the New York Yacht Club
for its 1903 season. The same year in Europe a parallel
move was delayed by a few years as the national authorities or
senior clubs of the yacht race nations sought to find an agreed
formula.

This new American rule, as has been seen, had appeared quite
frequently in discussions during the later unsatisfactory years of
the length and sail area boats on both sides of the Atlantic. Its
original and adopted formula was this:

Rating in feet = (L × (S)$^{1/2}$))/5 × (D)$^{1/3}$

In this case D is displacement; so at last this essential and vast
influence arrived in the rating rule. By using the square root of the
sail area and the cube root of the displacement, all dimensions were
reduced to linear ones and in feet. The rating was therefore in feet.

This set the pattern for many years: many sailors find it
convenient to visualize rating as a length in feet, because this can be
related to an envisaged speed. One can somehow think of a 40
footer (12.19m) (waterline not overall) sailing away from a 30

footer (9.14m). Further, the rating in feet of the yacht represented its (very) theoretical load waterline, which in basic naval architecture is directly proportional to the square of the maximum speed. This is expressed as

$$\text{Maximum speed} = k\,(LWL)^{1/2}$$

The constant k is about 1.4, though planing hulls, moving ballast and measurement-'cheating' waterlines, undoubtedly leave it in the theoretical category!

The Universal rule

With typical American enthusiasm and optimism, outflanking the European search for an 'international' rule, the formula was named in 1904, as mentioned, the Universal rule. Not only was it technically a big step forward, but it had the important negative effect of being fully acceptable in bringing the Seawanhaka rule to an end. It will be seen also to become an essential component of other later rules of the twentieth century when its own days are over. Most notable of all, it was the rule of rating used in the America's Cup races from the *Resolute* v. *Shamrock IV* races of 1920 until *Ranger* v. *Endeavour II* in 1937.

Without any national authority it was up to each club or regional association (such as the YRA of Long Island Sound) to adopt the rule, following the New York YC and the Seawanhaka Corinthian YC. Whether the rule did, in the event, prosper widely in the United States will be examined shortly.

There was a major change in attitude in the running of the Universal rule, when compared with the late length and sail area rule. The same phenomenon will be seen in the new European rule. The desperate search for a better kind of rule no longer prevailed; instead technical improvements were made to the existing rule to a greater or lesser amount. This is surely preferable to any 'sweep away the government and start with a clean sheet' moves, which are a sure cause of despair among owners.

In its first six years the Universal rule had some changes both in the basic formula and the measurements on which it was based. By 1904, the lower constant of 5 had been changed slightly to become 5.5. It is not clear why; perhaps to more closely equate the LWL of existing yachts.

As for L, this had an important method of measurement, for long advocated by Herreshoff. No longer was the dimension on the waterline, giving rise to long overhangs. Instead it used the quite well known concept of 'quarter beam depth'. The length was measured (**Fig 3.1**) one quarter of the greatest beam at LWL, out from the centre and one-tenth of that beam above the waterline. Any 'notches, jogs, curves or angles' (or, as would have been said in the 1980s, 'creases') would be ignored.

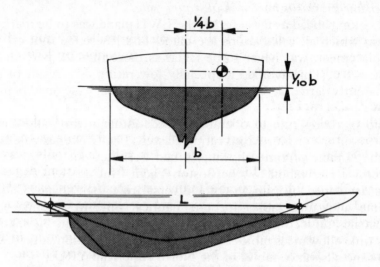

Fig 3.1 *Nathanael Herreshoff's accepted way of measuring length and adopted for the Universal rule to avoid the disadvantages of waterline. b is maximum beam; one quarter of the beam out from centreline was taken and where this intersected the ends was measured at one-tenth of the beam above the waterline. It was an important abandonment of very simplistic measurement.*

Displacement, D, was obtained by areas of cross sections along the LWL divided into five parts. There were limits on draft and sail area to prevent excesses seen earlier. Any excess of the square root of the sail area, $(S)^{1/2}$, over 135 per cent of rated L, was to be added to the rating. No vessel under the rule could have a draft of more than 18 feet, *excluding centreboard*, though this did not apply to yachts built before 1905. Draft of any yacht without penalty was limited to $(0.15 \times L) + 2.5$ feet, again centreboards were free.

In 1909, there was the last change (again a small one to the constant) to the basic formula, which remained for ever as follows:

Rating in feet $= 0.18 (L \times (S)^{1/2})/ D^{1/3}$

The same year there were small changes in draft limit, $(0.16 \times L) + 1.75$ feet; there was an alteration to measuring sections for displacement at ten sections rather than five. A change to L was: LWL plus half the excess of quarter beam length over the percentage of LWL given by $100 - (LWL)^{1/2}$.

Apart from the detail, it can be seen that there immediately developed problems in measuring the length of a hull necessitating amendments; this is known in all rating rules.

Looking ahead as far as 1913, the LWL plane was to be marked 'from which all calculations are made' and [the cube root of] D, displacement, was never to be taken as more than 20 percent of LWL + 0.5. This avoided a specially low rating as a result of an apparently large D. Thus stood the Universal rule just before WWI.[1]

For a rating rule to operate it needs either a time allowance system or one or more fixed rating classes. The Universal rule had both. A table of time allowances had been set out by the ever inventive Herreshoff for the Boston Yacht Club in 1877 and this was developed by him as the Universal rule took shape. Called 'Time allowance tables for one nautical mile in seconds and decimals', these, duly refined and accepted, became the New York YC time allowances tables and then, without alteration, after 1925 the time allowance tables of the North American YRU.

The tables are shown in Chapter 5, for they eventually will have a pronounced effect on the development of rating rules throughout the world.

As for fixed rating classes, there came about a number at rating figures under the Universal rule. They were known by letters, including S, R, Q, P, M, L and J (**Fig 3.2**). Class J was 76 feet under the rule and became used for the America's Cup (see below); the others were smaller.

Fixed rating or one-design

Records in the United States are peculiarly reticent about the progress of classes under the Universal rule from its inception in 1903 until, say, 1914. It seems that clubs created new classes as one-designs 'complying to the Universal rule', but there is no evidence that these raced against different designs using time allowances under the rule. Once again the lack of any national authority meant that clubs made their own racing classes. Herreshoff designed, for individual clubs, the Buzzards Bay 30 in 1902 (with his new rule in mind), the Bar Harbor 30 in 1903 and, specifically to rate to the rule, the New York Yacht Club 30 in 1905. At the big regattas the NYYC 30 raced as a one-design. Presumably the idea was that the class had a good rating when in a

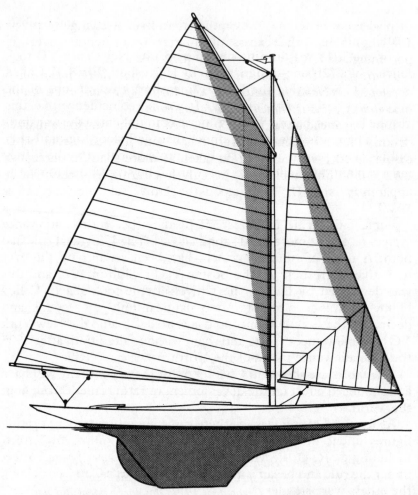

Fig 3.2 *One of a number of classes designed to the Universal rule at specific ratings. Each was given a letter; this one is the Q class of about 1910 at 25.0ft rating and about 38ft (11.6m) LOA.*

mixed fleet under time allowance.

The 'P-boats' (which was the American mode of talking about these classes) rated at 31ft Universal rule, were about 54ft LOA and about 34ft LWL with cabin accommodation. Two paid hands were carried. The Q-boat rated 25ft, was 28ft LWL and 40ft LOA. They seemed to have something of a peak year in 1907, when HM King Edward VII presented a cup for the class in connection with an international exhibition at Jamestown (first British settlement), Virginia. One report speaks of a race with P and Q-boats in it;[2] this implies numbers were not great and that time allowances using the

Universal rule were in use. R-boats were 20 feet rating and S-boats smaller still.

For the 1913 season nine members of the New York YC took delivery of a 72ft one-design, again by Herreshoff (**Fig 3.3**). Called the NYYC 50s (using the LWL dimension), this was one of the largest one-designs ever created.[3] It was no coincidence that this was the last year before WWI. America did not enter the war until 1917. 'There was keen racing under their gaff sloop rigs and club topsails every season until 1916. For a professional crew, the Fifties had a captain, two sailors and a steward. They continued to race as

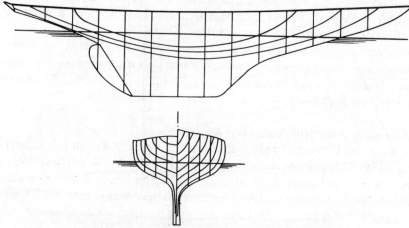

Fig 3.3 *Lines of the New York Yacht Club 50, which was 72ft (21.9m) LOA. Designed to the Universal rule, it was a one-design class. The lines show a moderate type: the skimming dish was now of the past. Created in 1913, this large yacht did not unfortunately long survive WWI.*

a class after the war, but crew costs presented a problem and income tax and inflation had come into existence'.

'The last sizeable Universal rule one-design was a fleet of fourteen yachts of the New York YC Forty Footers. These were 59 feet LOA'.[4] They were apparently comfortable cruisers, considered ugly because of their high sides. The class raced after WWI, when it was known as the 'Roaring Forties' because owners and crews prided themselves on racing hard and drinking hard. *Memory*, of the class, owned by Bob Bavier, won the 1924 Bermuda race, under a different measurement rule (Chapter 4). As the class broke up, the various boats sailed under ocean racing rules or went cruising.

There must have been reasons why the rich owners of the New York YC clubbed together and built one-designs, instead of fixed rating yachts to the Universal rule. There were reasons too why the club reported these boats as 'one-designs to the Universal rule' whatever that might have meant.

The author believes that the Universal rule was unsatisfactory because it (a) had no scantling control, (b) had a very difficult measuring problem in computing D, the displacement as defined, (c) had no national or even rule authority to control and promote it, except the NYYC, which however senior, well respected and indeed wealthy, was still a gentlemen's club. For instance, amazingly, a P-boat racing off Marblehead was actually a boat of different rating to a P-boat in Great South Bay.

It will be seen that in Europe these three problems were overcome early. The Americans were loathe to admit all this, but we shall see how the Universal rule eventually faded and how leading American yachtsmen began to sail under the European rating rule.

The new rule for America's Cup

Where the Universal rule was used consistently was in the America's Cup. This is not surprising since the New York YC had it very much in mind when they abandoned the length and sail area rule following the freaks of 1903. However there was a gap of 17 years before the next race. *This was due to arguments over the rating rule* and then just as the race was impending, the outbreak of WWI.

After his 1903 defeat Sir Thomas Lipton challenged in 1907 through the Royal Irish Yacht Club, Dublin. He asked that ? challenge be accepted by the NYYC using class J of the Universal rule without time allowance, for, as seen below, this was the kind of racing that was the new fashion in the United Kingdom and Europe. Sir Thomas asked if he could build two yachts and select the faster after trials. A letter to this effect was sent to New York by the SS *Umbria* with a cable to say that it was on the way.

Quite quickly the NYYC replied that the America's Cup was 'for the fastest and most powerful vessels that could be produced' and that there should be 'no limitation or restriction other than is implied in the limits on waterline length expressed in the Deed [of the cup] . . . no agreement should be made to produce a vessel of special or limited type . . .' There was more on these lines. The club declined the challenge. 'We adopt this mode of communicating by cable in order that the action may reach you officially in advance of any other . . .'

It was signed by some very powerful men: Cornelius Vanderbilt, Commodore, Cass Ledyard (who had led the expulsion of Lord Dunraven), J.P. Morgan, C. Oliver Iselin and others on the committee.[5]

There was not the slightest mention of the Universal rule, nor of class J. It all seems to confirm that the concept of a fixed rating to the rule, which the NYYC itself had adopted, was in 1907 totally alien.

Over the years sometimes frequently, sometimes with nothing happening for long periods, Lipton corresponded with the NYYC. Advised by British rule experts and designers, he urged the NYYC to agree to a yacht of 75ft limit on the LWL which would then be measured to the Universal rule and, of course, race on the NYYC time allowance. The club held out for a 90ft LWL (27.43m), as *Reliance* had been, but having made their point they conceded the 75ft (22.86m) and the challenge was on.[6] *Shamrock IV* sailed across the Atlantic in the summer of 1914; war broke out when she was on passage and she was laid up on arrival in New York, the races taking place in July 1920 in outer New York harbor.

Charles Nicholson the British designer of *Shamrock IV* was obviously not familiar with the Universal rule[7] and she had to give the defender *Resolute* 7 minutes 1 second on the 30 mile course.

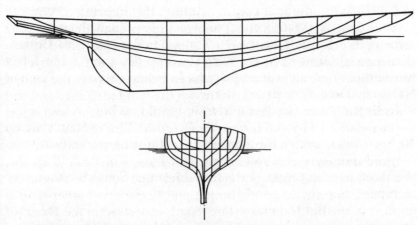

Fig 3.4 Resolute, *lines, cup defender for 1914 (postponed to 1920). The scow hull of* Reliance *had gone. Universal rule, maximum waterline 75ft (22.9m), time allowances applied. The defender was more carefully designed to the American rating rule than the challenger.*

The defender won, but only after being two down when a third win by the challenger would have taken the cup. This third race was a dead heat, but, of course, the corrected time made it a win for *Resolute*. The rules baffled the press and a wider public (**Fig 3.4**).

Once again discussions between and within the UK and the USA rumbled on for a long period, but in May 1929 came a formal challenge from Sir Thomas Lipton Bt in the knowledge that new conditions had been agreed for the cup challenge. These were radical. The whole contest was to move to Newport, Rhode Island away from the industrialization of New York; *the yachts were to be of class J under the Universal rule, which was 76ft rating* (there had been some talk of class K at 65ft rating)[8]; *there would be no time allowance*; construction was to be to Lloyds A1 scantling requirements to avoid throwaway machines and make it fairer for the challenger which had to sail on her own bottom from England to America; the yachts must use the new Bermudian or jib-headed mainsail (as called then in America and occasionally called there the Marconi rig after the new radio towers). The latter regulation was to prevent excessive cost of experimentation with developed gaff rigs, in a world where racing fleets were still a mixture of gaff and Bermudian.

To combat this last challenge of Sir Thomas Lipton, the finest fleet of big inshore racing yachts was built since the magic year of 1893. The Wall Street crash and depression was imminent, but the characters on our stage did not know this and it was still boom time in the USA. An important reason also was that British pressure had insisted on a fixed rating class, so owners now knew the sport they were entering. Built to the J class were *Yankee*, from Boston, *Weetamoe*, *Whirlwind* and *Enterprise*. The designers respectively were Frank C. Paine, Clinton Crane, L. Francis Herreshoff (son of Nathanael) and W. Starling Burgess.

In England Charles Nicholson designed and built *Shamrock V* to the J class rule for the ageing Sir Thomas[9]. She was launched on 30 April 1930. Unlike the Americans with their boat for boat trials (which were won by a sharpened *Enterprise*, launched 14 April), she raced handicap against the new 23-metre *Candida* built to the European rule (below) and the old, but up-dated *Britannia*, with great success. But the time allowances were dubious and the great optimism in England was misplaced. All the J-class were a few feet either side of 120ft (36.6m) LOA and around 80ft (24.4m) LWL.

Shamrock V was outclassed and beaten soundly by *Enterprise* 4-0 off Newport between 13 and 18 September.

For the last two America's cup races in J-boats, there is nothing to add on the subject of measurement and rating. There were inevitable minor additions and changes to the rule and more often to the race conditions. In 1934 T.O.M. Sopwith's *Endeavour* (Nicholson), as is well known, came close to beating the defender, *Rainbow* (Burgess), 4-3. The latter was the only boat built for the defence, it being the height of the depression in America and there were eighteen persons in her syndicate headed by Harold Vanderbilt (**Fig 3.5**).

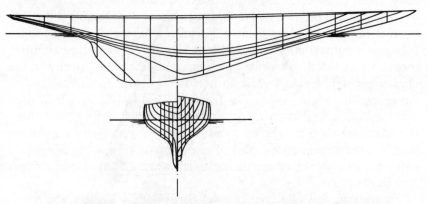

Fig 3.5 Rainbow, *class J (76ft rating) to the Universal rule and defender of the America's Cup in 1934 against* Endeavour. *Altogether 10 J-class yachts were built; some IYRU 23-metre class yachts were also converted to fit the rule.*

In 1937 Starling Burgess was assisted by two new young designers, Rod and Olin Stephens, to design the ultimate J-boat, *Ranger*, owned and steered by Harold Vanderbilt (**Fig 3.6**). She beat *Endeavour II*, again designed by Charles Nicholson by comfortable margins 4-0. One other British boat had been built to the J class rule, *Velsheda*, which helped as a triallist, but was never a contender for the cup races. She remains afloat and sailing today (1996), as do, after restoration *Endeavour* (I) and *Shamrock V*.

By the late 1930s, the J class had a poor reputation for the seaworthiness of its rigs.[10]

'The frequent loss of masts in the J-boats, which apart from their rigs were of such well proven excellence of design and construction, was causing widespread unfavourable comment; [this comment was] never so strong as when, on days which should have seen inspiring racing, the [J] class remained at its

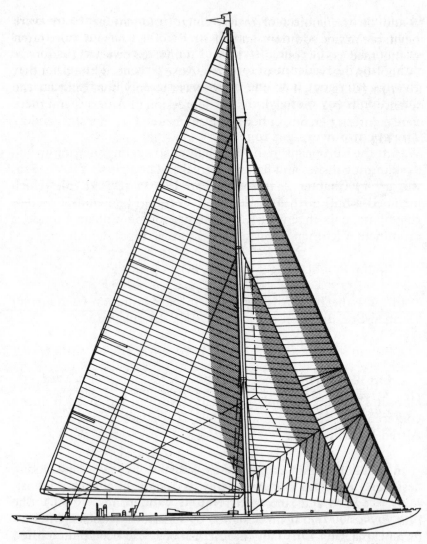

Fig 3.6 *The sail plan and profile of* Ranger, *designed by Starling Burgess with assistance from Olin Stephens. The 'ultimate J-boat' shows the huge rig and low freeboard allowed by the Universal rule. The yacht was scrapped in 1941.*

moorings for fear that a capful of wind would collapse the high rigs'.[11]

Only 10 J-boats were ever built, 6 American, 4 British, though in both countries a few other yachts were converted to fit the rule, including *Resolute* (the 1920 defender), *Britannia* owned by H.M. King George V and *Astra* (built in 1928 as a 23-metre). It was magnificent yacht racing, strictly of the inshore variety: as for the rating rule the reader must form his own opinions. The author may give his later, but now one must investigate if Europe managed these things any more wisely.

The great powers get together

We left the Europeans in the last chapter struggling to bring an end to skimming dishes and flat water freaks. The British YRA had, as we saw in Chapter 2, introduced in 1896 a revised rule which included a hull girth measurement, G (often known as Froude's rule by its main inventor, R.E. Froude, son of William Froude, a prominent Victorian naval architect in big ships), which was

$$\text{Rating in feet} = (L + B + 0.75G + 0.5(S)^{1/2})/2$$

In 1901 the British revised this in part imitation of a current German/Scandinavian rule. The 1901 YRA rule was

$$\text{Rating in feet} = (L + B + 0.75G + 0.5(S)^{1/2} + 4d)/2.1$$

For there had been a German/Scandinavian rule among senior clubs in Denmark, Germany, Finland, Norway and Sweden since a conference in Copenhagen in 1898. It was sometimes known as Alfred Benzon's rule:

$$\text{Rating in metres} = (L + B + 0.75G + 0.25(S)^{1/2} + d - F)/2$$

Here can be seen yet more factors intruding on the old Victorian misconception that the rule had to be a 'length' rule *or* 'cubic' rule *or* 'sail area' rule. Girth difference, d, (as explained) was there; also, for the first time in any rule, F, freeboard appeared. It was a minus quantity, so that the contemporary low freeboard now increased a yacht's rating. The rule was often known as the Copenhagen rule.[12]

Still the results, though showing promise, were not as intended and there was fiddling around with the constants in the different countries.

In England Brooke Heckstall-Smith saw that the rules both in Scandinavia and in the United Kingdom might with some changes at last solve the problem. He also saw clearly that power and politics were as important as the technical urgings of people such as Benzon and Froude. He later published a list of the numbers of sailing yachts in European countries, which showed one cause of his conclusion.

The numbers in Germany and Austria were 599, France 363, Norway and Sweden 300, Belgium and Holland 191, Denmark 107, but in the United Kingdom 2959 and her colonies 311. Furthermore the British yachts were larger with a tonnage of 57588 as against, say, France with total of 6300 tons.[13] Helpfully the schedules of the YRA, Copenhagen and the French systems (given in Chapter 2) all had an initial expiry date in 1907, so in 1904 the YRA approached its opposite numbers with a proposal for a rule conference in London in 1906. The boats that all had in mind, it should again be remembered, were for racing round the buoys, but in the bigger sizes they should be seaworthy for day racing in exposed water and for cruising between regatta ports, or for later use as cruisers. It was nothing to do with ocean racing.

Heckstall-Smith had written in 1903 under the heading 'Ocean Yacht Racing':

' ... there is no reason to believe this form of racing will ever commend itself to experienced yachtsmen ... it is proclaimed that the only real test of the skill of our sailors and the skill of our naval architects would be an ocean race; but I fear these opinions if carefully analysed will be found quite contrary to the fact ...'[14]

In March 1905 the council of the YRA met. It decided to invite the yacht racing nations to a conference in London in 1906, appointed the Prince of Wales as president and sent letters to Berlin, Copenhagen, Christiana, Genoa, New York, Paris, Pola (Austria-Hungary), Stockholm and elsewhere. For Britain the representatives were R.E. Froude, W.P. Burton, W. Baden Powell and several yacht designers.

Before the formal meeting there were many exchanges of views, but on 15 January 1906, the Langham Hotel, Portland Place, London, was once again the site for important yacht racing decisions. With no American authority, it was the New York Yacht Club that was invited to send delegates, but as the Universal rule was just getting settled down, with new boats building, the club could see no point in reopening the whole question. So the new twentieth century rating systems were to cross the narrow seas, but not the oceans.

The nations which eventually met in London decided that an authority was required to control the agreed new rule. After considering several names including the European Yacht Racing

Association, the title was agreed as the *International Yacht Racing Union* and that name remained with all its clarity until, most regrettably, it was voted out in 1994 (in favour of the International Sailing Federation, effective 1996). In using 'International' rather than 'European', it may have been that the delegates hoped that the United States would join, but that was not to be for another 46 years!

The founder countries were the following, most of which already had actual sailing federations, though in a few cases the name of the acknowledged senior national club was used: Austria-Hungary, Denmark, Finland, France, Germany, Holland and Belgium, Italy, Norway, Sweden, Switzerland, Spain, United Kingdom and colonies. Soon after the Russian Baltic ports also joined.

Some of these countries brought to London proposed rules, either existing or intended for wider use. Such rules were considered and some were used to reach the compromise decision. They included the rule of the *Yacht Club de France, the Swiss rule, the German/Scandinavian rule, British YRA rule of 1901* and (known but not represented) the *New York YC* rule (that is the Universal rule). (see Appendix I)

The chairman of this new IYRU was a vice-president of the YRA and the secretary was the secretary of the YRA, whose London office was to remain combined with that of the IYRU until 1975. The union was not actually in being, except when it came to meet each year. There was no staff other than Heckstall-Smith and the chairman was simply someone who took the chair at the annual meeting. The IYRU then was a file in a cabinet in the YRA office. (One reason perhaps that the USA did not join.)

Before looking at the rating rule that was agreed in 1906, it should be mentioned that the nations involved also unified their rules of racing, including right-of-way rules, at a further conference in Paris in 1907. The original IYRU rules which resulted were a single 'booklet', which included the racing rules and the rating rule with instructions for measurement. The rating rule was actually 'Part IV' of the rules. Many years later they were separated, but still there are traces of them in such rules as forestays being on the centreline.

The International rule

The rule on which the nations of Europe agreed is the longest living in history, as it remains in force to this day, still under the control of the IYRU/ISAF. Of course, the rule is greatly changed, but not entirely out of recognition. Nor can it be said to have been

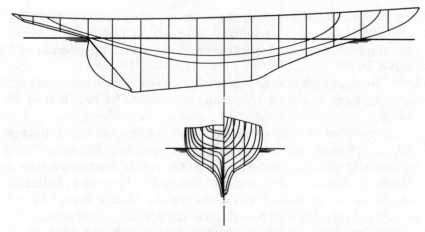

Fig 3.7 *An early design to the International rule of 1906: the 12-metre class* Nargie, *designed in Scotland by Alfred Mylne and built by R. McAlister. LOA 47.7ft (14.5m); LWL 39.3ft (12m); displacement 42,000 pounds (19,000kg).*

in use in much mainstream racing since 1945, but that story will be told later.

These men called it *The International rule*, just that, and it was to remain in force until 31 December 1917. The basic formula was

Rating in feet or metres =
(L + B + 0.5G + 3d + 1/3 × (S)$^{1/2}$ – F)/2

G is girth, d is girth difference, S is sail area, F is freeboard. In practice the ratings were always given in metres, but the boats could be measured in feet and then a feet to metres conversion made at the end.

If this formula looked very much like the previous rules with a few of the constants changed, there were important differences. The most important was political: having agreed on the compromise figures, then all agreed that this was the rule for the next eleven years, it replaced all national rules for first class yacht racing and owners could build new boats with confidence. And build they did to the 'classification' or what today would be called 'fixed' or 'level rating' laid down by the IYRU. There were also time allowances available (see below), but there is no record of them being used. The number of boats built to the metre classes from publication of the rule until war broke out in 1914 were: 23-metre, 3; 19-metre, 6; 15-metre, 19; 12-metre, 35, 10-metre, 54; 9-metre,

25; 8-metre, 174; 7-metre, 86; 6-metre, 328; 5-metre, 41. These were registered in 13 countries (**Fig 3.7**). Clubs were 'specially recommended to encourage 8, 6 and 5 metres, among classes of 10 and under.'[15]

These numbers may not seem big to today's reader, but yachting was far from the scale that developed in the second half of the twentieth century, so they were very creditable indeed. Additionally these 'metre boats' were soon racing in the waters of different European countries. For instance the yachting Olympic Games began in 1900 (the second modern Olympics after their start in 1896), missed out 1904, but in 1908 and 1912 used 6, 8 and 12-metre classes (also the 7 and 10-metre one in each year).[16]

At first the new metre boats were unfamiliar to yachtsmen, who were also able to have their old length and sail area yachts measured to the new rule. Until 1 January 1910, there were special conditions for these 'old boats', or what today might be called 'grandfathering'. In order to help sailors envisage the metre boats, Heckstall-Smith gave these examples of equivalents of the larger rated yachts.

LWL	1881-1886	1886-1895	1896-1907	1907-
50ft	20 tons	20 rater	52ft rating	15-metre
60ft	40 tons	40 rater	65ft rating	19-metre
80ft	85 tons	140 rater	75ft rating	23-metre

Thus was stated a reason for the legitimacy of the International rule. It was shown to be a logical step from lessons learned in all previous rating rules. This was judged important to gain acceptibility.

Creating a classic racer

The other important difference apart from the 'political' one, was that now, and in the future, the published formula was only part of the rule. What the letters meant, how they were measured and other restrictions were now agreed in 27 clauses, previously unheard, though a fraction of today's voluminous regulations. The most important innovation was to put an end to the flimsy old hulls and all yachts had to be classed at Lloyds, Germanischer Lloyd or Bureau Veritas, in London, Berlin or Paris respectively.

The International rule also featured these measurements and restrictions:

L was still waterline, but with additions for overhangs (**Fig 3.8**).

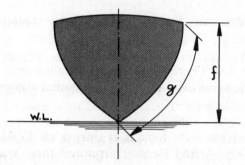

Fig 3.8 *Girth measurement in the first International rule. The girth was taken at the waterline; then 2 × (g − f) was added to the length and a similar system at the stern. This was to check full ends of the scow type.*

This was to require amendment in the future. There were detailed measurements for all types of sail to give a resultant S. There were minimum displacements for the 5, 6 and 7-metre classes only. The station at which the girth was taken was defined and here also freeboard was taken together with freeboards at bow and stern waterline to give a resultant F. Hollow masts were prohibited in classes above 10-metre.

There were rules for height within the cabin, cabin 'furniture', such as berths, tables, locker capacity, cooking stove and water capacity for boats of 9 metres (rating) upwards, the 8-metre had cabin height only. The 5, 6 and 7-metre simply had a maximum 'cockpit area'.

So yacht designers had plenty to get their teeth into and the age of the classic metre boats began in Europe (**Fig 3.9**). Again, as is almost always the case, many of the first metre boats did not look unlike the last of the length and sail area yachts. For instance if the freeboards were low, it was because they recently had been and designers took the F penalty as necessary. If the hulls were still a bit U-shaped, then they took the girth penalty. The result was, of course, shorter boats with less sail area to get down to the desired rating. Shorter and less than what? Later boats, of course, as designers got to know the new rule.

Time allowances (Chapter 5) had also caused trouble in the past and were given close attention. They were to be 'in proportion to the length of the course' and be used when there were amalgamated classes and old yachts. But it was the negative rule that had most effect:

'IYRU rule 4.4. There shall be no time allowance between new yachts of the same class in the International classes of 23-metre and under'.

Possible systems were looked at during an IYRU meeting in London of 1908. Alfred Benzon proposed three scales for light, medium and heavy winds, the break points being 5 and 8 metres per second (this unit is what the Scandinavians use for wind speed), but Professor Busley for Germany and R.E. Froude for UK said that clubs in their countries would invariably use a single

Fig 3.9 *Early 8-metre class racer. LOA was about 42ft (12.8m); coachroof and cabin accommodation were in the rule.*

time allowance for all conditions.[17]

Benzon said that in Scandinavia up to four scales had even been used. He was supported by M. Le Bret of France and the result was the publication of three time scales, though Heckstall-Smith immediately declared that in British waters only the medium scale would be used in all weather. No formula appears to have been published for rating against allotted time allowance, only tables. In these (medium scale) a 5-metre (the smallest) had no allowance, 6-metre 50 seconds and 8-metre 122 seconds. So in an amalgamated 10 mile race, the 6-metre got 122 – 50 seconds per mile from an 8-metre, that was exactly 12 minutes. But such cases are unrecorded among new metre boats.

Many years later (1933) Heckstall-Smith gave the time allowance between metre boats in seconds per mile as

$$(2160)/(r)^{1/2} - (2160)/(R)^{1/2}$$

In this R is the rating of the larger yacht and r the smaller. 'What is called the YRA time scale is compiled in this manner'.[18]

The big class from 1906
The numbers of yachts built to the metre boat rule mentioned above not only found regular racing at the main yachting harbours of Europe, but were followed by press and public. The best known owners and skippers in each country went to designers and builders so that they could compete in this modern and rational mode of yacht racing. Photography afloat became practical, so we can see today these elegant low freeboard, gaff rig racers with their bowsprits and two headsails, or even three if they used a jib topsail.

The three 23-metre class yachts to the International rule were all British. They were the Nicholson designed *Brynhild* for Sir J. Spender (later, 1909, sunk at Harwich regatta), the Fife *White Heather* for Mr Kennedy and *Nyria* which was actually designed by Charles Nicholson before the rule was published, but raced at the rating from 1907. *Britannia* was the same size, but was not being raced and in 1910 her owner King Edward VII died. *Shamrock II* also participated, though designed to the Universal rule. It cannot be said that the class was a success. By 1913 only *White Heather* was sailing and in a mixed handicap class of big yachts including *Britannia* with King George V as her owner.

Another rule
In 1913 there was published in England a rating rule, which had in

the event little immediate effect, but was to turn up years later in a rather important way. It was the product of the self styled Boat Racing Association, which met under the chairmanship of Lt Col J.T. Bucknill in November 1912.[19]

Its object was to cater for yachts smaller than those of the YRA, which were the IYRU metre boats. These were 'big' boats and the members of the BRA felt that the more ordinary racing sailor was not catered for. Initially there would be a class of 18 feet rating (not in the hated foreign metres!), which was smaller than a 6-metre. Others would follow between 12 and 20 feet. There were simple scantling rules and a draft limit of 1/10th LWL + $1\frac{1}{2}$ times average freeboard.

The BRA formula was

$$\text{Rating in feet} = \{(L + (S)^{1/2}) + (L \times (S)^{1/2}/0.75 \times (W)^{1/3}\}/4$$

The boat was to be weighed in pounds to obtain W. L was obtained by measuring 1/40th of LWL vertically above LWL and adding a reduced factor for overhangs. This length system was soon amended to use instead girths at the waterline endings. The rating in feet was also simplified to

$$(L + (S)^{1/2})/4 + (L \times (S)^{1/2})/ 3 \times (W)^{1/3}$$

Several designers produced designs to the 18ft rating, but the onset of WWI meant that the BRA never achieved a single full season. *Yet the formula will become much more significant than any of its long forgotten boats: it will be seen that the rule actually consisted exactly (less constants) of the form of two famous rating rules. Both were American: the Seawanhaka rule and the Universal rule.*

The war and after (1914-1920)

On 1 August 1914, the King was expected at Cowes Week. The Kaiser's racing cutter *Meteor* was on her way there, as was Frau von Krupp's schooner *Germania*. Guests of the Commodore of the Royal Yacht Squadron at Cowes included Prince Henry of Prussia and Admiral von Eisendecker, the Emperor's popular naval equerry. At the weekend Buckingham Palace informed the Squadron that the His Majesty had cancelled his visit to Cowes, while the German officers hurriedly departed. On 4 August Britain declared war on Germany. *Germania* was captured and interned in England; *Meteor* escaped in tow of a German destroyer. Dresden china and other prizes donated by HIM were locked away, to be eventually, with British Foreign office approval, returned to him, then ex-Emperor, in 1919.[20]

The first peace time season of 1919 was a shadow of its former self. Apart from the death and destruction, the whole structure of ownership of racing yachts and the support of the old European aristocracy was in disarray. British yachtsmen decided not to race against Austrian and German yachts for ten years (in the event this ban ended in 1925 with the Locarno Treaty).

Officially the International rule had expired in 1917 together with the IYRU itself, but no one had noticed. In October 1919 representatives met in London from Argentina, Belgium and Holland, Denmark, France, Norway, Sweden, Spain and Switzerland, as well as the United Kingdom and the IYRU was revived.[21]

The Scandinavians were the enthusiasts for the International rule and between the wars built metre boats of 5, 7 and 10, as well as the more popular 6, 8 and 12. Britain and France, except for the occasional owner (who did build as big as 15 and 19-metres) built to the 6, 8 and 12-metre classes only. But never again did the numbers approach the great surge between 1906 and 1914: the war had changed all that. Fewer people could afford classic yacht racing and as all the metre boats had carried paid hands, who now needed higher wages and social security, that also limited the bigger metre boats.

The conference amended the International rule to

$$\text{Rating in metres} = (L + 0.25G + 2d + (S)^{1/2} - F)/2.5$$

It will appear to be simplified, with B removed and some constants changed, but what was actually happening and would happen in further amendments was to put restrictions in sub-clauses instead. This was now possible since there were only a limited number of fixed rating classes and actual numbers could be given; for instance the height of the jib block on a 12-metre or the minimum beam on a 6-metre (which was then 6ft 6in). A 1922 6-metre design by Alfred Mylne had these dimensions LOA 33ft (10.1m), LWL 21ft 9in (6.9m), beam 7ft (2.13m), draft 5ft (1.5m), displacement 7390 pounds (3352kg) (**Fig 3.10**).

The war had hastened advances in technology including the early aircraft industry with its increasing knowledge of light weight materials and aerodynamics. A massive transition was in progress in the metre boats in the 1920s as boat after boat changed over from gaff to bermudan rig and new boats were designed to take the latter. As yacht racing gathered pace in the decade, these attractive racers

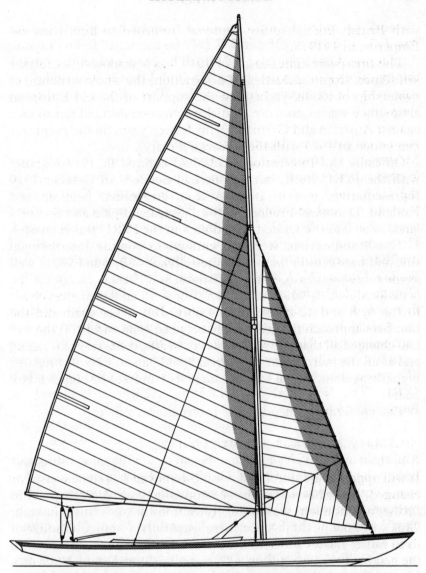

Fig 3.10 *6-metre class design of 1922. The Bermudian rig had just arrived; genoa jibs were as yet unknown. Later the class became longer, narrower and heavier under the International rule.*

were the primary classes at the main annual regattas around the coasts of Great Britain: Cowes, the Clyde, Burnham, Harwich, Plymouth, Dartmouth and many others. Ten years after 1922 the dimensions under the same rule of a 6-metre had grown to over 36ft LOA (10.97m), 23ft 2in LWL (7.06m), draft 5ft 4in (1.63m), displacement 8645 pounds (3921kg). The beam had reduced to the minimum 6ft 6in. So designers had found that it paid under the rule to be longer, heavier and narrower. The sail area stayed about the same.

America gets a national authority
Meanwhile in November 1925, the YRA of Long Island Sound invited other regional racing associations and unaffiliated clubs in the USA and Canada to a meeting at the Racquet Club in New York to try and coordinate racing rules (not rating rules). Once again the New York YC and the Eastern YC did not attend. Haltingly the conference issued a voluntary set of racing rules and drafted a constitution, calling itself the North American Yacht Racing Union (NAYRU): clubs and associations in the USA, Canada and Mexico could join. Clifford D. Mallory was elected first president and the next year went to London as an observer at the annual meeting of the IYRU. Thereafter senior American yachtsmen from NAYRU and also from the New York YC (quite separate!) usually observed at these meetings, joining in informal discussion about racing and rating rules. But NAYRU did not join IYRU. The New York YC will join NAYRU in 1942 and the Eastern in 1944.

And starts to race in 6-metre boats
American and British yachtsmen began to use the same rating rule before the formation of NAYRU. *It started with individual yachtsmen,* a scenario which the author never fails to point out as the most frequent conception of successful boats and events. In 1920 the S-class[22] arrived at the Seawanhaka Corinthian Yacht Club, Oyster Bay, Long Island Sound. They were to the Universal rule, but once again in America they were simply adopted as a one-design. One of the noted owners and helmsman in this class, Paul Hammond, had been in the US Navy in WWI and for some time had worked closely with the British. The boats were much the same size as a 6-metre.

So a group of American and British yachtsmen conceived the British-American Cup, the actual cup being bought between them. The idea was that a team race would be sailed in alternately British and American waters, using in Britain an International class, which was immediately decided as the 6-metre, and in America a Universal rule class. The first races were held in the Solent in 1921 for which the Americans designed and built four 6-metres. The Americans, new to the International rule, lost and then discussion began on the type of boat to use the following year in America.

At a meeting at the Royal Yacht Squadron, the Americans suggested possible Universal rule classes, but they were on weak ground because the rule was virtually voluntary in the US and the British claimed that the 1920 International rule had been amended to take account of lessons learned in America as well as Europe. After some hopeless talk about yet another new common rule between America and Europe, the US East coast sailors agreed sportingly to use the 6-metre in America for the next match. Over the next few years there was some attempt to use the Universal rule, the R class, for instance being very like a 6-metre in dimensions and appearance, but the American sailors liked the 6-metre and the authoritative control under which the rule was run. Better still their designers soon found they could design boats as good as, or better than the British, to the 6-metre rule. However the American sailor and designer Clinton Crane wrote that he was 'a strong believer in the International rule' but that there

> '*was strong controversy, almost amounting to bitterness, between the advocates of the two rules. A great many people, particularly in the New York YC, thought in supporting the International rule we were belittling our own Universal rule.*'[23]

What followed were classic years (this word is used advisedly, but there are surely certain groups or years in yacht racing which have given rise to *classic* racing) of 6-metre sailing, with not only the British-American Cup, but also other major trophies in this class including the One Ton Cup, the Seawanhaka Gold Cup, the Olympic games, the Scandinavian Gold Cup and many others in a number of countries.

By 1924 the Americans were welcome at the rule committees at IYRU, enough to be granted a request to prevent beam becoming too narrow. The Seawanhaka history says 'The old plank-on-edge tradition had hung on in England'.

All these exchanges were to be put on a formal basis at a meeting of the IYRU at the Royal Thames Yacht Club, London, on 8 and 9 February 1927. Such a step had become possible because at last America had a national authority empowered to negotiate. Shortly before this landmark meeting, the New York Yacht Club (as mentioned, not a member of NAYRU) made a last ditch stand. In the pages, strangely, of the *Christian Science Monitor*, its commodore, George Nicholls, defended the club's 'own' Universal rule:

'We have today the oldest active rule in the world and the only one that has not been successfully beaten – because there is nothing in it to beat. We measure driving power. We have stood at the head of the yachting world for 75 years because of our thoroughness, initiative and the freedom our rules have given us to exercise these qualities ... don't let us adopt a rule [the International] that stops progress and forces us to produce yachts that are one-design in everything but name. The present International rule was devised in 1920. In 1919 Sir William Burton and Major Heckstall-Smith came to this country and saw our yachts. They went home and spoke for our rule [in the IYRU]. They were beaten by the continental countries and the best they could do was to get a restricted rule ...'[24]

Thus spoke the politics of rule possession; the 75 years presumably refers back to 1851, but the America's Cup seems somewhat irrelevant!

The February 1927 conference inserted almost all the NAYRU suggestions into the International rule, including hollow masts (previously forbidden), centreboards (a perennial American tradition in all rules), maximum height of masts and maximum freeboard (though to modern eyes the freeboards are invariably low). The American delegates included Clifford W. Mallory, president of NAYRU, and Clinton Crane. Among the Europeans were Johan Anker, Alfred Benzon, Jan Loeff, the Marquis Paolo Pallaviano, Alfred Mylne and Charles E. Nicholson. Sir William Burton was in the chair.

In 1930 at the time of the America's Cup challenge mentioned above, Brooke Heckstall-Smith again went to New York with Norman Clark Neill, representing the IYRU and the British YRA. With leading Americans building metre boats and British challengers for America's Cup obliged to use the Universal rule, a wise compromise was reached with the New York YC. Rather than try and make a common rule for all sizes, it was agreed to build big boats to the Universal rule and small ones to the International rule!

In effect at this meeting and subsequent ones International yachts were no longer to be built over 12-metres, but sizes bigger than that would always be Universal classes J (76ft rating), K (65ft rating) and L (56ft rating). These classes would now adopt some of the European ideas on stronger scantlings. For 12-metres and below, racing between nations would be in 12s, 8s, 6s and a few of the other metres if desired.

In parenthesis, the M class, which was 46ft rating (= 14.0 metres and therefore the class one size up from the 12-metre) to the Universal rule was left out of any agreement, since a number of these 83ft LOA (25.30m) and 54ft LWL (16.46m) had been built in America in 1927 and over the next couple of years, said to be 'the finest racing class which this country [USA] has ever known'[25]: it is no coincidence that they appeared in the boom years just prior to the Wall Street crash and subsequent depression. The class then duly dispersed. The author saw a restored M-boat in England in 1990.

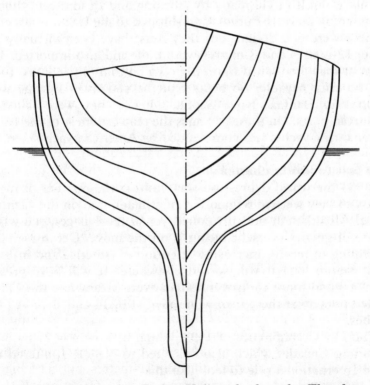

Fig 3.11 *Section of an R class Universal rule yacht. Though to modern eyes it is not unlike a 6-metre of the same period, that was not the opinion at the time and a Universal (American) versus International (European) rule debate took place.*

The K and L classes were too big to attract much interest and the J-boats trialled and, raced, as described, for the America's Cup until 1937. Writing in 1940, W.P. Stephens declared that

'. . . all classes under the Universal rule are dead, with no hope of speedy revival . . . the existing British system is well known to American yachtsmen, the terms '6-metre', '8-metre' etc. convey exact and definite ideas of the size and type of each class.' (**Fig 3.11**).

He perhaps spoke as a designer, when he implied that the rated classes of the Universal rule were killed by the over-adoption of one-designs by American clubs and the use of the International (European) rule by leading American yachtsmen when they wanted a yacht designed to a rating rule.

Apparently thirteen American owners even had International 10-metres built in Germany by Abeking and Rasmussen, though designed by Starling Burgess and shipped to the US; it is not clear if these were one-design, but they must have been virtually the same. 12-metres and 8-metres were built and also imported. If a yacht at that time sailed in on her own bottom to the USA, there was no duty payable. So boats built or bought in Europe were shipped to Halifax, Nova Scotia, whence they were sailed to American ports. On these passages the seaworthiness of the International rule yachts was commended by American yachtsmen.[26]

The last formula change
By 1933 the world depression was limiting the number of metre boats, so they were to remain few, if still admired on the yachting scene. Also though not mentioned yet in these pages, the whole centre of gravity of yacht racing is on the move. Ocean racing is beginning to receive increasing attention in America and in England; before long it will spread elsewhere. It will have greater numbers and more controversy than ever. Meanwhile the IYRU smiled politely at these men who sailed at night and slept in their clothes.

The IYRU conference of 1933, which by now was 21 nations, including Canada, which also belonged to NAYRU, altered the basic International rule to look like this

$$\text{Rating in metres} = (L + 2d + (S)^{1/2} - F)/2.37$$

Once again the improvements were in the written clauses and

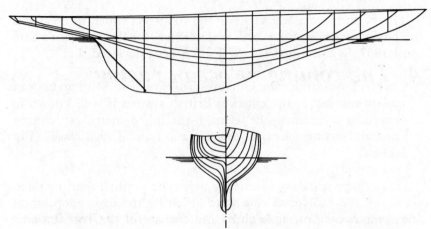

Fig 3.12 *Lines of the very successful 12-metre* Vim, *designed by Olin Stephens. An American designed and owned boat to the International rule, she beat the British 12s at Cowes in 1939. Then in 1957 she was the starting point for the USA when the America's Cup transferred to the 12-metre class.*

definitions. The old G, the girth around the hull invented to check the nineteenth century skimming dishes disappeared. Instead it was taken as part of finding d, the well established girth difference. The length, L, involved girths at the waterline ends, a plane above the waterline and freeboards. There was a beam limit with a penalty and ever more exact sail area measurements, which now no longer expected gaff rig.

This basic formula remains unchanged today, though with many supporting amendments. Meanwhile this chapter ends in 1939, the last season before WWII. With no further interest in the J-class, Harold Vanderbilt had Olin J. Stephens design a new 12-metre, *Vim*.[27] This yacht (**Fig 3.12**) he brought to England to sail against the strong British 12-metre fleet of about ten of these 73ft (22.3m) LOA sloops, including *Tomahawk*, the new Charles Nicholson 12 of his old Cup rival T.O.M. Sopwith. In 27 races against the British, *Vim* scored 19 firsts, four seconds and two thirds. Unlike 1914, Cowes Week was completed, with its 12s, 8s (including one American, *Iskareen*) and 6s, but a month later the metre boats of Europe were again hauled ashore for an indefinite period.

4 The coming of ocean racing

'Organized ocean racing in its present form, as far as Great Britain is concerned, owes its existence to the series of New London to Bermuda races. The Fastnet races were the first to be sailed here on a rating formula and time scale, as opposed to an arbitrary handicap; and the Fastnet race was promoted with the idea that, as far as circumstances allowed, it should be a counterpart of the New London to Bermuda race. The distance sailed is about the same and the measurement rule for both races is now almost identical, while size limits are similar.

Under the influence of the Ocean Racing measurement rule, as it is now framed, or as it may be modified, a type of ocean going yacht will be developed in which speed and seaworthiness will be combined to a degree never yet reached.' – Lieutenant-Commander E.G.Martin OBE RNVR, founder and first commodore of the Ocean Racing Club, in 1928.

MODERN OCEAN RACING appeared in the 1920s and owed little to the inshore keel boats of the International rule. By the 1930s, it had become their equal in status and enthusiasm. At the end of the 1940s the ocean racers far exceeded the maximum the rated keel boats had ever achieved in ships and men, in widespread interest, in world expansion and obviously in mileage sailed every year.

It has been seen how after WWI, the metre boats never returned to the expanding numbers that looked so promising in 1914; contemporary reports are chary of discussing the size of fleets, though a dozen entries in a race of, say, 8-metre or even 6-metre yachts, would be considered well supported. Yet any metre boat race would be regarded as important, for in these rated yachts were the best racing helmsmen and crews.

Earliest ocean racing

These pages are not intended for a step by step history of the arrival of ocean racing, because the aim here is to discuss the effect and adventures caused by rules of measurement and rating! The sequence of ocean racing progress is bound to be touched on, but there are excellent full accounts elsewhere.[1]

Such accounts show that modern ocean racing began in the USA in 1906, any earlier yacht racing across the oceans having been by large vessels with professional crews and that very occasionally. They were invariably some kind of challenge boat to boat, so that time allowances did not arise. Such a race was the British 188-ton, 108ft (32.92m) schooner *Cambria* from Daunt Rock, Ireland, to Sandy Hook, New York, against the American schooner *Dauntless* in 1870. *Cambria* was on her way to the first America's Cup challenge! In 1905 was sailed the famous transatlantic race for the Kaiser's Cup won by the 185ft (56.4m) schooner *Atlantic*, owned by the New York newspaper owner Wilson Marshall. Her record time from New York to the Lizard Point of 12 days 4 hours 1 minute still stands today (1996) for a monohull. Again there was no time allowance even though *Atlantic* was 135ft (41.1m) LWL and the smallest yacht *Fleur de Lys* was 'only' 87ft (26.5m) LWL.

The very few small (mostly under 40ft, 12.2m) yachts that sailed in the races of 1906, 1907 and 1908 from Brooklyn, New York, to Bermuda under arrangements by *The Rudder* magazine, did not find imitators, so the birth of modern ocean racing (moderate sized cruisers, sailed mainly by amateurs, for prizes of no great value) is fixed at New London, Connecticut, on 12 June 1923 with the course to a finish line arranged by the Royal Bermuda Yacht Club. Twenty-three yachts started, schooners, sloops, yawls: all were gaff rigged. Most were staunch cruisers, though some had origin-ally been designed rather loosely to the Universal rule. *Memory*, a New York 40 (Robert Bavier), was one of those. (She won the 'large' class, beginning an American tradition that even ocean races were for racing boats).

The Bermuda race was held again in June 1924, then in 1926, 1928, 1930 and every even year since then, to alternate, as will be seen, with the Fastnet race, itself on odd years.

The 1923 Bermuda race was not under the control of any particular organization or club, though clubs at each end helped. It was an initiative by Herbert L. Stone and other sailors. They were aware of the need for some kind of measurement, but the Universal rule called for knowledge of displacement and most of the cruising yachts participating had never been measured nor were their lines available.[2] For this race the organizers simply took the length overall and applied a time allowance to it.

Rating = LOA

The time allowance was 60 minutes per foot for the course distance of 660 nautical miles; this is $5\frac{1}{2}$ seconds per mile. There was apparently a span of 5 hours corrected time between the first six contestants, which was considered close![3]

After the 1923 Bermuda race, the owners found that most of them were already members of the very newly formed (on the lines of the Royal Cruising Club in Britain), Cruising Club of America (CCA). So the CCA agreed to run the Bermuda race of 1924 and has been the organizing club ever since. For 1924 and 1926, the same rating, LOA, was again used, but new time allowances were applied to it. For 1924 the New York YC time allowances tables of seconds per mile were used.

Evidently these were not popular because in 1926, an allowance of 45 minutes per foot of rating for the course (equals 4.1 seconds per mile) was in use.

Now 'rating equals LOA' was asking for trouble and it is surprising that it did not come sooner than the third race to use this 'formula'. Though unnamed in history, the race attracted the first yacht built to this 'rule'. 'She was a fine able vessel with a long LWL and short ends, a larger yacht for her LOA than all of the existing fleet. With ample sail, she was designed to be a fast reacher, beam winds being the conditions most likely to be encountered over this course, though there was [in 1926] considerable windward work'.[4]

For 1928 the CCA committee decided to examine a British rule (see below) which was in use for the Fastnet. As will be seen, this was in any case close to the Universal rule, with which all leading American racing men were familiar. For the Bermuda races of 1928 and 1930 and a transatlantic race from Newport, RI to Plymouth, England, in 1931 (won by *Dorade*, designed by Olin and Rod Stephens and sailed by them together with their father and three crew) it was in use as

Rating in feet = $0.2(L \times S^{1/2})/(B \times D)^{1/2}$

The main changes from the British were in the methods of measurement. In particular, from 1930, the CCA on the suggestion of Herreshoff measured length, L, on a plane 4 per cent of the LWL

Alarm *wins! The 193-ton cutter was launched at Lymington in May 1830 for Joseph Weld, who, in the absence of established time allowances, wanted a boat faster than anything else racing in the Solent in order to win. Therefore she had to be big and indeed won the annual King's Cup in 1830, 1831 and 1832. Her success (and that of others like her) hastened the search for 'classification' and time allowances.*

Vanessa, *20-ton English cutter, designed by Dan Hatcher in 1873 (11 firsts, 2 seconds): typical racer which was given time allowance against tonnage.*

Leonore, *plank-on-edge cutter* 1882. By this time the beam had narrowed and sail area increased. Designed by William Fife, prolific creator of racing yachts.

West

The big change. This 1890 40-rater, Creole *(designer George Watson), was the result of the 1886 YRA length and sail area rule.*

West

Extremes usually appear first in the smaller classes. Wee Winn *was an 1891 skimming dish ½-rater by Nathanael Herreshoff for an English owner.*

Beken of Cowes

When English owners first despaired of rating rules: the Solent One-Design class appeared in 1895.

Clyde ½-raters. The smallest inshore boats were built to rating rules until early in the 20th century. Note full length battens here, as well as skimming dish hulls.

Sakuntala, designed by Charlie Sibbick of Cowes for Captain Orr-Ewing in 1900 to the second YRA rule (Froude's rule): linear rating 36 feet. Still a skimming dish with long scow ends, fine bulb keel, lightly built, low freeboard, light displacement, large sail area.

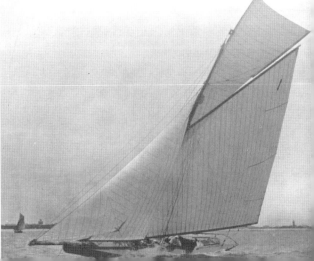

Europeans come together at the Langham Hotel, London, January 1906, and create the International Rule.

HRH The Prince of Wales who 'persuaded' senior clubs in Britain to unify racing and rating rules under the YRA. In America diverse customs continued for many years.

Brooke Heckstall-Smith, key world figure on rating rules 1898 to 1944.

Did yacht rating disputes help cause WWI? HIM Wilhelm II declared he was irritated by the time allowances allotted on some days to his Meteors by the Royal Yacht Squadron.

Reliance, *defender of the 1903 America's Cup and largest ever in the series. Even her designer Nathanael Herreshoff said she was a freak in all dimensions (including 16,160 square feet of sail). He urged the adoption of the Universal rule.*

Britannia *launched for HRH The Prince of Wales in 1893. Designed by Watson to the length and sail area rule, but successfully modified to several later rules, the last being the Universal, class J, in the 1930s.*

Annual decision time 1990s. The Offshore Racing Council, in London in 1991, adjudicating then on both IMS and IOR.

Rod and Olin Stephens (right) in about 1980. The latter had a major influence on all major yacht rating rules both by constructing them and designing to them between 1925-1990.

Kenneth Weller, Offshore Director US Sailing 1976 to 1994 and Chief Measurer ORC from 1984 to 1996.

Nicola Sironi, chairman International Technical Committee (for IOR, then IMS), from 1987 to 1996, thereafter he was IMS Chief Measurer.

John Bourke, the Irishman, who as chairman ORC 1987 to 1993, presided over the change from IMS to IOR.

One of the first yachts built, in 1909, to the International Rule of 1906. The fully restored (1995) 12-metre Cintra, designed by William Fife.

Pelly

6-metres in 1911. The International Rule was five years old and there were different ideas about hulls and rigs.

Beken of Cowes

Beken of Cowes

6-metres at Cowes in 1923. Genoas had not been invented. Despite girth measurements, overhangs were still long, though of different section to the old skimming dish.

The look of metre boats by 1951: still regarded as the apex of classic yacht racing, this is the British-American Cup in 6s.

*12-metres in 1964 (*Sovereign *and* Constellation*) before the start of the third America's Cup series to be sailed on the international rule.*

Eliminations off Perth, Western Australia, 1986, for the last America's Cup to be sailed using the International Rule at 12-metres rating: in effect the last development of the 12-metre (American Stars and Stripes; *British* White Crusader*).*

*Evolution of the 6-metre in 1995 (*Scoundrel*); still a classic rated yacht to the longest lasting rating rule.*

Farewell to the Universal rule. The American and British Js sail as a class after the 1937 cup matches: a sight never seen again and seldom seen before.

The RORC rule of rating was never the same after the appearance in 1947 of Myth of Malham; *owned by John Illingworth, designed to his requirements by Laurent Giles.*

Beken of Cowes

Jocasta, *a very successful ocean racer, designed to the RORC rule of rating in 1950 for G.P. Pattinson by Robert Clark of London. LOA 55ft (16.8m), LWL 40ft 10in (12.4m) displacement 45900lb (20300kg). With 'interior panelling of obeche' and rugged deck and rig, she raced in all weather.*

There was variety in the early years of IOR: Jiminy Cricket, *designed by Bruce Farr, which did well in the 1976 One Ton Cup, was considered radical.*

Author

IOR freak rig. The authorities upheld a protest ruling arising in New Zealand which allowed free sail set to leeward of the spinnaker. For some years attempts to rule on the 'blooper', 'big boy' or 'streaker' expended much energy. Sail limitation rules and fractional rigs eventually killed it.

IOR freak hull. The extraordinary **Warbird** *under construction in England.*

Although designed individually to a level rating (the One Ton Cup in IOR), designers of this 1974 fleet appeared to have arrived at similar solutions.

Once again owners tried to escape from rating rules: this time (1978) in the offshore classes. This was the OOD 34 class.

Typical shape of an International Offshore Rule yacht of 1981. This particular yacht was in due course involved in a serious rating and measurement tangle.

Most IOR boats could take heavy weather. A Danish and a Dutch yacht, respectively fractional and masthead rigged, meet testing conditions at the start of the 1985 RORC Channel race.

Bentley

1987 and IOR boats get more extreme (Decosol, ¾-tonner): large crew packed to windward, dinghy type control lines, hi-tech sailcloth (unrated), large cockpit with open stern. Note bagged sail to windward among crew.

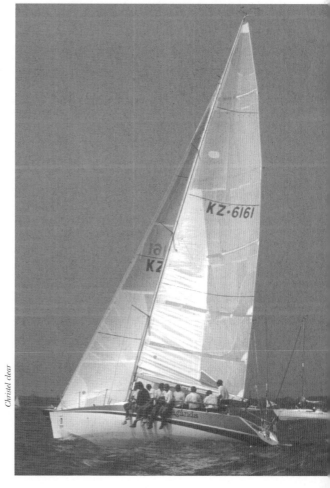

Christel clear

...te days in IOR. The New ...aland One Tonner, Propaganda, ...cing in 1989.

A short lived expensive class within IOR, the '50 footer' on a fixed rating. The Dutch Promotion VII *in the Mediterranean 1990.*

Christel clear

One of the first of the IMS rule beaters. The Argentinian Gaucho, *designed by Bruce Farr, appeared in 1992.*

Christel clear

Last of the IOR racers. The French 2-tonner Corum 45 *in 1991.*

Crack IMS racer 1994. The American Tripp designed 50ft Falcon. *What's the difference?*

The Moose: *1996 Australian crewed flat out IMS 32-footer designed by Judel/Vrolik.*

International 5.5-metre class in 1995; after 45 years still attracted discriminating owners, who wanted inshore racers to a rule of measurement and (fixed) rating.

An Open 60 class 1997, **PRB,** *skippered by Isabelle Autissier. No rule except: single handed, monohull, 60 feet overall and the oceans around the world. The huge stern width was one result.*

above the waterplane. The British, on the other hand, obtained their length from girth measurements at bow and stern, as had been developed in the International rule. *These diverse methods of measuring length will be unreconciled for forty years* (**Fig 4.1**).

Not many years elapsed before the effect of such measurements became visible. In general CCA boats had wide sterns on which there was no check and British boats had 'pinched in bows and sterns' to bring the girths inward.

D in the formula was depth of hull, as defined. The CCA also created a rig allowance which included sloops and cutters at 100%, gaff cutters and staysail schooner at 96% and gaff ketches at 90%; there were other rigs similarly specified.

For 1932 yet another rating system was tried and the very

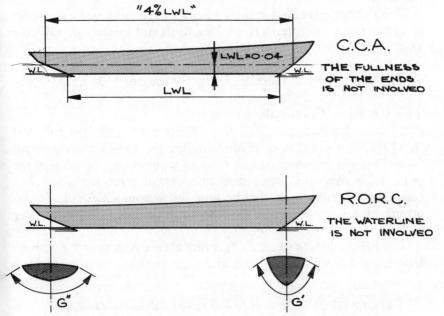

Fig 4.1 *Early on the CCA and RORC diverged on their measurement of hull length. The CCA measured on the centreline 4 per cent of LWL above LWL. The RORC followed the European mode of girths (shown here simply, but increasingly complex and multiple). The result for many years was that RORC boats had 'pinched ends' and American boats had 'wide sterns'.*

incidence of such change is significant. The CCA actually only ran one race, the Bermuda race, every other year. There were just occasional exceptions to this, like the transatlantic just mentioned, or one or two other courses at very infrequent intervals. Today and for many years now, the CCA has run the Bermuda race only. Essentially it is a cruising club: it makes cruising awards[5] and publishes members' logs. Most members never race.

This will have at least two effects. Firstly, there has always been a largely new committee for each Bermuda race and it will almost always change the rule, to a greater or lesser extent, among other preparations for the event. Such changes may well reflect the results of the last race: that is a single race in two years. Secondly, the ethos of the club will encourage the committee to seek a type of boat suitable for cruising, whatever that may mean at any period.

As a result, when it comes to talking to other ocean racing authorities in the USA and abroad, particularly the British, in the form of the Royal Ocean Racing Club, there will be much scope for misunderstanding.

The 1932 rule was based on the Seawanhaka with some elements of addition and subtraction for beam, draft and freeboard. The rule was

$$\text{Rating in feet} = 0.6(S)^{1/2} \times \text{rig allowance} + 0.4L$$

The Cruising Club rule

Again after the race the CCA was unhappy with its own rule and the 1932 formula was discarded. *Before the 1934 race, there was invented a new rule that had no relation to the rating formulae of the past.* It is this rule, with due amendment over the years but retaining a similar 'look' that became the famous CCA rule. It was often colloquially known in the US as 'the Cruising Club rule' (**Fig 4.2**).

The principle was to take a theoretical *base boat* starting with its length on 4% waterline plane and with controls to prevent long

Fig 4.2 Edlu *was one of the earliest boats designed and built to the 1934 'Cruising Club rule' (CCA). She won the 1934 Bermuda race; designer Sparkman and Stephens. Moderation seems to have been the watchword: the sections are not so different to the 12-metre or the R-boat in Chapter 3. Thus designers often reacted slowly to new rating rules and 'fought the last war'. The stern was reasonably wide and the ends 'short' for the time. LOA 56ft 2in (17.11m); LWL 40ft (12.19m); beam 13ft (3.96m).*

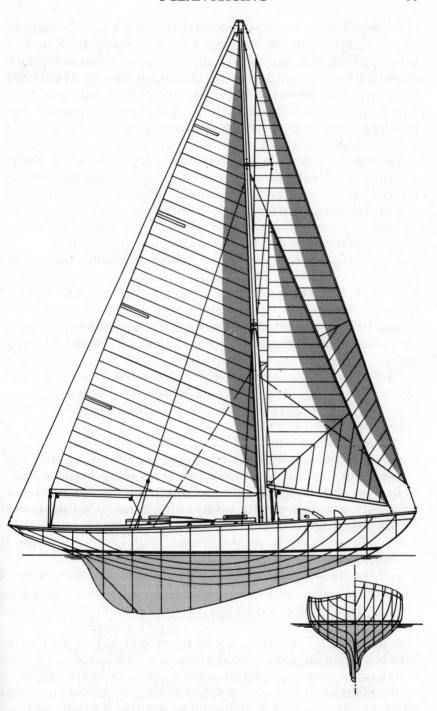

overhangs. Ratios were then worked out for this 'ideal' fast cruising yacht. Additions and subtractions were then made if a measured yacht departed from the base figures for beam, displacement, draft, freeboard, mast height and so on. Of course every yacht did need corrections and no such base boat existed. A base boat would not have prospered under the rule, as it was better to take a bonus or penalty for, say, draft, where the designer believed the boat would perform better than the rating.

Later more and more elements were added without technical difficulty to the rule: such features as iron versus lead keel, ballast ratio and factor for type of propeller.

This is what the early CCA rule looked like

Rating in feet = $0.6(SA)^{1/2} \times$ rig factor $+ 0.4(L \pm B \pm D \pm P$
$+ SB \pm F + A + C) \times$ propeller factor $\times R$

The symbols were as follows: L as already defined, SA sail area under Universal rule measurement, B beam at waterline, D draft, P displacement, SB a sail area penalty if SA is excessive in relation to some displacement figures, F freeboard, A bow overhang penalty, C stern overhang penalty, R ballast ratio.

Each of these factors had a paragraph or two (average about 160 words), which was not unduly long in 1934, that showed how the bonus or penalty figure was reached. Here is an example for B.

'If beam is less than $0.185L + 3.3$ (all in feet) then the latter is subtracted from beam, multiplied by 2 and inserted as $+ B$. (In other words there was a penalty if the beam was narrower than this norm). If $0.185L + 3.3$ is less than beam then the difference times 2 is subtracted; in other words a reduction in rating. However if beam exceeds $0.21L + 3.55$, an amount equal to the difference between $0.185L + 3.3$ and $0.21L + 3.55 +$ one-third the excess over $0.21L + 3.55$ shall be inserted as -B'.

All the other letters were on similar vein with adjustments and checks. These obviously gave scope for adjusting the constants every other year, as the CCA rule came up for review.

A major difficulty remained with the rule all its life. This, as in the Universal rule, was the need to measure displacement. Various methods were tried ranging from the owner's declaration in local racing to drawings and lines supplied by the designer and physical weighing. It is fair to say that none of these was satisfactory, though no one denies that displacement is a major speed factor.

The importance of the CCA rule was not merely that it was used for the then premier American ocean race. It was taken up by clubs around the United States and owners were obliged to obtain a CCA rating certificate before competing in specific cruiser racer events in many clubs. During the 1930s its use spread further to Canada and Mexico (which with the USA were members of NAYRU) and South America, where several ocean races came into being, such as the Buenos Aires to Rio de Janeiro. So in effect it was a national rule, or even international, but not acknowledged as such, for it was controlled by the committee of the Cruising Club of America. Thus it was a club (owned and run) rule.

It was quite common in the USA for clubs and local racing associations to amend the rule for a race or races. A typical reason was for the transpacific race where the course in the trade wind was guaranteed to be down wind for several thousand miles after a short beat following the start. As such conditions make it possible to design 'horses for courses' and also throw out the conventional time allowance scales, the rule would be amended.

But other bodies changed the CCA rule, more probably for the usual American reason that the clubs were very independent and were headed by men of strong opinions and with big boats. Thus the Lake Michigan Yachting Association in Chicago in 1936 headed its 'measurements for cruisers' as 'The Cruising Club of America rule for cruising classes, as amended by the special Cruising Rule Committee for adoption by the Lake Michigan Yachting Association'. The body had twenty-three member clubs.[6]

A common ocean racing rule?

In England in 1931 there was a meeting of E.G. 'George' Martin, commodore of the Ocean Racing Club, Malden Heckstall-Smith, brother of 'Bookstall', Olin J. Stephens, designer, who had just won the Fastnet in *Dorade* and Sherman Hoyt of the CCA. The subject was the way in which the American and British rules used for ocean racing might be amalgamated. Remember the 1931 rule used by the CCA was close to the British system.

Yachting World reported

'It is highly probable that the Ocean Racing Club and the Cruising Club of America will develop a common rule ... I believe yachts will be built to the new rule – the common rule – this must inevitably affect the design of all cruising yachts. Whatever rule is drawn up it should be one that will produce good, healthy, sea-going vessels'.[7]

However as described above, the CCA drew up a rule of total originality after the 1932 Bermuda race. This caused the British ocean racing designer J.Laurent Giles to write in 1933

'At the time of the last Fastnet race great hopes were raised that we were on the brink of a common [it should be noted that the word 'international' was not used] rule. Unfortunately the devotees of the sport in the senior ocean racing country [the USA] were unable not only to meet us, but were unable even to produce a common rule for their own country. So for the coming season there will be more rules applied to the competitors of long distance races than ever before.

In this country we can at least claim one rule, that one being the system of the only body organizing events of importance here. In America long distance races are run by many clubs with no body in control; the result is a diversity of rules and regulations'.[8]

The hopes of George Martin about a joint rule, in the words at the head of this chapter, were thus dashed. As will be seen, the rules did come together eventually – but *thirty-six years after* these words of Laurent Giles were written.[9]

The American ocean racer
Despite Giles's comments the CCA rule was effectively the American offshore rule, for North and South America, from its creation in 1932 until 1970. During that period its form as a *base boat rule* with correcting factors remained highly recognizable.

If you asked a keen American offshore sailor any time in that period, or even today, how many rating rules there are in the USA, he would blithely say 'about fifteen'. He would be about right, depending what you call a rating rule: one could indeed say, at any such time, the same number for Europe. However two American offshore rules were undoubtedly conspicuous, probably because, as well as the CCA rule, they were used by the same leading yachts in certain races. They were the *Off Soundings Club rule* and the *Storm Trysail Club rule* (Chapter 10).

Over the years some of the world's most magnificent ocean racers were built to the CCA rule. Many large yachts between, say, 50 and 70ft (15-21m) appeared (around 73ft, 22.2m, was usually the upper LOA limit for the rule). These were leaders in the increasing numbers of ocean races available after WWII, while owners in the recovering European countries were running smaller yachts.

It would be tedious to recount the many small changes to the CCA rules between 1934 and 1941, then from 1946 to 1970. There would be an advantage taken off centreboards here, a penalty taken off 1.7 genoas there, a rule cheating stern overhang regulated, a tax on concave sheerlines introduced, an adjustment one year and then another on the base freeboard and so on.

A supporter of the CCA wrote that after the races of 1934 and 1936

> 'the technical committee got busy and announced the 1938 rule, which was further modified for 1940. The trouble with the rule is that it is difficult to get agreement as to the best type of "normal" . . .'.[10]

By the late 1950s the CCA rule looked like this. As with the International rule (Chapter 3), the factors in the basic formula tended to disappear and be incorporated in restrictive sub clauses. For instance the old A and C for overhangs became part of the sub-measurement of determining L.

Rating in feet = 0.95(L ± beam ± draft ± displacement
± sail area ± freeboard – iron ballast)
× ballast ratio × propeller factor

L was 0.3 of the actual LWL + 0.7 of the 4 per cent waterline plane of the original rule. The typical CCA boat of the period had a wide stern, masthead rig and quite likely a centreboard. There was some advantage to yawls (or ketches, though at that time rudder heads, which define the difference between ketch and yawl were usually not far enough aft) under the rig allowances of the CCA, which were 'exceedingly complicated'.[11] There had been big revisions in 1950 and in 1957.

In its final form in the 1960s, before making way for an internationally agreed rule, the CCA rule was

Rating in feet = (L ± beam ± draft ± displacement ±
$(Sail area)^{1/2}$) × stability allowance
– prop allowance + draft penalty

By this time rule changes against beamy yachts had caused the latest boats to be distinctly narrow. The separate fin keel and rudder had also arrived, in particular the Cal 40 class of this type carried all before it.

At this advanced stage of the rule (mid-1960s) and owing to the huge area over which it was spread, it became evident that ratings were adrift because of different measurement practices. In 1964 it was possible for Gordon M. Curtis Jr, a leading committee man of the CCA to say

'It is vital to the success of ocean racing that a yacht be uniformly measured, whether in Miami, Seattle, Los Angeles or Boston . . . In those localities identical methods must be applied. Owing to a number of factors this has not been the case in the past. The CCA now intends certifying measurers on a national basis.'[12]

One important factor in all these years of the CCA rule must be noted. The rule, once clear of the early years, was used in conjunction with the time allowance tables of NAYRU, formerly the time allowance tables of the New York Yacht Club dated 1908. (Chapter 5). Never were they altered, while the factors in the measurement rule twisted and turned. There was an idea circulating that possibly the time allowance system might be graded for several different kinds of weather, but this was not pursued.

The rule makers of the CCA in its closing years tried to incorporate more and more numbers which were believed to affect a boat's speed. For instance the stability factor brought in the weight of the engine, the material of the ballast keel and mast and the assumed hull drag or resistance when heeling. The propeller factor gave numbers for a wide range of propeller types available made possible by the ingenuity of American designers and manufacturers to circumvent each previous propeller rating rule.

Some might think that the rating of propellers is little to do with the sport of yacht racing. Such moves placed the CCA rule under wide criticism in its closing years; so a new rule proposed with enough authority might be well received. And so it was at the end of the sixties. But those who were fascinated by all that made a boat fast or slow in different conditions continued quietly with their hobby. These Americans will emerge once more in the 1970s.

In higher latitudes
As the CCA ruled the shape of yachts in America from about 1930 to 1970, so the rule of the Ocean Racing Club of London, (from November 1931 the Royal Ocean Racing Club (RORC)), effected similar power in England. The two rules were dominant in ocean racing, as was acknowledged by other nations when eventually they

asked their respective owners to combine them. Anticipating matters, the RORC rule in due course spread around the world to all other countries which, particularly after WWII, were taking up ocean racing: Australia, New Zealand, France, Holland, Germany, the Mediterranean and other European countries and Hong Kong, Malta and British colonies. The exceptions were all of North and South America.

The first Fastnet race was in 1925 and as George Martin says at the chapter head, was in imitation of the Bermuda race. No club ran the race, it was a joint effort by the owners of seven staunch seagoing cruising yachts, who agreed to race from Ryde, Isle of Wight, down Channel, around the Fastnet Rock and finish in Plymouth Sound. Much of the encouragement had come from a yachting writer, Weston Martyr. The private committee which ran the race looked around for a rating rule suitable for heavy cruisers with their high freeboard. Malden Heckstall-Smith was approached and he proposed the old formula of the defunct Boat Racing Association of 1912, with a few minor changes.

Looking back we see that this choice was one of the most telling decisions in the history of rating rules, and so racing, and in turn cruising, yachts. A glance at the BRA rule in chapter 3 will show the relationship. This rule for the Fastnet was

$$\text{Rating in feet} = 0.1(L \times (S)^{1/2})/(\text{displacement})^{1/3}$$
$$+ 0.2(L + (S)^{1/2} - F)$$

The rating was to be 'taken in feet and quarters of a foot'. The time allowance per foot is not known, but it seems that for several of the early Fastnet races, as in the Bermuda race, a time in seconds per mile was announced shortly before the race. Indeed in 1927, Malden Heckstall-Smith announced it at a pre-Fastnet dinner in Cowes!

The symbols were IYRU measured sail area, F freeboard to top of rail, 'displacement' by designer's certificate (!). L was on the old American quarter beam depth principal, but 1/10th of waterline maximum beam out from centreline and 1/20th above the water-plane.

This exact rule will not outlast the first Fastnet, but its general form certainly will and become very important indeed. For what was this BRA and then Fastnet rule, but a summation of the Seawanhaka rule of 1883 and the Universal rule of 1903, both major rules from the USA; the Universal rule in 1925 was, of course, still in use (Chapter 3).

Immediately after the first Fastnet race in August 1925, at a dinner at the Royal Western Yacht Club in Plymouth, the Ocean Racing Club was formed. The original purpose was to run one Fastnet race each year. What eventually happened was that the club ran a Fastnet again in 1926 and 1927, then an additional race for smaller yachts in 1928, called the Channel race. The Fastnet continued every year until 1931; thereafter it was biennial (1933, 1935 etc), alternating with the Bermuda race. Meanwhile more events were added to the club programme each year, so that, for instance, by 1933 there was a Fastnet race, Channel, Cowes-Dinard, Burnham-Heligoland and Harwich-Maas race. This was quite a different concept to the CCA and the, by then, RORC had nothing whatever to do with cruising, rallies or inshore racing. Ocean or offshore racing was its only purpose. (This minimal history is essential to see what the rating rule was being used for).[13]

RORC rule development
The ORC rule (then the RORC from November 1931, though it will now simply be called the RORC rule, whatever the date) for the second Fastnet in 1928 was

$$\text{Rating in feet} = 0.2 \, ((L \times (S)^{1/2})/(B \times D)^{1/2}$$

The method of L was completely changed to a mixture of the old length between perpendiculars (from the old tonnage rules! But presumably it worked for these solid cruisers) and bits of any overhang. D was to become important later: it was the distance inside the boat 'from the top of beams to side amidships to top of floors'.[14]

B × D was, of course, an attempt to show displacement, as direct measurement and 'designer's certificate' had not worked.

This was the formula mentioned above in connection with the CCA, which the latter used for its Bermuda races of the time and which was in any case virtually Nathanael Herreshoff's Universal rule (Chapter 3). But as we have seen, the Americans in due course threw it out, and had never even measured the main factors (displacement, length and sail area) within it in any way that resembled the methods of the RORC.

This was the time that a common rule might have been settled; for the formula being the same, it would certainly have been worth trying to reconcile the measurement methods. Both clubs were also then using time-on-distance allowances.

Herreshoff as a designer had not found it difficult to determine a yacht's displacement or length above, say, 1/10th WL beam above the waterplane. In the United States designers then and later always had a big say in rating rules. In England this was not the case, where the RORC in the earliest days began appointing independent measurers, often retired Army and Naval officers with technical ability. They had to measure yachts as they found them and for which no plans were available. An early 'principle' was established that it must be possible fully to measure a yacht afloat and not necessarily in calm water. The theory was that a yacht could arrive from anywhere at an anchorage (no marinas then) for a race; then, provided there was time, she could be certificated without further ado. The British also ran a centralized measurement organization, so did not suffer lack of uniformity to the same extent as the CCA (above).

So Herreshoff's displacement disappeared for ever in the British rule and B × D was substituted (shades again of tonnage). Phillips-Birt commented in 1959

'This was intended to have the effect of assessing displacement without making this difficult measurement necessary. The BD measurement has been modified many times, but the principle has remained the basis of the club's method of assessing the bulk or speed reducing factor of a yacht ever since. It was to lead to many sorts of troubles and complications'.[15]

For the 1931 season the rule was considerably revised and reverted to the 'Universal plus Seawanhaka form'.

Rating in feet $= 0.15(L \times (S)^{1/2})/(B \times D)^{1/2} + 0.2(L + (S)^{1/2})$

In this form the RORC rule of measurement and rating remained until it ended in 1970. To this rule many outstanding ocean racing yachts were designed, built and sailed.

In stating that the rule lasted for another 39 years, apart from the sub amendments which by now we have seen occur with all rules at intervals, it was actually 'enclosed' finally, by calling the above rating 'measured rating' (MR) and then showing[16]

Rating in feet $=$ MR $\pm$ stability allowance $-$ propeller allowance $+$ draft penalty[17]

Such items were also seen above in the developed CCA rule.

However in 1931, the RORC established its method of measuring length (**Fig 4.1** again). A chain was placed around the bow, while the measurer stood on the foredeck (the boat could perfectly well be bobbing about) which was equal to half the maximum beam: where this fitted around the bow was the forward end of L. Aft, a similar operation was done using three-quarters of B. This had no relation at all to the methods favoured in America. With amendments, this was to remain the method of finding L throughout the life of the RORC rule.

The founders of the Ocean Racing Club actually wrote into its original rules that there should be a rule of measurement and rating for the Fastnet and then they made this emphatic by saying that any time allowances 'should not be on form' by which was meant handicap on known or estimated performance. George Martin had actually won the One Ton Cup, some years back, which was then annually in the 6-metre class. So he knew all about rated racing yachts, as well as Fastnet bound heavy cruisers. It is evident that he knew exactly what he was creating and that boats would in due course be built to the rule. After all, the BRA rule which was chosen for the Ocean Racing Club, had been intended to start a (small inshore) fixed rating class. Martin wrote

'The point has been raised that it may be against the spirit of ocean racing to "build to the rule" or, in other words, to build a vessel in which every advantage is taken of gaining speed that the rule allows. I should like to say that I am most strongly of the opposite opinion. The rule as it has been framed favours certain features which are factors for seaworthiness in existing yachts; to wit, short overhangs, freeboard and displacement. I believe that it is a shortsighted policy not to build to the rule, for the result of building to it will be to produce a type of ocean racing yacht which will be extremely fast without any sacrifice of seagoing ability. It seems to me not a foolish hope that the ocean racing yachts of the future may set a standard which will bring about an improvement in the form of cruising yachts ... *we shall see the development of a class of yachts more efficient in combined speed and seaworthiness than those which have hitherto been built in any class'.*

He went on to say briefly that despite 'the derision of class racing [metre boat] enthusiasts ocean racing will surely have an effect upon the International class'.[18]

The ocean racer takes shape
As with rules in the past, designers were slow to find a new shape

for a new rule. Additionally in this case, owners were more likely to look around for strong vessels that could cope with the gales along the route to Bermuda, or get around the Fastnet rock in a gale. Or they would build such vessels.

The 1928 Fastnet saw the first boat that was built as an ocean racer. She was not designed to the RORC rule, but did owe some features to the CCA rule (which we have seen was in transition), but was in the American tradition of fast schooners. *Nina* was a 59ft LOA (17.98m) vessel primarily for the transatlantic race.

There was an amount of uninformed comment in England, where some people tried to say that a boat built to the Fastnet rule (which she was not) was unfair, but this was not the view of the RORC. The British were slow in designing any boats to the rule, though *Maitenes II* (52ft, 15.8m) was an ocean racing type, though not designed to the rule, which entered the 1929 Fastnet. Yet any racing features were more likely to owe something to the International rule in profile, the shape of the ends, narrow beam and a steadily improving Bermuda rig (changing over from gaff remember in about 1928-1932).

To the Fastnet race of 1931 and 1933, winning the transatlantic race on the way, came the 55ft (16.8m) *Dorade*, designed and sailed by Olin and Rod Stephens. She outclassed all the British yachts, as did her direct same size successor *Stormy Weather*. An interesting sideline was a design competition organized by the Royal Corinthian Yacht Club in 1932 for yachts of 55ft and 35ft rating to the RORC rule. The thirty entries were received from a number of countries and judged by Malden Heckstall-Smith and Charles E. Nicholson. Since not a single RORC boat had yet been built, it is not surprising that many looked like offshore versions of metre boats: long ends, narrow, slack bilges, heavy displacement. There were even two entries with gaff rig, for the Bermudan rig was not quite universally acknowledged for offshore (**Fig 4.3**).

It is ironic that the judges commented that it had been said that the rule would result in short ends, but the entries did not result in that. Of course (in the light of later design) a boat should have had short ends, but then would the judges have favoured it?[19]

Yet Phillips-Birt commented later 'The collection of designs with one-third of the entries from architects under 30 years old [including Olin Stephens, Laurent Giles, Charles A. Nicholson] revealed how far thought had already gone beyond the ideas of the heavy displacement, gaff rigged cruiser with long keel and internal ballast, which seven years earlier (1925) had been the British conception of a suitable vessel for offshore racing'.

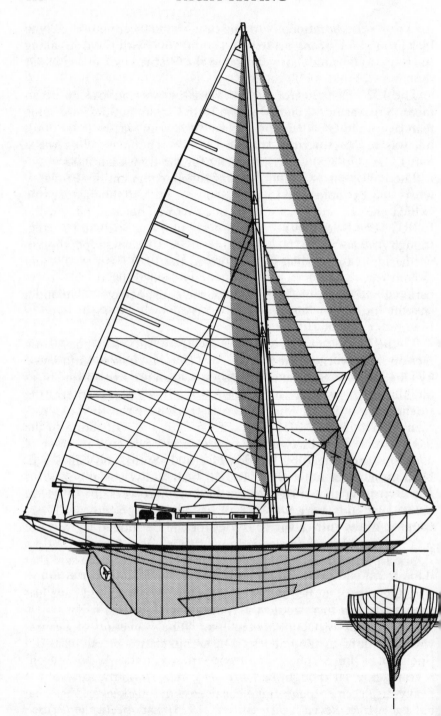

Following *Stormy Weather*[20], Olin Stephens designed several
boats to the RORC rule for European owners including *Zeearend*
in Holland and *Trenchemer* in Scotland in 1935. Then British yacht
designers pitched in with proper RORC racers at last in the mid
and late 1930s: *Ortac* by Robert Clark, *Foxhound* by Charles E.
Nicholson (who was at the same time designing Universal rule
America's Cup yachts – the *Endeavours*); *Maid of Malham* (42ft,
12.8m) by Laurent Giles launched for the 1937 season for a new
name in ocean racing, John Illingworth. The latter had a masthead
rig set well inboard giving large genoas. She was the archetypal
(and successful) RORC rule ocean racer immediately before
WWII.

In these years preceding the outbreak of war in September 1939,
each year saw a new crop of ocean racers to the rule of the RORC:
British, Dutch, German and French. 'The design for offshore in
British waters had been transformed. The new type of fast cruiser
was generally approved. Overhangs, short keels, moderate displacement and Bermudan rigs no longer struck chill into the heart of
blue water sailors'.[21] (**Fig 4.4**).

The 1937 Fastnet race had 29 yachts from five countries and was
won by a Dutch yacht to the RORC rule. The following Fastnets
1939, 1947, had very slightly fewer entries, but 1949 again had 29
and then each successive running of this famous course had greatly
increasing numbers. The last Fastnet under the RORC rule in
1969 saw 186 starters.

During 1938 and 1939 the RORC had run 17 other races in
addition to the Fastnet, but distance and passage races had also
been initiated by other clubs around Britain, in the Baltic and the
Mediterranean. The importance of these in rating terms is that by
about 1938, the many major races had changed from local handicapping to the rule of the RORC.

After 1945

This trend was even more marked after WWII for disruption in
Europe meant that it was convenient to look to the RORC, whose
club house had been bombed, but which had opened a new one in
1942 and was making postwar sailing plans. Similarly the CCA was
the logical leader for offshore racing in the Americas. Illingworth,

Fig 4.3 *The J. Laurent Giles entry in the Royal Corinthian
Yacht Club designing competition of 1932 for ocean racers rating
at 35ft RORC rule. This example was narrow and deep in the
English tradition. The rule was not pressed until some years later.*

whose war service ended in Australia, influenced the Cruising Club of Australia to run a race from Sydney to Hobart: being about 600 nautical miles, this became the third 'classic', equivalent to the Bermuda and Fastnet courses. The Australians adopted the RORC rule.

There was no question of the RORC trying to widen the use of its rating rule. Indeed there were reservations about allowing other organizations to use it. In a typical British manner, it spread by accident. Clubs elsewhere in Europe and elsewhere in the world, used the rule because they found it satisfactory. Control was in the hands of the RORC committee, or more immediately the 'RORC Rating Secretary', an unpaid post held by a retired English gentleman.

The CCA held the first post war Newport-Bermuda race in June 1946 and the first Fastnet was in August 1947. In yachting circles, ocean racing and passage races for habitable boats came to the head of the sport. Not only was this where the technical progress was to be found, but the numbers increased every year and were soon of an order never seen in the International classes. Even more than after WWI, the racing yachts of the International classes were reduced. In Chapter 9, it will be seen that they continued with small numbers and one of their classes began a renewed 'career' (in the America's Cup), but their place at the head of the sport and where the top racing men were to be found lapsed.

Looking at it another way, in the 1950s and 1960s, all kinds of sailing expanded enormously, but not in rated day keel boats. In Cowes Week, the principal classes were soon to be the larger RORC rated boats.

In 1948 the YRA made an attempt to return to the business of handicapping. It declared a 'speed figure' to be obtained from RORC rating. Of course this was just a time allowance under the RORC rule. If yachts were unmeasured they could count L as (LOA + LWL)/2, take beam and an amended depth measurement from Lloyds Register (an 'official' list of yachts and their stated dimensions), then put it into the RORC formula. Local handicappers were to be appointed to adjust such allowances.

As far as is known, this compromise scheme got nowhere. Clubs began to state that RORC ratings were needed for this race or that; or for small and known boats, a club simply used its own local

Fig 4.4 *Just before WWII the RORC rule was at last breaking away from the metre boat style*. Prelude, *a successful offshore boat by J. Laurent Giles, cut profile to reduce wetted surface, reduced*

displacement and had a genoa larger than the mainsail, but was still narrow. Stern was long, but pinched in for girth measurement. LOA 36ft 1in (11.0m); LWL 25ft (7.62m); beam 7ft 6in (2.28m).

handicapping allocation.

The Myth

The story of the immensely successful 38ft (11.58m) masthead
sloop *Myth of Malham* is told in several places[22]. She swept the
board from 1947 on, partly owing to the skill and attitude of her
owner, John Illingworth; partly owing to her design to the RORC
rule. At a bound, she convinced British ocean racing men, that for
success the pre-war 'fast cruisers which also rate well to the rule',
as designers preferred to call their new boats, was over. From now
on it was the flat-out ocean racer, as understood in each successive
season (**Fig 4.5**).

There was a strong rating aspect. The designer was Laurent
Giles, but the concept was that of Illingworth, who said

> 'I know he did not agree with a lot of things on which I insisted,
> but he drew them in faithfully just the same . . . When the lines
> were finished I said I intended to cut off the bow and stern,
> leaving the under waterlines untouched . . .'.[23]

Apart from the short ends, which reduced measured length,
there was a huge fortriangle since the rule was easy on headsails, a
short keel (though the rudder was attached to it), high freeboard
and light displacement. She had no engine.

What this did was to take advantage of the notorious RORC D
measurement. This was taken to the deck beams, so the rule
'thought' that the *Myth* had a big displacement, though much of
the D was in the freeboard (**Fig 4.6**).

The RORC did not hurry to amend its rule, unlike the CCA
(where the *Myth* was regarded with horror and a condemnation of
the British rating rule). Eventually after the *Myth* had swept all
before her for two seasons, in January 1949, the rule was changed
in respect of freeboard, depth measurements (which importantly

Fig 4.5 *One of the classic rule beaters in the history of yachting,*
Myth of Malham, *designed by J. Laurent Giles to the concept of
her owner Captain John Ilingworth RN. The RORC rule had to
undergo revision in several important areas, though 'the Myth'
continued to win races for many years. LOA 38ft (11.58m);
LWL 33ft 6in (10.21m); beam 9ft 3in (2.82m); draft 7ft 3in
(2.21m). She demonstrated that short ends, high freeboard, light
displacement, a mast amidships and other novel features were
compatible with speed.*

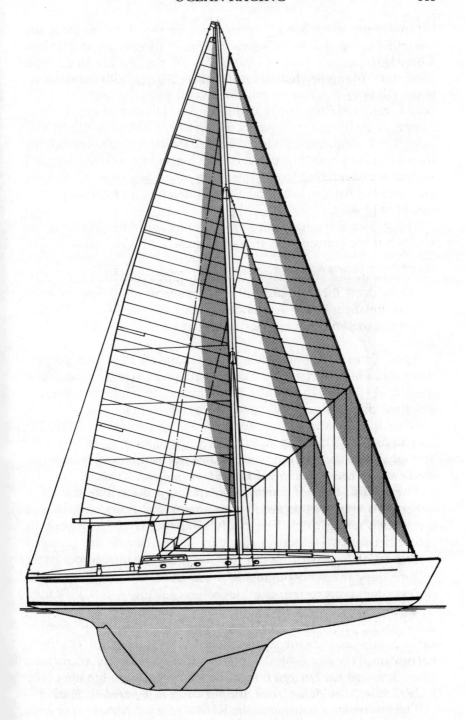

became 'immersed depth' by subtracting the distance from the waterline up to the deck (beams)), a small penalty on aluminium masts and measurement of snubbed ends. Some allowances were given for an engine. Sail area and the rule generally were to be looked at later.

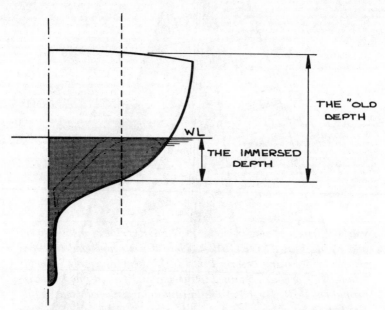

Fig 4.6 *Depth had been used to assess displacement without having to measure it. But 'the Myth' showed that measuring from the covering board gave freeboard and not just hull depth. So an 'immersed depth' was introduced, freeboard being subtracted. Much later this was further exploited by designing 'deepness' at the actual point of measurement and reducing displacement elsewhere.*

The RORC yachts, though none was as extreme as the *Myth* became very much distinguished from the fairly graceful vessels (forever being corrected into 'desirable cruising yachts') by high freeboard, sometimes with flat or convex sheerlines, masthead rigs, sometimes cutters and short even 'pinched' ends. Displacement varied. Strangely beam in the RORC was to remain relatively narrow until the late 1960s. Why this should have been is not clear, since B was on the bottom line of the formula; late in the life of the RORC rule B suddenly grew and, of course, lowered the rating.

The last major alteration to the RORC rule (each year there were small corrections, but the British policy was to keep them small and

THE ROYAL OCEAN RACING CLUB

RULE OF MEASUREMENT AND RATING 1957

Reprinted 1968

Amended to 31st December 1967

INTRODUCTION.

The object of the Rule of Measurement and Rating is to bring together by time allowance when racing together in open water, yachts of the widest possible range of type and size.

The intention is to assist in promoting Rule 2(b) of the R.O.R.C. by encouraging the design and building of yachts in which speed and seaworthiness are combined, without favouring any particular type.

It is not possible for the Rule to cover every eventuality and the Committee, therefore, reserve the right to modify the Rule at any time, or to deal with any peculiarity of design which does not conform to the spirit of the Rule, and to give such rating as they consider equitable.

I. RATING FORMULA.

I (1) Measured Rating, $MR = .15 \dfrac{L\sqrt{S}}{\sqrt{BD}} + .2(L + \sqrt{S})$

Where L = Length
B = Beam
D = Depth
S = Rated Sail Area

I (2) Rating, R = MR ± Stability Allowance (cor.) − Propeller Allowance + Draft Penalty.

I (3) All measurements, except dimensions of sails and scantling details, shall be in feet to two places of decimals. Dimensions of sails and spars for calculation of sail area shall be taken in feet to one decimal place, except battens, headboards and boom depth which shall be taken in feet to two decimal places. Sail areas shall be given in square feet to one decimal place. Scantling details shall be measured in inches and fractions or decimals of inches. Percentages shall be taken to one decimal place.

2

II. BEAM.

II Beam, B, shall be the greatest Breadth, measured to the outside of normal planking at a height not exceeding half the freeboard height at this position.

III. LENGTH.

III (1) Length, L, shall be found as follows:—

L = LBG − (FOC + AOC)

LBG = Horizontal length between FGS and AGS (see Rule III (2)) or AGS cor. (see Rule III (9))

FOC = Forward Overhang Component (see Rule III (7))

AOC = After Overhang Component (see Rules III (8), (9) and (10))

It is intended that L shall approximate to the distance between a point forward where the freeboard and the half-girth (see Rule III (3)) are equal, and a point aft where the freeboard and the half-girth is one-eighth B are equal.

Any case where L does not so approximate may be treated as a peculiarity of design under paragraph 3 of the Introduction to the Rule and, if the Committee so direct, alternative measurements shall be taken.

III (2) Girth stations, except in special cases dealt with under rules III (8), (9) and (10), shall be found as follows:—

FGS, Forward Girth Station, where the girth equals ⅓B

FIGS, Forward Inner Girth Station, where the girth equals ⅛B

AGS, After Girth Station, where the girth equals ⅓B

AIGS, After Inner Girth Station, where the girth equals ⅛B

GSDf = Horizontal distance between FGS and FIGS

GSDa = Horizontal distance between AGS and AIGS

III (3) Girths shall be chain girth measurements and, except in cases dealt with under Rule III (5), shall be taken from covering board to covering board, and the points on the covering board and the forward or after profile through which they pass shall be in the same vertical athwartships plane.

3

Fig 4.7 *Typical pages from the 1957 RORC rule of measurement and rating – the 'RORC rule'. Here it is as amended to 1968, shortly before being absorbed into IOR. Its Universal/Seawanhaka/BRA origins remained to the end and passed into the main formula of IOR. By today's inflated standards the rule was small. See* **Fig 7.4.**

let design run) was in 1957.

This took extra depth measurements and not only at the position of maximum beam. The scantling rule, which has hardly been mentioned here, but which started simply as 'according to Lloyds', which failed to cope with foreign visitors, was set down with figures for materials and thickness etc of components. Ideas from the CCA were introduced with a stability allowance including keel material, weight of engine and the scantlings; while another CCA system adopted was an elaborate propeller allowance for size and type. The CCA method of taxing rig aspect ratio came in, but was not so severe, as in America it had produced 'low' rigs, even some bowsprits. The RORC changed its previous policy that all measurement must be possible afloat, in the interests of accuracy (especially for freeboard, the new depth measurement and sails).

When the rule was announced, the RORC rating secretary/chief measurer since 1925, Ray Barrett, resigned and was succeeded by a

sapper Brigadier, David Fayle. Malden Heckstall-Smith, by then
aged 90, said he approved of the big rule changes.

There was no change in the basic RORC formula, as shown
above. As mentioned, it never did subsequently change from its
Universal/Seawanhaka/BRA form (**Fig 4.7**).

Affluence and the rules

Yacht racing is influenced by nothing, if not by economics. In
hindsight, it can be seen that however keen the sailors between and
after both world wars, the racing scene in bigger boats was severely
affected, though America always less than Europe.

By the late 1950s, nations were getting used to working together
for international sport, rather bigger boats were returning and
communications were become unimaginably better. In this revived
world there were several yacht racing novelties and proposals that
had a major effect on the rating rules of the CCA and RORC.
These were the relative events.

(1) In 1952 the NAYRU joined the IYRU. From January 1961,
after excruciating and lengthy controversy, there was also adopted
an agreed set of racing (right-of-way and so on) rules, based on the
American Vanderbilt rules. The metre boats, what was left of
them, therefore now had official American input, though, as
mentioned, there had been US 'observers' at the IYRU for most
years since WWII.

Of course, neither the IYRU, nor the national authorities in the
USA and the UK had anything to do with the ocean racing rules. *It
was now evident that America and Europe could get together on
yachting rules.*

The RORC was by no means the only offshore rule in Europe
and there were at least two others to which yachts were seriously
designed and built for established programmes of races. There was
the Swedish SHR, Svenska Havskryssar regeln, a base boat rule,
and the German KR rule. A rough description of the boats
resulting to these rules (or perhaps the conventions of Baltic
sailing) was moderate ended, low freeboard, moderate sail area
vessels. These rules did not spread outside the Baltic and as there
were two of them, numbers were split between them, not to metion
other Scandinavian classes such as the 'skerry cruisers', 30 square
metre yachts and the like.

(2) In 1957, some members of the RORC presented the Admiral's
Cup, for a three boat team race between British yachts and
American yachts, the latter usually coming over for Cowes Week
and the Fastnet. The races were two inshore events in Cowes Week

and the Channel race (about 250 miles) and the Fastnet. *This totally new concept brought international inshore racing into the ocean racing fleet.*

It also saw regular American entries in direct and high level competition with European and Australian offshore boats. The US boats were always designed to the CCA rule; when they arrived in England, *they were measured to the RORC rule and given an RORC rating. Despite this they often did extremely well.* The British claimed that RORC designs could not do equally well under the CCA rule, but numbers involved were too few to come to a conclusion.

(3) In 1965, the Cercle de la Voile de Paris, led particularly by Jean Peytel, previously an owner of metre boats, presented the One Ton Cup, which had been a very important annual international series for the 6-metre class for a series of inshore and offshore races for boats of 22ft rating in the RORC rule, with accommodation rules as in the IYRU 8-metre cruiser-racer class (see Chapter 8). This was at once greeted with wide enthusiasm. Now there were RORC boats to a fixed rating like the old International classes and they had even taken over their famous cup! *Now boats to the RORC rule were clearly the leading class of rated boat internationally. They had rated classes and were sailing around the buoys.*

(4) For many years there had been informal exchanges between the CCA and RORC. As seen, the RORC did try to incorporate some CCA ideas such as the way sails were measured, allowances for propellers and so on, but for designing a boat to the rule in a more competitive racing world, the results were very different (**Fig 4.8 and 4.9**). Continental Europeans having tidier minds than Anglo-Saxons (and prepared to lose the SHR and the KR in the process of unification) met in Bremen, invited by a German, Rolf Schmidt, on 5 June 1961. As a result an informal Offshore Rules Coordinating Committee (this said nothing about a common rule) from several nations met from time to time from then on. The chairman was an Englishman, E.P. 'Buster' de Guingand.[24] *Neither the British nor Americans really had their hearts in this, but it meant that technical people were examining the possibilities.*

(5) At the same time as, and not disconnected with, the One Ton Cup for RORC level rating, the IYRU was making noises about including ocean racing in the 1968 Olympic Games. Because of this the IYRU (which was the authority for the Games) asked the CCA and RORC if they could recommend a common rule for such a purpose. This was all rather strange, as the Olympics could have used one-designs and were in any case unsuitable for racing out of sight at night, *but this was a spur towards combining the two rules.*[25]

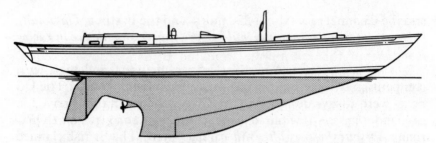

Fig 4.8 Palawan, *an 58ft (17.68m) S & S design to the CCA rule shortly before (1966) it combined with RORC. Beam to length ratio was 0.21. See* **Fig 4.9.**

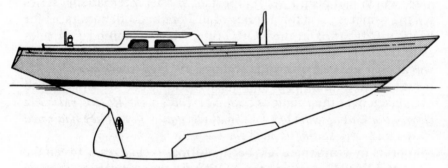

Fig 4.9 Quiver IV, *a 46ft 2in (14.06m) boat to the RORC rule by Camper and Nicholsons, designed at the same time as* **Fig 4.8.** *Beam to length ratio was 0.26, wider than the American boat, so after 60 years the British boats had actually become beamier than American (owing to the respective rating rules). Both* Palawan *and* Quiver IV *had big masthead rigs with the spar near amidships.*

(6) In the late 1960s some American designers were increasingly designing yachts to the RORC rule for European owners. These were successful. *Among the Americans, Olin J. Stephens and Dick Carter rather liked the way the RORC rule was administered, its continuity and rating policy* (in not favouring an envisaged cruising yacht).

(7) More level rating classes were invented in France to the RORC rule and they were quickly built to. The Half Ton Cup was 18ft RORC rating (from 1966), the Quarter Ton Cup was 15ft RORC rating (1967); the Italians began a Two Ton Cup at 28ft RORC rating (1967).[26] The RORC in its cramped committee room in London watched this cross border explosion with anxiety.

(8) As a result of all these moves, *an International Technical*

Committee (ITC) was formed under the chairmanship of Stephens to give a cutting edge to combining the CCA and RORC rules. Other members of this committee were the British rating secretary, David Fayle and his deputy, Robin Glover, Gustav Plym, Swedish sailor, designer and administrator and E. G. Van de Stadt, Dutch designer of many ocean racers. Dick Carter was the other American. The ITC worked intensively in 1968 and 1969. In November 1968, the ITC, meeting at the RORC in London, said it had a common rating rule on paper.

A prophecy recalled

There was much talk of the 'new rule' in the late 1960s. Of its prospects Douglas Phillips-Birt had something to say in magazine articles at the time. Much of what he said was prophetic.[27]

'It is questionable whether a common rating rule for international use is either philosophically desirable or even practicable. There is tidiness and logic, but that does not mean it is such a good idea as it may seem to those who assume the role of leading, with something less than the sweet music of Hamelin's piper [in Germany!], the regiments of the uniform and tidy-minded towards the wondrous portals of a world where everything is the same everywhere.

I have been unable to discover why a single international rating rule should be regarded as so desirable. One supposes that yachtsmen from the furthest shore of the curtained off Baltic to the sunlit harbours where the Pacific endlessly roars, are in a state of helpless confusion for lack of a common rating rule. Yet all that is heard is about technical improvements in rules, interesting but unconnected with the agenda.

A rule once internationalized becomes harder to administer and control. Even if class racing in a new guise, with an offshore racing element in it has appeared, the sailing waters of the world are numerous and of great variety. Why exchange having the CCA and RORC rules as twin norms in favour of the deadening uniformity of a single rule intended, it appears, to cater for every locality, for level and handicap racing, for inshore and offshore?

Combining the CCA and RORC is no less outrageous than supposing we might blend 'God save the Queen' with the 'Marseillaise' to produce an international anthem for the Common Market! The RORC rule may be open to criticism, but a private committee is rocked by less confusion than an international committee drawn at inconvenient intervals from the corners of the earth for a party'

Another contemporary wrote

'The new rule is bound to be the most complex formula to date. That it will be under broad international control is logical for the 1970s. The computer for rapid working of apparently lengthy arithmetic and the jet, jumbo, supersonic, or otherwise and the use of telex for rapid consultation between members of the controlling body of the rule, meet objections to this [complexity] feature'.[28]

In Chapter 7 this combination of the two great rules, American and British, will be described and the course of the rating rule which resulted will be followed.

5 Giving and getting time

'Fly envious time, till thou run out thy race' – John Milton
(1608-1674)

'At a tradition laden party in the fortress headquarters in Plymouth, there had been much hands-across-the-sea and discussion of the roughness of the Fastnet race just past. I begged the chair for leave to say a few words. I despaired the disagreement between the CCA rule, which is time-on-distance and the RORC, which is time-on-time. I felt that after the last race we could perhaps find some common ground for a rule based on time-on-motion. Since this was a very English joke, it was greeted with muted cheers' – William Snaith, owner of the successful American ocean racer *Figaro* after the 1957 Fastnet.

'The time is out of joint'. William Shakespeare, *Hamlet*.

WHAT IS APPLIED at the end of a race between two yachts with different ratings is a time allowance. This corrects the elapsed time and gives a result whereby the yacht with the shorter corrected time beats the other, whatever may have been the order of finish on the water.

In the first four chapters, time allowances have been looked at only briefly and where they directly affected the narrative. The assumption was made that a designer or owner wanted as low a rating as practicable for a yacht, because this would result in the most favourable time allowance. Now it is helpful to look at time allowances as they apply to rules both present and past. So the remarks which follow are no longer chronological, but an examination of how time allowances work and are derived and are developed. Rules will be mentioned that have not appeared in the previous (chronological) chapters, because before discussing more rules, it is necessary to catch up with these time allowances (TA).

Therefore when looking at later rules, the reader may want to refer back to this chapter.

A leap into the present

Time allowances are not always the same as ratings. One can have a time allowance without a rating, for instance in local handicapping, and one can have a rating without a time allowance, as in the International 6-metre class, or International Offshore Rule One Ton Cup.

There seem to be four sources of time allowances. (1) From *a rating figure in feet or metres*, which has already been arrived at by measurement and rating. (2) Out of the head of *a club or area handicapper*, who knows his boats, local conditions and results over a period. (3) From a performance system, usually national, where *production or one-design classes establish numbers* for the design with adjustments for alterations on individual boats, such as Portsmouth Yardstick or Performance Handicap Racing Fleet (PHRF). Both of these will be examined later. (4) Direct from *a measurement and rating rule which does not disclose a linear rating* (feet or metres), but issues a time allowance on a rating certificate. Here the time allowance is the rating. This is a relatively new fashion and is seen in the Channel Handicap System (CHS) (where there is a linear figure in the chain, but it is not disclosed) and International Measurement System (IMS), where the time allowance emerges from numerous measurements. Again both these rules will be carefully discussed in later chapters (10 and 11).

As much folly can be committed within time allowance systems, as in rules of rating. If the allowance per foot, is too 'big or small' one way or the other, then advantage is tilted to the smaller or larger end of a race entry. It was seen how in 1897 the YRA altered its 'scale of time allowance' so that for instance *Meteor* had to give to *Britannia*, under the new scale 13 seconds per mile instead of $6\frac{1}{2}$ seconds (enough to cause the Kaiser to complain personally to an Englishman visiting Berlin); other yachts were affected by similar huge changes. Several owners of big cutters withdrew from racing and 'the result of the YRA's legislation was a positive disaster'.[1]

Nearly one hundred years later, attempts to introduce a novel TA system, which varied with the weather, caused even wider difficulties for first class racing, whatever the validity of the rating rule (IMS) from which the TA came.

All time allowances have an inherent defect, which is well known, but worth stating here. Two yachts of different sizes, measured by a 'perfect' rating rule and sailed by crews who make no mistake (!) will arrive at a race mark at different times. On a leg of the course they will be in different water, one hundred metres apart or twenty miles. At any moment, or even when passing the same mark at intervals, the wind, current or tidal stream, or all three, may well be very different for each yacht. Thus on one day, the larger boat, say, could not, however well sailed, save her time against the competitor. This has to be accepted and is part of yacht racing. It makes it very difficult to decide what is 'fair'.

Early time allowances

The first attempt at some allowance was by the Royal Yacht Squadron; this was because the largest yachts invariably won every race. So in 1829 the Squadron yachts, which ranged from 40 to 140 tons, were released from the starting line in groups depending on the distance the group ahead had covered. The first class gave $\frac{1}{2}$ a mile to the second, so when the first group had sailed the distance, the next was released and so on for subsequent groups.

Slightly more advanced than this was to say, in 1838, that yacht

Tons.	Diff of Time	h.	m.	s.
Under 16	**60**	10	46	15
17	seconds	...	47	15
18	per ton	...	48	15
19		...	49	15
20		...	50	15
21	**55**	...	51	15
22		...	52	10
23		...	53	5
24		...	54	0
25		...	54	55
26	**50**	...	55	50
27		...	56	40
28		...	57	30
29		...	58	20
30		...	59	10

Fig 5.1 *As already shown at* **Fig 1.3,** *the scale of George Ackers made advances in its time, since it graded time allowance in steps rather than simply linear against tonnage.*

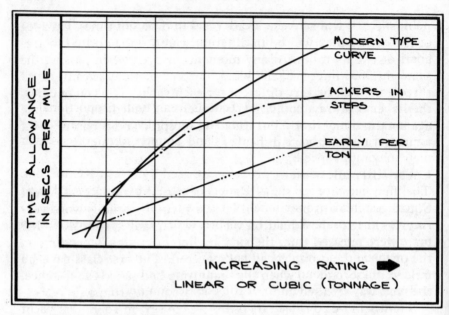

Fig 5.2 *Simple facts about time allowance: the very early times per ton were crude, Ackers went in steps, modern scales invariably run in a smooth curve per rating.*

A was allowed an allowance of, say, 9 minutes 40 seconds, on the Queen's Cup course, whatever that might have been. Then came the scale of George Holland Ackers of 1843, already shown in Chapter 1. (**Fig 5.1 and 1.3**) It will be seen that he moved his scale in steps; thus boats between 6 and 10 tons were corrected at 70 seconds per ton per mile, but boats between 21 and 25 tons were corrected at 55 seconds per ton per mile.

It is believed that Ackers compiled this from observation, though no doubt he consulted naval architects. This non-linear treatment has remained common to most time scales; one fundamental reason being that speed is not directly proportional to tonnage or length; also smaller yachts reach their maximum speeds earlier as the wind increases. (**Fig 5.2**)

The New York YC in its regatta of 1845 simply allowed 45 seconds per ton on the course; this was linear. Another crude time allowance, already mentioned, was that of the first few Bermuda races (early 1920s), where an allowance of so many minutes was given for the course, proportional to length overall.

No doubt there were a number of scales devised and then used to a greater or lesser extent, but among those known were the following which will simply be listed.

In 1871 the Seawanhaka YC devised the TA difference between two yachts of lengths (or linear rating) L (the longer) and l as:

$$0.4 \left((3600/(l)^{1/2}) - (3600/(L)^{1/2}) \right)$$

This is simply the number of seconds in an hour proportional to the square root of length or rating and multiplied by 0.4, this latter figure because the boats in Long Island Sound did not often reach their maximum speed.

The YRA rule of 1887, probably devised by Dixon Kemp[2] took the difference between the fifth roots of ratings by some weird logic which assumed proportionality between sail, beam and length. Anyway the result was an extensive table which showed seconds per mile against rating.

For instance a rating of 30 gave 177.67 seconds per mile and of 40 gave 187.87 seconds per mile. Kemp said subtract the difference and multiply by the length of the course in miles!

Time-on-distance in the USA

For many years all TA in America, Britain and elsewhere was stated as these seconds per mile. You simply subtract the difference between boats and multiply by the number of miles. This has continued as the almost universal TA system in the USA and some other places.

Here one must mention that since the 1930s and 1940s (details below), the British and some Europeans have used *time-on-time*. This means the yacht has a factor which when multiplied by the elapsed time, gives a corrected time.

Nathanael Herreshoff was experimenting with TA tables for many years and with the establishment of 'his' Universal rule, he suggested a time scale to go with it. The New York YC adopted this in 1908. *This one is important because, with some change in actual numbers, it has been the basis of time allowances throughout the United States (and places which follow) ever since. It was applied to the Universal rule, the CCA rule and then the IOR.* It is also used today where there are still linear rules and in principal for IMS and PHRF, where the figures come straight out as seconds per mile allowance for the yacht.

In 1908 the difference between two yachts of rating R (the larger) and rating r was given as:

$$TA = 2160/(r)^{1/2} - 2160/(R)^{1/2}$$

The top figure, 2160, is simply 3600 times 0.6, on the same principle as given above. This time the assumption is that yachts reach 0.6 of their maximum speed given by rating.

As developed later as the NAYRU time allowance tables, the TA was said to work well for a triangular course (closehauled, reach, run) and a wind between 8 and 25 knots.

For practical use time-on-distance systems need a table from which the allowance is immediately available for the rating. So with the NAYRU tables of 1908 (and in use until about 1991), a yacht of 25.5ft rating was 238.31 seconds. Then for, say, 36.8ft there was 166.63 seconds.

So for a course of 57 miles, the sum is simply 238.31 − 166.63 = 71.68 seconds; multiply by length of course = 4085.76 seconds = 1 hour 8 minutes 5.76 seconds. This time is subtracted from the elapsed of the smaller yacht to give her corrected time.

In order to make these sums practical for racing, it became the practice to show the yacht with the smallest rating (that is the 'fastest' yacht) in any race as 'scratch' yacht.[3] So her TA was 0 (zero) and each successive yacht was shown as the time difference from her. This makes it easier for the results to be worked out at the end and for crews to make a quick assessment on the water.

Fig 5.3 shows the TA tables of NAYRU, as issued after 1945 and as used today in any American rating given in feet. They remain almost the same as those issued in 1908; the difference is in the use of a constant, as follows to give the figure:

$$TA = (2160)/(R)^{1/2} + 183.64$$

The constant on the end appears to be an attempt to give a more precise figure for the expected seconds per mile for a yacht of rating R. However when the TA of any boats are subtracted, as above, the constant disappears anyway. It just means that the TA against rating in the tables is a different number.

Today's rules in the USA, particularly IMS and PHRF issue the 'seconds per mile' direct to the yacht from the rating certificate. Therefore the NAYRU tables are not required for finding it; the

Fig 5.3 *The notorious time allowance tables of NAYRU, as used in the 1960s (as well as afterwards and decades before). These caused Americans to have quite different perceptions of the same rating rules from Europeans and Australians, who were not concerned with these ancient tables. The left hand column is a rating in feet. So a 21.5 rater is allowed 289.48 seconds and a*

TIME ALLOWANCE TABLES

FOR ONE NAUTICAL MILE, IN SECONDS AND DECIMALS.

Rating	Allowance	Rating	Allowance	Rating	Allowance	Rating	Allowance
15.0	381.35	18.0	332.75	21.0	294.98	24.0	264.55
.1	379.49	.1	331.33	.1	293.87	.1	263.64
.2	377.65	.2	329.93	.2	292.76	.2	262.73
.3	375.83	.3	328.54	.3	291.65	.3	261.82
.4	374.03	.4	327.17	.4	290.56	.4	260.92
.5	372.26	.5	325.83	.5	289.48	.5	260.03
.6	370.50	.6	324.48	.6	288.40	.6	259.14
.7	368.76	.7	323.14	.7	287.33	.7	258.26
.8	367.03	.8	321.82	.8	286.26	.8	257.38
.9	365.31	.9	320.50	.9	285.20	.9	256.51
16.0	363.64	19.0	319.19	22.0	284.15	25.0	255.65
.1	361.97	.1	317.89	.1	238.10	.1	254.78
.2	360.31	.2	316.60	.2	282.07	.2	253.92
.3	358.66	.3	315.32	.3	281.04	.3	253.07
.4	357.02	.4	314.05	.4	280.02	.4	252.23
.5	355.39	.5	312.78	.5	279.00	.5	251.39
.6	353.79	.6	311.53	.6	277.99	.6	250.55
.7	352.21	.7	310.29	.7	276.99	.7	249.72
.8	350.64	.8	309.06	.8	276.00	.8	248.89
.9	349.08	.9	307.84	.9	275.01	.9	248.07
17.0	347.52	20.0	306.62	23.0	274.03	26.0	247.25
.1	345.99	.1	305.42	.1	273.06	.1	246.44
.2	344.47	.2	304.24	.2	272.09	.2	245.63
.3	342.96	.3	303.05	.3	271.13	.3	244.82
.4	341.46	.4	301.87	.4	270.17	.4	244.02
.5	339.97	.5	300.71	.5	269.22	.5	243.23
.6	338.50	.6	299.54	.6	268.27	.6	242.44
.7	337.04	.7	298.39	.7	267.33	.7	241.66
.8	335.60	.8	297.25	.8	266.40	.8	240.88
.9	334.17	.9	296.11	.9	265.48	.9	240.10
27.0	239.33	31.0	211.61	35.0	188.76	39.0	169.52
.1	238.56	.1	210.98	.1	188.24	.1	169.08
.2	237.79	.2	210.36	.2	187.72	.2	168.64
.3	237.03	.3	209.74	.3	187.20	.3	168.19
.4	236.27	.4	209.11	.4	186.68	.4	167.75
.5	235.52	.5	208.50	.5	186.17	.5	167.31
.6	234.78	.6	207.89	.6	185.65	.6	166.88
.7	234.04	.7	207.28	.7	185.15	.7	166.45
.8	233.30	.8	206.68	.8	184.64	.8	166.02
.9	232.57	.9	206.08	.9	184.14	.9	165.60
28.0	231.84	32.0	205.48	36.0	183.64	40.0	165.18
.1	231.11	.1	204.88	.1	183.14	.1	164.75
.2	230.39	.2	204.29	.2	182.64	.2	164.32
.3	229.67	.3	203.70	.3	182.15	.3	163.88
.4	228.95	.4	203.11	.4	181.66	.4	163.46
.5	228.24	.5	202.52	.5	181.16	.5	163.04
.6	227.53	.6	201.94	.6	180.67	.6	162.62
.7	226.82	.7	201.36	.7	180.19	.7	162.21
.8	226.12	.8	200.79	.8	179.71	.8	161.80
.9	225.43	.9	200.22	.9	179.23	.9	161.39
29.0	224.74	33.0	199.65	37.0	178.75	41.0	160.98
.1	224.05	.1	199.08	.1	178.27	.1	160.56
.2	223.37	.2	198.51	.2	177.79	.2	160.15
.3	222.68	.3	197.95	.3	177.31	.3	159.74
.4	222.00	.4	197.39	.4	176.83	.4	159.34
.5	221.33	.5	196.83	.5	176.36	.5	158.93
.6	220.66	.6	196.27	.6	175.90	.6	158.52
.7	219.99	.7	195.72	.7	175.43	.7	158.12
.8	219.32	.8	195.17	.8	174.96	.8	157.73
.9	218.66	.9	194.63	.9	174.50	.9	157.33
30.0	218.00	34.0	194.09	38.0	174.04	42.0	156.93
.1	217.34	.1	193.54	.1	173.58	.1	156.53
.2	216.70	.2	193.00	.2	173.12	.2	156.13
.3	216.05	.3	192.46	.3	172.67	.3	155.74
.4	215.40	.4	191.92	.4	172.21	.4	155.35
.5	214.75	.5	191.38	.5	171.76	.5	154.96
.6	214.11	.6	190.85	.6	171.30	.6	154.57
.7	213.48	.7	190.32	.7	170.84	.7	154.19
.8	212.85	.8	189.79	.8	170.40	.8	153.80
.9	212.23	.9	189.28	.9	169.96	.9	153.42

Time Allowance—Continued.

Rating	Allowance	Rating	Allowance	Rating	Allowance	Rating	Allowance
43.0	153.04	47.0	138.71	51.0	126.10	55.0	114.90
.1	152.66	.1	138.38	.1	125.81	.1	114.64
.2	152.28	.2	138.05	.2	125.51	.2	114.37
.3	151.90	.3	137.71	.3	125.21	.3	114.11
.4	151.52	.4	137.38	.4	124.92	.4	113.84
.5	151.14	.5	137.05	.5	124.62	.5	113.58
.6	150.76	.6	136.73	.6	124.33	.6	113.32
.7	150.38	.7	136.40	.7	124.04	.7	113.05
.8	150.01	.8	136.07	.8	123.76	.8	112.79
.9	149.65	.9	135.74	.9	123.47	.9	112.53
44.0	149.28	48.0	135.41	52.0	123.18	56.0	112.27
.1	148.91	.1	135.08	.1	122.89	.1	112.01
.2	148.54	.2	134.76	.2	122.60	.2	111.75
.3	148.17	.3	134.44	.3	122.32	.3	111.49
.4	147.80	.4	134.11	.4	122.03	.4	111.24
.5	147.43	.5	133.79	.5	121.74	.5	110.99
.6	147.07	.6	133.47	.6	121.45	.6	110.74
.7	146.71	.7	133.16	.7	121.17	.7	110.49
.8	146.35	.8	132.85	.8	120.89	.8	110.24
.9	145.99	.9	132.54	.9	120.61	.9	109.99
45.0	145.64	49.0	132.22	53.0	120.33	57.0	109.74
.1	145.28	.1	131.90	.1	120.05	.1	109.49
.2	144.92	.2	131.58	.2	119.77	.2	109.24
.3	144.56	.3	131.27	.3	119.50	.3	108.99
.4	144.20	.4	130.96	.4	119.22	.4	108.74
.5	143.85	.5	130.64	.5	118.94	.5	108.49
.6	143.50	.6	130.33	.6	118.67	.6	108.24
.7	143.15	.7	130.03	.7	118.39	.7	108.00
.8	142.80	.8	129.72	.8	118.12	.8	107.76
.9	142.46	.9	129.42	.9	117.85	.9	107.52
46.0	142.12	50.0	129.12	54.0	117.58	58.0	107.28
.1	141.78	.1	128.81	.1	117.31	.1	107.03
.2	141.43	.2	128.50	.2	117.04	.2	106.78
.3	141.08	.3	128.20	.3	116.77	.3	106.52
.4	140.74	.4	127.89	.4	116.50	.4	106.28
.5	140.39	.5	127.58	.5	116.23	.5	106.04
.6	140.04	.6	127.28	.6	115.96	.6	105.80
.7	139.70	.7	126.98	.7	115.69	.7	105.56
.8	139.37	.8	126.68	.8	115.43	.8	105.32
.9	139.04	.9	126.39	.9	115.16	.9	105.08
59.0	104.84	63.0	95.78	67.0	87.52	71.0	79.99
.1	104.60	.1	95.56	.1	87.32	.1	79.80
.2	104.36	.2	95.34	.2	87.12	.2	79.62
.3	104.12	.3	95.12	.3	86.92	.3	79.44
.4	103.89	.4	94.91	.4	86.73	.4	79.26
.5	103.66	.5	94.70	.5	86.54	.5	79.08
.6	103.42	.6	94.49	.6	86.35	.6	78.90
.7	103.19	.7	94.27	.7	86.16	.7	78.72
.8	102.96	.8	94.06	.8	85.97	.8	78.54
.9	102.73	.9	93.85	.9	85.78	.9	78.37
60.0	102.50	64.0	93.64	68.0	85.59	72.0	78.20
.1	102.26	.1	93.43	.1	85.40	.1	78.02
.2	102.03	.2	93.22	.2	85.21	.2	77.84
.3	101.80	.3	93.01	.3	85.02	.3	77.66
.4	101.57	.4	92.80	.4	84.83	.4	77.48
.5	101.34	.5	92.59	.5	84.64	.5	77.30
.6	101.11	.6	92.38	.6	84.45	.6	77.13
.7	100.88	.7	92.17	.7	84.26	.7	76.96
.8	100.66	.8	91.97	.8	84.07	.8	76.79
.9	100.43	.9	91.76	.9	83.88	.9	76.62
61.0	100.21	65.0	91.55	69.0	83.69	73.0	76.45
.1	99.98	.1	91.34	.1	83.50	.1	76.27
.2	99.76	.2	91.14	.2	83.31	.2	76.10
.3	99.53	.3	90.94	.3	83.12	.3	75.93
.4	99.30	.4	90.73	.4	82.93	.4	75.76
.5	99.07	.5	90.53	.5	82.74	.5	75.59
.6	98.84	.6	90.32	.6	82.55	.6	75.42
.7	98.62	.7	90.12	.7	82.36	.7	75.25
.8	98.40	.8	89.92	.8	82.17	.8	75.08
.9	98.18	.9	89.72	.9	81.99	.9	74.91
62.0	97.96	66.0	89.52	70.0	81.82	74.0	74.74
.1	97.74	.1	89.32	.1	81.63	.1	74.57
.2	97.51	.2	89.12	.2	81.44	.2	74.39
.3	97.29	.3	88.92	.3	81.25	.3	74.22
.4	97.07	.4	88.72	.4	81.07	.4	74.05
.5	96.85	.5	88.52	.5	80.89	.5	73.88
.6	96.64	.6	88.32	.6	80.71	.6	73.72
.7	96.42	.7	88.12	.7	80.53	.7	73.55
.8	96.20	.8	87.92	.8	80.35	.8	73.39
.9	95.99	.9	87.72	.9	80.17	.9	73.23

23.2 rater, 272.09 seconds per mile. The time allowance between these two on a 14 mile race, whatever the speed, and therefore time it takes, is (289.48 − 272.09) × 14 = 243.46 seconds = 4 minutes 3.4 seconds. The second decimal place is worth less than a second in a 600-mile race!

yacht does not have a linear rating in feet that makes this necessary. However the application of the TA remains the same (except where elaborate time systems from computer programs are used in IMS, described in Chapter 8) as shown on a race entry list[4], with a scratch boat at 0 and the others given successive times to subtract (**Fig 5.4**).

PHRF class 4 at Key West regatta 1996. Course length 8.1 miles.

Yacht	Rating	Allowance	
		seconds	min/sec
Aera	60	0	0 0
Diana	66	48.6	0 48.6
Banzai	72	97.2	1 37.2
Pooh	75	121.5	2 1.5
Sazerac	87	218.7	3 38.7
Affinity	99	315.9	5 15.9
Whisper	102	340.2	5 40.2

Fig 5.4 *Construction of race card (entry list) with PHRF time allowances in seconds per mile. Course length is essential to work out time allowances. Lowest allowance ('fastest' yacht) is scratch boat.*

William Snaith, a leading member and owner in the CCA,[5] who made the little joke in England at the chapter head quote, knew that the British had a very different TA system, but time-on-time was and is unknown to almost all American sailors. L. Francis Herreshoff in 1953 described his father's invention of the TA tables

'The Boston Yacht Club had honoured him *in 1877* for getting up the Tables, *which are today found in the back of most yacht club books throughout the world.* It is these tables which have made it practical to race yachts of different rating together with what is called time allowance'.[6] (Author's italics as usual).

This exactly demonstrates a general American belief that whatever the rating system and however it was changed over the years around the world, one had to use these tables, which by the end of the twentieth century were in tablets of stone.

This rigidity has been a major cause of today's rating difficulties, starting with unpopularity of the IOR in the USA and the blame heaped on the rule, while all the time the TA tables of NAYRU remained sacrosanct.

Time-on-distance rigidities

A chairman of the CCA measurement committee in the 1950s
wrote

> 'In spite of the variation between actual speed and tabular speed
> [in the tables], ratings appear to be equitable, provided the
> course is approximately equilaterally triangular and the wind is
> moderate, force 4, and constant in velocity'.[7]

This was an extraordinary statement by an official of a club
giving a race in a straight line which contained all the vagaries of
changing ocean conditions: calms, gales, currents and so on! What
was meant by equitable is not known, but it was typical of
'whatever is changed, don't touch the tablets – sorry, tables'!

At the same time Irving Pratt was well aware that the tables had
weaknesses, for instance, 'CCA ratings being somewhat higher in
relation to waterline than Universal or International rule ratings,
the speeds in the TA tables are relatively higher and therefore out
of line with actual speeds'. He seems to be floundering. Why revert
to waterline (whatever that is) when the whole point of the rating is
to give a fully derived equivalent figure? He certainly did know that
the TA were out of line in conditions other than 0.6 of maximum
rated speed.

The known rigidities are not so much in the tables as in the use
of time-on-distance itself. Therefore the same problems occur in,
for instance, PHRF, which does not use the old tables as such.

The serious disadvantages of time-on-distance are:

1. A beat to windward covers more distance than the course, so that
the smaller yacht runs out of the fixed time allotted to her.

2. If the TA is correct for the theoretically triangular course, then
the reverse must be the case on a reach or run.

3. Once the smaller yacht has 'used up' her allowance against the
larger, it can, in practice, never be recovered even in light air, when
the smaller may be sailing almost as fast.

4. The TA depends on knowing the exact distance of the course;
this poses problems when the course is shortened, or even when
corrected times are very close and might depend on an accuracy of,
say, 500 metres distance.

On the last point, committees using t-o-d usually give a figure in
the race instructions to be taken as the distance for the purpose of
the TA. This then sometimes leads to arbitrary figures. For
instance, if the committee believes that the course usually involves
much beating, it can give a very much higher figure than the

believed rhumb line distance: that will help the higher rated (smaller) boats. Or it may declare a shorter distance, if small boats have been winning this race too often; that gives the smaller boats less TA.

Even today an American official in PHRF admitted that his users would not understand departing from seconds per mile; he said 'Time-on-time seems to work better if race conditions are not "normal". If there is nothing unusual about the race, time-on-distance works equally well.'[8]

Time-on-time

In 1935 the Royal Ocean Racing Club race from Burnham-on-Crouch to Heligoland, 310 miles, gave exactly the kind of result predicted above as time-on-distance 'disadvantage no. 2'. The race was won in fresh reaching and running conditions all the way by the smallest rated yacht, a German double-ended ketch called *Hajo*, rating 22.6ft. The biggest yacht *Asta*, rating 78.7ft, manned by the Kriegsmarine, would have had to clock 16 knots average to equate the *Hajo* corrected time.

The time-on-distance (t-o-d) system in use by RORC was in principle the same as that of NAYRU. The only difference was that as winds were generally stronger in north-west Europe than in the north-east United States, the factor was 0.8 instead of the American 0.6, thus

$$TA = 0.8(3600/(r)^{1/2} - 3600/(R)^{1/2})$$

As in America, the actual figure in the TA tables had a constant attached, so the formula was the TA in seconds of a yacht against her rating in feet

$$TA = 2880/(R)^{1/2} - 288$$

For racing inshore it was recommended that 0.7 was used instead of 0.8. (2880 is simply 3600 × 0.8; 3600 being the number of seconds in an hour.)

The RORC asked Ray Barrett, the Rating Secretary, and Major Malden Heckstall-Smith to come up with a solution to this 'complete breakdown of the time scale'.[9] They rejected altering the nominated distance (which in this case would have had to be made shorter – and then what if the next Heligoland race was a beat to windward?) and decided on a new system. *This was time-on-time.* Instead of seconds per mile there would be corrected time based on minutes per hour. In a fast race there would be less allowance for the smaller yacht than in a slow race. The distance did not come into the calculations.

Time-on-time (t-o-t) has been used by RORC ever since, with two small exceptions, which will be mentioned. The club was followed by the rest of British cruiser and offshore racing rather later; by 1951 all British and many other countries outside America used t-o-t.

The mode of operation established for the RORC 1936 season was to derive a factor from the rating in feet. This factor, called the *time correction factor (TCF)* was, and is, multiplied by the elapsed time to give corrected time.

Corrected time = elapsed time × TCF

From 1936 until 1953, the formula for TCF was

$$TCF = ((Rating)^{1/2} + 2)/10$$

So for a yacht of 36.5ft rating the TCF was 0.8042. The higher the rating in feet of the yacht, the larger her TCF. If this yacht had an elapsed time over the course (of any distance) of 26 hours 45 minutes 20 seconds, her corrected time was 21 hours 30 minutes 0 seconds. The yacht with the shortest corrected time is the winner (**Fig 5.5**).

At the annual general meeting of the RORC on 5 November 1935, the time-on-time system was adopted. Malden Heckstall-Smith said he had

'examined the method exhaustively and found that it worked well in every way. It is so good that it should be adopted for inshore courses'[10]

'It will eliminate the anomalies produced by allowance tables in very fast or very slow races', said the commodore, T.P. Rose-Richards.

The advantages of TA by t-o-t are really the opposites of the negatives above of t-o-d. In slow races the smaller boats get more allowance. Race committees do not need to know the distance of the race. For both systems the inherent defects of any TA remain. A striking disadvantage of t-o-t is in calm or very light air, when the higher rated yacht is not sailing away from the lower rated; indeed both may be kedged on a foul tidal stream with the lower

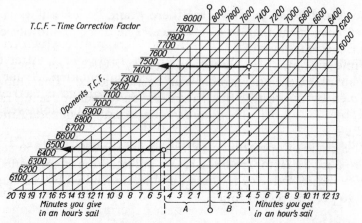

Fig 5.5 *In the days of the RORC rule and before the appearance of calculators, this graph was one system. From your TCF of 0.7000 at top, slide down curved diagonal to find what you 'get' from boat of 0.7500 and 'give' to a boat of 0.6500 (shown by arrows and vertical broken lines).*

rated yacht literally clocking up time. In light air races, there will usually be a win for the smaller yacht: in the 1981 Fastnet race with 244 yachts including top racers and maxi yachts tuning up for the forthcoming Whitbread Round The World Race, the lowest rated yacht in the whole fleet, the Belgian owned *Mordicus*, was the overall winner. There had been light air for the last several hundred miles of the race.

Changes in time-on-time
In 1953, after it was felt that smaller yachts were winning too high a proportion of the races, RORC changed its formula of 1935 to

$$\text{TCF} = ((\text{Rating})^{1/2} + 3)/10$$

This demonstrates the flexibility of the TCF system; in later years under IOR, while the NAYRU tables remained the same as ever, several changes to RORC TCF were made, but the given time scale always remained the same for at least a season. Other clubs could have adopted variations in determining TCF from rating, but in Britain they generally followed the RORC TCF.

When IOR was introduced in 1970 with a rating in feet, the rating for the same boat was rather different in magnitude from the RORC rating, so the TCF was revised to

TIME 135

$$TCF = ((Rating)^{1/2} + 2.6)/10$$

The body controlling the IOR had a committee which tried to put together the British and American TA systems. After three years it came up with a formula for experimentation. As far as is known only RORC and some Scandinavian clubs gave it a trial and that was for the 1974 season. No other British clubs followed suit, nor did the CCA which stuck to t-o-d.

The formula was complex. Briefly it gave each yacht a TCF from its rating, which was called 'yacht rating factor'; then each race course had a 'distance factor' which was distance divided by 2.75. At the end of the race corrected time was found by combining these. The detail is of no interest: the experiment was dropped and for the IOR, organizing bodies, as before, went on to apply their own TAs to the IOR rating.

After this for 1975, RORC produced another formula (R being the IOR rating in feet of the yacht)

$$TCF = 0.2424(R)^{1/2}/1 + 0.567(R)^{1/2}$$

This gave a yacht of 29ft a TCF of 1.000. Larger yachts were higher, smaller were lower than 1. The only point of this was to keep the corrected time numerically near the elapsed times for the known sizes which participated. 29ft rating was a kind of 'scratch yacht'. Since then, this has always been attempted by RORC.

The 1975 RORC TCF stood for some time, but in the mid-1980s, as will be recounted, when the IOR came under pressure, there were several adjustments to TCF derived from rating. Generally these arose from complaints that either 'large' or 'small' yachts were favoured. One cause of this was the entry into a particular level of professionals or specially designed yachts, which gave the appearance that 'size' was the cause. Not every change will be shown here. What the RORC decided on was a 'break point' or 'knuckle' at 23ft rating (**Fig 5.6**). Bigger yachts were given some easement.

The formula introduced in 1984 was

$$TCF = a(R)^{1/2}/1 + b(R)^{1/2}$$

R was rating of yacht and a and b were constants depending on the rating range as follows:

below 23ft, a = 0.4039, b = 0.2337.
23ft – 70ft, a = 0.2424, b = 0.567 (i.e. as for 1975);

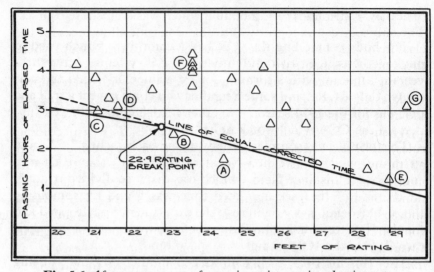

Fig 5.6 *After many years of experience in running the time-on-time system, the RORC put in a 'knuckle' so scales changed over slightly at 22.9ft rating. Explanation: the nearer the bottom of the graph, the better the elapsed time. Slope of line depends on formula for TCF against linear rating. A steeper line would help low rated yachts. A has best corrected time and would have won on any feasible slope for TMF. B would have been beaten by C if there was no knuckle. Dotted line, D, is if knuckle had not been used. E finished first, but failed to save her time on A, B and probably C. The group at F is a one-design class; same ratings, but slightly different finishing times. G is highest rated yacht, but had poor elapsed time and was last on corrected time.*

In 1986 things got more complicated: the above formulae remained the same, but another break was made at 30ft rating. Yachts above this figure were given

$$TCF = 2 + (R)^{1/2}/7.0249$$

In the dying days of the IOR, the TCFs below 30.5ft (changed from 30ft) remained the same, but those above (where the latest rule cheaters were racing) were given

$$TCF = 0.2885/(1/(R)^{1/2}) + 0.1019$$

Note that $\times ((R)^{1/2}/y(R)^{1/2} + k)$ is the same as $\times /(k/(R)^{1/2}) + y$

Today these figures are largely academic. They show an attempt to apply the rather elegant and flexible TCF against rating method to needle sharp racing, an amount of which was on inshore courses. The only logical end to this was to abandon time allowances for the class involved. This was indeed done for the Admiral's Cup, where these problems had particularly arisen.

Time allowances, if used, must be accepted with their known weaknesses; which is not to say that they should not be refined in the light of experience.

When the RORC dropped IOR in favour of two succeeding rules, CHS and IMS, the time allowances for these came straight off the rating certificate. For the first time there was no visible intermediate linear rating (in feet or metres). However, as mentioned briefly, the linear figure is within the secret CHS formula and so the time scale can be adjusted against 'rating' by those controlling it. The TAs under these rules will be looked at again in Chapters 8 and 9. *The method of obtaining elapsed time from corrected time by TCF however remained and remains exactly the same* (**Fig 5.7**).

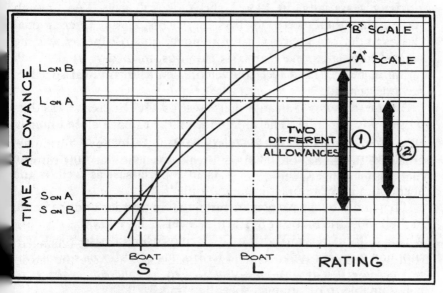

Fig 5.7 *Altering the time scale, for instance, to benefit 'the smaller boat' (BOAT S) against the larger (BOAT L). On B scale, a steeper curve, there is a bigger gap so BOAT L must sail faster for rating. The ratings have not changed, only the time scale. In practice, such changes (in CHS for instance) are small (a few seconds per hour).*

Last YRA time scales

The YRA, as seen, issued time allowances from the late 19th century. After about 1947, cruiser racers and ocean racers in Britain were required by all major regattas to have RORC ratings. Race organizers in theory could have used any time allowance system with an RORC rating in feet (and in later years an IOR rating). However they lacked originality, or more likely wanted to avoid argument, and in the United Kingdom and other parts of the world simply used the RORC TCF. There were from time to time variations in constants and factors used in Australia, Ireland and elsewhere.

When the International rule went into force in 1906, there were at the same time published TAs for ratings in metres.[11] As far as is known these were never used, since the metre boats began immediately as classes rating at level ratings. Of some interest today is the fact that such *ratings were in three tables, for light, medium and heavy wind speed*.

Examples: Between a 6-metre and an 8-metre in seconds per mile. Light wind: 145 seconds. Medium wind: 212 seconds. Heavy wind: 301 seconds.

Many years later, in 1936[12], the YRA still gave TAs, though stating that there were no TAs for yachts in the International classes under $14\frac{1}{2}$ metres (therefore none, since 12-metres was the biggest, thereafter the Universal rule was, in theory, used). Each rating in metres (and feet equivalent) had a 'theoretical speed in seconds per mile'.

A 6-metre was 515.0; an 8-metre was 452.1. Difference was thus 63 seconds per mile. The difference seems to have closed hugely since 1908! Theory is the operative word, but this does show how any linear rating can be allotted a TA, yet by contrast, the limitations and sidelining of TAs in top classes, as well as the abandonment of impracticable multiple TAs.

This might be the place to mention that in Sweden and the Baltic in the 1950s, the Baltic or SHR rule (Svenska Havskryssar Regeln), which in form resembled the CCA rule (using a base boat), was supplied with *five different wind force scales of TA*. *Once again this was because it was time-on-distance, with its inherent weakness* of being unable to distinguish speed in a race.

The YRA attempt in Britain to establish 'handicap classes' before its 'customers' fled to the RORC, was announced in 1948, the basis already being an RORC TCF. The YRA speed figure was

SF = 514.3/RORC TCF[13]

This was the potential time in seconds taken by a yacht to sail one mile. Unmeasured yachts were advised to obtain a rating by a crude formula from Lloyds Register, which was then an annual volume containing main dimensions of all yachts. There were some simple rig and propeller allowances. Local (regional?) 'handicap committees were to be formed with authority to adjust the SF, 'after *one or more* races'.[14] It will be seen that all it did for (RORC) measured yachts was simply to convert the TCF into a particular t-o-d scale.

By 1951, the system was a rather long-winded way of trying to adjust seconds per mile versions of RORC TCF 'to ensure a fair share of the prize money'.[15] As it had become dependent on having an RORC rating anyway, the YRA seconds per mile TAs faded from view, British yachtsmen totally ditching time-on-distance and using RORC TCFs for all racing of a certain level.

Time-on-time without rating
The alternative in a number of localities was, and still is, club allocation by knowledge of the boats on the water of TCFs. Some handicappers like to think of the TCF in percentage terms for correction of elapsed times with a 'middle' boat at 1.000. Its rival at 1.015 gives 1½ per cent of time, or 54 seconds per hour. It can nearly be done in the head. With modern hand calculators, TCFs are even more convenient than when created in the days of logarithm tables and slide rules.

Pursuit race. In a pursuit race, usually a club 'fun' event, yachts are released from the start line at intervals; first boat to finish is the winner. When run on t-o-t, it is necessary to stop the race at a suitable mark, when the time on which the 'seconds gaps' at the start was based runs out. On t-o-d, the yachts must run the distance however long it takes. This seems to illustrate rather well the differences between t-o-d and t-o-t.

In the Royal Naval Sailing Association/Whitbread Round The World Race of 1974, the last leg from Rio to England was run as a pursuit to try and get the yachts, which differed substantially in size and IOR rating, home at about the same time. However the TA was still applied to the elapsed time of each competitor. The experiment was not repeated in later races.

It is interesting that for these early round the world races, though they were organized and started in Britain, that time-on-distance was used, derived from IOR rating in feet.[16]

$$SF = 5143/(R)^{1/2} + 3.5$$

Later on for the 1989-90 race, the contemporary (above) RORC TCF was used. In the event this caused great dissatisfaction and was the last Whitbread Round The World Race to make any use of time allowances. Classes were subsequently arranged which raced level.

6 Keen racing, but no rating

'It is proposed to establish in Kingstown a class of sailing punts, with centreboards, all built and rigged the same, so that an even harbour race may be had with a light rowing and generally useful boat. Gentlemen wishing to consider the proposition can have full particulars on applying to this office.' – Irish Times, 18 September 1886.[1]

'A one-design class encourages men with limited means to indulge in the sport of boat racing without fear of meeting in their next year's contests some dark stranger of the 'sailing machine' type, or some boat designed or built in evasion of the rules of measurement with a view to defeating the champion boat of the previous year'. – Henry Coleman Folkard in 1901.[2]

'The objects of the association are to govern and to further the interests of the class e.g. (a) to maintain the one-design character of the OOD 34 . . .' - from the constitution of the Offshore One-Design 34 Class, 1980.

I F RACING under a time allowance is never fully satisfactory, then it should follow that sailing without a time allowance must be the answer. Unfortunately that simple concept is not the perfect solution to all the ills of rating rules. Yet a race in which the first boat to cross the line is actually also the winner has many attractions.

It is clear to readers, by this stage, that racing without time allowance will have to be in one of the following kinds of boat. (1) Yachts to a maximum permitted rating (Six-metre class, IOR One Ton Cup); (2) Yachts measured to maximum/minimum dimensions and weights with rules on equipment and mode of production (Whitbread 60); (3) All comers, no allowances, first home wins, as seen in the race of the schooner *America* on 22 August 1851: today seldom occurring except in single-handed ocean races and in very local, say, fishing boat regattas; (4) Yachts measured to specific dimensions, weights and equipment (Soling class, J24 class). This last, (4), is, of course, the one-design class.

Classes in category (1) are looked at under the rule from which they emerge (Chapters 3, 4, 7, 8, 10). Category (2) is known as a 'restricted class' or 'yacht in a box': of this see later in the chapter.

There are probably about 850 one-design classes in the world. This author collected about 250 together with short comment and a colour illustration profile of each:[3] that was about one-third of those that exist (whatever 'existence' may be). One class may be well known (used perhaps for the Olympic Games); another remains hidden on a little lake far away within some continent!

There is no agreed exact definition of a one-design, even if the IYRU and some national authorities may have their own criteria for recognition. Certainly it is not just any production boat where a builder has simply turned out similar craft. Minimum requirements might be (1) a controlling committee, usually of owners; (2) a class association of all or most owners; (3) rules and also drawings, to keep the boats the same; (4) specific racing fixtures which are duly supported each season.

In the kind of classes considered here, as active alternatives to rated boats, one would expect all and many more of these conditions to apply.

In this work, there is no intention of making a survey of one-design classes, nor even their effect on yacht racing in general. The question here is 'Does a one-design class solve the perennial problems posed by rating and time allowance?' One might as well give the answer immediately: 'No. One is left with advantages and disadvantages'.

As for measurement, a one-design has by definition to be measured, even though it is never rated. Measurement of a one-design may be more or less complicated than a given rule of measurement and rating (**Fig 6.1**).

The answer to the key question has to be taken separately: *inshore and offshore*. Each kind of sailing has reached a different stage in the evolution of its one-design boats and one-design racing.

When one-designs come together

Inshore or offshore, if one-design classes proliferate, then there will be times, especially at club level where they come together for racing. So one is back to time allowances for differing boats.

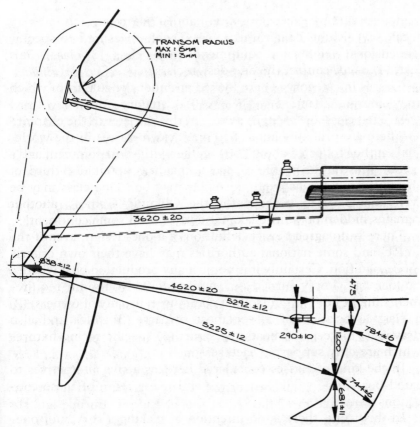

Fig 6.1 *The one-design principle is that a yacht is measured, as seen here from the rules of the RORC Mumm 36 class, but not rated, since all yachts must comply with the dimensions. (Of course, it can be measured and rated to another rule.)*

However this is not quite the same as a collection of cruisers or miscellaneous craft needing some system created for them to race together.

The one-design classes are already strictly controlled by their one-design rules. This immediately makes it attractive to allot ratings or time allowances against the known performance of the class (against other known classes). So logic drives us to *performance handicapping or numbers. These systems include the Portsmouth Yardstick and Performance Handicap Racing Fleet (PHRF)* described in Chapters 8 and 10.

In other words the strictly controlled one-design would appear to obviate the need for a formula type rating rule, even on the occasions differing one-designs come together to race.

The other side of the coin is when introducing a new one-design into present day offshore racing and cruiser racing. *It then needs to rate reasonably well to figure in corrected time results to stimulate interest in the class.* Examples of this are the Sigma 33 class which did well under IOR when it appeared in 1980 and subsequently prospered as a one-design: today it can still race CHS and IMS without great disadvantage (**Fig 6.2**). More recently the IMX 38 class did well in CHS and IMS on her rating when introduced in 1994 and so in the years that immediately followed became established as a one-design.

One-design classes which have failed to reach 'critical mass' simply have to continue to sail in the rated classes or can in due course get a number under a performance rating scheme.

Inshore

Today the only rated classes left inshore are either owned by a bunch of local enthusiasts, or are one of the select, now rarefied metre boat classes (8s, 6s and 5.5s: Chapter 10). *For mainstream inshore racing, that is to say in keel day boats (keel boats) and centreboard dinghies, rating is finished. Only one-design and restricted classes can be raced in the great inshore championships.*

The end of fresh inshore formula classes can be fixed at the time of the introduction of the International Rule in Europe and the Universal Rule in America (Chapter 3). Thereafter, with the isolated exception, these rules were the only 'non-one-design' and 'non-restricted'. As they waned, then, in effect, the formula class inshore faded with them.

Today there are 'too many one-design classes', but there is nothing we can do about it. The 850 world wide are in every different stage of development, some starting, some finishing, some steady, some making major changes. One can only rather weakly say 'the market will have to decide'.

In well developed yachting areas this class or that often depends on both the market and clubs of long standing for preservation. In

Fig 6.2 *This is the Sigma 33 offshore one-design, designed by David Thomas. By any standard it has been a huge success from the first one (in 1979). Among its many assets were a strong class association, suitability for cruising during and after racing life, no extremes, fitted relevant rules on arrival and since, concentration of boats in a few areas gave good racing, large numbers (309 built) meant numbers available for race fixtures.*

'emerging nations' the authorities may fund or even permit only certain classes, for instance those chosen for the Olympic Games. The fact that a class is approved or not by the ISAF makes little difference in advanced countries: their sailors are unimpressed. The ISAF shows 43 recognized one-design classes.[4]

The main criteria are as follows: 'active racing' in at least six countries on three continents; have a recognized measurement organization with class measurers; and continue to run an annual world championship. However there are some six pages of IYRU conditions, before even a single rule for the class itself is read. Thus it should not be assumed that the ownership of a one-design is necessarily always simpler than that of a rated yacht! Recall the fate of the venerable X-class described in the Introduction.

Today, other than in papers on yacht research or 'ideas' articles, no one would attempt to introduce a formula class inshore. A new restricted class is a very rare occurrence; its success even more so. Virtually all new classes by private groups, clubs, organizations, builders, designers or national authorities are, *in the inshore sailing world*, one-design.

The progress of the Olympic Games, which, of course, have always been all 'inshore' boats, is significant. The first games held in 1900 were in six rated classes. All classes remained as formula boats until the appearance of a one man dinghy one-design in 1920. In 1932 a second OD appeared, the Star class. By 1952 there were two formula designs (6-metre and 5.5-metre) and three ODs (Star, Dragon and one-man dinghy). In 1968 there was just one formula boat (5.5-metre) and the four other classes were ODs. That was the last year for the 5.5-metre and since then all classes, now inflated to ten or more, have been one-design.

As a reminder of the out of phase inshore/offshore chronology, just as the Olympic Games were beginning their first year in 1972 with no formula class, the ocean racing world was in the third year of a major new rating rule formula (IOR), which was to last for more than two decades.

Long lasting classes

There are one-designs that ran for a few years before they disappeared; there are also those which ran for some time, but also in due course disappeared. An example of the latter was the Y Class, based at Yarmouth, Isle of Wight. I used to watch about a dozen of these varnished carvel sloops of 21ft racing regularly off their home port. Then one day in the mid-1970s they were gone; what had happened was that after sixty years they were not worth repairing any more. Designed and built in 1913, they had been converted to Bermuda rig in 1936. But this is only one kind of end for a class; others may disperse or even all move to a completely new location, as did the so-called International One-Design class (a kind of frozen 6-metre) (LOA 33ft 4in, 10.16m) fleet at Cowes that was shipped in the 1980s to north-east Scotland, where it continued to give regular racing. Fleets of IODs also race in North America and Sweden.

Then there are ghosts. Whatever happened for instance to the Clyde 20-Ton One-Design class, LOA 50ft (15.24m) established in 1899?

'It was the outcome of the desire on the part of several owners to have a boat of medium (*sic*) size, speedy, strongly built and with good cruising accommodation. This combination being unattainable under the YRA rule, the principle of a one-design was adopted'.[5]

Five boats were built to the Alfred Mylne design; they were gaff cutters with topsails and the sail area was 1700 square feet (158 sq m). The winner of the first season was *Noyra* owned by M. Greenless, who chose the name to publicize his feelings about the rating rule. The class then had a busy second season in 1900, sailing on Belfast Lough and in Dublin Bay, as well as its home waters of the Clyde, Scotland. What happened after that is not known and there is no evidence that the class ever grew larger than the five original boats. If one or two boats in a class of five fail to turn out for a race, it is getting below 'critical mass'.

Maybe they dispersed, then suffered the indignity of being measured to the despised rule after all!

In contrast to these, the first one-design class of all still sails. The advertisement at this chapter head, which appeared in the *Irish Times*, received no response, but T.B. Middleton of Shankhill, Co. Dublin, who had inserted it, then tried a circular to all known local men, who sailed a mixture of open sailing boats in Dublin Bay. This met with more success and a meeting decided the main dimensions of a double ended Norwegian praam LOA 13ft (3.96m), beam 4ft (1.22m), with pivoting iron centreplate, sail area 75 sq ft (6.97 sq m), spinnaker 60 sq ft (5.57 sq m) (**Fig 6.3**). The first racing (and cruising) season followed in 1887.[6]

One has to spoil the story slightly by explaining that the 13ft praam is not in fact the Water Wag boat that sails today. This is a second design that was adopted by the same people without any

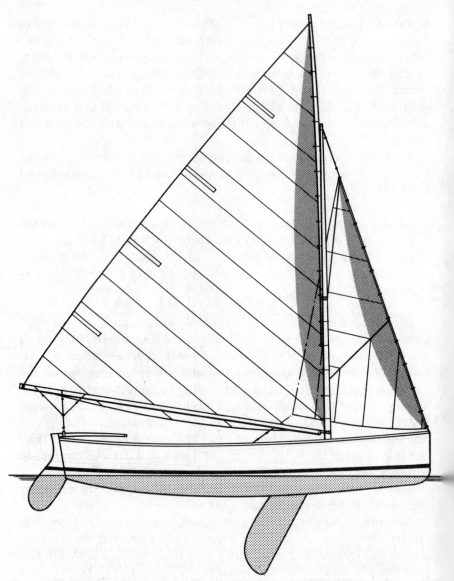

Fig 6.3 *The first one-design class in history: the Dublin Bay Water Wag of 1886. The class proves the durability of one-designs, by continuing to race every season (in a second design dating from 1900).*

break in sequence of seasons (indeed there was an overlap of the classes): LOA 14ft 3in (4.34m), beam 5ft 3in (1.60m), designed by J.E. Doyle of Dun Laoghaire (then Kingstown) or possibly mainly

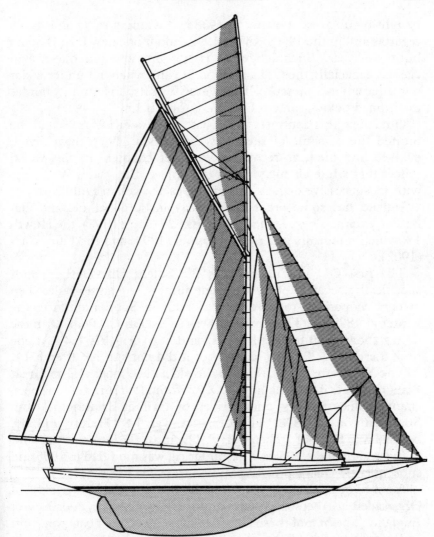

Fig 6.4 *First one-design class to be formed in Great Britain: the 33ft (10.06m) Solent One-Design. Starting in 1896 up to 20 raced in its eponymous waters (strangely the same length as the Sigma 33 above), but were not heard of after WWI.*

by his daughter. The first racing for the new design was in 1900. A few years later the new boats totalled 20 and to this day numbers have hovered around this figure: a thoroughly practical quantity for any local OD.

Continuity is demonstrated by one boat, *Pansy*, built in 1906, bought by its present owner in 1938 and winning races and whole regattas still in the 1990s. In the 1990s about one new boat is being built per year. Such longevity is not unknown in one-design classes, especially those of a local nature and when not under wider nor international pressure. The Water Wag itself is unique, but, as mentioned below, some others are not far behind.

Obviously this contrasts with boats built to rating rules and the limited life of some of the rules themselves. These have lived, evolved and died, as recounted in other chapters in this work: reflect that while all such events took place, the Water Wag class with its successive owners was racing each week in Dublin Bay.[7]

Ireland has some other noted early inshore one-designs that remain extant. There is the Dublin Bay 25 (since 1897), the Howth 17, which retains its gaff rig and topsail (1898) and the Fairy class (1902).

The first OD in England was the Solent One-Design, built specifically because of the current unpopular rating rule. Ten owners cooperated to have a batch built in Southampton in the winter of 1895-96. This keel boat was LOA 33ft (10.06m) with the then standard gaff mainsail, topsail and bowsprit (**Fig 6.4**). At one time there were 20 boats racing, but it did not survive after 1914.

The Yorkshire One-Design is the oldest keel boat OD in Great Britain still racing.[8] The hull, LOA 25ft 6in (7.77m), has not been changed since the first ones arrived by train at Bridlington from Southampton in 1898. The designer was J.S. Helyar and the builder was Field of Itchen Ferry. The most recent boat was built to the design in the 1950s. The gunter rig was modified in 1955 and subsequently changed to Bermudian in 1973 (**Fig 6.5**).

A survivor of equal longevity is the Seabird Half Rater class of ODs sailed at Abersoch, Wales and the River Mersey, north-west England. The first of these 20ft (6.09m) centreplate boats was built and raced in 1899. Since then 90 have been built and 70 are in existence; a few have migrated to America and Africa. The name is now the Seabird One-Design: names of the actual boats are invariably breeds of ocean or coastal birds. Of course, the Half Rater name comes from the rating of 0.5 under Froude's rule current in 1899.

OD ways

Another way in which the life of a class has lasted over one hundred years is that of the Bembridge Redwing. Bembridge is a shallow harbour on the north-east corner of the Isle of Wight. The owners are upper crust and for them Bembridge is a weekend and

Fig 6.5 *The Yorkshire One-Design, oldest class still regularly racing in Great Britain (on England's North Sea coast). LOA 25ft 6in (7.77m). The class, including some individual boats, dates from 1898. Thus some one-designs can last for 100 years, while rating rules work on a quite diffferent time scale.*

summer holiday village.

For the 1896 season the famous designer-builders Camper and

Fig 6.6 *Modern Bembridge Redwing with typical rig. The class was scrapped and then rebuilt in 1990 to the same design which had dated from 1937. The boats will surely then be sailed regularly at least until 2043. The class started in 1896 and was duly redesigned by Charles Nicholson for the owners in 1937. Thus do one-design classes regulate their racing. Another centenary racing class!*

Nicholsons produced a fleet of 22ft (6.71m), beam 5ft 5in (1.66m), iron keel 1120 pounds (508kg). However only the hull was OD: the rig could be any configuration of not more than 200 sq ft (18.6 sq m) actual area. Early pictures of the boats show them with and without bowsprits, different mast positions and big and small jibs! One other famous rule was (and is) that the sails be made of distinctive red cloth approved by the class.

In 1937 a new one-design hull was requested from Camper and Nicholsons, this time 27ft 11in (8.52m) and an inch (25mm) more beam. The optional rig rule remained and over the years all kinds of rigs were tried. The 'final' solution for most boats is surely more significant than any number of laboratory experiments!

In 1990 the Redwing fleet (wooden) was again phased out and a search made for a new design in new materials. After much investigation the owners decided that they could do no better than return to the 1937 hull with a new plug and hulls built of best glass and kevlar. The 200 sq ft rig in any configuration remains, though the forestay must stay on the centreline. Thus occurred one evolution of an OD with physically different boats over one hundred years yet with continuing ownership and rules which have remained the same in concept throughout (**Fig 6.6**).

One other characteristic of ODs is that they are sometimes found to be frozen versions of rated yachts. For instance a particular stage of evolution is represented in the 5.5-metre class (Chapter 10) (**Fig 6.7**) by the Daring class in England and the Safir class in Sweden (**Fig 6.8**). The 1930s International One-Design, as mentioned, is a frozen International 6-metre. Among small boats, the Olympic Games Tornado is a frozen B-class catamaran of 1967 (the B-class itself having meanwhile disappeared into the hi-tech stratosphere of wing sails and featherweight hulls). The Europe is a frozen International Moth. The two-man Firefly dinghy is a 1946 version of the National 12 foot restricted class; yet the latter continues to develop as a restricted class. So fifty years later owners of both are happy.[9]

Offshore one-designs
Because of the way in which ocean racing originated from cruising yachts using time allowances, any moves to one-design have been slow. One could say that offshore moves are sixty years later than the inshore fleets, where formula classes are confined to a few enthusiasts.

One must be sure to distinguish between boats with cabins or seagoing capability and similar boats of a class that are genuinely

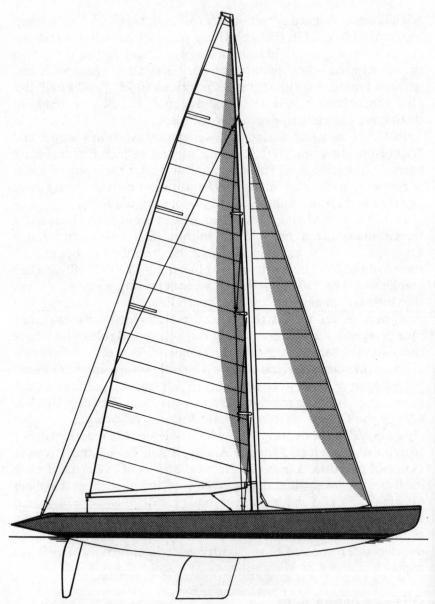

Fig 6.7 *A modern (1995) example of the IYRU International 5.5-metre class. The class was created after WWII as a 'cheaper' 6-metre and still evolves in a limited number of places with very keen owners who enjoy an inshore formula class (see also Chapter 10). It has been 'frozen' at times to create the Daring in England and the Safir class in Sweden. See* **Fig 6.8.**

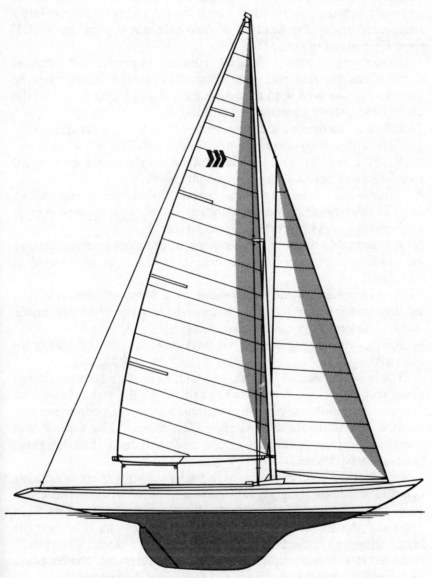

Fig 6.8 *The Daring One-design class. Raced regularly at Cowes,
this is a frozen example of a 1961 5.5-metre.*

used for ocean racing (even though they may also appear in big
day-only regattas, as do other ocean racing yachts). It is the latter
that come under the heading of 'offshore one-design' or 'OOD'
(two Os instead of one!).[10]

Commercial interests tend to claim series production boats as
one-designs; for that and other reasons the author listed, when he
was closely involved with the administration of OOD classes in the
early 1980s, these identifying features.

1. Effective owners' association controlling the one-design.

2. Class rules to ensure boats are alike.

3. Yacht complies with current offshore safety and equipment
regulations of national or international body.

4. Thus boats of the class are accepted in first class ocean races.

5. A regular programme of offshore, though also inshore events,
individually or within other regattas/races.

6. A reasonable number of the boats in the class concentrated in
one sailing area; a large number scattered over the world is
unhelpful.

7. Accommodation and equipment to a standard which is not
usually possible for flat out ('stripped-out') racers under rating
rules. The boat is genuinely habitable.

8. Recognition by regional or national authority, though this is not
essential.

It was in the late 1970s that the OOD classes began to emerge
conspicuously. The New York Yacht Club 40 was adopted by
some of its members, while in England a group of people met and
formed the Offshore One-design Conference. The author was
chairman and the committee of this body set about choosing three
boats as new classes.

As historical references in these pages recount, there is nothing
original about creating an OD class and even offshore there had
been some in recent years, notably the South Coast One-Design in
1956 and the Royal Yorkshire YC offshore class in 1970, but the
latter dispersed as the boats failed to beat newer racers. The former
races in class (in very small numbers) to this day, but the boats are
wooden 27ft (8.23m) and very old fashioned cruiser racers.

On the OODC committee was the late yachting journalist, Jack
Knights, with a wide knowledge of yachting, but not an offshore
man. Jack wanted to get away from the then current features of the
IOR ocean racers, but the author wanted to 'freeze' a good one, so
that the boats could race successfully from day one. The result was
the choice of the OOD 34 designed by Californian Doug Peterson
and built by the English south coast firm of Jeremy Rogers and the

Danish Aphrodite 101 a narrow Scandinavian 'keel boat' type. The third was the 28ft (8.53m) Impala OOD, as the smaller option. The 101 did not appeal to British sailors and did not rate well under IOR. When the committee failed to choose a David Thomas/late Angus Primrose design for a 35 footer, the Thomas design was reworked and built in Plymouth, England, as the Sigma 33, slightly smaller, lower priced and better IOR rated than the OOD34 and has been a tremendous success ever since (**Fig 6.2**, again). David Thomas famously said of the Sigma 33 and of his later Sigma 38 'The boats are what the rule makers actually intended that IOR boats ought to be, if designers had not outflanked the rule'.

This remark sums up appeal of the OOD generally, though it is slightly different from 'freezing' a rated boat. However it is not advisable to 'freeze' an extreme example under any contemporary rule (though see remarks below on the RORC Mumm 36 class of 1994).

OOD versus rating
The author sailed his OOD34 for five seasons and for part of that time was class captain. He then sold it in favour of a rated boat. Among reasons for this 'reversion' was the feeling that one should support the class programme in the OOD, but one's preference was for other races, in particular longer courses offshore.[11] There is a tendency for classes over the seasons to 'go inshore'. Six years after the arrival in Britain (in 1978-79) of several OODs, the author reviewed the state of play of offshore one-designs in Britain; therefore they were rated to the then rule, the IOR.[12] He looked at the current classes, their advantages and disadvantages.

The classes reported then were OOD34 (33ft 10in, 10.32m) (33 then active); Sigma 33 (33ft, 9.91m) (115); Contessa 32 (32ft, 9.74m) (285); Impala OOD (28ft, 8.53m) (125); Trapper 300 (26ft, 7.92m) (110); also two classes which are closer to inshore ODs: J24 (24ft, 7.31m) (110); Sonata (22ft 6in, 6.86m). The last two were and are IYRU and National (RYA) classes respectively.

The advantages of an OOD were in 1984 seen as follows (a) Cannot be outdesigned by another boat in the class, (b) Race results do not depend on basic design, (c) No expensive modifications (but depends on class committee), (d) No IOR rating problems, (e) Good social and like-minded owner network, (f) Potential second hand sale, (g) Designed as practical cruising yacht without 'stripped out' accommodation.

Reading these today, they seem a bit bland with nothing about exciting performance or attractive regattas.

Disadvantages then listed were: (h) Frozen design gradually less successful under IOR, (j) Owner may not be allowed to make chosen changes, (k) Racing programme restricted to class chosen fixtures, (l) Owner has to accept fixed layout and accommodation, (m) On the other hand, possible class modification that owner does not favour, (n) Current policies for age allowance can result in different time allowances for yachts of the same class. (j, l, m appear to be the same theme from different angles!).

This last factor, n, was caused by a rule which changed the time allowance on rating depending when the actual boat was launched, so that ODs in a general race might have one results order as an OD and a different one when the time allowance was applied. Even more fundamental was the IOR measurement of the OOD34s in particular when they first appeared (1978-79). The RORC measurers came up with slightly different ratings for each boat, which threw out the OD order in races with ratings. Outside ODs, sailors began to wonder about the variability of any rating.

To rectify this bad news for the then IOR, a standard rating was devised which roughly speaking measured a sample batch of a properly controlled OOD and then accepted these measurements, subject to checks and specific measurement of sails, as the class rating. Eventually the tail wagged the dog, as the IOR 'one-design rating' in turn regulated the OD class itself. This useful philosophy has evolved into later rating rules, especially CHS, though it is not developed outside Britain. In the USA class measurement prevails and the most used rule, PHRF, is a performance rule anyway.[13]

Though level rating classes are discussed elsewhere, the point should be made that when the rating of an IOR One Tonner (the classic level rater) did not come out at the expected level then some adjustment was duly made such as, say, more ballast, less sail area. If these changes were made on an OOD, it would have thrown it out of (one-design) class.

One more fact in the 1984 article[14] was the current number of all IOR rated yachts in Britain and how many of those had OOD ratings: these were given as 1278 and 253. So 20 per cent of IOR rated boats were already one-designs; how figures changed in later years will be mentioned below.

OODs not in charge

Twenty years on, the offshore scene still relies on the racers sailing under time allowances. On the other hand in many major offshore races and regattas for 'habitable' boats, if the OODs were removed there would be a massive gap in the event. In Britain, France,

REGATTA	DATE	RATED YACHTS	ONE DESIGNS	% OF OD's
SPI OUEST - FRANCE	1995	235	266	53%
KEY WEST - U.S.A.	1996	124	109	47%
COWES WEEK- ENGLAND	1995	311	INSHORE 210	30%
			OFFSHORE 180	26%
			TOTAL 390	56%
ROVER SERIES - SCOTLAND	1995	210	59	22%
FASTNET	1995	243	28	11%

Fig 6.9 *Numbers compared of one-design classes and rated classes at some important world regattas in mid 1990s. Right hand column shows percentage of one-designs.*

Ireland and USA, the biggest fixtures could be said to emerge with very roughly half rated yachts and half ODs. (Whether the smaller sized of these ODs is for 'offshore' under my definition is more doubtful.) The events in mind here include Key West, Cowes Week, Rover (Scottish) Week, Ford Cork Week, Spi Ouest and La Rochelle Week. **Fig 6.9** shows some figures for specific years.

Britain remains the only country formally to link specified OODs to the rating systems. In 1995 the classes receiving actual OD measurement from the Rating Office were Mumm 36, Sigma 33, Sigma 38; others whose ratings were standardized were Contessa 32, JOD 35, Lightwave 395, OOD34, Storm 33OD, X99. The numbers in the classes are vastly greater than 1984 above, but more important is what the proportions look like on the start line. In the 1995 Cowes Week the daily starters comprised 311 rated yachts on time allowance (CHS), 180 OODs and also 210 inshore one-designs, such as Dragons, Etchells and J24s. The same year Spi Ouest had 235 CHS boats on time allowance and 261 one-designs. The Jeanneau OD, JOD 35, is particularly well supported in French events often with up to 70 starters, while it also sails the long events of RORC and Union National pour la Course au Large. In the USA many one-designs flourish, but they are not conspicuous in long offshore events. Typical classes with offshore capability are IMX 38, J44, J39, J35, and J29.

Back in England major offshore races (say between 100 and 300 miles) typically have up to quarter of the starters as OODs, most likely the well proved all weather Sigma 33s and 38s. However a class will nominate one race or another in its programme and that is where the big OOD turn out appears. The 'most offshore' of OODs, the Sigma 38 had the following numbers in the mid-1990s (1995): *total number built 123, certificated per annum in Britain 85, major single regatta turn out 35. Its smaller sister, the Sigma 33 shows: built 338; registered (1996) 285; major single regatta turnout (at Cork) 60 starters.*

It does appear that there is a long way to go before one-designs are in the ascendancy in ocean racing, as they are inshore. What mitigates against the OOD actually displacing the rated yacht is the sheer size of the vessel, the difficulty in keeping the class geographically together (ocean racers cannot simply be trailed to regattas), the individualism of more monied owners, as well as inherent disadvantages set out in this chapter. On the other hand to what extent today's rating rules push owners into OODs is another matter.

Again it must be emphasized that the more OOD classes that proliferate, the more likely different designs will need to race together, particularly in the traditional ocean races, and thus the need for a time allowance system returns!

Mumm 36 OD

The particular case of the Mumm 36 OOD appears to break some of the assumptions on offshore one-designs that have just been made! The RORC wanted to introduce an OOD of about 36ft (10.97m) as one of the national competing classes in its biennial Admiral's Cup, which includes one race of about 225 miles in the English Channel and the 605-mile Fastnet race.

The new class was chosen with haste. A specification was sent out in mid-May 1993; six tenders were received by the closing date of 20 June and one of these was chosen on 26 July. This choice fell on the Farr 36, which was a state-of-the-art IMS rated yacht recently introduced in the USA. The class was sponsored (exactly

Fig 6.10 *The Mumm 36 class offshore one-design chosen by the RORC in 1993 as a class for the three boat team of each nation in the Admiral's Cup races of 1995 and 1997. Later it may be seen as a 'frozen' 1993 IMS design.*

how has never been clear) by the Champagne supplier Mumm, hence the name (**Fig 6.10**).

The designer is Bruce Farr and there are five approved builders in Argentina, France, New Zealand, South Africa and USA. There have been none in Britain although the class is controlled from London. There seems to be a contradiction between the need to group boats together for racing and the purpose of having one per nation for the Admiral's Cup in 1995 and 1997 (what happens after that is unclear at this writing). Only eight were required for the 1995 Cup races anyway, but a first world championship held just beforehand mustered 24. Held in very strong winds in the Solent, it was one of the most sensational regattas ever seen. True to the times it was recorded on video and one can still watch the broachings, mast inversions and knock downs which ensued. The wholly professional crews coped well in these very light displacement boats with sensitive rigs and stripped out accommodation. Such a concept is a far cry from the owner desirable OD which has shed the worst excesses of any rating rule.

There are boats in New Zealand and South America, but the mode of racing in 1995 and 1996 was to have circuits in the USA and in Europe. The fleets move to different locations (maybe by truck, maybe sailing depending on location) for long-weekend regattas, giving a seasonal series. This is reminiscent of the metre classes in the 1930s, or Formula 1 OD class, which ran for three years from 1989. It consisted of sponsored 'billboard' carrying large day racers which moved around the world to regatta sites in a ship. This positive idea and spectacle did not continue. Presumably the class could reappear. Whether the Mumm 36 will progress as a substitute for rated classes remains to be seen. More seasons are needed to see the success or otherwise of this particular concept.

By 1995, the 36 was inevitably in rating terms slightly outdated by newer IMS designs, but it has no cruiser racer or cruising potential unlike, say, the J39 or Sigma 38. In Britain, in theory the country of origin, it was, in 1996, virtually invisible. Perhaps the best outcome would be, as the price falls in time and when it is retired from the Admiral's Cup, for the boats around the world to concentrate in one or two areas with a group of new owners.[15]

Restricted classes

The Whitbread 60 is a restricted class, so is the International 14 footer, the National (British) 12 footer, and the International Moth. In a sense restricted classes are somewhere between one-designs and formula boats to fixed rating.

The rules lay down maximum and minimum dimensions all around the hull and rig and there are restrictions on materials and fittings – hence the name.

They are seldom adopted in the USA or the continent, but the British do have a few. Some of them will be reviewed in Chapter 10. The important difference from formula classes (such as as the IOR One Tonner) is that there is *no trade-off*. In other words the size of the jib is restricted in certain ways; making it smaller *does not* allow the hull to be longer or lighter.

The advantage over a formula system is that the rules are more easily understood and there is less chance of a breakthrough in design to outdate existing boats. The boats seem very alike on the water in any given season. However in successive years designs can keep abreast of new techniques.

There is an informed opinion that restricted classes are no more attractive than formula classes, because a very small increase in speed under the rule requires huge expenditure on design and refinement. Also because the rules are quite independent and envisage a certain kind of boat of limited dimensions, this is likely to suffer under any widely used rating rule.

The International Fourteen

There is a class which happens to be a racing dinghy that is an advanced hi-tech racing machine, yet has been in existence and racing every year since 1928: some seventy years. It is the International Fourteen Foot Dinghy and it provides lessons for offshore and habitable boats and a possible escape route from the problems of rating and formula classes.

In the words of the class historian, T.J. Vaughan, 'Change is what "fourteening" is, and always will be, about. As a concept it is not stuck in time. The class is fortunate in having a history that goes back to the origins of racing small open boats and a future that within its chosen constraints, is as limitless as human endeavour and ingenuity can devise'. Excusing his English syntax, the spirit of the Fourteen class comes through.[16]

It originated in the racing of the tenders of large yachts, that is heavy clinker open boats with a sail, as well as from the Decimal Three dinghy: a reference to 0.3 rating under Dixon Kemp's length and sail area rule. So in England in 1920 after WWI, there were two 14ft (4.27m) classes raced fairly seriously: the West of England Conference dinghy, dating from 1889 and the Norfolk dinghy. Both were by then independent of the current rating rules.

In 1922 some of the sailors called on the YRA to coordinate the
dinghy rules and a YRA dinghy committee was formed. Within a
year designers like Morgan Giles and Uffa Fox were designing to
the new rule and the class never looked back.

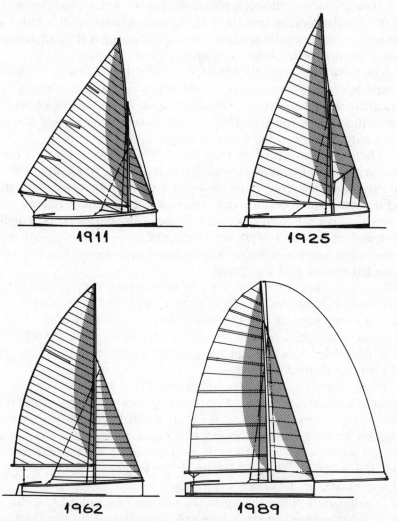

Fig 6.11 *To find a restricted class which has been superbly run for
nearly 80 years, it is useful to turn to the IYRU International
Fourteen Foot Dinghy Class. Its rules have been smoothly
changed to permit evolution, yet there is invariably an ample fleet
in any one year. Surely classes of larger yachts could be organized
in a similar manner!*

With boats being built in Canada and the USA, the IYRU declared it 'international' in 1927. So over many years the rules aspect has been a continuous effort of introducing new possibilities, restricting unwanted features, closing loopholes and allowing the latest techniques. Controlled by practical sailors, each change or veto has to be a matter of judgement for the progress of the class. The result is of new designs evolving, but older boats holding their own for an acceptable period. Critics have a point in that some of the major changes have occurred in fits and starts. Yet on the whole the class stays in the front rank, as highly developed as any racing dinghy (**Fig 6.11**).

Surely there is a profound lesson in the excellent way this class has thrived for so many years of this century through wars, economic cycles, the arrival of countless new designs and classes and huge changes in the sport of sailing and yacht racing.

The dimensions are LOA 14ft (4.27m), beam 6ft (1.83m), weight 180 pounds (82 kg), mainsail and jib area 200 sq ft (18.6 sq m), asymmetric spinnaker is unrestricted. After so many years the class (1996) is spreading even further outside the stalwarts in Britain, Canada, Australia, New Zealand and USA to Japan, Denmark, Holland and Germany. In 70 years it is believed that about 1800 boats have been built to the rules of this class.

7 For two decades: a world rule

'*I rejoice that America has resisted.*'- William Pitt, 1766.[1]

'*The rule that was meant to last a thousand years.*' – American journalist quoted in official paper circulated in ORC, 1973.

'*In 1906 the first international conference on yacht measurement was held. Thirteen nations assembled, all full of scientific talent and each with the best possible rule. Under these circumstances it was obvious that nothing but a compromise could be accepted with the usual unsatisfactory results. Thus was born the International Rule – or the metre classes. These boats are expensive to build, poor cruisers and are slow for their cost or sail area. They are required to be built under a scantling rule which makes it difficult for them to be strong or long lived. Personally I believe England was better off when she made her own rules and other countries bought her yachts or built to her rules.*'- L. Francis Herreshoff, 1946.[2]

THE LONDON MEETINGS of November 1968 announced that the new rule, combining those of the Cruising Club of America and the Royal Ocean Racing Racing Club, was ready for the 1969 season (northern hemisphere). It was recommended that all national authorities should use it.

The brave new world of yacht rating had apparently arrived with the better parts of each rule used, while removing aspects of both rules which had been due for revision. Never before, nor ever again would there be a move like this one. For the CCA and the RORC were to stop measuring to their own rules and switch on an allotted date to the *International Offshore rule (IOR)*. Thus the rule would start immediately with the combined fleet, already sited in many countries, of about 7000. 4000 of these yachts were in the USA and UK; the remainder were mainly RORC boats around the world principally Italy, Holland and France, in that order. These boats were therefore of three kinds: those designed to the CCA rule, those designed to the RORC rule and those of other designs whose owners found it acceptable to race to one of the two rules. *A fourth type of yacht was bound to appear soon after the new rule was published: that designed to the IOR.*

Yet just four years later a paper was circulated within the ORC which began

'Of all the views held about the present working of the International Offshore rule, two extreme opinions are heard which are impossible to reconcile. The first is that the IOR has achieved, on a scale and across the world, an ability never seen before and that the fair racing it gives to so many different types and sizes inshore and offshore is an undreamed-off success. The other is that it is something approaching a confidence trick run by a small "power elite" (an actual quote) who juggle it to give advantage to commercial interests and that it has eliminated sporting yacht racing. In addition, if some brave young fellow comes up with a helpful innovation for sailing men, this is soon crushed by the faceless rule makers.'[3]

So by 1973 something seems to have gone wrong with the IOR on which so many hopes were pinned. What that was exactly we shall see, but the fact is that thousands of boats and scores of major events continued to use IOR for over two decades, from 1969 to, say, around 1991, by which time sailors had largely moved over to other systems. After 1993-94 only isolated localities awarded IOR ratings.[4] One observation is that among such huge numbers (for instance the numbers using the International rule and its predecessors were a tiny fraction of the size of these offshore fleets) there were bound to be pools of discontent.

IOR arrives

The United States delegates were in a hurry to get started and declared that 1969 would be their first year for IOR, all CCA boats needing to convert. Then they would have time to settle down before the 1970 CCA Newport-Bermuda race. This was not however achieved. The RORC wanted more time to train its measurers spread around the world and decided 1970 would be the first IOR season; in a similar way the rule would be well in place before the 1971 Fastnet.

On 1 November 1969, the Offshore Rules Coordinating Committee (ORCC) turned itself into the *Offshore Rating Council, ORC*, with representation from those nations with rated yachts. Bernard Hayman, the editor of *Yachting World* wrote

'Before the details get buried, the principals in this saga of *the last nine years* need to be named. For first steps we should thank Hans Otto Schumann of Germany and Ola Wettergren of Sweden. On the technical side Olin J. Stephens stands head and shoulders above the rest. He has been helped by E.G. Van de Stadt (Holland), Dick Carter (USA), RORC Chief Measurer Brigadier David Fayle and great credit must go to chairman [of ORCC] Buster de Guingand (RORC). We now have a council consisting of Beppe Croce and Sandy Hawarth (IYRU), David Edwards, Robin Glover [a leading measurer, later chief measurer ORC, 1972-1984], Peter Johnson (UK), R.Hall, Arthur Homer, James Michael (CCA/USA), Sven Hultin, Ola Wettergren (Scandinavia), Hans Otto Schumann (Germany), Pierre Chambonnet, Francois Sergent [designer] (France and Spain), Marcel Leeman (Benelux), Dr A. Pierbon (Italy and Greece) and M. Davey (Australia) . . . Incidentally why don't we start using metres for the ratings from the word "go". In three years time we will all think in metres for everything'[5]

It was a repeat of 1906. A rule created, then an international body to administer it. Some politics impinged immediately. The ocean racing men did not want to be controlled by the IYRU which was then traditionally the world of metre boats, dinghies, the Olympics and the right-of-way rules. In particular the British had always run their ocean racing via the RORC and not from their national yachting authority, the RYA (Royal Yachting Association, previously the YRA). Anyway neither the CCA or RORC had any connection with IYRU. IYRU recognized the Offshore Rating Council as independent (but sent two delegates). A new chairman took over, who was to guide the ORC until 1978, the 38-year old commodore of the RORC, David Edwards. Within the USA the national authority, NAYRU almost immediately took over the running of IOR from the CCA, who wanted to get out of the rule business, though at first this meant much the same people were on the relevant rule committees. (See Appendix II)

The rule that was authorized in November 1969 was known as IOR Mark II, because Mark I published the year before had contained a 'hull strength factor', in other words scantlings, and this down to a certain size only. In Mark II this was abandoned as impracticable and all yachts were required to have an inclining test instead. This small angle of heel detected the relative height of the centre of gravity in every yacht, which showed, for instance, if the yacht had much of its weight in the keel and perhaps an unduly light hull. It was already a method well known to naval architecture. This centre of gravity factor, CGF, remained in one form or another in the life of IOR and was to cause many problems.

The British would have preferred a scantling rule, as in the RORC formula, but the Americans and Olin Stephens in particular would not have it. The RORC had in recent years allowed its scantling rule to be exploited and Stephens had discovered one of his designs in Europe with rule cheating iron rails and such like inside the hull for rating purposes, which he never forgot; so the British only had themselves to blame.

In its final stage, the RORC rule had been

$$MR = 0.15(L \times (S)^{1/2})/(B \times D)^{1/2} + 0.2L + 0.2(S)^{1/2}$$

This is shown because IOR Mark II was almost the same

$$MR = 0.13(L \times (S)^{1/2})/(B \times D)X^{1/2} + 0.25 + 0.2(S)^{1/2}$$

So from the RORC the Americans received back a rule which comprised the old American rules of the Seawanhaka and the Universal.

However the final form of the CCA rule was

Rating = 0.95(L ± B ± draft ± displacement ± S ± freeboard ± iron keel factor) × stability factor × propeller allowance

Some of these had already been borrowed by the RORC rule which deduced 'rating' (R), a further stage in the calculation, by adding or subtracting (±) stability allowance, propeller allowance and draft penalty to MR, the measured rating.

So the IOR also went on to calculate the actual rating, R, like this

R = MR + draft correction + freeboard corr. ± propeller drag factor ± centre of gravity factor

Immediately it must be said that this still looked more like the RORC rule than the now abandoned CCA rule. Therefore it was easier for the British sailor to accept the new rule. However the average American owner had probably never heard of the RORC, so he thought he was getting a brand new (and therefore much improved) rating system, which it was. Many of the sub-components were in fact from the CCA rule, or a compromise, or RORC paragraphs which had in previous years been borrowed from the CCA, or new items created by the International Technical Committee (ITC) with its two American designers, two British measurers and two continentals.

It must be remembered that the rating came out in feet and was converted in Britain to a TCF by the formula

$$\text{TCF} = (\text{Rating} + 2.6)^{1/2}/10$$

In America the NAYRU time allowance tables of seconds per mile against feet of rating were used.

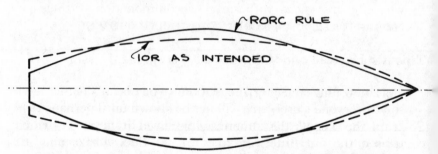

Fig 7.1 '*As a concession to the CCA*', *the British agreed that the IOR could include a check against the RORC 'pregnant cow' shape. Had the British been happy with it then?*

Features of IOR Mark II

There were many sub clauses to the main factors and David Fayle listed some of these at the time.[6] *Length* was much the same as RORC, being located by girth stations whose size related to beam; so the bigger the beam the more the girth station came inward and the rating 'thought' the boat was shorter. 'As a concession to the CCA, there was an additional stern profile measurement, to check the RORC "pregnant cow"' (**Fig 7.1**). The rule was not to use LWL (length waterline) in any way and never would, unlike some earlier rules. *Depth* (of immersed hull) developed in RORC subsequent to *Myth of Malham*, was in IOR, but had some complex bits and pieces attached.

Sail area was closer to CCA experience with taxes on high aspect ratio ('tall' rigs), long battens (being those over 10 per cent of the foot of the sail plus 1 foot) and certain kinds of rig (**Fig 7.2**). Best off for equal area was the large foretriangle, worst the fractional with small genoa. Rules on engines and propeller allowances were tightened up on the combined international experience. The motor must drive the yacht, but allowances for propellers were based on some tank tests in the US which later turned out to be unreliable and there would be systems designed to exploit propeller ratings.

Centre of Gravity factor was new to most yachtsmen. A tenderness ratio was found from small inclinations, crudely carried out with spinnaker poles, weights and spirit level measures. Fayle said, though he does not sound very convinced,

> 'the centre of gravity factor is to some extent a deterrent against very light construction and high ballast ratio. It also has, or should have, the virtue of giving more allowance to the owner who fills his yacht with heavy accommodation, fittings and comforts as against a similar boat stripped out.'

Bernard Hayman rallied his readers

> '... a new universal (*sic*) rule is about to be born. Whether it will solve everyone's problems will not be known until perhaps 1972, but if we consider the amount of high level brain power that has gone into it, it will be a tragedy if it does not cure some of the main anomalies'[7]

An earlier writer on an earlier rule (quote at chapter head), was less impressed with diverse amounts of brain power as such, while Hayman, whose otherwise wide knowledge of sailing excluded America, had in mind rating improvement rather than the task which had been completed of putting two existing systems together.

IOR Mark III and other moves

Many were the changes to IOR in its 'two decades plus'. The basic formula remained, but there were direct additions and its final form will be seen below. The sub factors and means of arriving at length and sail area were amended and complex. The reader can well imagine that the rule book became longer, but the quantity is staggering. *From an RORC rule of one sheet of A4 (298 × 210mm) in 1930 to a 32-page booklet measuring 185 × 125mm at the end of the rule (1969), the IOR required a manual of 60 pages of A4 in 1990, an increase of paper area of 304 times!* That did not include measure-

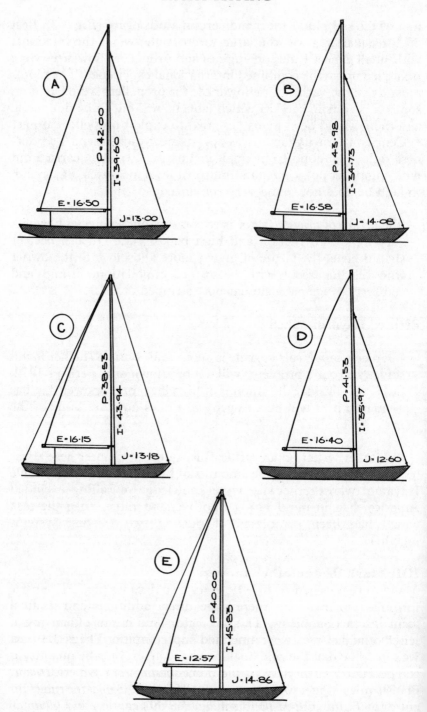

A
P = 42.00
I = 39.60
E = 16.50
J = 13.00

B
P = 43.98
I = 34.75
E = 16.58
J = 14.08

C
P = 38.53
I = 43.94
E = 16.15
J = 13.18

D
P = 41.55
I = 35.97
E = 16.40
J = 12.60

E
P = 40.00
I = 45.83
E = 12.57
J = 14.86

Fig 7.2 *How different rigs were rated at the beginning of IOR, mainly based on CCA practice, rather than RORC. The CCA also insisted on short battens, cutting down previous RORC practice. C was a typical RORC masthead rig of mid-1960s (Van de Stadt Excalibur class). A was an earlier RORC fractional rig which rated lower. B was a 12-metre rig which rated a lot lower (American Eagle used offshore) owing to low aspect ratio. D with old fashioned fractional rates lower still (pre-WWI West Solent class). E is S&S 34, latest RORC rule rig (1969) before rule change and rates higher than any: causes were big foretriangle taxed more under IOR than RORC and aspect ratio of skinny mainsail. All higher/lower descriptions are proportional.*

Fig 7.3 *The modest RORC rule book, as already shown at* **Fig 4.7.**

THE ROYAL OCEAN RACING CLUB

RULE OF MEASUREMENT AND RATING 1957

Reprinted 1968

Amended to 31st December 1967

INTRODUCTION.

The object of the Rule of Measurement and Rating is to bring together by time allowance when racing together in open water, yachts of the widest possible range of type and size.

The intention is to assist in promoting Rule 2(b) of the R.O.R.C. by encouraging the design and building of yachts in which speed and seaworthiness are combined, without favouring any particular type.

It is not possible for the Rule to cover every eventuality and the Committee, therefore, reserve the right to modify the Rule at any time, or to deal with any peculiarity of design which does not conform to the spirit of the Rule, and to give such rating as they consider equitable.

I. RATING FORMULA.

I (1) Measured Rating, MR $= .15 \dfrac{L\sqrt{S}}{\sqrt{BD}} + .2\,(L + \sqrt{S})$

Where L = Length
B = Beam
D = Depth
S = Rated Sail Area

I (2) Rating, R = MR $\pm$ Stability Allowance (cor.) — Propeller Allowance + Draft Penalty.

I (3) All measurements, except dimensions of sails and scantling details, shall be in feet to two places of decimals. Dimensions of sails and spars for calculation of sail area shall be taken in feet to one decimal place, except battens, headboards and boom depth which shall be taken in feet to two decimal places. Sail areas shall be given in square feet to one decimal place. Scantling details shall be measured in inches and fractions or decimals of inches. Percentages shall be taken to one decimal place.

2

II. BEAM.

II Beam, B, shall be the greatest Breadth, measured to the outside of normal planking at a height not exceeding half the freeboard height at this position.

III. LENGTH.

III (1) Length, L, shall be found as follows:—
L = LBG — (FOC + AOC)
LBG = Horizontal length between FGS and AGS (see Rule III (2)) or AGS cor. (see Rule III (9))
FOC = Forward Overhang Component (see Rule III (7))
AOC = After Overhang Component (see Rules III (8), (9) and (10))
It is intended that L shall approximate to the distance between a point forward where the freeboard and the half-girth (see Rule III (3)) are equal, and a point aft where the freeboard and the half-girth less one-eighth B are equal. Any case where L does not so approximate may be treated as a peculiarity of design under paragraph 3 of the Introduction to the Rule and, if the Committee so direct, alternative measurements shall be taken.

III (2) Girth stations, except in special cases dealt with under rules III (8), (9) and (10), shall be found as follows:—
FGS, Forward Girth Station, where the girth equals ⅓B
FIGS, Forward Inner Girth Station, where the girth equals ¼B
AGS, After Girth Station, where the girth equals ½B
AIGS, After Inner Girth Station, where the girth equals ⅜B
GSDf = Horizontal distance between FGS and FIGS
GSDa = Horizontal distance between AGS and AIGS

III (3) Girths shall be chain girth measurements and, except in cases dealt with under Rule III (5), shall be taken from covering board to covering board, and the points on the covering board and the forward or after profile through which they pass shall be in the same vertical athwartships plane.

3

---

ment instructions, just the rating rule. This is more than just a series of additions. It is rating rule super-inflation (**Figs 7.3 and 7.4**).

The IOR was the last visible descendent of the American and British rules of measurement and rating (**Fig 7.5**). Later rules did not draw on the pre-1970 formulae (see this caption and Chapter 8).

FORMULAE FOR DEPTHS

335.   Formulae for Immersed Depths.

The immersed depths at FD and MD stations shall be known as forward depth immersed (FDI), center midship depth immersed (CMDI), midship depth immersed (MDI) and outer midship depth immersed (OMDI) respectively, and shall be found from the formulae:

$$FDI = FD - FFD - CCF$$
$$CMDI = CMD - FMD - CCC$$
$$MDI = MD - FMD - CCM$$
$$OMDI = OMD - FMD - CCO$$

336   Formula for MDIA

.1   Midship depth immersed adjusted (MDIA) is found from the formula:
$$MDIA = 0.125*(3.0*CMDI + 2.0*MDI - 2.0*OMDI) + 0.5*OMDI*BWL/B$$

.2   Where MDIAS is available from the IORMP :
$$MDIA = MDIAS + (OMDI/B)*(BWL + 0.75*B)/2.0$$

MDIAS is the integrated area divided by B of the mid depth station below the lowest point of OMD and above a point distance CMD-MD below the lower point of CMD.

337.   Formulae for FDIC
Forward depth immersed corrected (FDIC) is found from:
FDIC = FDI or (0.2175*(MDI+CMDI)+0.5*FDI) or 0.475*(MDI+CMDI) whichever is the smallest.

338.   Formula for D
Rated Depth (D) is found from the formula:
$$D = 1.3*MDIA + 0.9*FDIC + 0.055*(3.0*FOC - AOCC) + (L + 10ft)/30. \quad (L + 3.048 \text{ M})$$

339.   Formula for BDR
Base displacement ratio (BDR) is found from the following formula:

$$BDR = (2.165*L^{0.525} - 5.85)^{0.375}/(L*B*MDIA)^{0.125} \text{ in feet}$$
$$BDR = (1.23127*L^{0.525} - 1.783)^{0.375}/(L*B*MDIA)^{0.125} \text{ in metres}$$
BDR shall not be taken as less than 1.0 in 340 or 0.94 in 1108.1.

340.   Formula for DLF
Displacement length factor (DLF) is found from the formula:

$$DLF = 1.0 + 5.7*(BDR - 1.0)^{1.75}$$
DLF shall not be taken as greater than 1.1.

Fig 7.4 *A page from IOR; it just grew and grew. Rule inflation appears to lead in due course to rule demise.*

Fig 7.5 *The family tree of principal rules of rating. After the tonnage rules were abolished, evolution flowed separately in Europe and USA. The British borrowed the Seawanhaka and Universal rules from America to create the BRA rule which was turned into the RORC rule and the 5.5-metre rule. It can be seen how in America there was a tendency to create rules from scratch; examples are the CCA and the MHS/IMS. After the USA joined IYRU, it had official input to the International rule, long after its own contemporary Universal rule had been abandoned. This key chart illustrates happenings in several chapters in this book.*

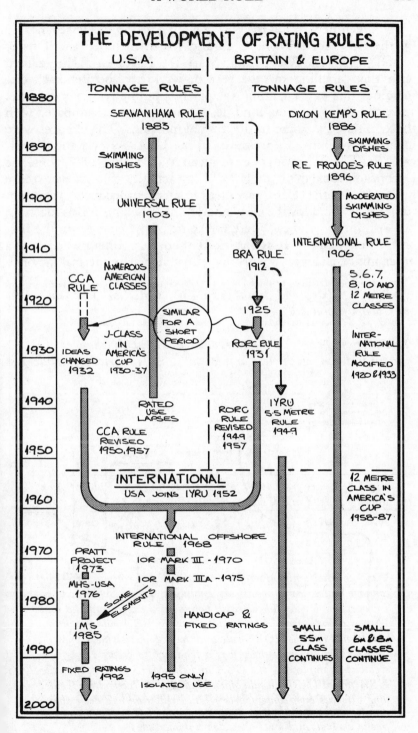

THE DEVELOPMENT OF RATING RULES

U.S.A.   BRITAIN & EUROPE

TONNAGE RULES   TONNAGE RULES

1880

SEAWANHAKA RULE   DIXON KEMP'S RULE
1883   1886

1890   SKIMMING
                                      DISHES

SKIMMING   R.E. FROUDE'S RULE
DISHES   1896

1900   MODERATED
                                      SKIMMING
UNIVERSAL RULE   DISHES
1903

1910   BRA RULE   INTERNATIONAL RULE
                         1912   1906

        NUMEROUS   5, 6, 7,
CCA   AMERICAN   8, 10 AND
RULE   CLASSES   12 METRE
1920   1925   CLASSES
              SIMILAR
              FOR A
              SHORT   INTER-
              PERIOD   NATIONAL
        J-CLASS   RORC RULE   RULE
1930   IN   1931   MODIFIED
IDEAS   AMERICA'S   1920 & 1933
CHANGED CUP
1932   1930-37

1940   RATED   RORC   IYRU
        USE   RULE   5.5 METRE
        LAPSES   REVISED RULE
CCA RULE   1949   1949
REVISED   1957
1950   1950,1957

        INTERNATIONAL   12 METRE
1960   USA JOINS IYRU 1952   CLASS IN
                                      AMERICA'S
                                      CUP
                                      1958-87
        INTERNATIONAL OFFSHORE
        RULE 1968
1970   PRATT   IOR MARK III - 1970
        PROJECT
        1973   IOR MARK IIIA - 1975
        MHS-USA
        1976   SOME
1980   ELEMENTS
        IMS   HANDICAP &
        1985   FIXED RATINGS SMALL   SMALL
                                      5.5m   6m & 8m
1990   CLASS   CLASSES
        FIXED RATINGS   CONTINUES CONTINUE
        1992   1995 ONLY
                ISOLATED USE
2000

In November 1971 at the ORC meeting in San Francisco, hosted by the St Francis Yacht Club and which included the Tinsley Island Cruise, the IOR became Mark III. IOR Mark III remained with that labelling for the rest of its life.[8] Looking back one imagines this new labelling was partly a public relations exercise, since the changes, though numerous were not vast compared with those initiated at some future annual meetings. The changes were mainly in response to pressures in the USA. As ever the Americans, in a hurry to change, introduced Mark III for 1972, while the Europeans took it on in 1973. This actually caused even more problems in the USA, as measurement procedures were not properly in hand for the early alterations. Looking at this meeting, but also jumping ahead, here are some of the changes in the first half dozen years of IOR (Mark II then III). There were always other minor changes in wording, substance or numerical factors.

*April 1971: Extra mid depths (**Fig 7.6**); 'water' or 'joke' sail under main boom prohibited*

November 1971: IOR becomes Mark III with changes to L, D (forward depth made less influential), S (foretriangle made less

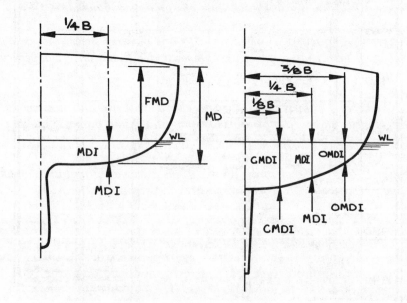

Fig 7.6 *Early repairs to IOR. Extra depth measurements were introduced to discourage the flat mid-section. But their effect was limited and flat sections continued and seemed to be fast. (C, M, O mean central, mid, outer DI, depth immersed.)*

influential) and CGF (cut off at .985, so tender yachts with big crews were not advantaged); bumps on hulls to take advantage were checked (but this saga went on for years); time allowance investigations (but they never got anywhere); moveable appendage factor (MAF) to regulate centreboards, swing keels, trim tabs and so on.

15 April 1972: Bloopers, bigboys declared legal.
This was the setting of a genoa to windward of the spinnaker. It had originated in a protest against *Wai-Aniwa* (New Zealand) during the Southern Cross Cup off Sydney, Australia. The ORC declared the protest dismissed. As a result special sails were developed as the area was free of measurement. It was an unwise decision as it added nothing to sailing except expense and a need for big crews. It was a throw back to the days of rules without rated sail area! The sail was eventually killed, after some ten years, by sail limitation and fractional rigs.

November 1972: The cat ketch outlawed (see below). Rules on tankage at measurement. Liferaft position at measurement.

April 1973: Propeller type factors altered (those tank tests were not so 'scientific'); adjustable leech lines on spinnakers banned.

April 1974: Rules changed on outboard motors; sheer line, bulbous bows. Further alterations on bumps at depth stations; blooper rule altered.

November 1974: Bloopers again reworded! Trim and stowage rules tightened; outboard platforms carrying stanchions banned; number of sails carried on board discussed for first time.

April 1975: Liferaft to be ashore at measurement; limitation of sails not agreed; USYRU measurement trim proposals rejected.

November 1975: IOR Mark IIIA introduced for existing yachts only. It gave a bonus to 'cruising' features. One reason for promulgating it now was to divert the threat by the organizers of the 1976 (June) Newport-Bermuda race to use its own modification of the IOR. In the event they rejected IOR Mark IIIA (see below).

November 1976: Mark IIIA widened in application slightly; stern measurements changed; blooper again affected (tack pennant!) the numbers of sails carried when racing gets agreed.

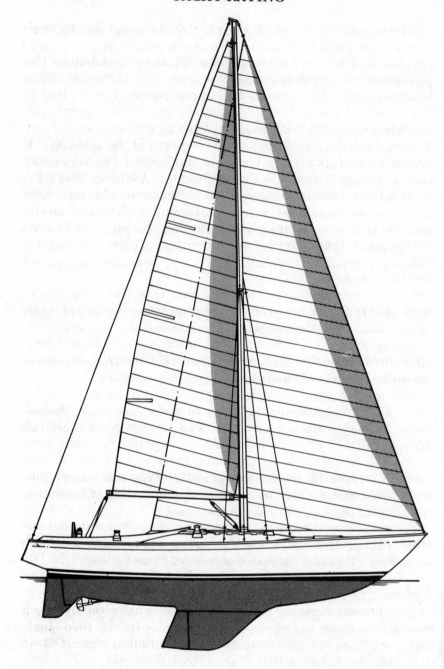

Fig 7.7 *Early design to the IOR.* Cervantes IV, *a successful British Admiral's Cup yacht designed by Sparkman and Stephens. LOA 40ft 2in (12.24m), displacement 20,000 pounds (9000 kg), nearly half of which was lead keel.*

And so it went on. Running a world rule with such numbers of yachts was a tough job.

As for the kind of yachts which were being produced under the IOR in its first years, one might look at the 1971 Admiral's Cup. Among the excellent turn out of 17 countries, only Britain, Brazil, Argentina and Holland had all IOR designed ocean racers: the others had some previous designs, though no doubt optimized and rerigged for IOR. The British yacht *Cervantes IV* designed by the current masters of the rule, Sparkman and Stephens of New York, was very succesful and in the British Admiral's Cup team (**Fig 7.7**). She was second AC boat in the Fastnet, which was won overall by the Australian *Ragamuffin*, a 1968 RORC rule design. All boats in the Fastnet race sailed under IOR (as they did until 1987, after which other rating rules were admitted).

World wide races
The impression should be corrected that IOR was hung up on disputes. In these early years of the rule there was world wide racing under it and designing and building to it. Later some of the fiercest controversy will be reviewed in more detail. Such debate arose almost always at the 'front edge' of IOR racing: lower down the ladder, happy racing prospered.

IOR worked particularly well where the competitors were of much the same standard, the boats of about the same age and expensive campaigns were absent. This applies to most rating rules, but as IOR was so widely used, it meant that top boats were 'sold down' to more local competition. Once again it helped if sizes were not far apart. If the number of starters was large enough, the boats could be split into near bands of rating and class winners made sense.

The practice in the USA of giving a corrected time order for the 'whole fleet', rather than a number of class orders, was not helpful to the rule. The same thinking meant and still means that in the US and Australia, the first boat to finish (the biggest?) is said to have 'line honours', while in Britain it is simply 'first to finish'.

The numbers of yachts with IOR certificates in the early years of the rule may never be seen again under a single rating rule, though they are approached with small sized (sailing dinghy) one-designs. *World*: 1972, 7100 yachts; 1973, 9363; 1974, 10815; 1975, 9484; 1976, 10193; only after 1981 did world numbers fall below 10,000.[9] What was happening was that many countries were increasing the number of rated yachts, though from 1975 on, the USA, with very much the biggest number, fell steadily. For instance *Germany*:

1973, 500; 1975, 950; 1977, 1290; 1979, 1348 (*peaked*). *UK*: 1972, 1232; 1974, 1834; 1976, 1888 (*peaked*). However *USA* showed: 1971, 2400; 1972, 2771; 1973, 3917; 1974, 4362 (*peaked*); 1975, 3416 (a massive drop); 1977, 2956.

Major IOR events

IOR was used from its inception until about 1993 in all major ocean racing events in the world, as well as inshore regattas for 'habitable' boats.

Ton Cups. Under the RORC rule, as recounted, the One Ton Cup, previously used for inshore classes, latterly the 6-metre, had been allocated to yachts of 22ft rating in 1965. The clubs at La Rochelle soon after gave the Half Ton Cup for 18ft RORC rating and the Quarter Ton Cup for 15ft RORC rating. In 1971 all were converted to IOR rating, the One Ton at 27.5ft IOR, Half at 21.7ft. Quarter at 18ft. There was a Two ton which was never very well supported at 33ft IOR, then 32ft in 1974. In 1974, the US delegates to the ORC presented a Three-Quarter Ton Cup at 24.5ft IOR. In 1978 appeared the Mini-Ton at 16ft IOR (**Fig 7.8**).

Level rating in effect, though not in name, was the maximum size yacht permitted in IOR. In the CCA rule it had been 73ft LOA (22.25m), but in the IOR it was quickly declared to be 70ft rating. Thus was initiated the famous 'maxi' class.

These level rating classes had well supported world championships in leading yachting countries in turn and invariably represented the very latest ideas in IOR design. Sometimes new designers made their names as a result. In the late 1970s the numbers of starters were likely to be between 30 and 35. Then there were all the boats in the class which sailed in the participating countries, but did not make it to the worlds. In each case the winner of the main trophy in this inshore-offshore series was a single boat, though there were other prizes for teams and separate races.

The last year that the One Ton Cup used IOR was 1994, similarly the Three-Quarter Ton Cup. Only the Quarter Ton Cup continued in 1996 as a class established on the Baltic coasts of Germany and Poland.

Southern Ocean Racing Conference. This series of winter weekends off the Florida coast dating from 1941 was famous for introducing each year the new designs and best offshore sailors with all the power of the American ocean racing scene. There were six races in

CHANGES IN RATINGS						
	TWO TON	ONE TON	THREE-QUARTER TON	HALF TON	QUARTER TON	MINI TON
1965		22ft RORC				
1966				18ft RORC		
1967	28ft RORC				15ft RORC	
1971	33ft IOR	27·5ft IOR		21·7ft IOR	18ft IOR	
1974	32ft IOR		24·5ft IOR			
1978						16ft IOR
1979				22·05 ft IOR	18·55ft IOR	16·55ft IOR
1981	SUSPENDED					
1984		30·55ft IOR				
1991	RESTARTED 35·05ft IOR					
1992						LAST EVENT
1993	LAST EVENT			LAST EVENT		
1994		LAST EVENT	LAST EVENT			
1995						

Fig 7.8 *How the Ton Cup classes, fixed rating under RORC rule then under IOR, were created, died and changed their ratings. A vertical column indicates fixed rating history including the year class was started, or changed and continues downward until different figures or 'last event' shown. The Quarter Ton continued locally in the Baltic, but ended in 1996.*

January and February in sub-tropical waters varying from 35 miles to 400 miles.

The magnificent fleet used the CCA rule rising from about 40 in 1961-63 to 99 in 1969, the last year for CCA. In 1973 the starters using IOR peaked at 124, the next year they were 111, declining slightly to about 70 through the early 1980s, but this was a fine fleet. In 1986 and 1987 there were 50 plus. Then suddenly it was all over with only 18 in 1988. Today the SORC remains as a local inshore regatta of one long weekend at Miami.[10]

Bermuda race. The previous importance of the Newport to Bermuda race waned in rating terms once NAYRU/USYRU handled the IOR. No longer was the result of this race the signal for the CCA to review its own rule. Again in the final years of the CCA the number of starters soared on each biennial event, for instance: 1954, 77; 1958, 111; 1962, 131; 1966, 167. The first year of IOR, 1970 saw 152 (the winner was *Carina*, a CCA design). 178 was the peak in 1972, when a British IOR boat, *Noryema*, won overall, the only foreign win in the history of the event. In 1978 the CCA allowed in a class rated to the new MHS rule, giving IOR 89 and

MHS 72. In 1980, following the 1979 Fastnet storm, the Bermuda race was for MHS only, though IOR was shadowed. In the years which immediately followed, IOR in decreasing numbers took second place to MHS.

Thus was betrayed by the Cruising Club of America its agreement with the Royal Ocean Racing Club to adopt a common rule. The great scheme had lasted just four Bermuda races (1970 to 1976), before the Cruising Club returned to its old biennial habits.

Sydney to Hobart. IOR substantially boosted the starters in this 615-mile event (purposely same approximate length as Bermuda and Fastnet), with over 100 yachts for the first time ever in 1975. Australia got on with IOR, sending teams to England for the Admiral's Cup and never suffered the problems of America. A peak of 212 IOR boats was reached in 1985. IOR was not completely abandoned until 1994.

Other Far East races based on Japan, Hong Kong, New Zealand and also the long established yachting nations such as Argentina and Brazil tended to lag 'behind' USA (certainly) and Europe (a bit). It is more akin to a cycle with these 'other' countries getting good support for IOR, while the early starters were in the down of the cycle.

Inshore events like Cowes Week, Block Island Week and La Rochelle Week drew hundreds of IOR boats throughout the mid-1970s. In 1975 in the annual Round the Island (Isle of Wight) race from Cowes, there started no less than 466 yachts on IOR rating. Offshore the regular classics such as Buenos Aires to Rio de Janeiro, Capetown to Rio, the Giraglia (Mediterranean) were run under IOR, as well as something undreamt of by the earlier rule makers, a race around the world.

RNSA-Whitbread race. The Royal Naval Sailing Association wanted to run an adventurous race particularly for yachts of the British armed forces; a sponsor was found in the Whitbread company, a long established brewer. Use of the IOR was undoubtedly an important element in the creation of this race. Robin Glover, IOR Chief Measurer, devised a special time allowance system for the long ocean courses. There were 19 starters for the first race which started off Portsmouth, England, on 8 September 1973, varying in size from 32ft (9.75m) to 80ft (24.38m) LOA. Legs ended and restarted at Cape Town, Sydney and Rio. As is well known the race has been repeated every four years since. Ports of call have varied. The last race using IOR was in 1989-90 without time allowances. This effectively meant only a maxi rated yacht could (and did) win. The combination of the nature of the course, the lack of attention to the rule (which bred huge near-freak ketches despite requests for rule correction) and high priced sponsorship caused this. However IOR is still the only formula that has been used in five great round the world events. Subsequent Whitbread races (the RNSA withdrew after 1994) and other round the world races have used restricted classes or one-designs.

Fastnet race and Admiral's Cup. The IOR was the successor to the RORC rule and the RORC itself stuck loyally to IOR only for these biennial events from 1971 until 1993 for the Cup and 1989 for the Fastnet race open to all qualified ocean racers. The Admiral's Cup attracted the foremost IOR boats of their day, which also appeared in its 'imitators' such as the Southern Cross and Sardinia Cup. The number of three-boat national teams reached its peak of 19 in 1975, 1977 and 1979, thereafter declining in fits and starts (**Fig 7.9**).

The detailed rules for the Cup have varied over the years. From 1973, the boats had to be between 29 and 45ft IOR rating; results used the current RORC time allowance system. The One Ton Cup boats were too small for the AC, but when the One Ton moved in 1983 to 30.5ft rating, this meant that the latest machines became eligible for the AC; the competitive pressure and therefore the strains on the rule became considerable. (See also Appendix III)

The next logical move was to abolish time allowances and in the final years of IOR, the teams had to comprise of a One Tonner, a Two Tonner (revived for a couple of years at 35ft rating, before disappearing) and a 50 footer (the latter was an owner initiated class, mostly American on a fixed rating and their own rules which existed from 1988 to about 1993. It was destroyed by professionalism and the demise of IOR). By restricting the classes in this way, the level of sailing reached a peak, but the number of countries, as can be seen, diminished. The crews were almost all professional.

The 1979 Fastnet storm
The facts are well known or at least available in book form.[11] 303 yachts, all IOR rated, from many nations set off on 11 August from Cowes to race round the Fastnet rock and back to Plymouth, 605 nautical miles.

In the storm which hit the competitors strung out between Land's End and Fastnet Rock, 5 yachts were lost, 19 yachts were abandoned and subsequently recovered and 15 lives were lost in

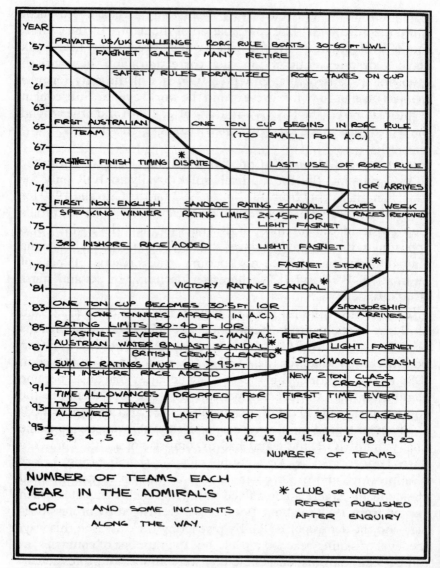

YEAR

'57 PRIVATE US/UK CHALLENGE   RORC RULE BOATS 30-60 FT LWL
     FASTNET GALES MANY RETIRE
'59
            SAFETY RULES FORMALIZED   RORC TAKES ON CUP
'61

'63

'65 FIRST AUSTRALIAN   ONE TON CUP BEGINS IN RORC RULE
        TEAM   (TOO SMALL FOR A.C.)
'67

'69 FASTNET FINISH TIMING DISPUTE   LAST USE OF RORC RULE

'71   IOR ARRIVES

'73 FIRST NON-ENGLISH   SANDADE RATING SCANDAL   COWES WEEK
        SPEAKING WINNER   RATING LIMITS 29-45 FT IOR RACES REMOVED
'75   LIGHT FASTNET

'77 3RD INSHORE RACE ADDED   LIGHT FASTNET

'79   FASTNET STORM *

'81   VICTORY RATING SCANDAL *

'83 ONE TON CUP BECOMES 30.5FT IOR   SPONSORSHIP
        (ONE TONNERS APPEAR IN A.C.)   ARRIVES
'85 RATING LIMITS 30-40 FT IOR
     FASTNET SEVERE GALES - MANY A.C. RETIRE
'87 AUSTRIAN WATER BALLAST SCANDAL *   LIGHT FASTNET
        BRITISH CREWS CLEARED *
'89 SUM OF RATINGS MUST BE >95FT   STOCK MARKET CRASH
     4TH INSHORE RACE ADDED   NEW 2 TON CLASS
'91   CREATED
     TIME ALLOWANCES DROPPED FOR FIRST TIME EVER
'93 TWO BOAT TEAMS
     ALLOWED   LAST YEAR OF IOR   3 ORC CLASSES
'95
     2 3 4 5 6 7 8 9 10 11 12 13 14 15 16 17 18 19 20
                              NUMBER OF TEAMS

NUMBER OF TEAMS EACH
YEAR IN THE ADMIRAL'S   * CLUB or WIDER
CUP - AND SOME INCIDENTS   REPORT PUBLISHED
        ALONG THE WAY.   AFTER ENQUIRY

Fig 7.9 *Rise and fall of the Admiral's Cup and some incidents along the way. In 1995 and 1997, the IMS rule was used. The comments by the graph may or may not be relevant to numbers. The time of greatest expansion was under the RORC rule. At the end of IOR, fixed rating classes appear to have made national teams difficult to recruit. Numbers never recovered to those which set out in the Fastnet storm, but the connection may be a coincidence.*

various circumstances. No yacht actually sank with crew, though a multihull, not permitted in the race, but sailing the course, was found capsized and with all hands missing. 85 yachts completed the course of the race which was won by *Tenacious*, 65ft (19.81m) owned by Ted Turner (USA). It remains the worst disaster in the history of yachting.[12]

Here we are only concerned with blame, if any, which was apportioned to the IOR under which all yachts sailed. The only verdict has to be in the *Fastnet Race Enquiry* by the RORC and RYA.[13] The most characteristic effect of the Fastnet storm 1979 on the ocean racing yachts was the number of alleged knock downs or even 360 degree rolls. On the rule the report equivocated.

'Trends which have been noticeable in yachts designed to the IOR have included light displacement, broad beam, shallow hull form and large sail area. In 1978 the ORC decided that these trends were reaching undesirable proportions. In particular boats of extreme light displacement and dubious ultimate stability were appearing: the rule was amended to penalize them and exclude potentially unstable boats from racing. The rule is under constant review by an (*sic*) International Technical Committee which is alert for developments which might reduce the seaworthiness of yachts.

'In considering the effect of the IOR on design it is difficult to separate the trends which have resulted from improved technology and general progress of yacht design, which are likely to occur whatever rating rule is in current use from the result of designers' endeavours to produce boats with the lowest possible rating and which are directly dependent upon the current rating rule.'

Later the report stated

'It has been alleged that in their quest for faster boats designers have gone to extremes which surpass the bounds of common sense and which ignore constraint *which should be imposed* by the requirements for offshore racing to be able to cope with any weather which might be expected.'

A search through the inquiry finds no verdict on the rule, rather so-called allegations followed by statistics from which one was expected to draw one's own conclusions. After nearly 20 years, one must regard this part of the report and maybe much of it as characteristic briefing by counsel.

In a final part of the report there was evasive verbiage

> 'We do not believe that we should make any specific recommen-
> dation ... We do recommend, however, that the finding of this
> section of the report should be placed before the ORC with a
> view to their considering whether further changes in the mea-
> surement rules might not be required'.[14]

As mentioned, the CCA did not waste much time on it. The
Bermuda race committee decided the rule was guilty and that the
limeys sailed in stupidly small boats! The 1980 Bermuda race
abandoned IOR and had a much higher minimum size than was the
lower limit in British ocean racing.

The ORC inserted into the IOR a displacement/length factor,
DLF, which altered the rating of certain kinds of apparently light
displacement boat: a few years later boats were as light and 'flat' as
ever.

IOR ocean racers

In the period in which IOR flourished, there were many magnificent ocean racers of all sizes. It is only possible to give here a few
drawings of examples which typify the profiles of their time (**Fig
7.10 to 7.12**).

Once again it must be emphasized that in such boats thousands
of enjoyable miles were sailed and hundreds of satisfying races
completed. We are about to look again at some detail of the rule
difficulties sketched out earlier in the chapter. As these were
debated so racing continued, though the higher the level the more
the uncertainty. The controversy did in the long run reduce the use
of the rule. **Fig 7.13** plots the rise and fall of IOR in the world,
which is the total at any time. All countries did not move in the
same direction, as shown in **Fig 7.14**; the most striking aspect is
that while the USA fell, taking the world total down with it, some
other nations increased their support of IOR. The number of

Fig 7.10 *Look of IOR racer by 1978, rule about eight years old
and just before Fastnet storm: huge foretriangle, pinched in stern
and pregnant cow still lives. Such shapes proved difficult to steer
when running. There is here an open accommodation and flush
deck. This was* Irish Mist *by Ron Holland, designed and built in
Ireland. LOA 41ft 6in (12.65m) and fitted Two Ton rule of that
time.*

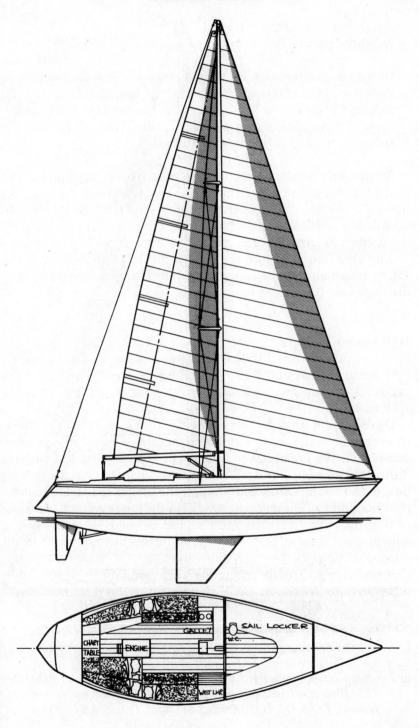

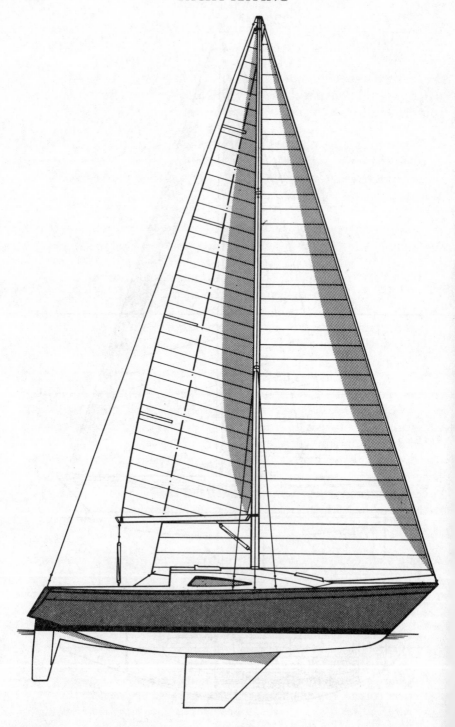

certificates in any rule does not necessarily have a direct relationship with the number of starts in races.[15]

American reservations
After two full seasons of the 'new' IOR, a leading offshore racing
commentator in New York[16] wrote in February 1972

> 'When the CCA endorsed the newly formulated IOR on 22 May
> 1969, there was relatively little vocal opposition . . . Now almost
> three years later, most ocean racing events around the country –
> and the world – are run under IOR.'

A number of people, it was said, were unhappy: builders,
designers, owners. One builder was quoted

> ' "NAYRU marched in on this and pushed IOR off on us. The
> IOR has little benefit for US yachtsmen or US boat manufac-
> turers. Because the boats we built were to the CCA rule, there
> was no market in Europe for our boats, but the IOR did open the
> US for RORC boats". A designer, Gary Mull, later to join the
> ITC, says "My dissatisfaction stems from the ITC operating
> behind closed doors. Many designers think Olin Stephens,
> chairman of ITC, has an inside track". Britton Chance Jr
> [another designer] says "My main objection to the IOR is its
> complexity of measurement. It is possible to have a better
> handicapping rule with few measurements"
> '. . . the governing body of the Storm Trysail Club approved a
> series of modifications to IOR. These take data from the IOR
> certificate and *also fresh information from the yacht's designer* . . .
> the club feels that lateral plane is an important factor of boat
> speed and should be measured . . .'

Among such controversy Gary Mull remarked that calls heard for
an 'owner-oriented rule' amused him

Fig 7.11 *Contention 33 production class under IOR originating in
1975 to a design by the Californian Doug Peterson, was a popular
and successful IOR racer and also a cruiser. It fitted the Three-
Quarter Ton level in a period when many European IOR boats
were built to Ton Cup ratings. Large masthead genoas were the
norm, set on a two-spreader rig. Despite the rule the mainsail
appears skinny.*

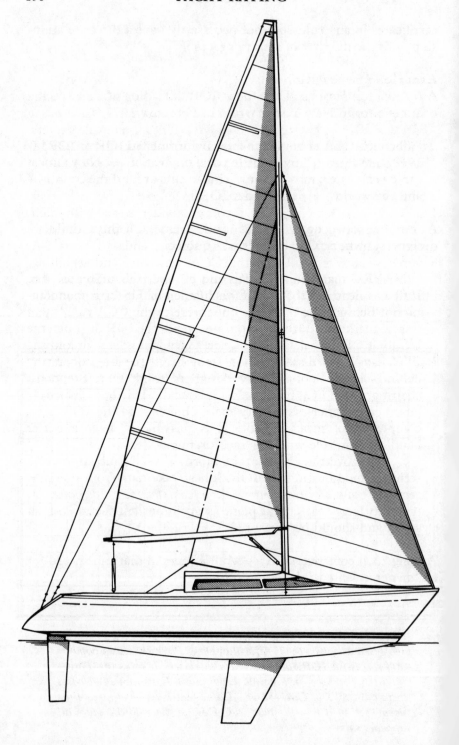

Fig 7.12 *A beamy (9ft 1in, 2.78m) flat, Quarter Tonner of 1978 designed by Ed Dubois. Unusually for the period,* Starflash *had a low fractional rig. LOA 25ft 7in (7.81m), displacement 1950 pounds (885 kg).*

'. . . *the owner does not want a boat that is rated fairly. He wants a boat that will beat the rule – a rule beater*. There were rule beaters under CCA and those boats are now losing out under IOR: I think they are getting justice'.

Olin Stephens's immediate defence in 1972 to these and other comments was (1) The CCA favoured tender boats with high centres of gravity, which were not desirable; (2) the CCA also favoured a scow type, while IOR had sharper ends; (3) the CCA favoured narrow beam;[17] (4) the CCA waterline and weighing measurements had been in disarray; (5) wetted surface is too difficult to measure; (6) IOR does not encourage stripped out boats, but racing does; (7) as for the inside track

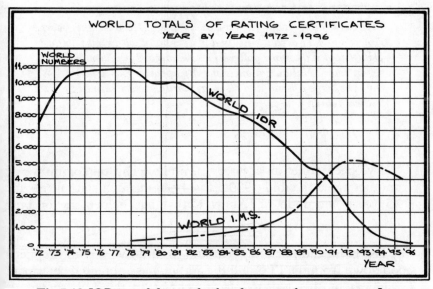

Fig 7.13 *IOR served thousands of yacht owners for some years. It had the unique advantage of accumulating immediately all yachts already rated to the important CCA and RORC rules world wide, but after about 1978 it began a slow decline in total numbers, though the best yachts and events increased in race potential. After 25 years of the rule, IOR was confined to a few scattered ports in the eastern Baltic and Mediterranean.*

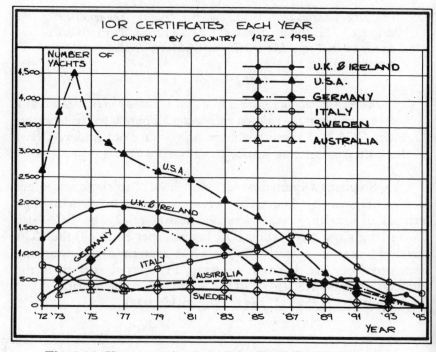

Fig 7.14 *How countries reacted to the IOR over the years. Americans embraced it quickly and dropped it with some rapidity. UK followed the same pattern more moderately. German decline began later. Italian sailors went the opposite was and by 1987 were the biggest world user. The authorities never seemed to react to these telling figures.*

' "I've been either an adviser or on one technical committee or another since the mid-1930s. I've been on such committees for 35 years and I do not know if that has helped me or hurt me . . ." '

The last point did not disappear and in mid-1973, Olin Stephens stood down from the ITC and the author was appointed chairman. To an extent this was to placate circles in the US, though it resulted in Englishmen holding the major appointments, the other two being the ORC chairman, David Edwards and the international chief measurer, Robin Glover. A contributory cause was the sensational appearance of the 'cat ketch' *Cascade*. She was one more in the historic line of rule freaks – in this case perhaps a 'rule mocker' (**Fig 7.15**).

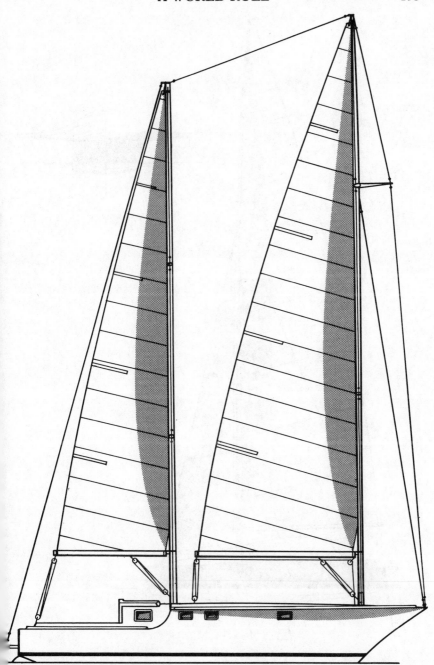

Fig 7.15 *The profile of the cat ketch* Cascade, *another historic rule cheater. The effect was to cause major rule controversy in America. Her designer Professor Jerry Milgram, was later involved in the creation of MHS/IMS.*

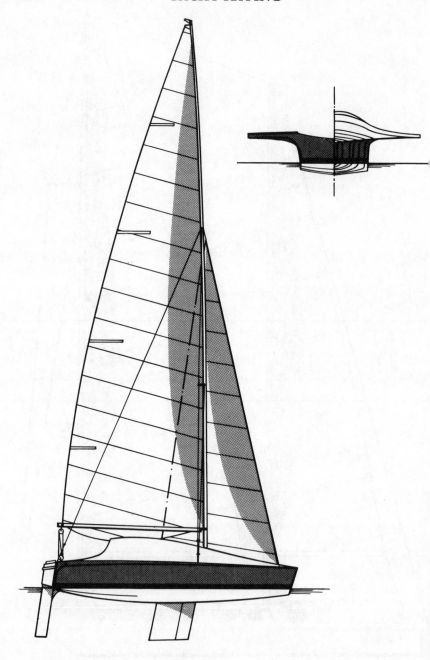

Fig 7.16 *The British could also mock the IOR. The Quarter Tonner* Warbird *(1973) had beam and crew leverage extended by platforms, extreme rig and hull shape. Though built, she was not a practical racing proposition.*

The designer was Dr Jerry Milgram of Massachusetts Institute of Technology (MIT), Cambridge, Massachusetts, where he had a Ph.D. in naval architecture. The yacht with two masts and no 'headsails' was 38ft (11.58m) LOA, but rated only 21ft IOR! She nearly swept the New York Yacht Club cruise (a series of races) of late summer 1972, then appeared at the SORC in January 1973, where, despite an arbitrary 10 per cent increase in rating, she won three of these big events. At the April 1973 meeting of the ORC a new rating for rigs moved her rating to around 27ft, which a boat of her size would expect. The ketch without headsails had found a loophole in IOR which rated the actual 800 sq ft (74 sq m) as 300 (28 sq m) and advantages were also found in the engine and propeller factor, as well as pieces taken out of bow and stern profiles. Of the new rating Milgram said in reply to the question 'Do you think that 27.2 [feet rating] will kill *Cascade*?', 'Sure'.[18]

As a result similar designs were not built, but Milgram went away to think further about rating rules.

Another freak
About the same time in England, a Quarter Tonner (i.e. 18ft level rating IOR) was being built called *Warbird*. Most Quarter Tonners were then about 20ft (6.10m) on the waterline, but this one designed by Gordon Thrower of the Southampton College of Technology came out at 29ft (8.84m). The beam was a massive 13ft (3.96m) and the crew sat on wings to keep the boat upright for there was a low ballast ratio and light displacement. Though 'wings' had been banned after Paul Elvstrom tried them in his Half Tonner the previous year, that was only if they began aft of the forward girth station (FGS). Never mind the details; of course, these began forward of such a station. *Warbird*, built for David Potter, took advantage of other clauses in IOR concerning the transom stern, the rig proportions (as *Cascade*). Some of the dimensions were on a knife edge in relation to the rule; by that it is meant that if the freeboard at FGS was raised by one inch (25mm), the rating would shoot up to 90ft![19] This was because of critical divisors, as any mathematician would guess (**Fig 7.16**).

The boat was cheered on by British enthusiasts who could see her lifting the Quarter Ton Cup which was soon to be held in England. In the event Robin Glover visited the boat building, found serious flaws in the expected measurement and anyway as Chief Measurer IOR was entitled to issue holding clauses until the next international meetings. As the debate on the design intensified one letter said

'The design is a most interesting experiment. Would it not be better to get this boat sailing and place less emphasis on the rating problems?'[20]

However it did not ever get sailing. A much milder version of the concept was designed by Stephen Jones for Jack Knights, who had written much about *Warbird*. She was an unusual looking boat called *Oddjob*. She had several big successes, then was little heard of, yet was racing happily under other rules in 1995 and probably later: a case of remembering that rating is not everything and low rating by unconventional means may not result in beating the rule.

Both *Warbird* and *Cascade* stoked up rule controversy with those who were glad their existing boats had been protected against outlandish design under the rule (these people generally being unheard) and those who felt that the innovators should be allowed to design to the letter of the rule. A leading American racing man and author of an outspoken book[21], John J. McNamara Jr wrote a long open letter to the ORC, the IYRU and the yachting press in Britain and the USA, though nominally addressed to Olin Stephens.

'The re-rating of *Cascade* takes on the aspects of a maritime Dreyfus Affair with too many vested industry interests serving on the drumhead court martial . . . The present credibility of the offshore sport hangs in very delicate balance [examples were then given of recent rule changes]. If the pattern keeps up then your committee will find itself in the same position as those who presided over the last days of the CCA rule; namely that of the little Dutch boy at the dyke who ran out of fingers . . . Dr Milgram's *Cascade* has been done in for the wrong reasons . . . the IOR is a flat out development rule in an escalating spiral of hulls of the month and rigs of the week; it has become a paradise for committee member designers and a Nirvana for sailmakers. The time is at hand for the ORC to re-think what has been wrought and to set down in clear terms a rule with a healthy and desirable philosophy, in which the printed word of the rule is kept'.

Rereading years later the 'letter' of some 2200 words of which the above is only a part, it is strangely contradictory; which is a characteristic of much but not all rating rule criticism. McNamara seems to say that the wording of the rule must not be changed so that *Cascade*, an innovation, may duly take her place. Then he

accuses the rule of allowing boats which quickly outdate those
already racing.[22]

Blooper blues

The summary of rule changes by years earlier in this chapter
mentions a number of alterations to the blooper (or big boy,
shooter and other names). For reasons mentioned, the ITC should
never have permitted it.

It was an example of how changes, for the best of motives to
make this sail's shape and limits 'fairer', simply upset those who
had already bought such a sail. Owing to the large number of all
sails carried on IOR boats (and also kept ashore) before sail
limitation was instituted, sailmakers were intensely watchful of the
rule.

A headline in an American paper read

'NAYRU Phones Run Hot As Blooper Decision Spreads.
The howl of protest from owners and sailmakers that greeted the
ORC action [in changing the rule on the shape of the sail] could
yet lead to official recognition of bloopers, shooters and
streakers. The executive (sic) committee of ORC was due to
consider the question, three days before the rule change outlaw-
ing the present generation of bloopers was due to take effect...
"Never have I seen so much mail on any one subject and I've
never seen the phone jump off the hook quite so much," said
Ted Jones, offshore director of the North American Yacht
Racing Union...'[23]

Comments from letters received by NAYRU were typically

'I have made a considerable effort to stay in ocean racing under
the IOR, but I feel very badly used with this kind of tampering
with the rule...'[24]
'I am really shocked and exasperated in the extreme by the
proposed amendment... ill conceived measure in terms of
trying to limit the definition of the Shooter... kind of behaviour
which is driving more and more people away from this type of
competition...'[25]

In the event the rule change went ahead and the blooper or big
boy, familiar in old photographs but no longer on the water, duly
ived and died.

Threats and diversions

One must venture for just a shade longer into American yachting –
or more precisely – International Offshore Rule politics. For the
consequences were considerable for the future of yacht racing
world wide.

In passing one might ask, what about Europe, Australasia and
elsewhere? As seen in earlier chapters the USA is unique in
yachting terms in its size and spread and weak national authority;
at least weak relative to European authorities, whose decisions may
sometimes have been queried, but at the end of the day were
accepted – and certainly not forever being re-opened. In Britain
the RORC had acted for the national authority in offshore racing
and rating matters for fifty years (from 1925).

In New York a staunch supporter of IOR, Ted Jones, a resident
of Norwalk, CT, was running the NAYRU Offshore office. In June
1974 his president, James Michael of San Francisco, had written to
David Edwards in London to warn him that if changes were not
made in the IOR, there would soon be a number of different rules
in the USA, with IOR confined to the top international boats only.

Meanwhile Jones had warned Edwards and the author that the
old guard of the CCA led by Michael and Lynn Williams,[26] were
maybe trying to take charge of offshore ratings, for had the senior
men of the CCA not traditionally had that role?

As chairman of a self styled committee to the board of governors
of the CCA, Williams circulated an 11-point memo, calling for rule
changes. It ended

> 'These adjustments must be made, and very soon, if the Rule
> (*sic*) is to have continued acceptance in North America. Absent
> such timely action by the ORC, we believe it will remain the
> obligation of the CCA to initiate such measures.'[27]

As so often in looking back at these calls for change, the specific
items seem slight. Preliminaries about 'desirable boats', 'fairness',
'checking obsolescence' and so on are always there in resounding
texts. The changes of which Williams made so much of were
principally (1) Stronger scantlings; (2) the rule to be adjusted
frequently; (3) big sail area must be further penalized; (4) bow
down measurement must be stopped, as it forced moveable gear aft
when racing; (5) measurement points such as depths were too
sensitive. Amazingly that was about all.

It will be remembered that it was the CCA which refused to
incorporate a scantling rule (as used by the RORC) into the IOR

and frequent rule changes were a major complaint of users. Sail area was probably a fair criticism, but was as much due to improved sailing techniques as the rule, while bow down trim was duly limited by rules on gear placement or removal at measurement.

In November 1975, the ORC had urgently introduced IOR Mark IIIA which helped boats already in existence. The timing, at least, was to prevent the CCA from using its own modified IOR for 1976. NAYRU had become USYRU (United States Yacht Racing Union), Canada and Mexico forming their own national authorities affiliated to IYRU. USYRU still spoke for Canada at ORC, or had a joint delegation.[28] In another move, Ted Jones was removed as Offshore Director and the CCA seemed to be synonymous with USYRU on rule representation. Its representatives on ORC were Lynn Williams, Olin Stephens, Gordon M. Curtis and Mark Baxter.

Taking over from Jones was Ken Weller, described then as a computer specialist. On his appointment he said

'I think it is wrong that IYRU (*sic*) and USYRU are thought to be supporting the IOR, as though it is their rule. Actually it is not the national authority's job to support only one rule. *The USYRU should help to broaden the rule base*'.[29]

ORCA

Fig 7.17 *ORCA, symbol of a breed of whale. The Ocean Racing Club of America was modelled on the Royal Ocean Racing Club (and its 50-year old* Seahorse *badge), but did not prosper against the Cruising Club of America and its way of doing things.*

At the same time Ted Jones and some leading ocean racing men formed ORCA, the Ocean Racing Club of America. It was intended to support IOR and obviously to provide a rallying point for those who did not like what the CCA was trying to do, it included Dave Allen, Jeff Hammond and Norm Raben. To some extent its model was RORC, though it would not have done to say so; indeed its logo was a whale (breed *orca*) rather than a seahorse (**Fig 7.17**). Unfortunately the new club only lasted a few years.

In the event, the next biennial Newport-Bermuda race (1976) which as we know is the only full length ocean race that the CCA runs regularly, used the long threatened club modification of IOR. Out west the Ocean Racing Fleet of Southern California based in Los Angeles made its own modifications to the IOR. These penalized high masts, extra big headsails, modified forward depth measurement (to prevent 'bow down trim'). A list of 39 yachts which raced with the fleet, mainly between 35ft and 55ft (10.66–17.76m), showed rises of rating of 1.6ft (though most were less) and falls as big as 3.6ft. No doubt those whose ratings fell were happy until their main rival fell even further!

It is easy enough to proclaim a rating rule, if no one is going to build to it. Having said that, all this is within the American tradition of modifications to a central rating rule, especially as distances increase in hours of flying time from the NAYRU office.

When David Edwards was asked by Jeff Hammond why the IOR seemed to be accepted around the world, yet in the US there was 'debate, resistance and criticism', he seemed genuinely to understand it, rather like William Pitt in the eighteenth century, a chapter head, for he said

'It is historical in origin: there have always been a number of rules in America. The Storm Trysail Club had its own rule and over the years there were a number of big upsets in the CCA over its own rule. Here [in USA] there is a belief that you can solve the problem of the obsolete boat by the rule. In other countries it is a hope, here it is a belief – it's a religious difference.

'Another problem is that IOR is regarded here as a foreign sort of thing, a European thing. Many people started with an antipathy to the hull measurements because they were based on the RORC rule. That was reinforced because the last generation of CCA rule boats tended to rate high under IOR, higher than the owners thought they should – and probably rightly, too. Our attempts to cope with this did not work out well. We just created new problems.[30]

A peace is bought
Enough of tensions and their examples! Lynn Williams and his friends were never going to be happy with the IOR or indeed working with those of the RORC tradition. As early as 1973, not long therefore after the *Cascade* row – for a row it was – senior members of NAYRU/CCA asked MIT, Cambridge, Massachu

setts, to initiate a research programme for a possible new rating rule. Funds were duly provided for this, from these American racing yacht owners, who were then one of the most wealthy circles in the world.

Dr Jerry Milgram was one researcher. Another was Professor Nick Newman MSc ScD, Professor of Naval Architecture at MIT. In March 1975 Newman came to Southampton University, England. There he proposed a new kind of what he called 'handicapping'. This would be based on

> 'hypothetical performance predictions determined by hydro-dynamic and aerodynamic theories, empirical towing tank tests and *full size results from existing race data.*'

There would also be 'special instruments and techniques for measuring boats'[31]

The British, who thought this was going to be a relaxed academic survey, were suddenly told that work was well in hand to make this the basis of a new 'handicapping' system in the USA. A year later USYRU resolved at its annual meeting for

> 'a handicap rule to parallel the IOR development (*sic*) rule'

Extremely optimistic forecasts were made by Lynn Williams and others[32] of work already undertaken at MIT. Many readers will recognize these events as the birth of the Measurement Handicap System (MHS), which in due course became the International Measurement System (IMS). Its further course, including that in the 1980s which was in parallel with the fully operating IOR, will be traced in the next chapter.

In December 1975, Williams invited David Edwards to come to MIT Boston and discuss the new system. He said

> '... the variable time allowance system is already very close to being usable'[33]

At the meeting would be the technicians and also Olin Stephens, C.W. Lapworth, J.A. McCurdy, Gordon M. Curtis Jr and Mark Baxter. Strangely this was a CCA group and not USYRU. Edwards sent his reply as chairman of the Offshore Rating Council

> '... I am disappointed that the CCA does not feel able to adopt IOR Mark IIIA for the Bermuda race ... this breach is bound to

be viewed with great concern by those responsible for the rule.

'I do not feel it would be right for the ORC to appear to be negotiating with the technical committee of any club, even one so important as the CCA. Therefore I do not think that the meeting which you propose in Boston ought to take place . . .'[34]

So the CCA and subsequently USYRU in the person of Ken Weller and his small staff proceeded with MHS. The ORC and the rest of the world and indeed many in the USA raced on under IOR, though each year reducing in numbers. From the latter the pressures of these American yachtsmen, who had never been happy with it, were removed.

But in parallel with the change (above) in the Bermuda race, the agreement to combine the two great rules which had come together in the 1960s was undermined.

IOR in the 1980s

There were disagreements about IOR in other places than America, but they were simply not conducted at the same intensity. For instance *The Daily Telegraph*, London, ran lengthy letters in its main correspondence column, 'for' and 'against', which would be unlikely today. The original letter by Bruce Fraser was full of the customary allegations: the boats broached, could not be converted to cruisers, needed costly electronics and winches, scores of sails, the rule was complex and dominated by American designers.

Replies quickly came, among others, from Dick Carter, Nahant, MA (agreed to separate classification, but the rule was seaworthy), Mark Baxter, Chicago (the rule was fine, but the CCA was trying other systems!), Hugh Evans, Cowes (smaller crews should be compulsory), A.J. Coleman of the Folkboat Association (IOR boats were unseaworthy; people should write to the RYA) and a reasoned defence from Mary Pera[35]. Fascinatingly came a letter from Anthony Heckstall-Smith, mentioning that he was now over 70, but recalling his father, Brooke Heckstall-Smith and his uncle Malden Heckstall-Smith.[36]

'. . . I found myself in a storm of controversy that raged between my father and my uncle. The former who held that ocean racing was a dangerous sport, *pointed out that any rating rule, however well intended, was bound to stimulate designers to 'cheat the rule' in order to win with the result that they would produce expensive racing machines. My uncle as first secretary of the Ocean Racing Club had devised the first ocean racing rule, a formula to rate a motley group of cruising yachts.*

'*History has proved my father right. This is not the first time in the past 100 years that a rating rule drawn up by designers (in the case of the IOR, two of them American) has produced thoroughly undesirable and impractical boats. One immediately recalls the famous J class, built to the American Universal rule, some of whose bones are to be found in the mud around our shores*'.

Thus an eye witness of history gave pause for reflection.

Earlier in this chapter were mentioned well supported major events using IOR. The numbers given there show that such IOR support did not really fall off until about 1986-87. After that it was down hill all the way.

The graph of numbers of teams in the RORC Admiral's Cup is particularly important (**Fig 7.9 again**). After all it represented the ability of many countries to field three boat teams of the latest IOR yachts. The USA, where there was so much feeling against the rule, actually provided a team every year until 1993, the last year of IOR, but perhaps this was a result of the size of the country.

As MHS was introduced into the big races in the USA, it turned out that fleets were often about equally split. But the waters were muddied, for IOR could not be loudly castigated year after year without serious doubt and damage, yet the new MHS was soon seen to be even more complex, certainly more expensive and not appealing to most racing at area and club level. The latter boats increasingly turned to a system that had for a number of years been used locally on the west coast, Performance Handicap Racing Fleet (or, in its early days, Pacific HRF), or PHRF (Chapter 9). PHRF expanded rapidly in the US in 1979-80.

So we see in the Marblehead to Halifax, Canada, race, first sailed in 1905, the following numbers of starters in IOR, PHRF and MHS respectively for 1983, 35, 35, 19; 1985 21, 39, 19; 1987 20, 28, 35. It was not a satisfactory sight.[37] Robert Johnstone of J-Boats fame quoted the following classes appearing for a regatta on Narragansett Bay in early 1980: 7 PHRF A, 8 PHRF B, 5 IOR, 8 PHRF C, 5 MORC A, 4 MORC (Midget Ocean Racing Club rule) B, 12 J-24 ODs.

Who's in charge?

In 1978 David Edwards handed over the chairmanship of ORC to John Roome, like himself both a London solicitor and a previous commodore of the RORC. Both were also members of the Royal Yacht Squadron, Roome later actually becoming commodore of that exclusive body. Roome was ORC chairman for nine years (the longest so far of anyone). He sailed a Contessa 38, an 'evergreen' S & S design of early 1970s vintage which he raced to great success under RORC, IOR and later rules. His successor in 1987 was an Irish member of the RORC and RYS, John Bourke, whose record will be examined later.

The British in the persons of members of their most elevated clubs did not rule quite as it might appear! As mentioned, Olin J. Stephens II returned to the chairmanship of the International Technical Committee in 1976 at the age of 68. He handed over to one its members, the busy yacht designer and wit from San Diego, California, Gary Mull. The latter virtually paralleled Roome, handing over in 1987 to Nicola Sironi, an Italian.

Some would say that the international Chief Measurer, Robin Glover had more influence on the rule and certainly its detail than anyone. He had a high knowledge of computers before they were in general use and being unconnected with any design office or commercial side of yachting and also working full time for the ORC, he was as impartial as anyone. He also got on extremely well with Stephens. (In the tradition of the American designer/British measurer combination). After 12 years in the job he handed over in 1984 to Ken Weller, who as we have seen was already the US chief measurer. Weller combined both jobs from USYRU offices in Newport, RI. The previous British Rating Secretary (1977-82) with extensive technical qualifications, Keith Ludlow, was made his deputy (see also Appendix II).

As for the council of the ORC, this had always comprised representatives from countries using the IOR. Unlike the IYRU which consisted of all the world's yachting authorities, it comprised single or groups of ocean racing nations, though not necessarily because they had just a few IOR boats. For instance the USA and UK had three representatives each, France had one and two persons looked after Germany, Austria and Switzerland. The council seldom disputed (disputes) the long and detailed technicalities of minor or even major rule changes (if the difference is detectable) recommended by its principal officers.

The rule over which these gentlemen presided battled on quite successfully and acceptably 'against' the latest designs particularly in the level rating classes which they also controlled and regulated. In the mid-eighties another difficulty was the encroachment of other rating rules for ocean racing. All that need be said in this chapter is that the most loyal institution to IOR, the RORC, installed a second rule in conjunction with its French opposite number Union Nationale pour la Course au Large (UNCL), the Channel Handicap System (CHS). CHS was intended for cruiser racers and outdated IOR boats. That was in 1984, but (as will be seen in Chapter 9) it began to erode the British and French IOR events.

The ORC and Gary Mull in particular viewed CHS and other regional rules with alarm as world numbers of IOR certificated yachts fell each year. In a panic measure in 1985 with the cooperation of USYRU and particularly recommended by Gary Mull, the American MHS was adopted by ORC as a second rating rule. It was renamed the International Measurement System (IMS). The ill starred intention was that it would mop up the cruiser racers, leaving the IOR to cater for the out and out racers. In the next chapter, it will be seen what actually happened.

The final formula
Although the IOR manual expanded to the inflationary dimensions mentioned above, the basic formula towards the end of its effective life looked little changed; the old combination of the Seawanhaka and Universal rules. However there were many added factors as well as immensely complex sub-formulae for arriving at the main visible components.

As it had been for many years, the formula was split into MR (measured rating) which was then inserted in a further formula to give R (rating). So IOR Mark III read[38]

$$MR = \{(0.13L \times SC)/(B \times D)^{1/2}) + 0.25L + 0.2SC + DC + FC\} \times DLF$$

$$R = MR \times EPF \times CGF \times MAF \times SMF \times LRP \times CBF \times TPF$$

Here is a kind of potted history of the rule and its antecedents. Each factor was added to bar some rule cheater or unwanted emerging developement. Remembering that each factor has extensive club clauses, the symbols represent:

L rated length; SC sail value; B rated beam; D rated depth; DC draft correction; FC freeboard correction; DLF displacement length factor ('penalizes' light displacement); EPF engine and propeller factor; CGF centre of gravity factor (as invented for IOR); MAF moveable appendage factor (trim tabs, twin rudders, bilge boards); SMF spar material factor (carbon fibre and exotics penalty); LRP low rigging penalty (chicken stay penalty); CBF centreboard factor (credit for board, but not on new designs); TPF trim penalty factor (the old bow down problem).

The huge number of factors and measurements involved in the rule are shown in a reproduction of an official listing in **Fig 7.18**.

In the same way that attempts were made to correct rules at the turn of the century by altering constants, it is worth noting the kind of changes solemly debated by 'break-away' fleets from IOR. Again it has to be said that it is 'easy' to run rules, when there is no possibility of their being designed to. For instance one of the Bermuda race changes altered the factor of L from 0.13 to 0.115, while the Southern Californian organizers chose the same constant at 0.09 and removed the 0.25L altogether. The fact that these authorities published at the time a list of the resultant changes of the time allowances of their regular competitors gives a clue to how such fiddling was arrived at.

A selection of the look of the last racers to be designed to the IOR including a yacht that started in round the world races in 1989 and 1993 is seen in **Figs 7.19-7.23**.

Corrections, many of them over the years to the rule are one thing, but there was another feature which arose from time to time. This is the 'rating scandal' when some boat, usually a winner, is found later to have been carrying a grossly incorrect rating to her advantage. (No one worries about a disadvantaged one except its owner). There were several of these. While some technical aspects of measuring were to blame, it is fair to say that it was more a function of rule complexity and the geographical spread of measurers and rating offices.

After the 1981 SORC in Florida, two top notch yachts with crack crews selected for shipping to England for the Admiral's Cup, *Williwaw* and *Arcadia*, both 40ft (12.19m) LOA, were remeasured and found to be 1.0 and 1.2ft respectively higher in rating. Another boat which had actually won the circuit, *Louisiana Crude*, was disqualified when found incorrectly measured, though this was disputed by the owner. *Williwaw's* owner was initially banned from racing for two years, after it was found that a member of the crew had loaded the bilge with water at measurement. Cross law suits followed with various outcomes, but the incidents in such high profile competition obviously did not help the rule.

In 1982, the 44ft (13.41m) *Victory of Burnham*, a British team member in the previous year's Admiral's Cup was found to have been carrying an IOR rating over one foot too low, 33.1 against the correct 34.5, when measured in America. British measurers flew out to double check with their American colleagues and it was revealed that the depth measurements were the culprit owing to

ALPHABETICAL INDEX OF SYMBOLS IN THE RULE

Suffix S on freeboards FFS, FAS etc. 1005.   Indicates standard or measured ashore.
Suffix A on sail areas or rating, RSATA, RA ,1105.   Indicates Mk III A.

Symbol	Para.	Meaning	Symbol	Para.	Meaning
ABS	209	American Bureau of Shipping	CGF	712	Center of Gravity Factor
ACG1	332	AOCG Factor	CGFA	1108	CGF Mark III A
ACG2	332	AOCG Factor	CGFB	712	Calculated CGF of the Boat
AFPM	APX8	Aft Flotation Point Freeboard (Meas.)	CGFM	712	Minimum CGF
AFPV	APX8	Aft Flotation Point Vertical Offset	CMD	326.1 B	Center Midship Depth
AGO	327.3	After Girth Overhang	CMDI	335	CMD Immersed
AGS	311.2 A	After Girth Station	CPD	APX7	Pendulum Deflection
AGSL	332.4	Aft Girth Slope	CRM	APX7	Righting Moment 1 Degree
AIGS	311.2 B	After Inner Girth Station	CSF	711	Crew Stability Factor
AOC	332	After Overhang Component	CW	APX7	Inclining Weight
AOCC	333	AOC Corrected	CWD	APX7	Weight Distance
AOCG	332	AOC Girth	D	338	Rated Depth
AOCP	332	AOC Profile	DB	508	Base Draft
APD	APX7	Pendulum Deflection	DC	511	Draft Correction
APH	609.1 A	Aperture Height	DF	611	Propeller Drag Factor
APSL	332.5	Aft Profile Slope	DLF	340	Displacement Length Factor
APSLC	332.5	Aft Profile Slope Corrected	DLFA	1108	Ditto Mark III A
APB	609.1 B	Aperture Width Bottom	DM	324	Draft Measured
APT	609.1 B	Aperture Width Top	DMC	324.1	Draft Measured Correction
ARM	APX7	Righting Moment 1 Degree	DMT	324	Draft Measured Total
AW	APX7	Inclining Weight	DPD	APX7	Pendulum Deflection
AWD	APX7	Weight Distance	DRM	APX7	Righting Moment 1 Degree
B	319	Rated Beam	DSPL	509	Displacement
BA	321.3	Beam Aft	DW	APX7	Inclining Weight
BADS	877	BAS Schooner Foresail	DWD	APX7	Weight Distance
BADX	879	BAS Schooner Foresail	EDL	609.2 C	Strut Drive Length
BADY	854	BAS Mizzen	E	836.1	Foot of Mainsail
BAI	321.4	Beam Aft Inner	EB	865,875	Distance Between Masts
BAL	836.2	Sheet Limit Main Boom	EBC	881	EB Corrected
BALF	873	Sheeting Limit Schooner Foresail	EC	836.3	Foot of Mainsail Corrected
BALY	852.2	Sheet Limit Mizzen	EF	873	Foot of Schooner Foresail
BAPSL	332.5	Base Aft Profile Slope	EFC	873	EF Corrected
BAS	838	Boom Above Sheerline	EM	604	Engine Moment
BBS	318	B below Sheerline	EMF	605	Engine Moment Factor
BCOR	1202	BWL Corrected	EPF	601	Engine and Propeller Factor
BD	841	Boom Diameter	ESD	609.2 J	Exposed Shaft Depth
BDF	873	BD Schooner Foresail	ESL	609.2 A	Exposed Shaft Length
BDR	339	Base Displacement Ratio	EW	602	Engine Weight
BDY	857	BD Mizzen	EWD	603	Engine Weight Distance
BF	321.1	Beam Forward	EY	852.1	Foot of Mizzen
BFI	321.2	Beam Forward Inner	EYC	852.3	EY Corrected
BHA	323.1	Buttock Height Aft	FA	328.3	Freeboard Aft
BHAI	323.2	Buttock Height Aft Inner	FAI	328.4	Freeboard Aft Inner
BL1-5	845	Batten Lengths	FAM	329.A	Freeboard Aft Measured
BLP	840.1	Batten Leech Penalty	FB	402	Base Freeboard
BLPS	873	BLP Schooner Foresail	FBI	328.7	Freeboard Base of I
BLPY	856	Batten Leech Penalty Mizzen	FBM	328.9	Freeboard at BMAX (also 320.1A)
BMAX	310	Maximum Beam	FC	401	Freeboard Correction
BPD	APX7	Pendulum Deflection	FD	326.1 A	Forward Depth
BRM	APX7	Righting Moment 1 Degree	FDI	335	FD Immersed
BS1-5	873	Batten Lengths Schooner Foresail	FDIC	337	FDI Corrected
BSC	317	Beam Sheer Correction	FDS	313.1	Forward Depth Station
BW	APX7	Inclining Weight	FF	328.1	Freeboard Forward
BWD	APX7	Weight Distance	FFD	328.5	Freeboard Forward Depth
BWL	320	Beam Waterline	FFI	328.2	Freeboard Forward Inner
BWL1	1202	Ditto Calculated	FFM	329.A	Freeboard Forward Measured
BY1-5	861	Mizzen Batten Lengths	FFPM	APX8	Fwd Flotation Point Freeboard (Meas.)
CBDA,B	706	Centerboard Center	FFPV	APX8	Fwd Flotation Point Vertical Offset
CBF	512	Centerboard Factor	FGO	327.2	Forward Girth Overhang
CBFA		Ditto Mark III A	FGS	311.1 A	Forward Girth Station
CBLD	507	Centerborad CG Lateral	FIGS	311.1 B	Forward Inner Girth Station
CCAI	323.4	Curve Correction Aft	FJ	328.8	Freeboard Foremast Stay
CCC)			FM	403	Measured Freeboard
CCF)			FMD	328.6	Freeboard Mid Depth
CCIC)			FOC	330	Forward Overhang Component
CCIM)	326.2	Curvature Corrections at	FSP	814	Forestay Perpendicular
CCIO)		Depth Stations	G	APX7	Gaff Length
CCM)			GD	311.3	Girth Difference
CCO)			GDFI	311.1 C	Girth Difference Forward Inner
CD	504	Centerboard Extension	GF	APX7	Foresail Gaff

Fig 7.18 *Rule inflation in IOR. Symbols for measurements and derivations from measurements on just one of two pages. Over twenty years, factor after factor was added.*

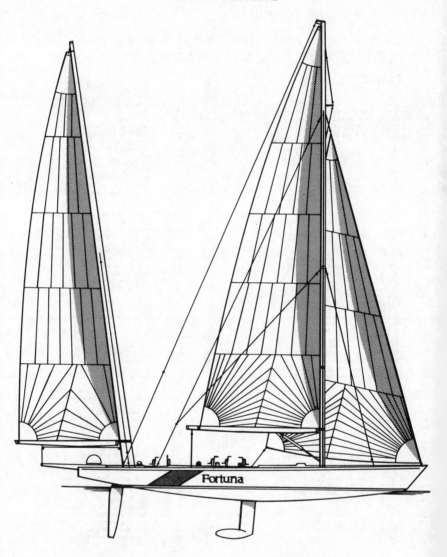

Fig 7.19 *The reader by now has seen that the end of rating rules is signalled by the arrival of freaks, often quite expensive ones. Here is* Fortuna *a ketch built for the 1993 Royal Naval Sailing Association Whitbread round the world race. The rating authorities were warned some years earlier that ketches with excessive sail plans would appear, but refused to act.* Fortuna, *a Spanish entry with an English skipper, lost both her masts on the first leg of the event.*

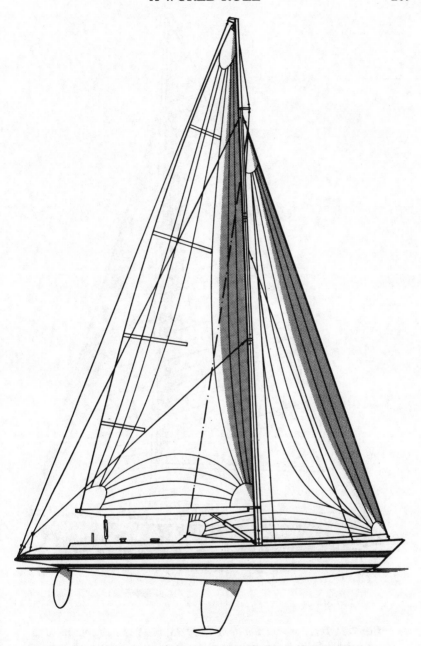

Fig 7.20 *An IOR design for the Whitbread round the world race 1989-90,* Satquote British Defender, *LOA 81ft (24.7m). French design (Francis/Faroux), built in England. By this time profiles in IOR all showed narrow keels with bulb and substantial sail area.*

Fig 7.21 *IOR production design, SJ 35, in 1981 and continued to sail successfully for a number of years when in competent hands. Design by Stephen Jones, LOA 34ft 7in (10.56m), beam 11ft 5in (3.49m), displacement 7600 pounds (3450 kg), said to have half displacement on lead keel. Note foretriangles and sail proportions and aspect ratio have moderated since 1970s, but area is actually as large or larger.*

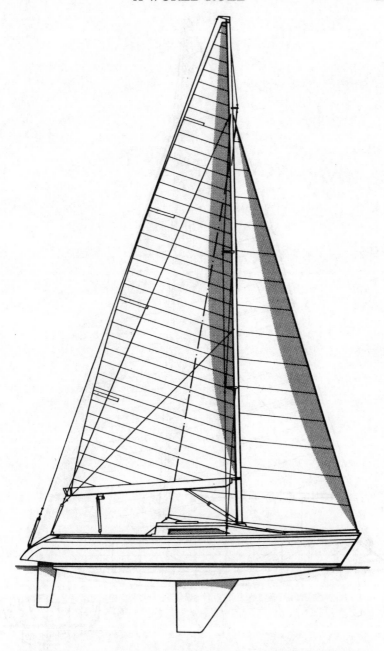

Fig 7.22 *Admiral's Cup 1983 design,* Justine IV *by Tony Castro. It rated 30ft IOR which was the cup minimum rating (LOA 40ft, 12.19m), displacement 12,500 pounds (5670 kg);* compare this weight with the 1971 Cervantes *of same LOA in* **Fig 7.7** *(nearly half!)*

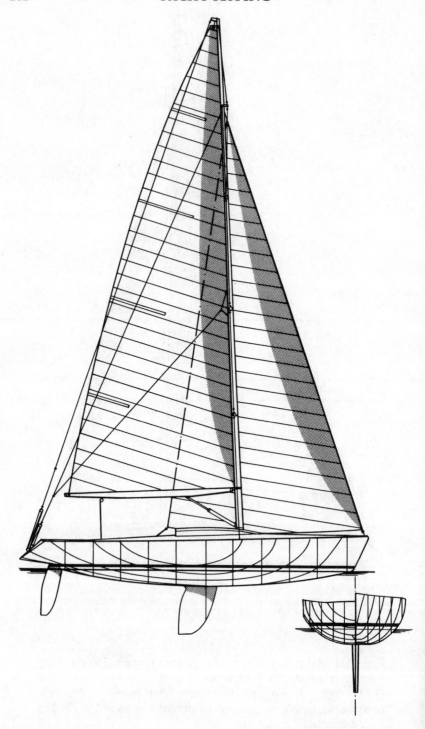

inaccuracy and incorrect stations on the hull. The RORC instituted an enquiry, chaired by David Edwards, which found the original owner, Peter de Savary, and designer, Ed Dubois, who had earlier queried the favourable figures, were exonerated, but the measurer on the ground was largely to blame together with his immediate superior, Keith Ludlow, the RORC rating secretary. The latter two therefore resigned their posts.[39]

The contrast between the English participants accepting the enquiry by members of the London club, while the Americans briefed their lawyers is instructive.

A year later *Szechwan*, an Australian member of the Southern Cross (Sydney-Hobart international team race) team, was found to have been rating one foot too low at 29.1ft IOR, the discovery being made as she was about to be shipped to Hawaii for international racing. The error had arisen from computer calculations of the freeboards. There were a number of other cases over the years, mostly in more local racing, which attracted attention in their respective countries. One must declare however that they were a tiny minority in what was still the biggest number of boats by far ever to be measured to a single rating rule.

Fig 7.23 *The ultimate shape of IOR, 1989 and 20 years after the rule was first announced. Compare this hull shape, rig size and proportions with all earlier IOR racers. This is* Jamarella, *50ft Admiral's Cup successful contender, owned by Alan Gray, designed by Bruce Farr OBE, a New Zealander based in Annapolis, Maryland. Features in IOR boats of this final stage included light displacement, latest keel and rudder profiles as shown, internal ballast, large sail area with fractional rig, wide open cockpits, large crews which lined the weather rail, mild depth measurement and point measurement distortion; indeed there appears to be a distinct whiff of the skimming dish.*

8 Scatter

'*To innovate is not to reform*' – Edmund Burke, 1796

'*Although possession was of greater value than principle, nevertheless, the greater was thrown away for the less, the unworkable pursued at the sacrifice of the possible*' – Barbara Tuchman: The March of Folly[1]

'*Rule 01.00.00 Introduction: In January 1976 the Offshore Committee of USYRU adopted a resolution for a new handicapping system for those yachtsmen who prefer a handicap rule, as opposed to a design rule. The system was called the Measurement Handicap System or MHS. It provides for measuring and the calculating of predicted speeds and intrinsically provides for derivation of time allowance without the use of tables . . . The purpose is to protect the existing fleet rather than encouraging investment in a new rule beating yacht . . .*' – from IMS Rule Section 1 1989

'*I do perceive a divided duty*' – Shakespeare, Othello Act I Scene 3

I T SEEMED DIFFICULT to escape from that haunting logo of the child in a broad rimmed hat. It was not only the tee-shirts, belts and baseball caps, but somehow the stickers were in the cars, the clubs and an amazing number of roadsigns. Some were still there years later; the local authorities maybe finding them inoffensive (**Fig 8.1**). *Jamarella* was just the name of a boat. It was neither commercial nor aggressive. *Jamarella* in summer 1989 was the big boat of the British Admiral's Cup team and her owner Alan Gray was team captain. She had been designed that very year by Bruce Farr and built in England, the latest IOR race machine. She also fitted the rules of the IOR 50 class, a self organized mainly American division within the IOR rule with a limit of 41ft rating.

The pretty face and her summer hat were a symbol of an all out

214

Fig 8.1. *Then impossible to escape from: the logo of* Jamarella.
'Last' of the great campaigns by the British for the Admiral's Cup under IOR.

campaign with permanent shore base in the Solent area, professionals in key positions on board and a determination to beat the
other thirteen nations which came to England to take part in the
Cup races. In the event this was achieved.

Admiral's Cup '89

If IOR was giving way to other rating systems for ordinary racing,
it still seemed to be attracting the best for the top events. Andrew
Preece, an offshore correspondent, sailing on an Irish team boat,
Hitchhiker II, wrote

> 'The Champagne Mumm Admiral's Cup shows little sign of
> suffering the decline experienced in other areas of IOR. This
> year's competition will be as closly fought as ever. True there are
> fewer teams but the standard is high'[2]

Other remarks at the same time are revealing

> 'The addition [over previous years] of a long inshore race shifts
> the points emphasis to the inshore races. The significance of the
> Fastnet race is reduced from 37.5 per cent in 1983 to 35 per cent
> in 1985-87 and to 31 per cent now [1989]. *Changes in the TMF
> mean that a 50ft class will give around 40 seconds an hour less to a
> One Tonner, which is as much as an hour in a typical Fastnet race.
> However the leading One Tonners beat the 50 footers by as much as
> four hours on corrected time in 1987.*
> 'A look around the fleet discloses more older boats than in
> 1987, partly because age allowance has been introduced to

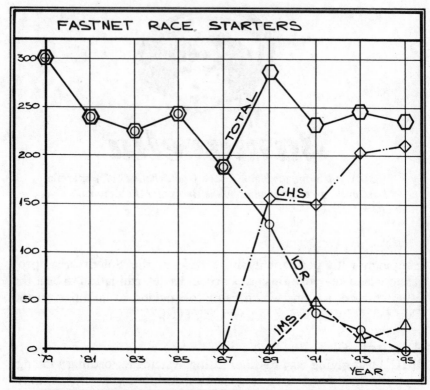

Fig 8.2 *Change over in the Fastnet race and also (right) its amazing overall growth since inception. The total numbers columns can probably be divided into three periods: slow growth to 1957; rapid increase from 1959 to 1973; then slight drop after 1979 storm and steadying to about 250 each year. The other graph (above) shows how IOR was swapped for CHS, after the 1987 Fastnet suffered from the decline of IOR.*

Admiral's Cup racing...

'The Admiral's Cup remains the pinnacle of offshore racing. At this high level the IOR is entirely satisfactory and is providing for top level sailors racing of a standard that has never been bettered'

In fact out of the 52 starters, 22 were built in 1988 or 1989; that is since the last Admiral's Cup. One reads above yet again the influence of time allowances and age allowances beyond that of the actual rating rule. Yet this was to prove the last major turn out of the IOR. The famous fixtures went on: the One Ton and other Ton

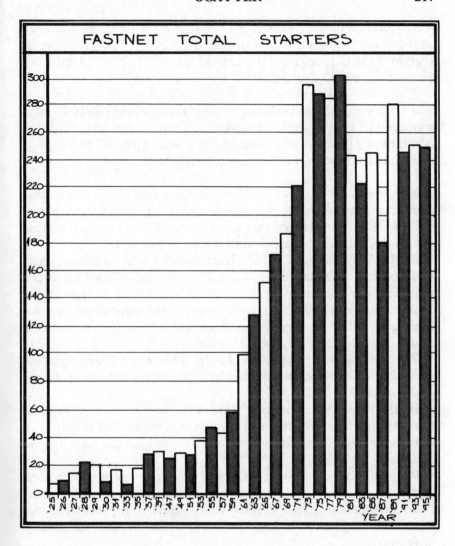

FASTNET TOTAL STARTERS

Cups, the Kenwood Cup in Hawaii and the Admiral's Cup itself in
1991 and 1993, with 8 and 7 full teams respectively (**Fig 7.9**,
previously), but the world overall numbers, we already know, fell
fast, while in the USA they were all but gone, just a few enthusiasts
turning up at the international meetings, albeit with excellent
individual boats.

End of IOR
The IOR was a long time dying. The last IOR One Ton Cup was at
Marseille in 1994, the last Half Ton, Bayona, Spain 1993. The

Two Ton had been recreated in 1991 at 35.05 ft IOR, but was only sailed three times until it terminated in 1993. The last year in regular RORC races for IOR entries was 1991. **Fig 8.2 and 8.3** show the change of rating use in the Fastnet and other races.

The causes of the world wide eclipse of IOR between about 1990 and 1994 were as follows. Some of these reasons apply to IOR only; some will be seen to apply whatever the international rating rule for ocean racing (anticipating matters, they will apply to IMS racing, though the authorities did not necessarily admit this).

1. Kevlar was allowed in sails (1985) without additional rating: this drove out a number of owners (and caused the resignation of one British ORC delegate) who were not prepared to re-equip with this expensive, difficult to handle and (then) fragile cloth.
2. At the 1989 Admiral's Cup, John Bourke, who, we have seen, had become chairman of ORC, held a meeting of owners to ask their opinion on the rule. They asked him not to change it. Of course they did, since all their boats were optimized to take legitimate full advantage of the current rule. *He almost immediately declared a six-year freeze on IOR changes.*

The 'rule cheaters' had taken charge! This was a green light for designers to explore and exploit any possibilty for lower rating without fear.[3]
3. In 1985 the ORC adopted MHS/IMS as a cruiser-racer rule, thus inviting race organizers to split their entries. This might have attracted more boats, but more often than not simply reduced the IOR entry in a race.
4. Regional and local rating rules and handicap systems increased in use, on the principle that once over a critical mass they attracted boats away from IOR. Typical were PHRF (long established), CHS, Danish Handicap. In some cases, see below, they eventually took over.
5. World economics: these are never decisive, but assist in pushing at an open door. The 1987 stock market crash had no immediate effect, but we now know that after a two year delay it did so. The property market collapsed in many ocean racing nations from 1990 on, as did asset values.
6. The design of IOR yachts from mid-eighties on became wholly unsuitable for conversion to cruising boats in deck and cockpit layout, accommodation, tenderness, keel configuration, amount of inside ballast and rig. They were therefore potentially unsaleable.
7. At its November 1989 meeting the ORC was presented by the RORC with a proposed revision of IOR to correct outstanding

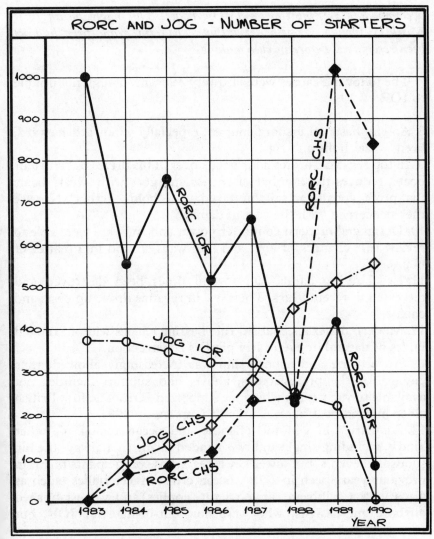

Fig 8.3 *How IOR support waned between 1983 and 1990 in its use in England in races of the Royal Ocean Racing Club and Junior Offshore Group.*

unpopular features, including some of the above. *A proposal to examine it was rejected by the the council by one vote, after American opposition and lobbying. The RORC was expected to try it out in Britain, but instead declared IMS to be a second rule for its races. This sequence as much as anything spelt the destruction of IOR. The ORC then declared it was looking for a new 'grand prix' rule, which would*

accommodate existing top level IOR boats. This might be an IOR
Mark IV though no one believed that. The term 'grand prix' had not
been recognized before in rule making.

The following causes were also very relevant, though not unique
to IOR.

8. An emphasis on inshore courses, especially windward-leeward,
bred 'weak' hulls and rigs.
9. In top regattas, professionals took over. This drives out amateur
boats, reduces the number of entries and goes with 'weak' boats
that professionals can sail 'on the edge' or 'hold together'. Nor are
they concerned with the cost of damage.
10. Designers' modern computer power and software were able to
review rule changes, if any, and find ways around in a matter of
hours.
11. Level rating bands had several times been destroyed and
recreated in recent years. Their use in regattas drove up costs and
choice.
12. Modern materials enabled rule beating shapes without the old
limits of natural or even early plastics construction.
13. Advertising and sponsorship was increasingly allowed, thus
paying for the professionals, above, and support facilities not
available to yachtsmen who once supported IOR. The first British
all sponsored boat in an Admiral's Cup was in 1991.
14. Popularity in genuine offshore and ocean racing of 'other
kinds', including single and two-handed racing (not always the big
sponsored events, but lower key races, whose participants might in
previous years been in IOR), ocean cruiser racer rallies (such as
Canaries to Caribbean, same stricture applies) and well established
offshore one-designs, who were now out-of-date for IOR, but
continued on their own merits.

IOR ended not with a bang but with a whimper. For instance
countries late in the cycle went on IOR racing and there was the
mysterious list of IOR yachts, never previously accounted for, on
the coasts of Russia, the ex-Soviet Baltic states and Poland. As a
result the Quarter Ton Cup continued in the Baltic until as late as
1996, the boats being oldish ones of similar performance. Maybe
like other rating rules in history IOR will continue in one or more
small pockets, regulated by the owners (and rightly so), preserving
the long used formulae of American and British rule makers of
yesterday in waters far from their original shores.[4]

The return of Jerry Milgram
Not in person, of course, all those years after the great row over
Cascade, but the rule in which he and his colleagues took their
revenge on the IOR came in due course centre stage.

In the previous chapter it was mentioned briefly how, at the
urging of Gary Mull, chairman of the ITC and other Americans,
MHS was adopted as an international rule. This was simply done
by transferring the authority for MHS from USYRU to ORC and
naming it the International Measurement System, IMS. It was
done in a hurry and there was no 'bargaining', as had occurred in
the creation of IOR. The American rule simply became 'international'. Some Americans who had been running it joined the
ITC, which expanded from its old six or seven to ten. It would
henceforth control both IMS and IOR.

IMS had never proved popular in the US remaining at around
800 certificates each year since 1978, so some in USYRU thought
that making it 'international' would increase interest (it did). The
European members of ORC hoped it would provide a cruiser racer
rule under their control, as in the early days of IOR and recruit
owners who were disappearing rapidly into regional and national
rules (it didn't). Much was made of this 'new rule'. It was not.

Let it not be forgotten that IMS is almost as old as IOR. Moves
towards it started almost as soon as the first adverse reactions to
IOR occurred in the USA, as early as 1973. The USYRU
Handicap Committee, which was seeking a second rule to IOR,
issued in 1975 its statement of objectives and procedure. Abbrevi-
ating the full wording of its six points they were: to reduce cost;
protect existing yachts; to encourage dual purpose yachts; to match
each factor to actual effect on speed; to adjust handicapping [no
doubt meaning time allowances] to weather conditions; to prevent
exploitation of loopholes. These were the objects of experienced
American ocean racing men. One has to say now it was a vote for
motherhood. *No one argues with most of these ideas: the difficulty was
and is how to achieve them.*

No reason was advanced for a great leap from these objectives by
expecting them to be achieved by adopting the H. Irving Pratt
Ocean Race Handicap Project at MIT and turning it as quickly as
possible into a rule of measurement, rating and time allowance.
Dislike of IOR by a few leading American sailors, mainly as we saw
members of the CCA, turned this very forward yacht research
project in the university laboratory, but only a piece of research
among others, for political reasons, into a rating rule. It was said

'In *the new* handicap system it is intended *to rely* upon measuring apparatus *recently devised* at Massachusetts Institute of Technology that allow quick and accurate one time hull measurement... *This will end the problems... once the lines are taken no further hull measurement will ever be required.* (Words in author's italics should have been a warning even then).

'Another part of the research is the Velocity Prediction program, VPP, an elaborate computer program based upon wind tunnel tests, instrumented sailing trials, tank tests, full scale towing tests... The VPP provides a quantitative standard for the effectiveness of any proposed handicap formula...'.[5]

Such was the policy of hope over experience.

When Nick Newman came to talk to the British at Southampton University in 1975 he reported two years work, based on established naval architecture tools such as tank tests, wind tunnels and instrumentation on full size vessels – in this case racing yachts.[6] He declared that more of this work was needed and in order to utilize them that instruments should be developed for measuring hulls. However he had already faired and drawn lines plans of hulls on a computer, thus it would be possible to abolish the point measurements in IOR. *He spent a lot of his lecture in comparing time allowance systems. He did not propose any revision of known rule formulae, for with VPPs they were no longer to be pursued.*

Being the scientist he was, he ended by warning that more input was needed before 'developing a handicap system on the potential speed of each boat'. He warned that results obtained

'so far must be treated as preliminary and utilized with caution'.

Who was suggesting that they be 'utilized' at all? Possibly the professor and his colleagues, Jerry Milgram, Justin 'Jake' E. Kerwin and D.D. Stromeier. In April 1976, Newman sent a message to the USYRU Handicap committee, which was read out there

'in which *he urged an approach from zero base as distinguished from modifications of a pre-existing [existing?] rule.* Mr Stromeier suggested a two step approach; first a revision of IOR *and then a wholly new rule...*'

During 1976 somehow the MIT project became MHS, for the statement more than a decade later, at this chapter head, implies that the decision to measure, rate and race with MHS was taken in that year.

What IMS looked like
And what it looks like today and indeed when first used as MHS in 1976! There have been quite numerous numerical and measurement changes, but the principles have remained the same. These are quite different from all the rules of rating and measurement that we have so far met.

So in November 1985, when MHS changed its name to IMS and came under control of ORC, it had a rule book, computer programs for both measurement and working results and a low key history of development, based on certificates held by 77 yachts in 1978 rising to 926 in 1985, all, of course, within the USA. In 1985 it was said

'Since that time [1976-78] the system has been refined, with more complete modelling of the sail aerodynamics and improvements in *the estimates of* the hull resistance and restoring moment. The description of the VPP developed by the Pratt Project in 1978, has had changes in detail and remains the most complete description of the MHS available. There has been generally good acceptance by the dual purpose boat owners for whom it was intended.'[7]

So the rule which was about to be thrown into the international arena, albeit as a cruiser-racer rule with IOR there to take the keenest racing pressure, had ticked over for a small (in US terms) number of boats and races and without much change on parts of the US east coast and Great Lakes, though not in the west.

It was thought from the earliest days (allegedly unlike IOR) that

'As improvements in speed prediction are developed, they will lead to prompt system changes . . . to protect the existing fleet.'[8]

Why this should have been thought to work for IMS, though it has not for other rating rules, is unknown. Presumably because the speed predictions would correct the rating of every boat. But the very language admitted and still admits that the predictions are not the last word.

IMS is not immune from the problems of all other rating rules. Once the change is made 'to protect the existing fleet' or for any other, perhaps technical reason, designers will input the new elements and come up with the best design for the new factors.

The IMS rule book is devoid of formulae in the old manner, though some sub-formulae do appear that are also within the computer program which calculates the rating. In its own words, for hulls:

'04.00.01 Lines Processing Program accepts data in the form of a set of hull offsets obtained from measuring machine encoded data. It accepts flotation and inclining test data. From these it calculates all hull characteristics required by the VPP, for example it finds displacement, righting moment, sailing lengths, wetted surface and beam to depth ratio. The formulae are expressed in imperial units'.[9]

As mentioned there are few visible formulae on paper and those that appear contain calculus or symbols with complex derivation. For instance the formula for Sailing Length, L is

$$L = .3194 \times (LSM1 + LSM2 + LSM4)$$

LSM1 is for yacht in sailing trim floating upright; LSM2 is for yacht in sailing trim floating with 2 degrees heel; LSM4 is for the yacht in deep (*sic*) condition such that compared to sailing trim it is sunk 0.025LSM1 forward and 0.0375LSM1 aft floating upright.

Again Effective Hull Depth, T is

$$T = 2.07 \times (AMS2/B)$$

B is effective beam arrived at by a long formula including calculus and LSMO (length in measurement trim upright); AMS2 is the area of the largest immersed section for the yacht in sailing trim floating upright, which is in turn found by a formula including the Naperian constant 2.7183, LSMO, defined depth in a vertical direction and working by calculus.

These items are enough to show the reader the character of the rule book, itself only part of the rule, of which the program is a major block plus reference to other rules, especially for sail area, such as IOR in places and IYRU sail area measurement regulations.

Measuring machine. There were two designs of machine originating in Germany or the USA and central to IMS in order to take off complete hull lines, offsets or, to the layman, shape of hull. This is a slow matter and space is required around the boat. However offsets exist for standard classes. As for the physical constraints

'The limitations are what the measurers can take in terms of cold and rain, rather than in the machine. As there is not much guidance internationally for measurers, we [the British] have developed our own mode of accuracy; we believe that this is more stringent than existing practice in the USA. Much time is spent setting up the machine and we use a theodolite to position it each time. This is preferable to tapes which visitors trip over. For a 40ft (12.19m) boat we might take twenty interleaved sightings per side. It can take one day or a day and a half'.[10]

Measurement in the water. This is much the same as IOR, which is unfortunate since freeboards measured physically in all weather conditions and the inclining test were always areas of weakness never fully solved. All these IMS hull readings are entered into a hydrostatic computer program called the LPP (lines prediction program).

Rig measurement. Sail area as in previous rules, especially IOR, is measured with spars, girths, limitations on shape and so on.

Accommodation rules. These were essentially part of the rule, which depended on the boat being a 'proper' cruiser. In later years, the letter of rule was exploited to give fairly empty interiors.

IMS certificate. All the above are processed to create a VPP, velocity prediction program, for the yacht which has been measured. This consists of figures on the rating certificate (**Fig 8.4**). This has on it the usual limitations and dimensions (as seen on IOR and, later, on CHS), draft, displacement, results of inclining test, limit to the number or weight of crew and so on.

But unlike any other rating rule it has a set of speeds for different angles to the wind, close hauled, reaching and running and in different wind speeds from 6 to 20. Then comes to the most important part of all to the user.

Thirty-six numbers giving different time allowances for winds and courses: these are instead of a fixed rating figure of any sort, though here is a single derived allowance called GENERAL PURPOSE HANDICAP (GPH). It is actually the linear random course at 10 knots wind speed.

The kinds of courses listed for each of the different wind

```
IMS RATING CERTIFICATE NO. 2402          IMS AMENDED TO JANUARY 1996        VPP: 14/AUG/96 11:13:15
Based on: FULL MEASUREMENT (Metric)      Offshore Racing Council                 14/AUG/96 12:12:54
                                   [GPH] 19 St James's Place, London
NOT VALID AFTER 31/12/96           564.1         Copyright 1996
```

```
IMS AMENDED TO JANUARY 1996
Cert No 2402                                     SYCORX.OFF  29/APR/96 09:55:10
OFF Meas'd: 00/00/00
            CENTERBOARD AND DRAFT
ECM   0.000   CBRC  0.000   CBMC  0.000   CBTC  0.000
WCBA  0.0     CBDA  0.000   KCDA  0.000   ECE   0.000
WCBB  0.0     CBDB  0.000   ENDPLATE ADJ (KEDA)  0.000
            PROPELLER AND INSTALLATION
PRD  0.420  STI 0.042  ST4 0.112  ST5 0.240  EDL  1.570
PIPA 0.0055
                 FLOTATION DATA
FFM  1.285   FFPS 1.168   SFPP  0.150   SG   1.023
FAM  0.990   AFPS 1.033   SAFP 11.980   WD  13.050
W1  23.000   PD1 41.000   PLM 1510.000  PL 1505.437
W2  46.000   PD2 82.000   GSA 19.400    RSA 6400.0
W3  69.000   PD3 122.000  RM   194.8    RMC  194.8
W4  92.000   PD4 163.000  SMB   7.760
RM2 202.5    RM20 180.0   RM40 143.1    RM60  97.8
RM90 45.9                 CREW ARM (CRA)  1.466
CALCULATED LIMIT OF POSITIVE STABILITY: 123.4 DEGREES
RATIO STABILITY CURVE AREAS, POSITIVE/NEGATIVE 3.936
      HYDROSTATICS    --MEASUREMENT TRIM---SAILING TRIM--
KEEL DRAFT                 (DHKO)  2.594   (DHKA)    2.637
2ND MOMENT LENGTH          (LSMO) 10.918   (LSM1)   11.333
DISPLACEMENT (WEIGHT)      (DSPM)  6896    (DSPS)    7996
WETTED SURFACE             (WSM)  30.90    (WSS)    33.04
VCG FROM OFFSETS DATUM (For CLUB RM)       (VCGD)   -0.222
VCG FROM MEASUREMENT TRIM WATERLINE        (VCGM)   -0.189
INTEGRATED BEAM ATTENUATED WITH DEPTH      (B)       3.134
MAXIMUM SECTION AREA                       (AMS1)    1.465
BEAM/DEPTH RATIO                           (BTR)     4.579
EFFECTIVE DRAFT                            (D)       2.318
 2° HEEL (LSM2) 11.338    25° HEEL (LSM3)  11.487
SUNK     (LSM4) 13.295    AVG LENGTH (L)   11.488
TRIM: 1mm/12.319m-kg      SINK: 1mm/23.175kg
```

```
SAIL AREA: MAIN + FORETRIANGLE + MIZZEN (SA)   91.46
MAIN:  49.68 SPIN: 138.69 GENOA: 63.19 MIZ N:   0.00
     --FORETRIANGLE--      -----MAIN-----   ----MAST-BTNS----
IG  17.115   SPL  4.837   HB   0.210   TL   2.800
MW   0.163   J    4.837   MGT  1.18    MDT1 0.130
GO   0.208   LPG  6.98    MGU  2.00    MDL1 0.203
ISP 17.170   FSP  0.064   MGM  3.45    MDT2 0.121
IM  17.276   LP   7.04    MGL  4.79    MDL2 0.163
HBI  1.040   SFJ -0.010   MSW 25.0     BATX 1.570
MXSL 16.95   MXSMW 8.71   P   15.190   BL1  1.840
SL   16.80   SMW  8.64    E    5.400   BL2  2.920
SPS   4.015  BAL  0.150   BAS  1.775   BL3  1.660
CPIS  2.180  BD   0.180   BLP  3.20    BL4  1.650
CPW          MWT  0.00    MCG  0.00    BL5  0.000
                  ------MIZZEN------
IY   0.000   EY   0.000   BYI  0.000   MDT1Y 0.000
EB   0.000   EY   0.000   BY2  0.000   MDL1Y 0.000
YSD  0.000   BADY 0.000   BY3  0.000   MDT2Y 0.000
YSF  0.000   BALY 0.000   BY4  0.000   MDL2Y 0.000
YSMG 0.000   SMGY 0.000   BY5  0.000   TILZ  0.000
HBIY 0.000   HBY  0.000   MGMY 0.000

ILC WEIGHTED AVERAGE: 634.3                     TMF: 1.0636
```

```
---- YACHT DESCRIPTION ----               RATING OFFICE:
Name:    SHAKESPEARE'S FLOOSIE            Issued:    ROYAL OCEAN RACING CLUB
Sail No: GBR 1991 R                       14/AUG/96     SEAHORSE BUILDING
Class:   BH 41                            Measured:          BATH ROAD
LOA:  12.460m   Beam(MB) 3.670m           11/JAN/96   LIMINGTON, SO41 9SE
Designer: MURRAY
Builder:  BASHFORD                        Revalidation Authority: RORC
Rig:      MASTHEAD SLOOP 146% Jib         Measurer: JULES
Keel/CB:  FIXED KEEL
Propinst: STRUT DRIVE FOLDING             "I CERTIFY THAT I UNDERSTAND MY
FwdAccom: YES    SPIN: SYMMETRIC           RESPONSIBILITIES UNDER THE IMS."
Hullcnst: LIGHT  RudCnst: STNDRD
Forestay: ADJST AFT  InrFstY: NONE        OWNER:..............................
Spreaders: 3 Sets  Jumpers: NONE          MR. WILLIAM PLOOSE
Runners:  2 Sets   Battens: LONG          20 HAMLET WAY
Dates:    AGE:11/1995                      STRATFORD ON AVON
COMMENTS                                    WARWICKSHIRE, CV1
```

```
------ LIMITS AND REGULATIONS ------
Limit of Positive Stability: MEETS REQ    Measurement Inventory: 11/JAN/96
Minimum Displacem't 3854kg:  MEETS REQ    Accommodation Length:  11.927m
Maximum Crew Weight:        845 kg.       Accom Certificate: CRUISER/RACER
Stability Index:           126.6          Plan Approval:           YES

NOTE TO OWNER: The range available to revise crew weight is 529- 977 kg.
```

---- TIME ALLOWANCES IN SEC/MI BY TRUE WIND VELOCITY & ANGLE ----

Wind Velocity:	6kt	8kt	10kt	12kt	14kt	16kt	20kt	CHECKSUM
BEAT ANGLES:	46.0°	43.7°	41.5°	40.1°	39.5°	39.4°	39.6°	289.8
BEAT VMG:	938.1	784.5	714.7	678.8	659.3	648.5	637.4	(5061.3)
R 52°	595.3	510.8	478.3	463.2	454.4	449.2	441.6	(3392.8)
70°	549.4	481.1	457.8	445.8	438.3	432.6	424.4	(3229.4)
A 95°	514.8	458.5	436.0	424.4	416.4	409.9	399.8	(3059.8)
C 110°	524.6	456.2	437.5	412.9	397.0	392.3	380.7	(2973.0)
H 125°	569.4	455.4	435.1	413.6	397.5	371.3	357.8	(3000.1)
135°	650.4	520.7	465.3	432.4	407.3	386.2	349.3	(3226.8)
150°	805.5	625.4	533.0	474.1	457.7	456.2	303.8	(3673.7)
RUN VMG:	930.1	726.8	615.8	545.1	489.3	454.4	406.1	(4168.0)
GYBE ANGLES:	138.5°	141.6°	146.7°	155.6°	166.4°	171.4°	172.8°	(1093.0)

NOTE: To convert any time allowance above to speed in knots: Kt = 3600/TA

WIND-AVERAGED TIME ALLOWANCES FOR SELECTED COURSES

	6kt	8kt	10kt	12kt	14kt	16kt	20kt	CHECKSUM
Windward VMG	1043.5	852.8	754.8	701.6	672.1	655.3	638.5	(5318.6)
Leeward VMG	974.9	758.7	634.4	554.9	500.4	461.0	407.2	(4291.5)
Olympic 6-leg	945.4	762.1	664.3	607.8	573.1	550.1	520.3	(4623.1)
Circular Rndm	767.9	624.0	547.9	504.2	477.1	459.0	434.7	(3814.4)
Non-Spinnaker	854.8	684.2	591.2	536.0	501.4	478.4	450.0	(4096.0)
Ocean for PCS	886.9	694.8	586.3	519.1	474.3	442.4	398.1	(4001.9)

Fig 8.4 *The rating certificate of a yacht under the International Measurement System. The most striking difference from measurement certificates in all other classes is the unprecedented choice of time allowances (in seconds per mile) for varying wind velocities and theoretical courses.*

velocities were: Windward-leeward, Olympic, Circular random, Linear random, non-spinnaker. Later was added an ocean racing course, which assumed the kind of highly variable weather met offshore over a period of time. Linear random was removed.

Circular random meant that in theory the yacht sailed a circle with the wind staying, say, due north the whole time. Linear random assumed a straight line course with the wind going all around the clock equally.

As IMS was invented in America, all these time allowances are in seconds per mile (Chapter 5).

The reader will say immediately, 'Life is not like that; last weekend the wind headed us the whole race, until the last leg which was one sixth of the course and that was a dead run. Also the tide was against us virtually the whole time!' The author will say, 'Right!' We shall be looking at this and related problems.

How the race was conducted

The time allowances vary with each boat and design of boat, so that theoretically there is compensation for conditions that do not suit her. She is not rated on her totality, but on the components which give her a certain performance on a point of sailing in a wind speed. So a boat will receive a better rating in conditions in which she is not so good. In 'her own weather' the rating will 'penalize' her.

Whether you think that is how racing should be conducted is another matter: it is the way IMS is intended to work. **Fig 8.5** shows how main boat features affect different points of sailing. For instance high sail area helps in light weather, but not at all in heavy weather when it is largely reefed. A big mainsail helps reaching, but a big foretriangle helps light to moderate beating.

To run the time allowances at their most basic, the race committee chooses the wind speed and course most closely to fit the description e.g. 16 knots of wind windward-leeward and applies the time allowance for each competitor shown against that on her certificate.

The strongest proponents of IMS would now (1996) admit that such an approach is totally unsatisfactory for well known reasons. Elaborations therefore now exist; these are described below.

IMS progress

Following ORC adoption of the rule, time was needed for distribution, translation and national decisions. By the end of 1988 there were 1160 IMS boats in USA and Canada, 235 in Holland, which had centrally switched all IOR certificates to IMS, 210 in Ger-

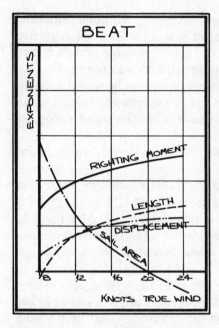

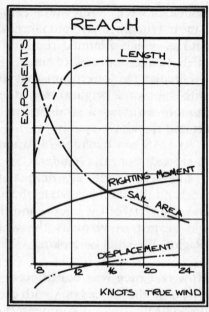

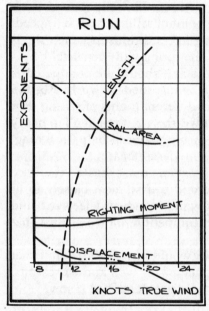

Fig 8.5 *One way of looking at the argument for variable time allowances based on different features of a yacht as derived for IMS. The graphs show how on a beat, reach and run, increase in wind speed benefits or otherwise performance caused by length, displacement, sail area and righting moment respectively.*

many, another country with centralized strong national authority, 110 in Argentina (strong US influence), 29 in Finland, 25 in Britain and other small numbers around.

In Britain the RORC recorded the results in its races where yachts had IMS certificates by 'shadowing' them. So they raced on other rules (IOR or CHS) and the IMS was on paper as an experiment. Everyone waited for the report on this test and the RORC Secretary told the author after the season

> 'I think you can forget IMS; the experiment showed it offered us nothing . . .'.[11]

Imagine the surprise therefore when at the RORC annual dinner, in front of guests, wives and girl friends, the commodore, Jonathan Bradbeer, announced in a speech that in 1989 IMS would become a rating rule in use by the club, starting in the annual Morgan Cup race in June. Efforts would be made to attract entries in the IMS class. Nothing was ever published of the 'results' of the 1988 'IMS trials'. So in 1989 the RORC would run three rating rules in a single race (CHS, IMS, IOR). In the 1987 Fastnet there had only been IOR; in 1989 there were CHS and IOR with IMS shadowed but with prizes and points.

Anticipating here the progress or otherwise of IMS in RORC and Britain, from the season of 1990, a separate class start was given for IMS. This continued for two more seasons, but owing to lack of support and no visible difference in yacht types between those in IMS and those in CHS, the IMS class reverted to being shadowed, though with proper prizes and points, from 1993 onward. From 1995, the RORC abandoned the use of the multiple ratings on the IMS certificate and deduced corrected time of an IMS yacht from a single TMF extracted from the GPH. There is more on IMS time allowances below.

Other race organizers in Britain and Ireland gave IMS trials in a number of races between 1989 and 1992, but after that all gave up using the rule. In early 1993 the director of a very major annual British regatta wrote

> 'We are continually under pressure from the IMS class. Our experience is that these "more than ever" numbers [of entries this year] are a mirage, rather than any practical forecast, but we have said we will provide one class for 1993 and must stick by that'.[12]

The turn out of starters was derisory and that was the last time for an IMS class in Cowes Week.

In the period in which IMS became effective in Europe generally (say, 1988 to 1993), some pleasant cruiser racer yachts were designed and built. Sometimes these were described as 'non-IOR', since they represented offshore experience without the distorting hull or rig features of IOR, rather than any attempt to extract advantage from the minutiae of IMS (**Fig 8.6 – 8.7**).

Running the rule

In November 1988 the Offshore Rating Council met in London. For three years now it had been in charge of two world rules, IOR and IMS. Numbers in IOR continued to fall fast. The more the advantages of IMS were extolled, the less attractive IOR looked. However the ORC under its chairman, John Bourke, attempted to maximize both rules. Yet to most owners it was 'either-or', or even something else nearer home.

A contemporary report by Andrew Preece[13] gave the last appeal of David Edwards (by then 'Hon. President'). Edwards pleaded with the ORC to grasp the issue that mattered and take the required action. He was the most effective speaker of the day. If some of Preece's report was over dramatic, it is fair to quote it as contemporary comment:

'Offshore racing, what there is of it, is a complete and utter shambles... The 50ft class [IOR fixed rating] having been offered a Ton Cup, have said "Thanks, but no thanks", preferring instead to run their own events... it would seem that the ORC has lost its way... then there is the IMS lobby. The Americans are dead set on IMS, the system in which the race officer decides afterwards which sort of race it has been... In this country there is no IMS racing and we know of no plans to hold any. There is therefore this massive rift between the American contingent and the British who wish to modify the IOR as 'IOR 90'. The RORC was virtually told to keep itself to itself by Olin Stephens from the floor, [and not to bring] another variation on to an unsuspecting world, when a perfectly good rule like IMS already existed. In reply John Allenby [for RORC] was disappointed that its carefully developed proposal had been merely brushed aside'.

'The IMS versus IOR battle with no one quite sure which rule is for what and in what direction either or any rules are desired to be heading...'.

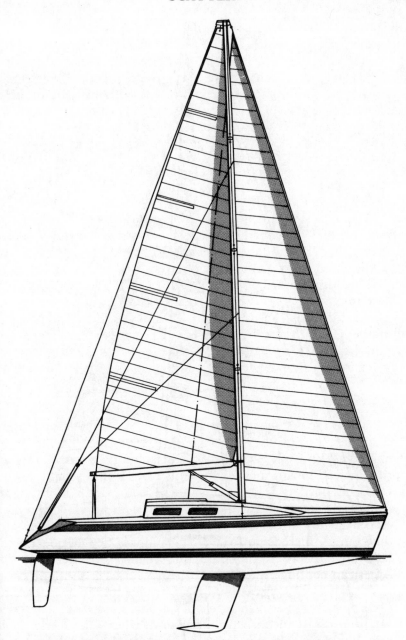

Fig 8.6 *IMS production design after the rule was made international. The Tripp 36 of 1991 designed by Bill Tripp and built in Newport, RI, raced in America and Europe. Intended to do specially well under IMS, it was duly outclassed by later designs. As so often seen previously, the designer did not really get away from the habits of the previous rating rule (IOR)!*

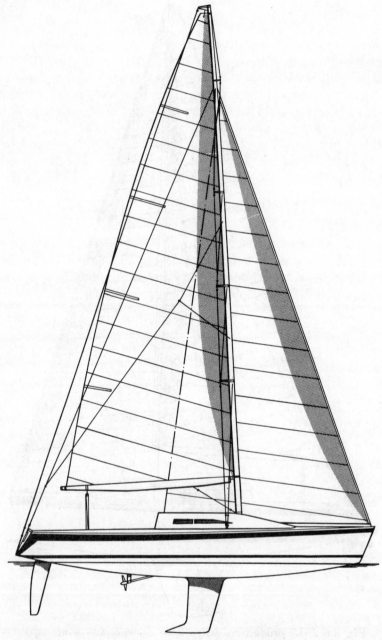

Fig 8.7 *IMS one-off 38ft (11.65m) of 1992. Megalopolis designed by Rob Humphreys was intended for an IMS international series in England, but the yacht may have been compromised to rate reasonably under CHS, where most of her racing actually took place.*

Which rule?

1990 was the year in which the increasing number of IMS rated yachts in the world came to equal the decreasing number of IOR (even if some of these were in the statistic the same boats) (**Fig 8.8**). The problem with keeping IOR for what was becoming known as the 'grand-prix' contests was that there were just too few of them, while numbers of IMS starters were slowly improving (**Fig 8.9**).

At the November 1992 ORC meeting, it was acknowledged that IOR was dying and some new rule was essential for grand prix racing. Modifying the IOR had already been defeated by the Americans. John Bourke spoke to Malcolm McKeag who wrote

'Bourke's answer is to define the characteristics of the yacht that people [which people?] say that they want, then create an entirely new rule to meet it. Simply switching to IMS for grand prix has to be ruled out: the IMS is unsuited to level rating racing and, worse, grand prix pressures would harm the sport of

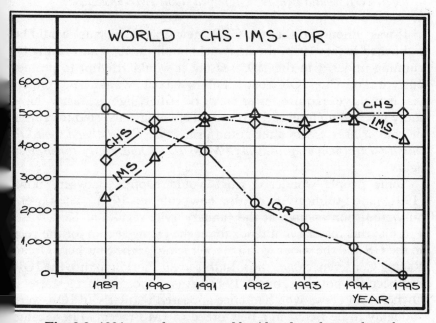

Fig 8.8 *1991 was the year world wide when the number of certificated IMS boats first exceeded IOR registrations. IOR subsequently collapsed; in practice the number of certificates held on, though there were few IOR races. CHS was also in the picture being more or equal to IMS.*

YEAR	ADMIRAL'S CUP TEAMS	SARDINIA CUP TEAMS	BERMUDA RACE IMS	BERMUDA IOR
1985	18	~	~	~
1986	~	12	82	42
1987	14	~	~	~
1988	~	7	99	20
1989	14	~	~	~
1990	~	5	145	0
1991	8	~	~	~

Fig 8.9 *The Admiral's Cup and Sardinia Cup were under fading IOR. The Newport – Bermuda race used IMS and IOR, but the former is seen to take over in 1990.*

the cruiser racers for whom IMS is intended. *All the ills that befell IOR would simply be dumped upon IMS instead*.[14]

It was announced that the GPR (new grand prix rule) would be published in late 1993, the first yachts built in 1994 and racing be running under it in the 1995 season; it would attempt to protect current Ton Cup IOR boats. The new boats would be stronger, less expensive, require fewer crew, be stiffer, lighter, faster, have more internal volume and be capable of being converted to cruiser or club cruiser racers after grand prix days. *The author listened to this list with mounting disbelief! Motherhood had really taken over again.*

Some people wondered what would happen between 'now' (1991) and publication of the new rule in 1993. They were answered soon enough at the January 1992 regatta at Key West, Florida; this major event tends to set the racing season for the year in the US and the wider world of top racing (as the Southern Ocean Racing Conference once did). In this great Florida fixture the IOR had been the hot class, but in 1992 it was reduced to just 9 starters. Owners and crews who had once appeared regularly in IOR were suddenly to be found in a new breed of IMS racers. These came and conquered.

Their owners were not going to hang around waiting for ORC to cogitate. In particular the Farr designed *Gaucho* with plumb ends very deep draft and virtually stripped out despite the IMS accommodation rules was conspicuous. Anger, panic, urgent consultations followed. *IMS, the science based rule which was different, had been breached as had all the rules of old.*

The ORC held an emergency meeting in London on 5 May 1992. It put on an immediate draft penalty and declared that in future

'appropriate corrections might be made in the IMS hydrodynamic model for effective keel draft for application as early as 1993'.[15]

In the event the penalty was either too little or draft could be slightly lessened to avoid it. The new breed of grand-prix racer had arrived to the dismay, yet remarkable complacency of the ORC. If there was ever a time when the council could have come down like a ton of bricks to restore IMS to its proclaimed role was then. It failed lamentably in respect of will and technical application.

After the meeting John Bourke wrote

'We will also have to preserve IMS with the successful introduction of the grand prix rule, which I hope will be able to take place sooner rather than later.' But it was too late already.[16]

Comedy

The RORC had decided in 1991 to run a kind of mini-Admiral's Cup to encourage IMS rated yachts. It would be for three boat teams from any nation, a combination of inshore and offshore races, would be based in Cowes and unlike the Admiral's Cup which ran on IOR (until 1993 remember) the essential aspect was that it was on IMS rating. Some members of ORC, the Germans for instance, did not like this, as they saw IMS being pushed into too hot an arena. However John Dare, the new commodore of RORC, who was also then honorary treasurer of ORC, made a series of pronouncements in writing[17]

(July 1991) 'For the future is an international regatta for cruiser racers under IMS. The object of the exercise is to provide a truly international and highly competitive event for the rest of us – the non grand prix types to enjoy'.
(October 1991) '. . . we expect the Commodores' Cup to be a showcase for the latest cruiser racers as the Admiral's Cup is for grand prix yachts.'

(February 1992) 'Many critics of the Admiral's Cup say it has become élitist and moved beyond the reach of the average yachtsman. This is probably true and is why we have initiated the Commodores' Cup. As it is under IMS, dedicated amateurs, if I may use that term, will be able to compete in their cruiser racers, just as they did in the early days of the Admiral's Cup'.[18]

Although the 1992 Key West machines had appeared, the news had not been absorbed in *May 1992*.

'The Commodores' Cup . . . I am greatly looking forward to it. What pleases me is that so many fine sailors, who for various reasons cannot participate at grand prix level, are getting hyped up about their season's new focus.'

Then came some doubts:

(June 1992) 'Speaking of IMS, you will have read of some new designs putting the system under pressure. This *(sic)* has been anticipated – after all, what are designers paid for?
(August 1992, just before the event) ' . . . some pros turn out. So what wrong with that? In my view nothing. If some of the best sailors in the world are there, along with some exciting new boats from the top designers, you have the ingredients for a world class event . . .'.

Among 160 years of the words of rule keepers versus rule beaters told of in the present work, this sequence surely must stand out.
The British and others built new boats to the IMS rule, such as the attractive Dubois designed *Impulse* (**Fig 8.10**). There was a big turn out of some 36 boats, partly aided by splitting Britain into teams from England, Scotland, Wales and Jersey and having two teams from USA, but others came from Argentina, Finland, France, Holland (2) and Hong Kong.
In the end USA 1 swept the board with USA 2 4th. Argentina with new US designs came 2nd. It became known as the 'Comedy Cup', but this was mainly because of the breakdown of the time

Fig 8.10 *Successful Ed Dubois designed IMS one-off* Impulse *of 1992. LOA 39ft 7in (12.10m), beam 12ft 7in (3.83m), displacement 10,912 pounds (4950 kg), ballast half this. Compare with IOR designs of previous years: designers seemed able to exploit light displacement and big sail area in IMS as much or more than in IOR.*

allowance system, and the resulting chaos in issuing results. There was also difficulty in matching the IMS certificates issued in different countries.

At the end of the five race series of 20 to 30 July, (a sixth abandoned in calm, the weather being fine and warm throughout), the individual boats at the top were *Califa* and *Gaucho*, both Farr 44s, then a Nelson Marek 46, then came two Tripp 40s, then *Impulse* and *Numbers*, a Taylor 42. All these except for *Impulse*, being the names of American designers and of the type which had swept Key West (**Fig 8.11**). The rest of the competitors, including earlier IMS boats such as *Apriori* and *Old Mother Gun* (roughly a bigger *Apriori*), converted IOR and some production yachts, followed.

After July 1992 IMS was never the same, for as David Pelly wrote

'Although the RORC has been tinkering with IMS for the past couple of years this was to be the first major test of IMS at a major British regatta. If the RORC had planned it as a means of

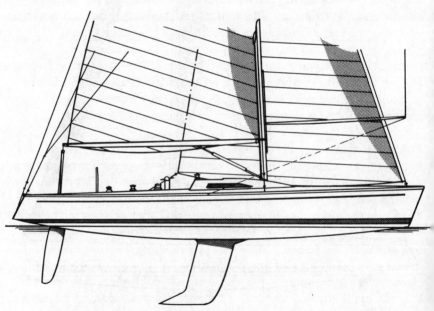

Fig 8.11 *Although the appearance did not differ from other IMS boats,* Gaucho *was designed closely to the rule and was seen to outdate her IMS rated competitors by her performance at Key West regatta in early 1992.*

destroying all credibility in the system, they could not have done a better job, as the early part of the regatta was characterized by results that were so bizarre and were changed so many times that they might just as well have been picked out of a hat.

'By the end of the event things had improved, but by then the damage had been done: 'Comedy Cup' T-shirts were appearing and the 'International Mystery System' was the joke of the beer tent'.[19]

If 'damage' means not building again to the IMS rule, Pelly was correct, for after summer 1992, no more IMS boats were built by British owners, though they were to be in Europe and, of course, America, Australia and elsewhere.

On a more technical level, the RORC Director of Rating, Commander Tony Ashmead CEng MIMechE RN, made a report to the club after the series, which (it is believed owing to a misunderstanding) was published.[20] The main points were (1) measurement needs refinement, for instance as between supposed standard hulls, (2) rating software needs improvement; changes must be possible without access to computer data, (3) new designs are able to sail faster than their VPPs, especially in surfing conditions, (4) there are still major deficiencies in both American and German measurement machines, (5) displacement is not properly measured, (6) rating software did not cope with small changes and software did not match certificates of boats arriving, (7) the ORC emergency penalty on draft has been proved ineffective and, lastly, a personal view, (8) time-on-distance, as currently integral in IMS, is unsatisfactory in strongly tidal waters.

Decision time

When the ORC met again in November 1992, its earlier plans for a grand prix class by 1994 were scrapped. It was declared that *far from a new rule being created to protect the cruiser racers of IMS, IMS was the new rule*. There was to be no other rating rule beyond it!

Central to the use of IMS would be new fixed rating classes, the grand prix boats for the major regattas. Meanwhile IOR Ton Cup classes were 'guaranteed' fixtures until 1996 (though they were not around by then; see above). The new classes were to be called ILRR, International Level Racing Rule: the first ones would probably be about 35ft (11m) and 42ft (13m). This was voted unanimously! Unlike the old classes a single rating would not be extracted from IMS with its multiple time allowances. Therefore there would be VPP 'envelopes' controlling the VPP at 'three points of sail and three wind velocities (*sic*) to control the class's full performance spectrum', while there would also be some overall linear dimensions and 'parametric limits of beam, stability and so forth'.

'The chairman noted that great strides forward had been made in the accuracy of the VPP and that it was a far more accurate (*sic*) tool than previously'.[21]

Thus it was supposed the boats would sail extremely close!

With IMS now suddenly launched as a rule for flat out racing, something had to be done for the cruiser racers, to whom it had promised so much for so long. One idea was to split fleets in regattas, but where the number of entries was too small (usually!), a percentage factor might be given to cruiser ratings. Later this was done at 1 per cent – a curiously crude method for a rating rule of such alleged precision. Accommodation and layout rules, many pages of them, distinguished between the 'racer' and the 'cruiser'.

In April 1993, the ILRR sub-committee[22] stated the first level rater would be between 11.5m and 12.5m LOA and there would be a change of name to ILC 40, International Level Class.[23] Later a second class was declared to be the ILC 46; others before long were projected at 70, the new maxi, and at 30.

Now it was known where IMS and its position in world ocean racing lay. For the years immediately ahead, the principles of what in chapter 1 might have been called 'classification' (!) were presumably set out. The first ILC 40 championship was scheduled for 1994, but that proved too early, so Denmark first saw 10 ILC 40s gather and race in 1995,[24] which mostly went on to England for the Admiral's Cup starting in July 1995. This was the first Admiral's Cup to use IMS (following the final use of IOR in 1993), the classes being the ILC 40, a bigger IMS boat on time allowance and a modern one-design, the Mumm 36. Only eight of each class turned up (**Fig 8.12**). In 1996 the ILC40 world championship was in Greece: nine boats came to the line, mostly Greek and Italian. The first ever ILC 46 championship was under the flag of the Storm Trysail Club at Newport, RI. However only two boats, both American, showed up. The fact was that this class, imposed by the ORC, was of minimal appeal. Following this fiasco, the RORC cancelled its announcement that the next edition (1997) of the Admiral's Cup would have the ILC46 as a class; it reverted to a boat of about that size using time allowance (as for 1995). Chapter

**IMS RATING CERTIFICATES IN THE WORLD WITH
SELECTED COUNTRIES**

	1988	1990	1992	1993	1995
Argentina	0	87	158	81	66
Australia	0	210	250	349	315
Denmark	1	25	29	30	6
Germany	179	391	632	657	647
Italy	0	101	1004	960	930
Netherlands	212	419	578	613	615
UK	10	88	145	48	31
USA	1161	1351	1055	873	700
WORLD	**1634**	**3538**	**5481**	**5288**	**4494**

Fig 8.12 *IMS boats in the world by nation and total, which peaked in 1992. These are certificated and (1) may in many cases hold other rating certificates and race under their rules, while (2) these numbers have no relation to IMS activity, such as actual number of starts. Among these are presumably, after 1994, some ILC fixed rating yachts. (Source: ORC statistics).*

11 looks at other late developments in the story of IMS.

Time allowances in IMS
The history of time allowances and their difference from rules of measurement and rating were described in Chapter 5. It is very necessary to mention how they have been handled in IMS.

It will be remembered that there were in effect two main systems, whatever the different numbers used over the years, which were applied to the linear rating of a yacht in feet, whether IOR or any other rule: (1) time-on-distance using USYRU tables and (2) time-on-time using a time correction factor (TCF).

Back in 1964, when most of America was using the CCA rule, Gordon M. Curtis Jr, a leading member of that club wrote

'The time allowance tables are subject to error ... until now it has been accepted that all evens up in the long run, but this is not true ... A method is being developed by the measurement committee [of the CCA] which will greatly minimize the error in computing handicaps where race speed varies widely from the conditions on which the time allowance tables are based. It is hoped to try this out ... in some races in 1964 ...'.[25]

It has been mentioned in Chapter 5 that in the early days of the metre boats and even in the nineteenth century, scales of varying seconds per mile were introduced for different wind strengths, such as 'light', 'medium' and 'heavy'. It is believed that the CCA experiments were conducted, though the problem was obviously that competitors could always calculate what their corrected time would have been on the 'old' system. Therefore of any two boats in competition, one was potentially unhappy. Alternatively there was no change in order so 'What was the point of changing anyway?'!

Now we heard the comments of Nick Newman when MIT created MHS. He was very concerned with time allowances; this was surely and rightly because of the inflexibility of NAYRU tables, as appreciated by the CCA (see chapter head quote).

Therefore the multiple time allowances were a clever solution to both the 'table' problem and making use of the research results of VPP.

Olin J. Stephens II, later an advocate of IMS, was at first not sure about this approach

'My personal opinion is that, while IMS speed predictions are remarkably good, turning them into time allowances and race results is difficult'.[26]

It is is generally agreed that any lack of popularity of IMS since its adoption by the international body in 1985 is owed in great measure to its time allowance system. How this appears has already been mentioned and is visible on the certificate (**Fig 8.4, again**). Because there is no single, especially linear, rating, race committees have no alternative. Admittedly there is the single GPH (general purpose handicap) shown, but this was and is heavily talked down by the promoters of IMS. In other words, this was quite different from offering a linear rating and saying 'Here you are, apply any time scale to this suitable for your waters and your tradition'.

All kinds of ways were devised for handling this mass of numbers on the IMS certificate. In many clubs and organizations mathematicians and computer buffs popped up and suggested ways of handling them. Often such schemes were tried. *As late as 1996*, John Marshall, chairman US IMS committee was able to write

'I suspect [that so many brilliant people working on programs] is more to do with human nature than a technical problem. When smart [clever] people are given the opportunity to make something perfect they are tempted to persist. IMS offers that opportunity with post-processing. Yet experience shows that any slight benefits that approach yields are far outweighed by the negatives'.[27]

So twenty years after USYRU promulgated the rule, the time allowance system is in as much disarray as ever.

The basis of the problem has always been quite evident. To allot time allowances before the race, it is necessary to choose the course type and wind speed: this will almost always be wrong. To wait until after the race to collect information on the course time and wind speed (if agreed!) means long delay in publishing results. For post race allowances try this for the 1991 259-mile Port Huron-Mackinac race on Lake Huron

'For the first 38 hours of the race there was little or no wind; then an 18-knot north-easter kicked in.

'The race committee created confusion, fired up tempers and reopened debate about the integrity of the IMS rule when they posted three different results. Tim Woodhouse, who sailed the Tripp 40, *Rumours*, at one point was listed as the winner of class B, but ended up second and said "This is killing IMS". Race officer Jim Dundas said that the wind speed was changed from 12 knots to 10 knots so that the whole fleet could be scored in the same wind strength'.[28]

If this statement baffles the reader, it baffles the author! One could quote scores of similar scenes, such as in the Commodores' Cup of 1992 and, still unsolved as late as 1996, the Sydney-Hobart race, where

'The race has shown *yet again that something has to be done about the method of calculating the results for offshore races under IMS.*

'Never before have the letters IMS stood more for international mystery system or international misery system.[29] It took 48 hours from the time *Sayrona* [new ILC 70, first to finish] crossed the finish line for any results to be announced. Mumblings around the docks and bars was all about what a mess this year's system was ... and there may have been a glaring error'.[30]

There was more and later the Cruising Yacht Club of Australia announced a conference on the subject to be held shortly.

A recommended method

To be fair to the ORC, it did have a recommended method for some years before this, but for unknown reasons it has seldom seemed to become accepted as practical. It was called *Performance Curve Scoring (PCS)*. This was available as a computer program but can be represented in graphical form. **Fig 8.13** tries to show this together with an explanation.

The author will use his best endeavour to explain PCS. The principle is that for the speed of a yacht as it appears on completion of a race, there must be an equivalent VPP. However it is still necessary to select what course configuration has been sailed (or obviously the nearest one to what actually occurred). So there is an implied wind; in other words, the targeted VPP thinks that there was a certain wind speed which predicted it. Each boat has a curve as on the graph (**Fig 8.13 again**). The actual (elapsed time) speed of boat is read off at its position on the boat's own curve. The boat with the best implied wind is the winner.

As there is a wide aversion to giving corrected times as wind speeds, these are converted in the program to a corrected time in hours, minutes and seconds and a results order. However both the implied wind and the corrected time have no meaning that can be related to anything except what is hidden in the software.[31]

There are additional methods of applying time allowances which take in current and tidal stream, which will not be discussed here because (1) methods were fluid and remain so (as John Marshall, above) and (2) the stream varying along even a leg of the course, is difficult to measure accurately and boats may sail towards best water for tactical reasons.[32]

Enough has been said to show why IMS has, for all its existence, been ill served by its time allowance systems.

Time-on-time

At the ORC meeting in London in November 1994, the RORC asked if a time-on-time system could be approved as an alternative time allowance system. The reason for this was that Alan Green, RORC Director of Racing, had worked a series of results by ORC recommended methods including PCS and also by a TCF derived from the GPH on the IMS rating certificate. He found that there was little difference in the corrected time order. The cause of this equivalence is not far to seek. Much of the difference in time allowance between boats of different rating in IMS at different wind speeds, 8, 10, 12 knots etc. is not caused by the boat measurements, but simply because slower speeds (in lighter winds

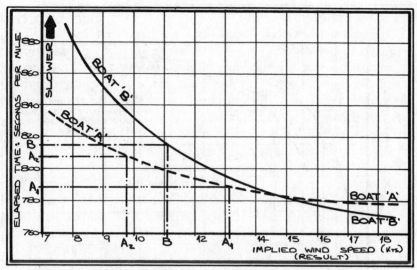

Fig 8.13 *Time allowances in IMS. The perpetual problem was that however logically deduced, the conversion to corrected time was never possible to envisage. This graph tries to show the so-called performance curve scoring, though the calculation was actually within the computer and impossible for crews to check. It is based on time-on-distance. The curves come from the certificates of boats A and B. B has an elapsed time of 816 seconds per mile. So hit curve B and go down to 'implied wind' speed of 11.1 knots. A's result A1 of 788 secs per mile hits A curve and gives implied wind of 13.2 knots, so she beats B (because she has had 'better' wind speed). A2 result of 808 secs per mile loses to B at only 9.8 implied wind. Sailors did not like all this.*

or in long beats to windward) stretch the time between them (**Fig 8.14**).

However this is exactly what time-on-time does, as described in Chapter 5.

The ORC in the form of a sub-committee chaired by Hans Zuider-baan, long time a Dutch member of ORC, and its main council confirming that said that this 'single-number' time allowance was not to be recommended.[33]

For the first time for years, RORC disregarded ORC rulings. For the 1995 season it instituted for (its much depleted) IMS class (which was as mentioned shadowing CHS) a TCF.[34] Thereafter races were calculated, exactly as in the days of the RORC rule, IOR and the current CHS!

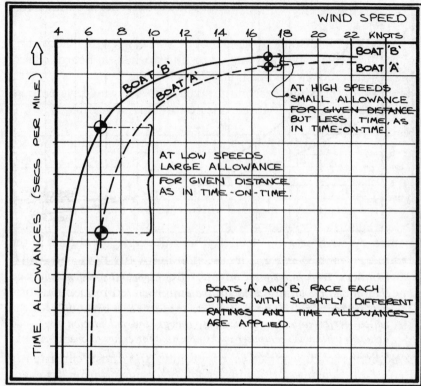

Fig 8.14 *The author contends that IMS variable time allowances are a roundabout way of arriving at time-on-time, but made acceptable for American users. The IMS rule rather gives away the game by saying it uses a system 'which does not require the use of tables', which were never used in Europe anyway! This graph shows how boats A and C are given a number of time allowances in seconds per mile for increasing wind speed (as found on their IMS certificates). But this is largely due to conditions at different speed, which time-on-time (using a TCF) allows for anyway. At slow speed time-on-time magnifies difference, which is all that the elaborate time-on-distance variations are showing. High speed is opposite (see comments on graph). Thus when time-on-time (minutes per hour by TCF) was applied to same race as IMS variable seconds per mile, it was not surprising that the results of the races in corrected time boat order were very little different.*

Corrected time = Elapsed time × TCF

What relief! No distances, no elaborate software (which according to Alan Green crashed anyway),[35] results worked on board, checkable by the crew at the finish and FAST.

For 1996, for which season the same time allowance system ran, the formula from the IMS certificate for a given yacht was

TCF = (600/GPH) less $1\frac{1}{2}$% cruiser allowance where applicable.

When a yacht was rated to more than one rule (i.e. CHS and IMS), it became possible to calculate which rule was most favourable to her, as against any other yacht. This is covered in the following chapter. As with previous RORC TCFs the constant chosen in the formula gives a TCF of 1 in the middle of the fleet with other figures above and below it, and not 'too far away' from elapsed time. This has no significance, but is appreciated by competitors.

This satisfaction for the British customer was a bit much for the ORC (international) chief measurer who wrote

'So long as the object is to provide the most consistently equitable scoring for a wide range of designs within an event IMS/PCS is the best system available. To the degree that the yachts are of similar size and design, the superiority of PCS over single number systems is diminished, but never to the degree that PCS produces inferior scoring.

'... there are some very important differences [in using TCFs]. These are differences which do make a difference and the result is the IMS/PCS will use time in a way which will produce more equitable scoring than a TCF, especially for fleets of diverse design ...'.[36]

The reader will be spared any more of this.

9 *What sailors did*

'Our life is frittered away by detail. Simplify, simplify' - Henry
David Thoreau, Concord, Massachusetts, 1848.

*'There is also the problem of fixing suitable time allowances to the
competing boats which often vary considerably in size and sail area and
indeed in all factors affecting their speed. Time allowances are
therefore given on a rating, that of each yacht being found by a
formula . . . When a yacht has been measured – a very simple matter
which can be done afloat in a few minutes – and has had her rating
worked out, a table is referred to, which shows the number of seconds
that a yacht of any particular rating should in theory take to sail a
given distance under average conditions'* – Robert Somerset DSO[1]:
Ocean Racing, The Lonsdale Library, 1935.

ON 20 APRIL 1989 the author sent a letter to the Rating
Secretary, Royal Ocean Racing Club, Commander F.A.H.
Ashmead MSc CEng MIMechE RN. It read:

'Dear Tony,
'IMS measurement.
'It was most kind of you to offer to measure my boat *Highwayman* at a reduced price of £200 including VAT and to refer to
her as "a leading edge boat".

'The fact is, I am afraid, that the boat is now eight years old
and cannot be considered of high racing potential. Family and
crew agree with me that spending £200 on a new rating would
not be appropriate now. As you know, I have allowed also my
IOR rating to lapse, having stayed faithful to IOR within RORC
up to and including last season. Apart from the ISC Round the
Island race, all my other races have been on CHS.

'However the 1988 IOR class in the Round the Island was a

farce and I am virtually forced into CHS in that race.

'In any case the only potential races for IMS in 1989 appear to be the RORC ones at the end of the season. Besides the range of boat in a single class for IMS may be so wide as to mean little, while I gather that no time allowance system has yet been decided. If there are class divisions, we do not know what these are. *Highwayman* because of her age goes for class success and any overall result is always a bonus!

'Thank you again for kindly writing to me about this.

'Yours sincerely, Peter Johnson'[2]

Looking back at this letter it seems to touch on all the reasons, why British yachtsmen (and French and Irish) were then and are still to be found favouring as the principal national offshore rating rule the Channel Handicap System (CHS) and spurning the now chronic effort to enlist them in the International Measurement System (IMS). The same goes for sailors in many, but not all, countries where other regional or local schemes are used for regular racing fixtures; especially this is the case in the United States in respect of Performance Handicap Racing Fleet (PHRF).

This chapter will look at CHS and PHRF, under which so many sailors have raced so many thousands of miles, through the 1980s and, at the time of writing, most of the 1990s.

As for the letter, because it was based on practical experience it inevitably picked up the preferences for CHS. These included (1) price, £200 being cheap for IMS, now five times that for the size of yacht, but then ten times the CHS price; (2) that IOR was followed, but lack of entries eventually made this pointless; (3) lack of IMS events, thus making rating fee uneconomic per race; (4) that the boats would not be close in rating in any IMS race; (5) that there was no decided time allowance system (which by now readers will know is endemic to IMS).

A second national rule

Origins of the Channel Handicap System remain obscure and undocumented, but in February 1984 some sailors read this piece of news:

'RORC and its French sister UNCL[3] plan to introduce a simplified rating system [in 1984] for those who want to race offshore, to be called the Channel Handicap System (CHS). The idea of buying a CHS certificate for £5, rather than an IOR certificate for £125 (approx cost for 25 ftr) seems likely to prove popular. It will be interesting to see if race organizers on both sides of the channel, which they share and after which the rule is named, adopt it . . .'.[4]

It was the French, always less hidebound than the RORC and its several committees, who initiated the idea, in particular Jean-Louis Fabry a speaker of excellent English, who had sailed thousands of miles in RORC races and elsewhere offshore. Robin Aisher, then commodore of RORC, was delighted to cooperate. The British were immediately able to hand the project over to their established RORC Rating Office (at Lymington on the south coast of England), while UNCL set up a desk under Jean Sans, a mathematics teacher in Brittany, with a part time certificate issuing office in Paris.

Unlike the birth of MHS/IMS, there were no ringing declarations, no grants for research and no proclaimed new technology. It was essentially an empirical operation and low key: just alternative ratings for those who were unsatisfied with IOR. By 1984-85, as we have seen, IOR had some time to run, was in full use in some cases, though numbers 'at the bottom' were falling away.

It remains unknown whether the arrival of CHS caused yacht owners to leave IOR, or if they would have left IOR anyway. But now they had somewhere to go, so probably the answer is a bit of both. However as numbers and available events increased in CHS the effect was accumulative. **Fig 9.1** shows the changeover projected to the present time, with equal number of CHS and IOR certificates in Britain in 1986. By 1988, there were more CHS rated boats in Britain than there had ever been in IOR; by 1990 the levels had stabilized and CHS numbers have not fluctuated much since then. It should be realized that under all rating rules owners and yachts come and go and it is not the same 2250 (or whatever the figure) boats each year. In France (and later some other countries) the same effect was to be found.

CHS was to be surprised by its own success and the offices were unprepared for its early appeal. Tony Ashmead to whom the author wrote in the above letter took charge of the RORC Rating Office in 1986. He remembers

'The day I arrived at the rating office, applications for CHS were flooding in, forms were all over the floor, there was total computer failure, the CHS program did not work and our French friends were urgently appealing for help. On top of this major international events with IOR problems were impending.

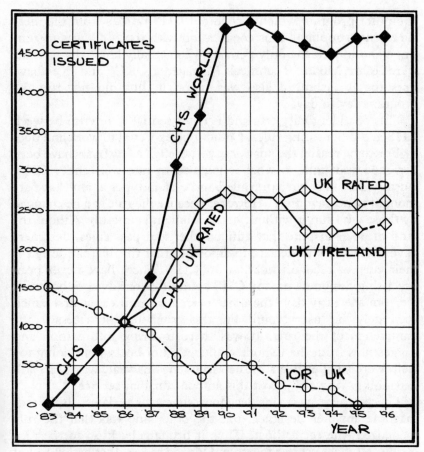

Fig 9.1 *The really remarkable growth of Channel Handicap System ratings in the 'home countries' of UK and Ireland; also in the world. As IOR fell, the main change over was between 1984 and 1990. After 1986 CHS was the principal rule for France, Ireland and UK.*

'John Moon, my no. 2, felt we just had to try and make it all work. Some how we managed it . . . Whatever may have been the intention for CHS in the early days, racing in Britain, France and Ireland and a number of places elsewhere depends on this Anglo-French rule'.[5]

An early helper in all this was the national authority, the RYA (the old YRA of the early chapters) in the person of its Technical Manager, Ken Kershaw. He provided important aid in devising a computer program which turned out CHS ratings from the measurements supplied. This cooperation with the RYA was to continue and indeed the only persons who actually knew the formula were John Moon, Technical Manager RORC, and Kershaw. Presumably Ashmead also was in on it, but did not run the program day to day.

This confidentiality was and is the essential difference between CHS and other rating rules. Could it be expected to work and does it? For some reason the answer is yes, though a few boats have been designed and built to what is guessed to rate well under CHS. Locally they may have prevailed and certain types at any stage are thought to be 'favoured'. However because the rule can be changed by those who run it without notification and certainly without the kind of open dispute that afflicts other and past rules, designers have no security to declare to an owner that this or that design is their current recommendation for CHS. There have never been practising designers on any CHS committee or advisory body.

From the early days there has been a committee, at first called accurately the 'user group', but this group had no access to the parameters of the rule. It was there to bring information and suggestions from the regions: which kind of boats were doing too well, were smaller boats in the ascendent this year, was CHS still expanding, why did it cost this amount for that service?

The 'secrecy' was one weapon 'against' the latest IOR race machine and her designer, but the other one was that the rule 'penalized' the racier boat. Thus it brought back on to the race course, all those cruiser racers and indeed racers, that had in recent years been outdated. A comparison of an IOR TCF and a CHS TCF shows that a 1989 One Tonner (this comparison is in 1989) gave to a five year-old fast cruiser racer 3 minutes 16 seconds per hour in IOR, but 6 minutes 28 seconds per hour in CHS (**Fig 9.2**). No longer did the less new boat face defeat, rather the 'hot shots' were driven to keep away from the all round fleet, for fear of 'middle placing' in it. Of course, circumstances varied in different racing areas, but this was the general and intended effect of CHS.

CHS operates
This is an outline of how CHS operates at the time of writing: the principle has not altered, though the factors and dimensions requested change gradually over the years.

A number of measurements are taken, the extent of which can be seen on the CHS application forms (**Fig 9.3**). There are also important particulars about the type of vessel because from this the

	IOR·TCF	CHS·TCF	
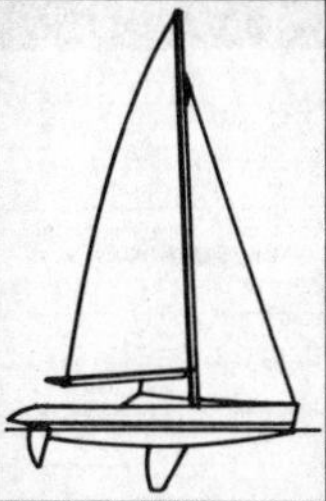	1·020	1·101	1989 ONE TONNER (IOR 30·55)
	3MIN 16s	6MIN 28s	MINUTES PER HR.
	0·9572	1·002	36FT 5 YEAR OLD CRUISER/RACER
	1MIN 17s	2MIN 37s	MINUTES PER HR.
	0·9470	0·960	37FT HEAVY CRUISER

Fig 9.2 *The important point about CHS, at the time it was introduced, was to restore the time allowance of a reasonable boat against the latest rule creation. It managed to achieve what the IOR authorities had failed to do: that is increase the rating of the latest machines. This picture shows the more practical time allowances granted by CHS. Those are the numbers shown for CHS and for IOR in the line 'between' the ratings of each type. Thus the 'outrated' yachts returned to racing.*

rule inputs hull factor and rig factor, which are extremely important to distiguish 'racy' and 'cruising' types and all the shades in between. Unlike many rating rules the sail material for each sail is rated (as indeed is the hull material with what that implies for hull

● State all measurements in metres and kilograms to 2 places of decimals

RIG DETAILS

RIG

☐ Bermudan ☐ Gaff ☐ Wishbone ☐ Sloop ☐ Yawl ☐ Ketch ☐ Cutter ☐ Schooner ☐ Cat ☐ Other ....

☐ Masthead ☐ Fractional

FORE AND AFT SAILS

	main or forward mast	mizzen or after mast	SOURCE OF INFORMATION
Main hoist	P	PY	....
Main foot	E	EY	....
Foretriangle base	J	JY	....
Forestay length	FL	FLY	....
Headsail luff length	LL	LLY	....
Jib perpendicular	LP	LPY	....

DOWN WIND SAILS

When racing the yacht carries on board: ☐ A spinnaker or whisker pole or poles   ☐ A bowsprit only   ☐ Both

Length SPL ....

☐ Symmetric spinnakers (How many?   )   ☐ Asymmetric spinnakers (How many?   )

Symmetric spis: SLU ....   SLE ....   SF ....   SMG ....

Asymmetric spis: ASLU ....   ASLE ....   ASF ....   ASMG ....

Ketches/yawls: Mizzen staysail   LLY ....   LPY ....

CLOTH

Do any sails carried contain Hi-tech sailcloth?   ☐ YES ☐ NO
If YES, please state which sails (eg. Mainsail, No1L, No1H, No.3, etc.)
....

LOFT

Name of sailmaker(s) loft(s) ....

FEATURES

MAINMAST MATERIAL: ☐ Alloy ☐ Carbon ☐ Wood ☐ Other ....

SETS OF SPREADERS .... JUMPER STRUTS .... RUNNERS .... CHECKSTAYS ....

SPREADER SWEEP BACK ANGLE: ☐ less than 5° ☐ 5° to 10° ☐ more than 10°   Does the yacht have rod rigging?   YES/NO

Does the rig have any unusual or non-standard features? (eg. additional rig controls, extended roach mainsail, hi-tech materials, linked winch systems/
coffee grinders, in-mast/boom furling, etc.):   YES/NO

Describe ....

DAYBOATS

Is the yacht a dayboat (see CHS Rule 9.3)?   ☐ YES ☐ NO

ENGINE/PROP

ENGINE: ☐ Inboard ☐ Outboard ☐ No engine   Make/Model ....   Weight ....kg

PROPELLER: ☐ Folding ☐ Feathering ☐ Fixed ☐ Variable pitch   No of blades ....

DECLARATION

I confirm that I have read and agree to be bound by the Class Rules of the Channel Handicap System.
I certify that the information provided is true to the best of my knowledge. If I make any changes to the yacht or discover any of the information to be
incorrect, I will notify the Rating Office immediately. I am prepared to make my yacht available for check measurements at any reasonable time. I am aware
that the RORC will maintain my rating details on its computer database and I confirm that I have no objection to these data being maintained and used for
the purposes of analysis and information.

Signed .... (Owner)   Date ....

I have checked the above figures to the best of my ability and confirm that I believe them to be correct.

Signed .... Status (Club Officer, Measurer, etc.)   Date ....

I enclose the fee of LOA ....m x £5 = £ .... (plus endorsement fee if applicable)

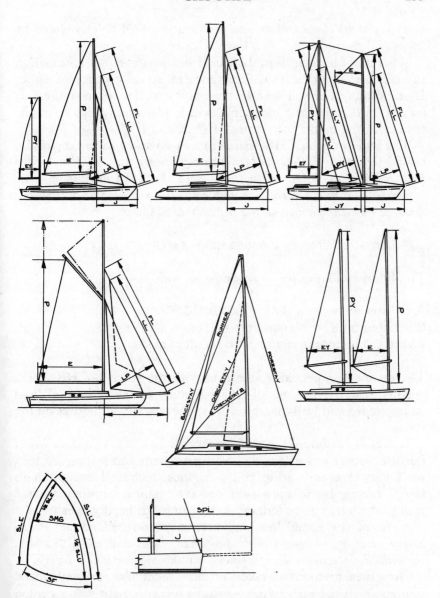

Fig 9.3 *The data required on the CHS application forms gives a clue as to characteristics that determine a rating. The letters on the form (left) correspond to those on these sail diagrams. There is another form for hull details. The rating offices also often have existing information about production boats and their inevitable variations.*

qualities of stiffness and weight distribution). All Kevlar would be 'high'; all dacron would be 'low', with stages betwen.

Wherever the yacht is in the world and whatever her nationality, the completed application form goes to a rating office in either Lymington or Paris. These are the only two calculation stations. It means uniformity of processing, which has simply not been the case from the many outstations of IMS and IOR.

The data for each CHS boat is processed and a rating certificate issued (**Fig 9.4**). *This provides a rating simply as a TCF, which is used just like the TCFs of previous rules. In CHS there is no other rating (e.g. a linear rating) though conversion is possible to time-on-distance (used sometimes in the Mediterranean).*

Corrected time = elapsed time × TCF

To obtain an allowance in seconds per mile (t-o-d):

Time allowance (TA) = 5513/((TCF × 10) − .88)
Corrected time = elapsed time − (TA × CD)
where CD is course distance in nautical miles

The owner is expected to conform with the rules of CHS which occupy nearly five pages of A4, although one and a half of these pages are rig and hull diagrams to aid the entering of figures on the form.

It may be wondered what a secret rule has to say to the owner, but the clauses cover loading at measurement and sailing (as seen we know in every rating rule), engines, technical exception to ISAF racing rules, crew and protests against another yacht's rating, the latter quite lengthy in wording but hardly ever used.

Some of the actual headings are: *length waterplane and draft, empty weight, engine and propeller, keel/centreboard/rudder, rig/sails, down wind sails, equipment/loading, seaworthiness/safety.*[6]

How measurement is taken on any yacht has gradually been tightened. In the earliest days owner's measurement was accepted (approved by a 'club official'), but as many yachts had IOR certificates, or at least recently discarded ones, the dimensions could come straight off those and they had been officially checked. Then clubs and race organizers had the option of requiring more stringent checking; so, for instance, at Ramsgate where the fleet was cohesive, the authorities measured all their competitors for CHS. Later some races required measurement by RORC measurer, as in the days of IOR (or as for IMS). One proposal about

RORC
Seahorse Building
Bath Road
Lymington SO41 9SE

 UNCL
Face au 36, Quai A. le Gallo
92100 Boulogne-sur-Seine
Paris

CHS - CHANNEL HANDICAP SYSTEM - CHS

```
YACHT    : RIDE THE WILD WIND      SSS BASE VALUE ....  30
SAIL No. : GBR1666R                ADJUSTMENT VALUE ..   6  c)
CERT No. : K- 6666 /96             SSS NUMERAL .......  36


                    TCF  =   0.992



Design: FIRST 35s5          Series date: 1988   Hull factor:  8.4
Type  : Bermudian Sloop     Age  date  : 1988   Rig factor :  1.02
                            Crew Number: 8       O/h factor :  1.010

Issue : New application
Notes : Std hull data
Sails : Sail data from sailmaker
-------------------------------------------------------------------
Hull:               Main:        Mizzen:       Spis: Sym:        Asym:
LOA.............. 10.60   P.... 13.00  PY.... 0.00   SLU... 12.52  SLU... 0.00
LWP.............. 8.95    E.... 4.60   EY.... 0.00   SLE... 12.52  SLE... 0.00
Beam............. 3.60    J.... 3.40   JY.... 0.00   SF.... 6.35   SF.... 0.00
Weight (empty).... 5000   FL... 13.10  FLY... 0.00   SMG... 6.35   SMG... 0.00
CHS Displacement.. 5660   LL... 12.75  LLY... 0.00
DLR.............. 220     LP... 5.32   LPY... 0.00   SPL... 3.20
Draft............ 1.80 : Low vcg Iron single keel
-------------------------------------------------------------------
Inboard engine  : Weight.... 159 Kg.   2 blade folding/feathering propeller
-------------------------------------------------------------------
Any Hi-tech sail not identified in the Sails Note shall NOT be carried
Spinnaker pole(s) only
2 Spreader (sets)    0 Jumper (sets)    0 Runner (sets)    0 Checkstay (sets)
Weight incl. batteries/cushions      No water ballast carried
-------------------------------------------------------------------
Certificate issued by the RORC Rating Office and VALID from 06-08-1996 (11:54:32)
Expires 31-12-1996 unless superseded or invalidated by CHS Rules and Regulations

I accept the dimensions shown on this certificate and
agree to report all subsequent changes and any errors
found at a later date to the issuing Authority.


Signed: ................................ (Owner)


  A M Howes                      A copy of this certificate
  44 North Lane                  shall be kept aboard the yacht
  East Sellington                when racing.
  YORK
  YO23 8DX                            (C)  RORC/UNCL 1996
```

Fig 9.4 *The CHS rating certificate. The actual rating figure is the TCF in large type, upper centre. It includes all dimensional, material, age and other input of the rule. Following the RORC experience with TCFs of IOR, the TCF figure of 'middle-size boats' is close either side of 1.000; thus corrected times numerically are not far away from elapsed times.*

1991 was for something called CHS(M), measured CHS, but this was turned down by the main committee of the RORC in late 1989. It thought that CHS was getting above itself and that IMS was 'the measured rule', (see CHS v.IMS, below). In 1993, a new grade of CHS(E), CHS (endorsed), was introduced without another veto and became required for the Fastnet race and certain regattas, indeed wherever the race organizer called for it.

What endorsement implied was a complete check by the rating office from all its sources of the data supplied by the yacht; this might or might not require more physical measurement, inspection and weighing (below). At the end of the process, the yacht had a CHS(E) certificate with a high validity.[7]

The *Entente* and other problems
Unlike the International rule and the IOR which formed councils (IYRU and ORC respectively) to administer the rules, CHS with only two nations should have been very controllable with such a bilateral agreement. It was, but for a time it had difficulties even so. After a few years it was found that practices were diverging in England and France particularly for measurement of waterplane, calculation of weight and sailcloth. Similar production boats in France turned up with lower ratings than those in Britain.

Obviously there were conferences (on the north coast of France or south coast of England – beside the common Channel!), but solutions were not always found. In 1990 Director of Rating[8] Tony Ashmead reported

'The RORC had now sent representatives to France on three separate occasions in the last three months with the hope of dramatically improving UNCL/RORC liaison. The return for this cost and effort proved to be disappointing. The CHS administrative work load had been doubled and revalidation delayed while attempting to achieve agreements. Common TCFs can only be acquired from agreed common data and a uniform approach.

'UNCL must realise that CHS development in the UK since 1984 and the growth of overseas had placed greater demands on the administration. The RORC success had been based on rapid certification and immediate decision making. Any requirement for prolonged debate and committee compromise would make CHS unworkable in the UK. The Group [meeting of regional users in UK] upheld the view that the current standing of CHS in the UK must not be jeopardized'.[9]

A couple of years after this most differences had been reconciled, or were so small as to be technically ignored.

'*International*'. That just two countries working together was found difficult shows that reducing the numerous participants using an international rule would not necessarily help (for instance for IOR in its disputes). Despite the common waters of the Channel, for which CHS was created, and visits to each other's coasts for occasional regattas, the value of so-called international rules is much exaggerated. *In the case of CHS, the vital policy of the User Group, above, was to prevent any upset among the balance of ratings of competing yachts, in, say, Scotland, where no French boat ever came, in the interests of 'compromise' to meet the French kind of CHS.*

The common races where both British and French yachts sailed, though high profile, could be counted on one hand. The same goes for other rating rules, particularly IMS and IOR. Thus to accommodate the problems with American top boats in the Florida based SORC, in its day, the balance of IOR ratings was upset, for example, in the southern North Sea. (Meanwhile in the northern North Sea, it so happened that the sailors carried on using their own rule of measurement and rating!)

Weight. CHS uses displacement (that is 'weight') in its secret formula. By the time the reader has reached this chapter, he knows that displacement has always been very difficult to determine, at least to use as an accurate comparison in a rating formula. Thus awkward methods like depths/freeboards and laser shape reading/freeboards have been used. Notional displacements or rated displacements appeared on IMS and IOR certificates, but they were relative.

In 1990, CHS unhindered by bureaucracy and precedent or even accountability to designers, looked for a solution. Up to then weight/displacement could be quantified from several sources:

(1) IOR DSPL which depended on immersed depths, BWL, B and L, but by 1990 there were few IOR certificates about.

(2) IMS DISP. Same problem and expensive to measure; numerous figures in input make it subject to error.

(3) Manufacturer's figures. Notoriously wild and promotion driven. Even with good will, scope for error in transcription.

(4) Designer's figures. Experience shows these are not reliable. Builder may have altered design, used more or less material and so on.

(5) Slings or crane at builders. These were checked in research and even British Ministry of Defence specifications were found to be well out owing to poor calibration of instrument, wind on the day and errors from angled slings. For yachts as found in the CCA rule in the 1960s, the loading of the yacht was often changed after launching and practices varied across the USA.

The solution was found in CHS. With a controllable number of yachts, calibrated load cells were employed hanging the yacht from a single point (instruments on angled slings were hopeless). Only a few chosen official measurers were allowed to use them. The loading of the yacht was ruled and meticulously enforced by those same measurers. When a yacht was not weighed, its displacement was taken on the light side (i.e. less well rated), thus giving an incentive to weighing which took time and money.

A number of examples of a production yacht, alleged to be the same by designer and builder, were often found to weigh very differently. The well known J35 cruiser racer has been found to vary by 1325 pounds (600 kilograms).

Rule changes

These cannot be promulgated in chapter and verse and are not a victim of arguments about notice (one year's time and so on), but were and are announced in general terms. These might be 'some relaxation for light displacement yachts' or 'more account taken of keels with bulbs'. In 1989 there were complaints from the regions of some light displacement yachts being unduly penalized by their ratings. As an example of how CHS changed from year to year **Fig 9.5** shows what happened to typical well known classes and one-off yachts, when there was a change (unknown except to Kershaw and Moon) of formula.

Sail cloth has been something of a battle throughout the life of CHS. It will be recalled how the IOR authorities 'gave in' to Kevlar, losing in the process a number of owners. These same

Fig 9.5 *When a rating rule is changed, some go up and some down. Here is what happened when CHS altered its secret formula at the end of 1989. The new and old TCFs are compared and in the right hand column is shown the change for the yacht in minutes and seconds per hour; this will be relative to other yachts which have or have not changed. For instance the Folkboat and S&S 34 did not alter in relation to each other, but the First Europe and Jacobite (a medium displacement Oyster 43 masthead cruiser racer) changed quite a lot.*

CHS RATINGS 1989 AND 1990 (BRACKETS INDICATE HAS TO 'GIVE' MORE TIME)			
CLASS OR BOAT	1989	1990	PER HOUR
STANDARD BARRACUDA	1.176	1.137	1m 48s
BARRACUDA of TARRANT	1.193	1.238	2m 11s
FIRST EUROPE	1.120	1.068	2m 24s
J 24	0.942	0.932	40s
OOD 34	0.973	0.971	7s
SIGMA 33	0.945	0.945	No CHANGE
SIGMA 41	1.024	(1.028)	(14s)
SIGMA 38	1.020	1.021	(4s)
SIGMA 36	0.978	(0.986)	(30s)
X 99	1.024	1.021	10s
GRP FOLK BOAT	0.836	(0.845)	(40s)
SWAN 39 R	1.032	(1.035)	(11s)
SUN STONE	0.943	(0.950)	(27s)
HIGHWAY MAN	1.003	(1.005)	(7s)
APRIORI	1.034	1.021	46s
O.M. GUN	1.083	1.077	20s
S & S 34	0.907	(0.917)	(40s)
CONTESSA 32	0.908	0.904	16s
JACOBITE	1.035	1.035	No CHANGE

owners were welcomed into CHS – 'the rule with the white sails'.

Various sail cloth moves occur from time to time. The obvious one is simple pressure from sailmakers to remove the penalty: this has been resisted. Then there is the production of new materials that are not 'hi-tech' (i.e. Kevlar or equivalent) but midddle material or mylar and other developed film. The rating offices hastened to rate such material. Meanwhile down wind sails (spin-nakers, gennakers) are limited to three per yacht; any extra sail means a little higher rating. Owners really like these effective steps against the sail wardrobe arms race. Sailmakers have to put up with such rules.

Here are some rules changes as announced year by year:[10]

For the 1991 season: *No rating change allowed during a 'short' series. Electrical or powered equipment for sail etc. handling allowed, if race organizer approves and rating is amended via rig factor.*

1992: *Hydraulics freed from rating. Change in permitted sail cloth. New sail area algorithms result in changes to some TCFs. Trade off altered between SL, SMW and SPL (spinnaker dimensions) and spinnaker pole length differently rated. LWP (length waterplane clarified [the 'French' problem, above].*

1993: *Age allowance limited to 20 years, begins at 3 years, its rating altered slightly. Crew limitation, still no rule, but a new recommenda-tion to race committees. New ways of measuring down wind sails and asymmetric ones for the first time. Rig factor enlarged (more items affect rule). Sail cloth changed again.*

1994: *Time scale (not rating, but relationship is not published) altered to help smaller yachts, so some relative TCFs change. Modern retractable bowsprits differentiated from spinnaker poles, so yacht rated according to type and length of pole. If yacht carries both symmetric and asymmetric (which in turn has new published definition in the rule) spinnakers, the rating will be higher. Water ballasted yacht may apply for CHS, but rating office reserves right to refuse rating.*

1995: *Definition of day boat [CHS always gave ratings for Dragons 6-metres etc, if required] is revised. The rating of hi-tech sails in yachts over 35ft is slightly altered to their benefit in a sliding scale o_ yacht size. Hull factor change to result in some small TCF changes Crew number now shown on certificate, but only if in use if invoked by th race committee.*[11]

1996: *Definition of a day boat extended. Loose footed mainsails and self tacking jibs no longer declared* [presumably any rating on these removed]. *During a regatta on consecutive days, crew number must remain the same, nor must SAIL WARDROBE be changed. Further changes on symmetric and asymmetric spinnakers.*

1997: *Amendments caused by revision of linked ISAF racing rules. Easing of tax on hi-tech sails, which will eventually be phased out. Rating of articulated bowsprits less severe.*

All the above were published, as well as some other small detail, but there were surely also unpublished changes to the rule. However any major changes in relative TCFs must be accompanied by explanations of a general kind, in fairness to the users.

Running down the rule
Like all the other rating rules in this book the Channel Handicap received its share of general abuse, sometimes both strong and repetitive. The most common criticisms found in 1992 and the replies to them then were as follows (the words in square brackets are today's additional comments):[12]

'*a simple rule*' – as the rule is secret, no one can say if it is simple or not. Certainly the rig algorithms are more sensitive than IMS and IOR. [However it is a virtue to be simple for the end user, the sailor, who invariably echos Thoreau, at chapter head.]

'*a non-measurement system*' – depends on what race organizers accept. [In later years CHS(E) came into force. There were increasingly grades of measurement. Did an ocean racer even in 1935 (chapter head) ever only take a few minutes?]

'*not international*' – correct in that it has no polygot committees, but it is used in many countries. [See remarks above on 'international'.]

'*not fair; under pressure*' – no rating rule is universally fair; all rules of any significance are under pressure, that is why they need day to day professional management.

'*won't last*' – all rating rules in history have eventually terminated or been changed out of recognition. In that sense no rating rule lasts.

'single figure TCF does not give a proper chance' – there is no
difficulty devising a dual or multiple time allowance system for
CHS (or IOR). IMS currently has multiple figures, but could be
run on a single allowance. [As the reader here knows, but this was
the reply at the time]

CHS v. IMS

The last comment above actually hinted that the IMS multiple
time allowance is 'better' and is just one aspect of the battle in the
UK and Ireland, to some extent France and occasionally in Hong
Kong and elsewhere, of whether to use CHS or IMS.

At the annual dinner of the RORC in 1991, the guest speaker
was Chay Blyth OBE BEM. He started his speech by announcing
that he was wondering whether to talk about 'CHS versus IMS' or
about his 'forthcoming round the world race in 67 footers'. Loud
laughter. The most appreciated jokes have a strong element of
truth. (He talked about the race!)

Four years later John Bourke, RORC commodore,[13] told his
club

> 'Both systems [CHS and IMS] are doing a first class job for their
> respective fleets. It has become rather popular to decry one or
> other system. I prefer to be in favour of both'.

Apart from the fact that by then in the CHS countries (assumed
as Britain, France, Ireland plus the countries listed in **Fig 9.10**),
there were no 'respective fleets' the statement is difficult to fathom.
IMS was, as described in Chapter 7, being shadowed in RORC
races and not used elsewhere in Britain. In France CHS ruled,
though some one-off regattas were billed for IMS. There the
position was complicated in that the national authority, FFV,
embraced IMS and some friction ensued with UNCL, which ran,
as described, CHS; UNCL was also the hands-on organization for
most national racing. France also had a local rule HN (Handicap
National) for standard production boats; this was at the same level
as PY in Britain.

Proponents of IMS said it was meant to attract 'the top of the
fleet', but this was never defined and was probably unable to
support its own rule. In fact CHS and IMS are there to rate the
same type of yacht, or at least they have a huge 'overlap'.

If the RORC was bold, it might have said, in say 1990, that its races were all on IMS. However it feared a lack of entries, failed to show the courage of its convictions, so struggled on, presumably with the rallying cry 'we favour both rules'!

The authorities have showed a marked reluctance to analyse the results of races in which a boat uses both rules. One might have thought it would have provided excellent data for decision making. Perhaps the resulting exercise would not have been to their liking. So it has been left to the author and others to set out the facts.

Among conclusions reached are *(1) that if the rules are split in the same race/regatta, it actually lowers the number of entries (because of the uncertainty and unequal sizes of yacht in a division); (2) if one rule is shadowed, the results are invariably much the same under CHS and IMS*. (While we have already seen that multiple t-o-d and single t-o-t in IMS produce 'the same' order!) (**Fig 9.6**).

There are changes in order at times, but not always what might be expected. The IMS Farr 40.7 class *Bounder* (Chris Little) was campaigned very fully in CHS/IMS simultaneously. After the 1993 season her skipper wrote

> 'The interesting thing about the season was the way the IMS boats were only very competitive in CHS; under IMS we were down the pan, strange really. I hope the problems that owners get, with having some rocket scientist publishing the results hours later, can be overcome'.[14]

Prizes. In the RORC an attempt was made to encourage owners into IMS racing in 1990 by giving the main prizes to IMS rated yachts. That season it was running the three rules (CHS, IMS, IOR) in its races. The then commodore, Jonathan Bradbeer wrote

> 'We are in a dilemma with three rating systems running at the same time, all of which have a particular reason for being maintained. We have become (*sic*) committed to IMS for our principal system for the next few years. [It is] a definitive rule which given time, we believe, will provide some extremely good and fair racing for a highly disparate fleet... We are all very concious of how successful CHS has been ... it is our intention to award major prizes to both CHS and IMS'.[15]

However when the prize allocation was published it showed eight important races giving their traditional trophies to IMS and even some to second in IMS. Just two overall prizes went to CHS. Complaints ensued.

The commodore wrote again:

Overall corrected time order in Fastnet race 1995.

Actual IMS order	CHS order of IMS rated	Actual CHS order
1. Nicorette	Nicorette	Nicorette
2. Deerstalker	Deerstalker	Deerstalker
3. Sunstone	Twee Gezusters	Sureema
4. Twee Gezusters	Buckshot	Clarionet
5. Blue Jane	Sunstone	Twee Gezusters
6. Buckshot	Course I Can	Stormy Weather
7. Course I Can	Kusima	Buckshot
8. Kusima	Deadbeat	Sunstone
9. Raspa [31]	Arbitrator	Course I Can
10. Deadbeat	Securon III	Kusima
11. Red Dragon	Billy J Whizz [22]	Deadbeat
12. Katie Uptick	Redcoat III [17]	Rumour
13. Xantor [32]	Yeoman XXVIII [18]	Delires
14. Arbitrator	Katie Uptick	Arbitrator
15. Securon III	Red Dragon	Securon III

Notes: (i) [ ] indicate place on 'the other' rating, where this is beyond 15th. (ii) Had all CHS boats been IMS rated positions would have looked even more similar on both rules.

Overall corrected time order in RORC St Vaast race 1995.

Actual IMS order	*CHS order of IMS boats*
1. Deerstalker	Deerstalker
2. Redcoat III	Redcoat III
3. Five Star	Serendip
4. Serendip	Dabula Manzi
5. Dabula Manzi	Billy J Whizz
6. Xantor	Dansos
7. Billy J Whizz	Five Star
8. Dansos	Xantor

Fig 9.6 *Some results from actual races of CHS and IMS order: who is to say which is 'correct'?*

'... it was our intention to do as I described, but the main committee overturned its previous decision and allotted the prizes as you see them now ... the commodore is not an autocrat ...'.

Records show that the vice commodore was then John Dare and the rear commodore was Tom Jackson. *For the owners and sailors, the arm twisting did not work and over the next couple of years, as numbers of IMS starters proved derisory, the trophies returned to the CHS competitors.*

As for the three rating rules, it is a strange argument to say that one can make no decision in a matter because each course of action has merits!

As the 1990 season opened, *The Daily Telegraph* commented

'The RORC has split its middle market fleet into two groups. Of the two Hustler 35s entered in the Cervantes Trophy race, one is sailing CHS and the other IMS. Alan Green, RORC Director of Racing, admits "I'm not very happy with three rating systems. I don't think our [number of starters] is big enough to sustain them". A few influential RORC committee members are blamed by competitors for IMS as well as CHS being offered in Britain and some sailors see the club's decision to switch their principal trophies from CHS and IOR to IMS as arm twisting. Britain's biggest race, the Round the Island [not RORC] will not be offering IMS'.[16]

After three seasons of IMS disinterest and the disastrous Commodores' Cup (Chapter 8), the same Alan Green was prepared to announce (and so reverse Bradbeer's statement above).

'For 1993 CHS has been adopted as the main system for RORC races . . . IMS results will be calculated as an additional feature to the main result on the CHS'.[17]

CHS had long been in use for all major regattas in Britain and IMS dropped except in the RORC's own races. Yet with John Bourke, coming direct from ORC, as mentioned, as commodore, the club still struggled to enlist entries, quite who they were was not certain, into its shadowed IMS. As late as March 1996, his 'IMS committee chairman' sent a letter round the yachting press

'. . . IMS is the only way to go for the serious racing yachtsman. CHS and PHRF cannot bear the burden of dedicated, competitive winners (*sic*) . . . IMS is well able to handle the strain of the inquisitive innovative yachtsman . . . yacht clubs will be advised and assisted, where necessary, in trying to encourage their amateur racers with the professional approach to opt for this measured system'.[18]

There was much more on this vein. It was an old cracked record, unbelievable to see after so many (eight!) years. What was he trying to say? CHS actually penalizes 'hot boats' more than IMS, so why should 'ordinary boats' go into the latter. So then who do the 'hot boats' sail against? And which one of those is advantaged in IMS? Thus ran the confusions of two rating rules in one race for the same boats, oddly unique to the RORC.

Once the RORC had moved IMS to TCFs, it became possible to see which rule suited one boat against another. If boat A has CHS TCF 1 and IMS TCF 1, he can find which rating suits him better against boat B, which has CHS TCF 2 and IMS TCF 2. Solve the following simple formulae:

$$y = \text{IMS TCF 2/IMS TCF 1}$$

$$z = \text{CHS TCF 2/CHS TCF 1}$$

If y is more than z, then IMS is more advantageous for boat A. If y is less than z, CHS is more advantageous for boat A. This is against B. It is not possible to look at an entry list as all the boats will move about in the TCFs of the two rules. Presumably the interesting other boat is a close and persistent rival.

Channel Handicap 1996 and its predecessors gradually homed in on a number of reasons for CHS success, eventually 14 in number. These are listed in **Fig 9.7**. Most of them show the opposite effect in IMS, though as published annually this was for obvious reasons not emphasized. It is simple enough to work out the contrasts, such as cheap/expensive, quick decisions on rule/slow international bureaucracy, age allowance/no age allowance, direct weighing/ tricky displacement calculations, and so on!

In a paper to a high level seminar organized in London by the RORC in September 1995,[19] the author showed a table (**Fig 9.8**) of time allowances under CHS and IMS for a range of then well known boats, each against each. As might be expected the latest IMS machines do well in IMS against earlier IMS designs and others. The times are there for all to see, the only way to compare the TCFs being to work out corrected time after an hour (or elapsed time needed to equate on corrected time, though the latter would have been more complex to calculate for many boats). The question posed after inspecting these figures is: *which is the 'fair' rating system here?*

Fourteen reasons for CHS success
Secret formulae: no designed exploitation or calculated trade-offs.
Low overall price: no levies for layered administration.
Certificates worldwide issued from only two rating offices, cutting out variations in application.
The rule is one of measurement and rating: it is not performance based, so does not tax good sailing.
Admits developing materials and techniques, such as carbon fibre spars, asymmetric spinnakers and water ballast: rating rather than banning them.
The time allowance is in the form of a TCF which is instantly applicable by race committees and crews and does not depend on any assumed distance.
CHS committee directly represents each region in the UK and elsewhere, giving input from sailors on the water. Designers and commercial interests have no direct role.
Has the most accurate and well tried method of determining yacht weight of any rule, by measurer controlled, calibrated load cell.
There is international use of CHS especially in Britain, France, Hong Kong, Ireland, Italy, Portugal, Turkey and the Far East; also in warm water round the world races.
Allows for offshore and cruising features, including sail-by-sail rating of cloth material.
Age allowance is part of the rating.
Substantial numbers certificated mean worthwhile entry sizes and narrower rating bands. Day keelboats are specially rated.
Rule changes can be made speedily and confidentially: no prolonged international wrangles and expensive meetings.
Race organizers can opt for level and cost of measurement, even within events, including CHS(E).

Fig 9.7 *Fourteen reasons for CHS success as given in its annual publication. Some of the advantages appear to be stated as the antithesis of features in IMS.*

CHS world
Many large regular fixtures are now (1996) dependent on CHS ratings for the participants. These include Gran Canaria to Barbados (ARC transatlantic) 50 boats, Solent spring series at Warsash and Lymington 120, Cornell organized world rallies (warm water routes) 40, Spi Ouest, La Trinité, 240 (maximum CHS allowed plus equal number ODs, Round the Island (of Wight) 510 (many more unrated and ODs), Clyde Scottish Week 125, Ford Cork

Week 350, Cowes to St Malo 220, Cowes Week 220 (and many OD classes), Fastnet race 240, La Nioulargue 130 (and other classes), King's Cup, Phuket, Thailand 60, China Sea race 75 and many regular weekend events all round the coasts of Britain, France and Ireland (**Fig 9.9**).

To assist all this lot there are 13 representatives around the coasts of the United Kingdom: Cornwall, South Wales, North Wales, Scotland, Northern Ireland, Channel Islands and so on plus some people for sailing schools, and specialized offshore organizations. Overseas there are CHS representatives stationed in Australia (various areas), Bahrain, Brunei, Cyprus, Dubai, Hong Kong, Iceland, Ireland, Kuwait, Madeira, Malaysia, Malta, Philippines, Portugal, Singapore and Thailand.

Paris has its own representatives around 'the hexagon' and others in Italy, Greece, Spain and Turkey, whose applications go to France. For some of these countries and the world the detailed numbers of certificates are shown in **Figs 9.10** and **9.11**. By way of comparison, some peak years of IMS and IOR in respective countries are listed.

As for the designs that have done well, it really is a huge range. Designers have tried at times to fit CHS, but, as mentioned, they simply cannot offer an owner 'the latest boat to the rule'. Winners and placed boats have included RORC rule, IOR rule of all stages, 12-metres, One Tonners, lots of Half and Three-Quarter Tonners, production boats like Beneteaus, J-35s, J-39s, converted maxis (in

Fig 9.8 *This table compares the time allowances for a number of actual yachts of recognizable type under CHS and IMS respectively. As it is misleading to compare directly TCFs under each rule, the figures are deduced on what happens for an elapsed time of one hour for each yacht. The figures are minutes and decimals of a minute and represent what the yacht ON THE LEFT GETS from the yacht ABOVE in the table. A minus sign indicates that the yacht on the left GIVES time.*

Examples are as follows: The Sigma 38 gets virtually the same time from the J35 under both rules; Sunstone gets substantially more time under IMS against all boats until she comes up against the ILC40, which is specially designed to IMS; the J39 is particularly badly favoured in IMS compared with CHS; IMS designs from the early 1990s are better off under CHS when racing against the latest IMS designs.

This table was presented to the RORC at a seminar in 1995 to demonstrate the limitations of IMS and ask: which rule is 'correct'?! No answer was ever given.

their weather), mini-tonners (in *their* weather!), light displacement flyers (given a long fast reach/run), Swans (given a long moderate beat). CHS maybe 'favours' the medium to heavy displacement, older boat and when these are well manned they are formidable.

YACHTS ON THE LEFT GET TIME FROM YACHTS ABOVE.

	SIGMA 33		SUNSTONE		SIGMA 38		J35 (FIONA VIII)		SIGMA 400		IMX 38		J35 (JACKDAW)		SWAN 46 (NEGRA)		OLD N.G.		1 TON (IOR '89)		TRIPP 40 (IMS '92)		MUMM 36 (IMS '93)	
	CHS	IMS	CHS	IMS	CHS	IMS	CHS	IMS	CHS	IMS	CHS	IMS	CHS	IMS	CHS	IMS	CHS	IMS	CHS	IMS	CHS	IMS	CHS	IMS
ILC 40 (IMS '95)	15.72	13.36	14.52	14.74	11.82	8.93	9.48	9.56	8.44	5.60	8.10	9.95	7.02	3.18	7.86	6.14	9.96	4.45	6.12	4.22	6.06	2.93	4.44	2.18
MUMM 36 (IMS '93)	10.86	9.57	8.66	10.45	6.96	5.44	4.62	2.77	8.13	1.81	3.24	2.16	2.16	-0.61	3.00	1.35	2.1	0.66	1.26	-0.43	0.86	-1.20		
TRIPP 40 (IMS '92)	9.66	10.43	8.46	11.31	5.76	6.00	3.42	3.63	2.88	2.67	2.04	3.02	0.96	0.25	1.80	2.21	0.90	1.52	0.06	-1.29				
1 TON (IOR '89)	9.60	9.14	8.40	10.01	5.70	4.11	3.36	2.34	2.52	1.38	1.98	1.73	0.90	1.04	1.74	0.92	0.84	0.23						
OLD N.G.	8.76	8.91	7.56	9.74	4.86	4.48	2.52	2.11	1.89	1.75	1.14	1.50	0.06	-1.27	0.90	0.66								
SWAN 46 (NEGRA)	7.86	8.22	6.66	9.10	3.96	3.74	1.62	1.42	0.82	0.46	0.40	-0.81	-0.84	-1.86										
J39	8.70	10.18	7.50	11.06	4.80	5.75	2.46	3.38	1.62	1.91	1.08	1.72												
IMX 38	7.62	7.44	6.42	8.29	3.76	2.98	1.38	0.61	0.54	-0.35														
SIGMA 400	7.08	7.76	4.97	8.44	3.18	3.33	0.84	0.97																
J35 (FIONA VIII)	6.24	6.79	5.04	7.67	2.34	2.85																		
SIGMA 38	3.90	4.43	2.70	5.31																				
SUNSTONE	1.20	-0.89																						

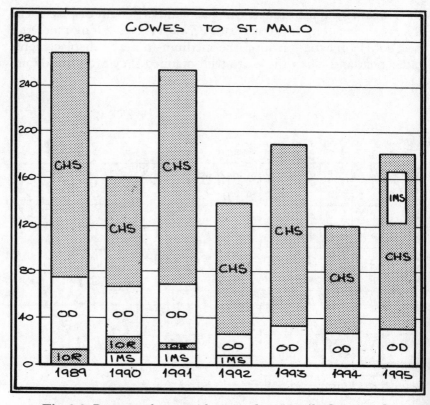

Fig 9.9 *Progress of a annual event, the 155-mile Cowes to St Malo race, popular with British and French yachts as well as other nationalities. For this kind of event CHS took over in an overall slightly decreasing entry. OODs are also rated CHS for results. IOR finished in 1991; IMS was not a separate class after 1992. Non-Fastnet years got less support, as there were alternative regattas; in Fastnet years the race was used by many as an optional 'qualifier'.*

Fig 9.10 *(Opposite page top) Where CHS boats were rated during the 1995 season (as at November 1995). (Sources: British and French rating offices).*

Fig. 9.11 *(Opposite page bottom) The maximum number of yachts ever rated in several countries and what year that happened, under three offshore rules: CHS, IMS and IOR. Brief comment in the right hand column on the circumstances in each country.*

CHS CERTIFICATES BY COUNTRY IN 1995

UNITED KINGDOM	2022	PHILIPPINES	22
FRANCE	800	ICELAND	19
ITALY	579	AUSTRALIA	17
SPAIN	528	MALAYSIA	17
IRELAND	242	USA	12
PORTUGAL	107	SWITZERLAND	12
TURKEY	99	MAURITIUS	12
BELGIUM, GERMANY,		SCANDINAVIA	11
NETHERLANDS	89	KUWAIT, BAHRAIN,	
HONG KONG	82	QATAR	7
GREECE	35	MONACO	6
MALTA	34	LUXEMBOURG	4
THAILAND	28	NEW ZEALAND	3
DUBAI	27	BRUNEI	2
SINGAPORE	23	COSTA RICA, TAIWAN,	
		ST VINCENT 1 EACH!	

TOTAL 4842

MAXIMUM BOATS EVER BY COUNTRY

COUNTRY	CHS	IOR	IMS	REMARKS
UK AND IRELAND	2264	1850	137	MORE IN CHS THAN EVER IN OTHERS
	1995	1977	1992	
FRANCE	800	664	152	SAME PATTERN AS U.K.
	1995	1974	1994	
ITALY	579	1319	999	LATE SUPPORTER OF I.O.R. BIG PLAYER
	1995	1988	1992	
HOLLAND	28	813	613	DIRECT SWAP IOR TO IMS BUT NOT ALL
	1995	1980	1993	
AUSTRALIA	43	539	372	NO RETURN TO IOR NUMBERS
	1991	1986	1994	
BRAZIL	0	132	91	FOLLOWS U.S.A.
	~	1973	1994	
U.S.A.	22	4000	1351	FIRST IN, FIRST OUT IN IOR AND IMS
	1993	1973	1990	

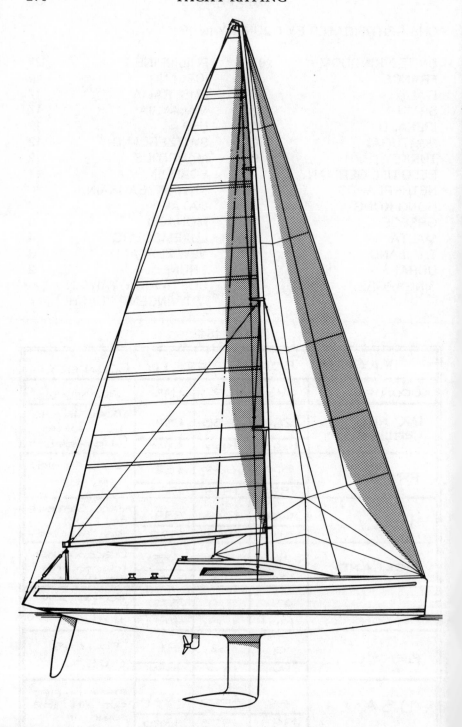

Fig 9.12 *There is no world 'successful shape' in CHS, mainly because of its secret formulae. Various boats do very well in different sailing areas. Left hand page shows* Mustang Sally *designed by John Corby of Cowes in 1995 specially to race CHS. With no inclining test in the rule a heavy bulb on the keel was used but this itself attracts unknown factors! There is masthead rig, full length battens and moderate displacement. Near vertical stem became the practice in virtually all rating rules in mid-90s. For most of the century there had been arguments to rationalize bow overhang: the reader knows it sprung from LWL measurement one hundred years earlier!*

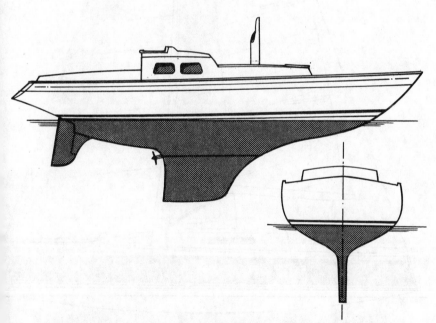

Fig 9.13 *The S&S 34 (LOA 34ft, 10.4m) a design from 1968 to* the RORC rule. *Several of these in different hands have had major offshore successes in CHS, 30 years later. Some say boats of such type are rated generously, but this Olin Stephens design keeps going in all weathers offshore.*

Strangely this appears also to apply to IMS! **Figs 9.12** to **9.14** show a few successful CHS profiles.

If the author seems to enthuse over CHS, it is only because it appears to work and attract the sailors. But he is not starry-eyed; experience shows that rating rules can go into a nose dive quite quickly. As he writes, he hears of plans to 'expand the use of CHS'. That could be inviting in the Trojan Horse: it could prove folly.

As for the Paris rating office, Anglo-French upsets seem long over, with a report from the RORC Rating Office that its

'. . . chairman and Technical Manager had travelled to Paris for the annual meeting with UNCL. This had been very productive with a number of significant decisions taken. Relationships between the two clubs were very good'.[20]

PHRF
The big one
The essential assets of the Performance Handicap Racing Fleet system of rating are that it is very large indeed and that it has worked for many years.

Unlike CHS (and IMS and IOR), this is a system for offshore and 'habitable' yachts based on the observed performance of the 'class' of production boat or one-design. In that sense it is closer to Portsmouth Yardstick (Chapter 10). It has proved eminently suitable for the way yacht racing has always been organized in the USA and is used right across the continent including Canada with just a few outstations in Hawaii (a US state anyway), US Caribbean and New Zealand (which runs its own version).[21] The number of yachts rated to PHRF is given as 20,000 plus another 20,000 using it without membership. The rounded off figures may be unconvincing, but were confirmed in 1996.[22]

This makes PHRF by far the world's biggest rating rule, though in the US the word 'handicap' is preferred. This is a word which has been used with a more restricted meaning in this book, but it will be found here in reference to PHRF, because that is what the users in the USA call it.

Fig 9.14 *A 1996 concept by Rob Humphreys, a leading race design office, for both CHS and IMS racing. There are design concessions to a wider cruiser/racer public in this* Yachting World *H35 boat with masthead rig, coachroof, medium displacement and moderate ends.*

In 1996 there were 114 'fleets' across the US, together with groups such as New England, which covered Maine, New Hampshire and Massachusetts with 1000 registered yachts.[23] There may be small variations in the rating of a similar standard yacht between groups; this poses no problem, as when the same yacht races with another group, her rating figure is adjusted to remain the same relative to competitors in the fleet. Figures from two Long Island Sound groups tend to average 3 to 9 seconds per mile higher than most other PHRF groups. North West, Chesapeake Bay, Lake Michigan and Lake Erie tend to be lower than most.

PHRF was not a reaction to IOR. Amazingly it was begun as early as 1958 in Southern California 'disenchanted with the built in cost and obsolescence of the rule of the Cruising Club of America (CCA)'.[24] With the arrival of IOR in 1970, we have seen the big move into it, as the rule to solve the problems of the CCA. When IOR itself began to lose support in the US, the adherents looked for somewhere else to go. PHRF was the answer for them, but now not only on the west coast, but across the shores and lakes of the continent.

Totally in character
The way PHRF is run remains totally in character with race organization in the USA. Once again we see a benevolent and weak national authority content to leave final authority with regions or localities, which themselves are separated by great distances. There too are variations in methods, but a remarkable reservoir of organizers and handicappers in areas and groups, rightly proud of their competence and independence. Their extent is probably unique to the US and there are very few other places where it would be possible to run such a system. The fleets do not want a centralized bureaucracy (which would happen in Europe) and a sailor with a rating problem in Chicago would not dream of calling the national authority, US Sailing, in Newport, RI.

US Sailing does have a PHRF Committee, but it has a coordinating rather than executive role. It helps all areas by publishing an annual US-PHRF handicap book, with assigned handicaps obtained from outstations. Then there is an update, the US-PHRF monthly bulletin with the latest figures.

There is no danger of centralization, if only because of the varying figures, which are best left to adjustment as a boat arrives. There is a strong 'hands off' element about US Sailing. As for international authorities (except for Canada which is integrated for PHRF) they are on another planet. Says a commentator

'The establishment has never understood PHRF. They don't grasp how a bunch of amateurs can control 98 per cent of the offshore racing in this country. Look at any PHRF group and you wonder who these guys are. They are unknowns. The "powers that be" would love to get their sticky, slimy fingers on PHRF. There is no way that would happen ... We in PHRF have considered multiple handicaps, but the race committees do not want any part of it. Many competitors have told us that the secret to success is "to keep it simple".

'At least one PHRF group has made annual contributions to IMS research, in hope that it would be successful and keep the rock stars out of PHRF. But alas they keep shooting themselves in the foot...'.[25]

How it runs

A PHRF yacht comes to the start line with a handicap – or as more usually called in this work, a time allowance of so many seconds per mile. Time-on-distance, as we know, prevails throughout the USA. A Tripp 36 might have a figure of 75 seconds per mile and a Jeanneau OD 35 in class would be 81. In the US the sailors would simply call this 'a handicap of 81'. The higher the figure, the better the allowance and the slower (presumed) the boat. Therefore on a 6 mile race the Tripp 36 gives the JOD35 36 seconds. As with other t-o-d, a class may show a scratch boat with simply the handicap on her, so here the Tripp 36 is 'scratch' and the JOD35 has 6; this might be 36 if the committee knows the race is 6 miles (a fixed distance is more likely in a passage race, port to port, so for 150-mile fixed course, the JOD35 gets exactly 900 seconds or 15 minutes.

When a known production boat enlists, her handicap is read straight off from the fleet list. Some fleets are big, over 2000 in Southern California, nearly as many in Northern California, 1000 in New England, 500 in Narragansett Bay on Rhode Island's shore.

An unknown production boat may be found on the US Sailing listing and adjusted for the local scale. A new production boat needs more care, but the first attempt will be to equate her to a known design. A form is sent by the owner to the handicapping committee. US Sailing also has a list of dimensions of some 4000 known boats, which again helps equate the new one. Once that has been done and if the production boat is known, but has been altered, variation from *base* is taken (another traditional American concept). Typical PHRF bases count a 150 per cent genoa (more or less affects rating), standard supplied spars, spinnaker pole as base of foretriangle, accommodation must not have been 'stripped' and propeller type would be applied. PHRF is prepared to handicap any self righting single-hulled sailing yacht complying with at least ORC category 4 special regulations.

When performance (the word at the core of this system) is observed, it has to be assessed clear of extreme crewing (brilliant or lousy), dirty bottom, very old sails and age.

If central data from US Sailing cannot help, then another PHRF group may be able to do so. Displacement remains a problem to determine, as in all rating rules.

Other inputs for the group handicapper to construct a figure, which is the 'handicap figure', include IMS certificates, other rating rule certificates (e.g. Midget Ocean Racing Club, MORC) and even old IOR ratings. The level of reputation of designer and builder for racing boats plus the manufacturer's claim for PHRF figure. If the company wants to make their boat sound fast, it claims a low number; this in turn is bad news for the new user. It can go the other way, where a small builder might want a high number to produce early results. As the committee homes in on a handicap, it knows that up to 3 (seconds per mile) is a common adjustment then, or later after observation; up to 6 is a significant change; over 6 means that something has gone wrong.

John J. Collins, chairman of the US Sailing PHRF Committee, says that it is useful to have someone from the marine industry advising a handicap committee. It all sounds hit and miss, yet he declares:

> 'Nevertheless I am usually heartened to see, when the dust has settled, how close an initial handicap comes to the actual speed potential of the boat'[26] (**Fig 9.15**).

Numbers for boats

Has there been in some strange way a reversion to those days in the nineteenth century in America and England when each club ran its own handicap system, yet the boats were all the same? For here is some well known production boat, say the Swan 40, which has one allowance under IMS (or a number!), one under CHS and one under PHRF, not to mention other rules. However the named three are big ones.

Yes, following the disintegration of IOR and its gradual non-acceptance, early in the USA and later in Europe, the yachts have fallen into such rules. It is where the sailors went, what the sailors did. Since many production boats are sold around the world, it

Last Name   Initial
COLLINS, J

PHRF-NE

Year
1996

Fleet
MARBLEHEAD

THE PERFORMANCE HANDICAP RACING FLEET OF NEW ENGLAND

HANDICAPS
66   78
Racing Cruising
HANDICAPPER USE ONLY

PRESS DOWN - FILL OUT COMPLETELY - USE BALL POINT PEN

SAIL #	YACHT NAME	HULL #	YEAR
42029	SHAMROCK	29	86

Make & Model (e.g. C&C 24): HINCKLEY 42C   Rig: SLP   Designer: McCURDY + RHODES

Masterand/or Owner: JOHN J. COLLINS

Address: 23 PILGRIM ROAD

City: MARBLEHEAD   State: MA   Zip: 01945

Home Phone: 617-639-1648   Alternate Phone: 508-475-9090

List 5 Headsails by % of LP
Type (e.g. 170% Reacher, Blooper)
Check off 3 Head Sails for Cruising Class

1. 164% ☒   2. 135% ☒
3. 105% ☒   4. ☐
5. ☐

STORM TRYSAIL ☒ STORM JIB ☒
HEAVY WEATHER JIB ☒
MIZZEN STAYSAIL ☐   MIZZEN ☐

SPINNAKER (Maximum 3)
SPINNAKER #1 .75 OZ.   OVERSIZE ☒
#2 1. OZ.   #3 1.7 OZ.   ASYMMETRICAL ☐
SPINNAKER POLE LENGTH 19.17   WHISKER POLE LENGTH

REQUEST RECREATIONAL HANDICAP ☐

REQUIRED:
Roller Furling
No KEVLAR/SPECTRA
1 Nylon Spinnaker Maximum
1 Jib ≥ 160% Maximum
1 Jib < 110% Maximum

BOAT MEASUREMENTS

I	FORETRIANGLE HEIGHT	57.75	LOA 41.0
J	FORETRIANGLE BASE	17.75	LWL 31.25
P	MAINSAIL LUFF	50.49	DRAFT 7.7
E	MAINSAIL FOOT	15.47	DISPL. 24,000
	BEAM	12.5	KEEL BALLAST WEIGHT 8,500
	KEEL BALLAST MATERIAL	LEAD	INTERNAL BALLAST WEIGHT NONE
	IMS GP	627.2	IOR/MORC

HAVE HULL, RIG, OR APPENDAGES EVER BEEN MODIFIED? (If YES Explain):   YES ☐   NO ☒

FOR HANDICAPPER USE ONLY

BASE HANDICAP	75
LP Adjustment	−6
Spin. Adjustment	−3
Rig. Adjustment	
Prop. Adjustment	
Recreational Adjustment	
Misc. Adjustment	
TOTAL:	66

Handicapper Notation & Initials

R.Wbss 22Jan96

I understand that it is my responsibility to notify the handicapper of changes to this yacht which affect measurement points, handicap adjustments, or would alter her from a standard boat.

It is an acknowledged responsibility of each owner and skipper to determine that his yacht is adequately equipped and maintained for ocean racing and assumes liability.

I certify that the above information is accurate.

Owner Signature (REQUIRED)   Date 26 Jan 96

MEMBERSHIP DUES
☐ NEW   ☒ RENEWAL

VARIABLES

ENGINE
☒ INBOARD
☐ OUTBOARD
☐ NONE

PROP. INSTAL.
☐ IN APERTURE
☒ EXPOSED SHAFT
☐ SAILDRIVE

RIG
☒ MASTHEAD
☐ FRACTIONAL
☐ OTHER
3 SETS OF SPREADERS

RUDDER
☐ KEEL ATTACHED
☐ SKEG
☒ SPADE
☐ OUTBOARD

PROP. TYPE
☐ FOLDING
☒ FEATHERING
☐ SOLID 2-BLADE
☐ SOLID 3-BLADE

KEEL
☒ FIN
☐ FULL
☐ CENTERBOARD
☐ WING ☐ OTHER

PRINT and PRESS HARD for Clear Copies

Fig 9.15 *Example of a PHRF rating certificate issued by one of the many PHRF fleets across North America.*

RATINGS COMPARED UNDER SIX RULES

CLASS OF YACHT	PHRF	CHS	PHRF 'TCF'	PY TCF	CYA	IMS TCF	DH TCF
J24	168	.928	.902	1.063	0.771		0.876
J29	117	.963	.977	1.148	0.847		
J35	71	1.045	1.057		0.868	0.9753	
J39	45	1.094	1.106		0.869	1.0166	
Albin Ballad	183	.877	.883	0.999			0.892
Contessa 32	180	.892	.887	1.014	.735 (n/s)		0.892
Sigma 33	144	.942	.936	1.078		0.8468	0.917
X119	42	1.110	1.112			0.992	1.050
Baltic 43	63-57	1.070	1.076		0.695 (B42)		1.070
X412	60	1.086	1.077				1.066
JOD 35	81	1.054	1.038				
Tripp 36	75	1.056	1.049			0.952	
Sigma 38	-	1.006	-	1.189	0.849	0.9206	
Melges 24	102	1.024	1.002		0.863		1.070
Swan 40	75	1.042	1.048		0.885		0.950
Swan 46	60	1.071	1.071		0.930	0.9837	1.074
Tripp 40	48	1.102	1.094		0.940	1.0206	
Boomerang	-75	1.398	1.419		1.072	1.3190	

becomes possible to compare the rating of a 'class' under the different rules. *It might also lead to some conclusions.*

What matters on the water is the time allowance, as we have seen in comparing CHS and IMS in **Fig. 9.8**.

Fig 9.16 compares what is offered to some designs and production boats in CHS and PHRF. Additionally for a few, their allowances in IMS are also compared. *There is a remarkable match for many boats between CHS and PHRF, despite their derivation from apparently quite different methods. This would seem to undermine the theory that an international rule is needed for when yachts visit other countries. In fact several European and Far East yachts, which have been in the habit of racing CHS have been happy to race in US regattas on PHRF and with success.*

To convert PHRF t-o-d to a TCF the following formula is used:

PHRF TCF = 606/(PHRF number + 500)

This can be compared directly with CHS for the Swan 40-2 like this:

PHRF is 75. CHS TCF is 1.042. Therefore calculating the PHRF TCF is 606/(75 + 500) = 1.044. So in the case there is only 0.002 difference between CHS and PHRF, or 0.2% or 7 seconds in the hour.

To convert IMS to PHRF, take the GPH (general purpose handicap) on the IMS certificate and subtract 550.

For the Swan 40-2, the IMS GPH was 625. In its case PHRF = 625 − 550 = 75, which is PHRF handicap!

An adjustment for age, not allowed in IMS, but to help a better PHRF handicap is to subtract 555 ± 20 for a new boat built in the year 1996, − 545 ± 8 for 1995 and − 550 ± 10 for 1994 and earlier. The extra ± amounts are PHRF 'fudge' for features on the yacht which IMS does not rate.

Fig 9.16 *Ratings of some common types of boat under several rules. Time allowances between well known and often sailed classes are likely to match (try them by applying TCFs): the problem for any kind of rule is the 'unusual' or novel. Among rules at top: PY is Portsmouth Yardstick, CYA is Caribbean Yachting Association, DH is Danish Handicap.*

10 Take your pick

'The world is so full of a number of things,
I'm sure we should all be as happy as kings.'
- Robert Louis Stevenson (1885).

IT WAS 1939 at the end of Chapter 3 when we left the metre boat classes of the International Yacht Racing Union. For the second time in their history, war stopped their progress; for the second time they re-emerged diminished. Cowes Week 1939, you remember, had ten 12-metre yachts competing and the great *Vim* had shown them the way.

Now in 1946, metre boats around Europe had either been destroyed, or their moderate wooden scantlings had not survived six years of damp lay up and neglect. In America the metre boats were of excellent design, but few. Well preserved were the light but habitable Baltic cruiser racers of the German forces, (the 100-, 50- and 30-square metres), rather than International rule boats. They had been rated under the German KR rule. These were seized, sailed back to England and split among the British armed services who had to use RORC or local rating.

Cowes Week 1946 saw two 8-metres, half a dozen 6-metres, but no 12s. Clyde Fortnight that year turned out four 8-metres and a couple of 6s. Meanwhile, as we know, the young men of action, demobilized from the war, went for ocean racing.

Ocean racing was however nothing to do with the IYRU. But its International classes retained a grip on important trophies, which included the British-American Cup, the One Ton Cup (until 1962), the Canada Cup and others particularly in Britain, Scandinavia and Long Island Sound. Thus the metre boats resumed their position as the aristocrats of inshore racing, where designers could still wrestle with the rule. Numbers were moderate, indeed by modern standards small at any regatta (six or a dozen), but this had already been the case in the 1930s. Some new boats were built, planked up in wood and duly launched with ceremony down a slipway, and made (yachting) news.

Still looking for formulae

The gentlemen of the IYRU were not so different from their fathers, for they still appeared to be in search of formulae which would either rate boats 'better' or produce a 'better boat' or even result in a 'less expensive' boat.

The first gathering of the International Yacht Racing Union since November 1938 met in London in December 1946. The British and the Scandinavians had proposals for new rules; the USA, as previously mentioned, was not a member.

'The Scandinavian Yacht Union, particular Norway, is submitting [proposals for] new international rating rules, while Britain will propose a new class to a rating rule which incorporates the best features of the 6-metre and 30 square metre classes. Charles E. Nicholson is behind this and he has the assistance of his old friend, Malden Heckstall-Smith, possibly the greatest living authority on rating rules'.[1]

The classes which emerged from these ideas took some time, more than three years in fact. While the IYRU deliberated with its international committees, sailors were piling into the ocean racing classes whose rules were run by hands-on clubs. In early 1950 however the new classes were announced, the British 'idea' being the 5.5-metre (a proposed 4.5-metre was rejected as too small) and the Scandinavian scheme creating metre boat cruiser-racer classes. See below.

6s, 8s, 12s

Meanwhile a select but influential number of owners in several countries kept the old metre boats going at a high standard. The 6-metre continued to be used in the Olympic Games until 1952. The British-American Cup for the same class was sailed in 1949/51/53 and last in 1955 (twenty years later revived in one-design classes) and the last 6-metre One Ton, as mentioned was 1962. This indicates the demise of the International Rule in first class yacht racing, the keenest owners having migrated to the increasing ocean racing fixtures.

There was a revival in the 1980s and 1990s, as a reaction to the problems of the IOR. Today 6s and 8s race regularly in modest numbers in several countries, coming together for championships with a respectable turn out. Often the fleets are divided into classics and modern designs. The International Rule is therefore the longest lasting active rating rule in history.

The 1995 International 8-metre class championship sailed in the Netherlands saw 14 starters from 6 countries (Belgium, Finland, France, Netherlands, Sweden, USA) in 6 races and there is no reason why the class will not continue for another 90 years. It is more likely to prosper if it does not become too widespread. 14 starters is of the same order as was seen in the 1930s and probably even pre-WWI, when, as we know, the class was expanding the most quickly.

A major revival of the 12-metre class occurred when it was adopted as the class to be used in the America's Cup starting in 1957. It has been too well chronicled to be discussed here, but in rating terms, it meant that the rule was under scrutiny and in good repair for thirty years until 1987, when the International 12-metre was used in the America's Cup for the last time. The number of 12-metres built post war was as follows: in the USA 27, Australia 14, Britain 7, France 7, Italy 4, Canada 3, New Zealand 2. Not bad for a 1906 rule of rating (**Fig 10.1**).

Today the IYRU keeps the rules published and available under the authority of the respective international class associations. 6s, 8s and 12s all have the same basic formula, unchanged for many years.

$$\text{Rating in metres} = (L + 2d - F + (S)^{1/2})/2.37$$

d, girth difference; F, freeboard, L, length, S, sail area.

As always there are many sub-clauses to support these main symbols, but despite allowing modern materials and the use of computers for design, the International Rule has not inflated like IMS and IOR. For instance the 6-metre rule of 1995, takes just 24 pages of A5 (148 × 105 mm) including measurement diagrams and such matters as sail numbers.[2] It was 10 pages plus extra measurement instructions in 1908, when the formula itself was actually longer (Chapter 3).

Even some major factors, it will be noted, are not in the formula. These are taken care of in such ways as this (for 6-metres; 8s and 12s having different numbers): displacement shall not be less than

$$(0.2 \text{ LWL (in metres)} + 0.15)^3$$

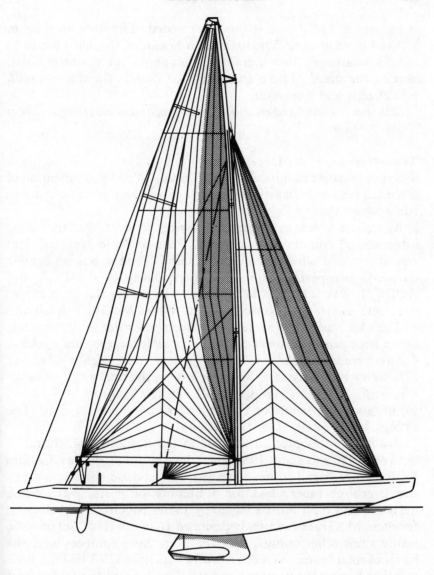

Fig 10.1 *The final profile of the 12-metre class after 80 years of moulding by rule makers (the IYRU) and designers. This is a typical competitor in the America's Cup of 1987 (the last time the 12 was used). The class had taken on an intense and rarified life since 1957, when it was first used for the Cup. Existing 12s race today (1996) at times, but there is no incentive to build a new one. Note here wing keel, trim tab, low rig, distribution of displacement in hull shape.*

A penalty is added to L if this is exceeded. The minimum beam allowed is 1830 mm. The maximum height of the sail plan is 13 metres measured 'from a point 90 mm above the covering board abreast the mast'. There are quantified clauses for the mainsail, foretriangle and spinnaker.

With such refined and relatively simple measurement, the metre boat classes continue.

The attempt at cruiser-racers

There is no point in mincing words on this IYRU promulgation of intended post-war classes, which stands as a lesson on how not to run a rating rule.

As seen, it took some three or four years to create the rule, while international committees wrangled. Then a whole range of sizes was announced which diluted each class. Then it was up against currently prospering club rules, particularly of the CCA and RORC. It was said that the rule itself was mainly the work of two designers, Bjarn Aas, Norwegian, and James McGruer, Scottish.

The idea was to revive the metre boats of earlier in the century, *but to have proper accommodation and enable them to race offshore. Classes were to be at the certain fixed (or level as we might say) ratings in metres,* which also were the lower limit of the waterline (whatever that was!). There was an upper WL limit, which for the 9-metre, for instance, was 9.45m or $1\frac{1}{2}$ feet longer than the lower limit. The ratings were 7, 8, 9, 10.5, 12, 13.5, 15!

Boats were designed to the rule in the Scandinavian countries between 1950 and about 1965 when the combining of the CCA and RORC rules began to be envisaged. In Scotland there was an 8-metre cruiser racer class for a number of years, eight being designed and built on the Clyde by James McGruer and three in Sweden. McGruer eventually designed 16 of the class, not only 8s, but at a few other ratings, (**Fig 10.2**) but these numbers were the kinds of total found. At a guess world wide (the USA had not been asked and was not interested, though Olin J. Stephens II designed one or two to the order of European owners), about 50 were ever built of all numbered class; and at some levels (7-metres, 15-metres?) none.

The rule (last published by IYRU in 1964) looked rather like that of the CCA, with a base boat upon which beam, draft, overhang components and so on were 'added' as plus or minus, the whole lot then simply being multiplied by a propeller factor. The fixed figure of rating in metres had to be equal or less than

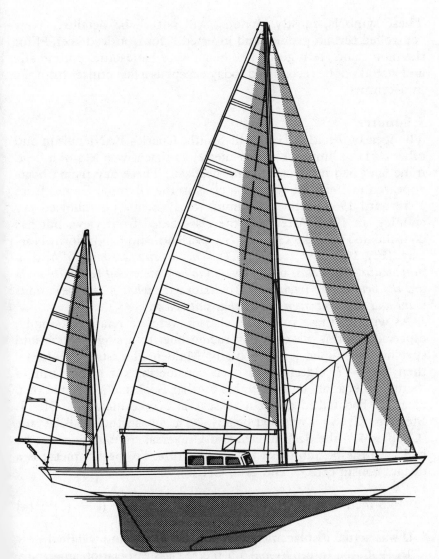

Fig 10.2 *One of the larger classes of IYRU cruiser racer rule, a 13.5-metre of 1962, designed by James McGruer in Scotland. Built in mahogany and teak with some steel frames, LOA was 66ft 9in (20.34m), LWL 46ft (14.02m) (therefore overhangs were equal to 45 per cent of the waterline, but went without comment at the time); beam 15ft 6in (4.72m). The two-masted rig was not common.*

$$1/2(L + (S)^{1/2} - F \pm B \pm D \pm P + A \pm H + C - K) \, Pf$$

These symbols, mostly obvious, will not all be detailed. They controlled certain profiles and inserted K for iron/lead keel, Pf for the motor and stern gear. The boats were handsome, undramatic and would not be recognized today except as a fast cruiser from the mid-century.

5.5-metre

The idea by Malden Heckstall-Smith, Charles E. Nicholson and others was to 'improve' the 6-metre, so that it was less of a 'lead mine' and had no overlappping headsail. These day racing boats appeared in 1951. They were a class in the Olympic Games from 1952 until 1968, with a maximum of 19 boats (one allowed per country) in 1960. After that the class faded from view, but has consolidated in Lake Geneva, Switzerland, and Oslo Fiord, Norway. (**Fig 10.3**, also see **Fig 6.7**). *This a prime example of how an 'unpopular' rated class once expected to be widespread (actually what did the originators intend?) provides exactly what a few enthusiasts want and can control in a way that suits them.*

As with all these rules, the clauses were/are relatively simple, especially as this was/is a day racing boat to a single rating and specific sub-dimensions. Actually Malden Heckstall-Smith, by then (1946-47) elderly, had been considering for a long time a 'better' rule, as an antidote to his brother Bookstall's International rule. He had talked about it to several people including Olin J. Stephens II.[3] So it was that he advised as a basis the old BRA rule (Chapter 4) – the Seawanhaka and Universal combination – as he had with the beginning of the RORC rule. So the 5.5-metre is a distant cousin of IOR and even CHS!

$$5.5 \text{ metres} = 0.9 \left[(L \times (S)^{1/2})/12 \times (D)^{1/3}) + (L + (S)^{1/2})/4 \right]$$

D was actual displacement, the boat simply being weighed.

In 1996, the International 5.5-metre class association amazingly claimed 120 boats in the world with valid certificates (renewed annually). Championships on Lake Geneva, Switzerland, in 1995 and at Crouesty, France, in 1994, saw 41 and 42 starters respectively. This is a big turn out by any standard. In 1997 major events were scheduled for Australia. National letters on sails include Bahamas, Finland, Germany, Norway, Sweden, UK, USA. In 1996 two new boats were building in England; carbon fibre spars were allowed and the old Lloyds scantlings (as decided as a reaction

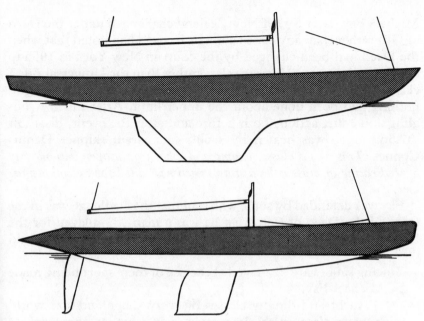

Fig 10.3 *The 5.5-metre has a particular niche among rating rules. Largely the work of Charles E. Nicholson with Malden Heckstall-Smith and his favourite combination of the Seawan-haka and Universal rules (as found in the RORC rule and then IOR), it was intended to replace after WWII the International rule 6-metre. Top profile shows an early design (about 1952), certainly lighter than the 6. Bottom profile is of a 1995 boat, rules having been changed some years back to allow a separate rudder (see also Chapter 6 for 'frozen' 5.5-metre boats). Typical modern LOA is 29ft 8in (9m).*

to the skimming dish in 1906) were dropped in favour of specific rules.

OTHER FORMULA AND RATED CLASSES

There are a number of classes which are not in the popular stream of racing, or which appeal to a minority. These use ratings, or at least have formulae or limits, which can and have to be designed to. The purpose of this chapter is to list them, with or without their actual rule basis.

America's Cup

The use of 12-metres was destroyed when the 1987 winners from San Diego dithered over the arrangements for the next series.

Michael Fay (later Sir) of New Zealand challenged under the Deed of Gift rather than any class rule. His lawyers had noted that when the Deed had been changed by the court in New York in 1956 to enable racing by the 12-metre class rather than the Universal rule J class, by means of a decrease of minimum waterline length, nothing had been done about the upper limit. After much wrangling and court actions both before and after the event, his 123ft (37.5m) sloop was beaten by a 60ft catamaran, skipper Dennis Conner. *This was a classic example of what can happen without any agreed rating or class rule, a state sometimes called for by commentators.*

Fay was defended by some who said that the challenge was in the spirit of the Deed of Gift, that he was a man who played for the highest stakes and so on. But a letter in a London newspaper said

'Racing sailors are dismayed at the use of their sport being made by Michael Fay.

'... yacht and dinghy classes of every shape and size world wide have class rules. It matters not whether these are of international status or agreed between a few local owners. They enable the sport to operate either "boat for boat" or by some form of acceptable handicap.

'From 1870, when a British owner first challenged for the America's Cup, the rules for each challenge have been agreed between challenger and defender. Sometimes there were lengthy periods while these were resolved...

'Mr Fay chose to overturn this tradition... he built a boat which belongs to no racing class. What then were his opponents expected to do?'[4]

It was no surprise that many interested parties then had a series of meetings to ensure that for the subsequent America's Cup events there would be an established class. The world was now

Fig 10.4 *America's Cup yacht: the 1990s saw a rating rule devised for Cup use only. First races were in 1992; second were in 1995. The boat was intended to be testing (and so 'extreme'). Called the IACC, the formulae rates in at 24-metres, very close to the 76ft rating of the J-class, but the new class refers to LOA not waterline. These dimensions on an actual yacht are about 75ft/ 55ft (23m/17m). For high performance inshore racing only, it is a reversion to an intentional skimming dish. In 1995 one boat broke in two and sank in seconds.*

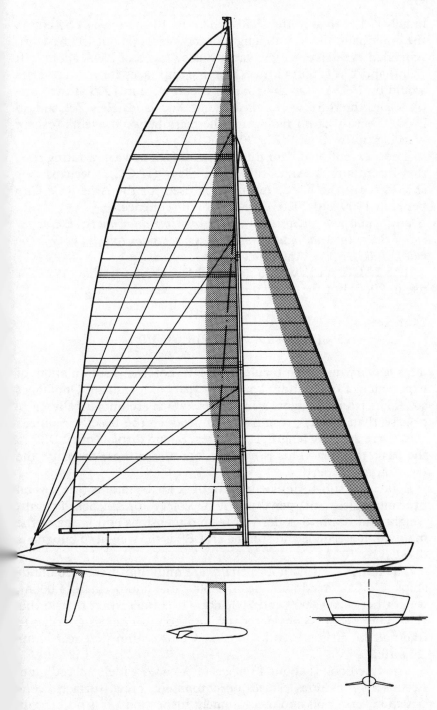

hugely richer than in the 1950s when the 12-metre was chosen; on the other hand the overall length of the J-class (about 135 ft, 41 m) remained excessive. A new yacht was evisaged of LOA about 75ft (23m) and LWL 55ft (17m). The first cup races for the new class would be 1992 at San Diego; the second were in 1995 at the same place and the third were scheduled at Auckland, New Zealand, in 2000. There was no racing for the class between events (except working up for them) (**Fig 10.4**).

Thus, exceptionally for the age, was developed a new rating rule, the International America's Cup Class (IACC). Perhaps one should recall the list of rating rules used for the America's Cup between 1900 and 2000. These were in sequence:
Seawanhaka rule; Universal rule using time allowances; Universal rule J class; International 12-metre class; reversion to Deed of Gift (no rule); IACC. (See Appendix III)

The IACC starts with a good old fashioned formula (1997 for use in 2000, but the basic formula has never changed).

24 metres $< =$
$$(L + 1.25 \times (S)^{1/2} - 9.8 \times (DSP)^{1/3})/0.679$$

This a very important rule for is it not the accumulation of experience of one hundred and fifty years of formulae? One hopes so. Apart from constants and factors, which are numerically more precise than usual, presumably to produce the exactly required size, there are only length, L, sail area, S, and displacement DSP in the basic formula. This is entirely logical, for these three are the basis of yacht speed.

L includes sub-formulae for length at girth stations (see several previous rules) and penalties, if necessary for freeboard, draft, weight and beam. S is derived from dimensions and limits of the mainsail, foretriangle and spinnaker. DSP is the weight in kilograms divided by 1025.

The dimensions without penalty are minimum freeboard amidships 1.250m, maximum beam 5.500, maximum drafts 4.000m, weight between 16000 and 20000kg. (It is interesting that in this class more beam is considered advantageous). The designer has to trade off his primary and sub dimensions within practical limits (**Fig 10.5**).

The rule book is about 42 pages of A4 with widely spaced type. As this also includes clauses on equipment, crew, surfaces, construction, materials and measurement/inspections, it is not unduly complex. The IACC rule has the advantage that the boats are

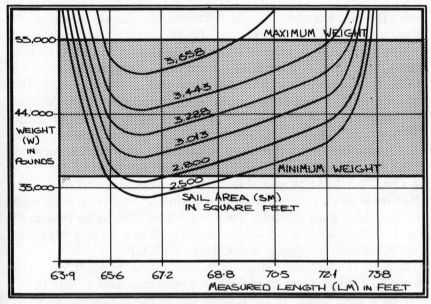

Fig 10.5 *Limits and trade off in the IACC rule. Within the weight (displacement) zone allowed, there is choice of rated sail area and measured length. The rule allows a masthead spinnaker and overlength pole.*

intended as flat out inshore racers, so there is an absence of conflict about accommodation, use for cruising and 'seaworthiness'. Because the America's Cup is on a known periodic cycle, three, five or whatever interval may be decided, then the rule can be adjusted for each impending contest. Thus the rule places its three primary factors all on the top line of the fraction to give a single fixed rated yacht. The authority for the rule is the America's Cup Class, recognized by IYRU, but not officially 'international'.

In former times the class might have been named the '24-metre'. One can reflect that the biggest class under the International rule was 23 metres and under the Universal rule, the 76ft rating of the J equals 23.14 metres, although those were approximate waterline and new rule is near LOA.

Caribbean Yachting Association (CYA) rule

This rating rule is in force for most of the Caribbean regattas and local racing, with the notable exception of the French islands. There are now big events each winter season to which numerous American and European boats come, as well as charter fleets based in the area. Racing includes that in Barbados, St Lucia, Antigua, St Maarten, British and US Virgin Islands.

The evolution is interesting. It started in the 1960s with a 'simplified' version of the RORC rule, therefore time allowance by TCF was the custom and has remained so.[5] In the late 1970s, the rule moved to a simplified version of IOR. In the 1980s, the rule had deserted IOR and was completely rewritten and called the CYA rating rule. It claimed that unlike most rules which take length as a key dimension to be adjusted, it took displacement as central and adjusted it by draft, beam, freeboard and so on.

The CYA has established its own measuring organization with chief measurer and outstations in the islands. Yachts arriving with other ratings such as CHS, IMS and PHRF, must be measured from scratch for the Caribbean fixtures. They receive a proper certificate with the rating in the form of a TCF.

In 1990 the rule was computerized and began to work like CHS in that all subsequent amendments were secret and a 'rule book' was no longer available to designers. The CYA publish a list of nearly 550 individual yachts with CYA TCFs.

Danish Handicap (DH)

A most efficient and highly developed formula is that run by the Dansk Sejlunion (Danish Sailing Association). It is no coincidence that it began in 1984, the same year as CHS. It also has historical roots from Scandicap (1973), Nordic Length (1927) and even, it is claimed, the Copenhagen rule of 1898, which was eventually a main contributor to the International rule. (Appendix I)

It is a published rule of some length and boats are measured at club level by one of 260 measurers in Denmark! It takes about two hours to measure a boat. However there is a widely applied scheme for standard hulls and boats. Boats are weighed by load cell of which there are five official ones in the country. The rating certificate, which also gives the Baltic LYS number (see below), lasts two years and there are a remarkable number of yachts: for 1994-5 these were 5483 Danish, 353 Swedish and 313 German. Polish yachts were possibly enlisting in 1996. Total is thus over 6000.

Time allowances are by time-on-distance, which has long been customary in the Baltic. There are also formulae available for time-on-time. The preferred t-o-d system is:

Performance factor = (t × length of course)/ET

where t is time allowance, l is actual length of course in nautical miles, ET is elapsed time. The boat with the largest pf (performance factor – should it not be 'result'?) is the winner. The time t in seconds per mile is:

t = 1450/0.44R where R is the rating.

The rating itself is derived from a long formula. Unlike some rules, many factors, some more than once, are inserted into this rather than 'subbed'. It is therefore more practical to mention most of the factors than show such an extended list of plus, minus and multiply. So they include length, beam, chain girth, hull factor, sail area, rig factor, hiking factor, displacement, keel weight.[6]

Scandicap was founded in 1973 when IOR boats were found to be far from the Swedish tradition. It looked more like a pre-International rule formula and suited the narrow long ended racers of the Baltic. It faded around 1988 and its users switched to DH and LYS.

The Storm Trysail Club, headquarters Long Island Sound, has long had its own formula for specific races. For many years this amended the IOR, using the latter's certificate. It was the typical case where it is possible to devise a rule knowing it will not be built to. It stated that it did not favour any type of yacht, but perhaps contradicted this by saying that it was suitable for yachts whose owners could cruise them. Rating was linear and then reverted to the old time allowance tables of seconds per mile.

MORC is a rule for offshore racing yachts below 30 feet (9.14m) LOA, boats of the Midget Ocean Racing Club, in a number of places in the USA. It was started in the 1960s, using chosen parts of the then CCA rule and amending others for the small JOG type yachts. It remained unmoved by the introduction of IOR and later IMS by US Sailing. The rule remains a base boat rule with an envisaged type and scope for correction from time to time. It remains an open formula which can be designed to, but few do as changes are inevitable.

MOCRA rule
The Multihull Offshore Cruising and Racing Association of the UK has a rating rule, which succeeds a long line of rating rules for multihulls over the years. Despite much work, none of these really

commanded wide international support. Still officially in existence is IOMR (International Offshore Multihull rule), but it is complex and awkwardly presented. It lacks the wide support internationally, which it was created for, but is used in Denmark and Sweden. With local modification it is also seen in Australia.[7] The MOCRA rule is derived from the IOMR of 1975, the MOCRA/IOMR relationship is rather like CHS/IOR, especially as 'power factors' are kept secret in imitation of the success of CHS.

For multihulls, which by definition have no ballast keel, total weight is primary. MOCRA has a load cell for weighing. Like CHS there is a system of self measurement and endorsement. A TCF is allotted derived from rated length, rated sail area, propeller factor and hull factor all multiplied on a top line of fraction and divided by rated weight.

{a × (rated length ^ p) × (rated sail area ^ q × PF × HF}/ rated weight ^ r = TCF [Here the symbol ^ means to the power of the letter, which, as stated is secret].

MOCRA also runs a 'yardstick', in other words a performance derived figure for a boat.

NSR and SBR are derivatives of CHS and both are secret and run by the RORC Rating Office. Nautor Swan rating (NSR) dates from 1988 and is used in regattas organized specifically for the famous Swan cruiser racers built by Nautor, Finland. Each boat receives a certificate, which looks almost the same as a CHS one with the TCF shown in large figures to three places of decimals. In America the rule has only been used in one Swan regatta some years ago, since when pressure to make use of IMS has prevailed.

The RORC/RYA Sports Boat rule (SBR) was devised in 1996 to allocate a TCF in the UK to the increasing breed of small light weight performance boats such as Melges 24, Cork 1720, H22, Fremantle 8, Mumm 30, Hunter 707 (**Fig 10.6**) because CHS 'favours' the cruiser racer type. There are definite clauses for qualification. TCFs are awarded either to classes or to individual boats.

These sports boat classes each want to be an established one-design, but the more that appear, the less likely that is for each succeeding one; therefore they need to be able to sail against each other. At the time of writing nothing is known of the effectiveness of this rule, which was to be intensely monitored, presumably a events which chose to use it for a sports boat class instead of CHS

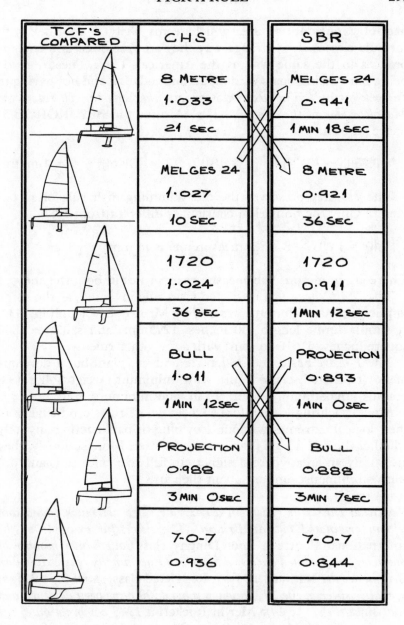

TCF's COMPARED	CHS	SBR
	8 METRE 1·033	MELGES 24 0·941
	21 SEC	1 MIN 18 SEC
	MELGES 24 1·027	8 METRE 0·921
	10 SEC	36 SEC
	1720 1·024	1720 0·911
	36 SEC	1 MIN 12 SEC
	BULL 1·011	PROJECTION 0·893
	1 MIN 12 SEC	1 MIN 0 SEC
	PROJECTION 0·988	BULL 0·888
	3 MIN 0 SEC	3 MIN 7 SEC
	7-0-7 0·936	7-0-7 0·844

Fig 10.6 *The difference between TCFs under the Sports Boat Rule (SBR) and Channel Handicap System (CHS). The margins in minutes and seconds represent the elapsed time allowed to the 'smaller' boat, if the 'faster' boat takes one hour elapsed. So add the margin time and such an elapsed time would result in exactly equal corrected times.*

Model yachts are an area which seems likely to continue with formula classes. In a strange way they are free of certain encumbrances in the same way as the America's Cup. These include being pure racing boats without accommodation and not having to be 'seaworthy'. The four classes are *the 'A', the 10-rater, the Marblehead and the 1-metre*. The 'A' uses the BRA/RORC/5.5-metre pattern:

$$0.25(L + (S)^{1/2}) + (L \times (S)^{1/2})/12 \times (Displ)^{1/3} <= 1 \text{ metre}$$

The *10-rater* preserves the old skimming dish rule of Dixon Kemp! Only the numerical constant is different from 1886.

$$10 = LWL \times S \times 8 \text{ (measurements in mm)}$$

There are numerous sub-measurements/rules in both the above.

The *Marblehead* is a restricted class rule invented, as the name implies, in Massachusetts, actually by Mr Roy L. Clough in 1932. It simply limits length (50 inches, 1275mm) and sail area (800 square inches, 51610 sq mm) with a few other rules.

The *1-metre* has a one-design rig and sail plan, but a development (restricted class) hull, with minimum weight 4kg (8.8 pounds), maximum (420mm, 16 in) and minimum draft,

Model yachting is therefore a world where rules can be taken to their logical extremes without drowning or bankrupting anybody whether the due design is a winner or a loser. More seriously, they are surely an area where designers to full size rules can (and do) learn an immense amount about their use.[8]

Restricted classes or 'yacht-in-a-box rules' are not much found and seldom originated outside Britain. The successful example of the International Fourteen Foot Dinghy class *sailed in a number of countries, was pointed out in Chapter 5. Other dinghy classes found in Britain are the* National 12 Foot Restricted class, *started in 1936, as a smaller sister of the 14, of which some 3500 have been designed and built since then; the 14ft* Merlin Rocket, *a 1949 combination of the* Yachting World Merlin *(1946) and the* Rocket *class, for fifty years an opportunity for dinghy designers. The* Norfolk Punt, *a local class dating from 1923 started as a restricted class, evolving from genuine gun-punts (for shooting wildfowl) and becoming a one-design to an agreed model in 1952. What is most unusual is that it then freed up into a restricted class in 1986; this has since attracted leading dinghy designers and builders. LOA has to be between 18ft (5486mm) and*

22ft 2in (6756mm); beam is between 5ft (1524mm) and 5ft 10in (1778mm); minimum weight is 220 pounds (91kg) and so on for other dimensions. 23m) LOA, with low freeboard and big sail area for inland waters.

There are however some recent restricted classes in ocean racing, which have attracted support in various parts of the world, namely the Mount Gay/Whitbread *series*.

Whitbread 60

The organizers of the Whitbread Round the World Race (which had begun in 1973 by using IOR with time allowances) decided they wanted a level rating class for their 1993-94 race at about 60ft (19m). This was because they had dropped time allowances from the main prize of the previous races, all run using IOR, with the predictable result that huge yachts for speed regardless of rating ensued, so long as they complied with the permitted top size/ rating limits of IOR. In 1990 at Fort Lauderdale during the race, the organizers met designers and journalists and began work on a restricted class to be fast and modern with water ballast, the Whitbread 60. Ten of these started in 1993 together with four IOR maxis. For 1997, Whitbread 60 class only would compete. It has no class racing (except for work-up) between events.

The rule is all limits and dimensional restrictions. There are no trade-offs (with one small exception: a simple formula to determine shape of the bow and stern, a penalty on which would be added to sail area, but it is a check and let-out rather than a trade-off). The rules produce a yacht with a big rig and an extreme, deep, narrow keel (maximum draft 12ft 4in, 3.75m). Typical dimensions are LOA 64ft (19.5m), beam 17 ft (5.25m), draft at stated maximum, weight 29700 pounds (13500 kg), mast height 85ft (26m).

Mount Gay 30 and others

In 1993 the Royal Ocean Racing Club held a designing competition for what was called the Whitbread 30 with water ballast. In effect this followed the same ideas as the 60, but was for ocean racing over courses between 60 and 300 miles. A number of entries was received from around the world and prizes awarded for the designs, but then nothing happened. The ORC had announced it would introduce an ILC 30 using IMS numbers and the RORC appeared to be unable to decide which 30 footer should be supported.

Private initiative built a 30ft boat to the W30 rules which sailed in a 1994 race around Britain and Ireland with a small crew and water ballast. It did moderately under CHS, but very well in terms of actual passage times. In 1995 Mount Gay, a brand of rum, declared sponsorship of the renamed Mount Gay 30, also announcing a Mount Gay 25 and a 40 (**Fig. 10.7**). At the time of writing, boats were being built in Australia, America and elsewhere, but it remains to be seen if such a restricted class can obtain international support; the 'Fourteen' does, of course, but for a select and skilled section of sailors.

Open 60 is used for the Vendée Globe race, a single-handed course around the world without stopping and the BOC race, which has some stops (since re-named). The rule is simply: maximum LOA 60ft (18.29m), no outriggers. The nature of the course keeps the boats seaworthy or eliminates them! The French organizers sometimes deplore that the Whitbread and the Open have different rules: in this they have a point (**Fig 10.8**).

*Performance rules, the third type after formula and restricted (***Fig 10.9***) are legion. Every local club handicapper who hands out a time allowance is using his estimate of the yacht or sailing dinghy. The biggest rule of this type was reviewed in Chapter 9 – PHRF. Others are to be found all over the world, so perhaps the author will be excused if he mentions a few geographically near him. These might be the Echo in Ireland ('east coast handicap organization'),* Leading yardstick performance (LYSTAL or LYS) *in the Baltic,* Handicap National *in France and* Portsmouth Yardstick *in Britain and parts of America. The American version, having received the system from England many years ago, runs it own numbers.*

Portsmouth Yardstick

This system, based on observed performance, has numbers available for the rating of standard classes in Britain. Many of these classes are widely known around the world. Portsmouth has been in use since 1946 and so is refined by long experience, but every new boat is a challenge. Instructions for using the rule are issued each year by the national authority, the RYA. Despite the simple concept, the detail is in effect quite complex to grasp. It is to be found in 20 pages of A4, consisting of small print and rating figures.[9]

Originally the rule was used for racing dinghies. This was highly effective because each was controlled by its own class one-design rules and there were no variations permitted by boats of the same mark; later came day keel boats, then cruisers where there are variations, so adjustment figures assist with the latter.

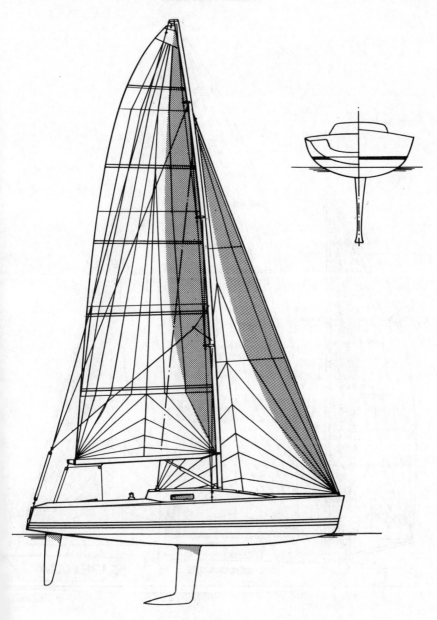

Fig 10.7 *Design to the Mount Gay 30 restricted class; springing from the Whitbread 60, both have no trade offs. In theory this avoids many problems of rating rules, but at time of writing, there is no rush into the 30. The 60 is required in order to enter the Whitbread Round The World Race every fourth year: 1997, 2001.*

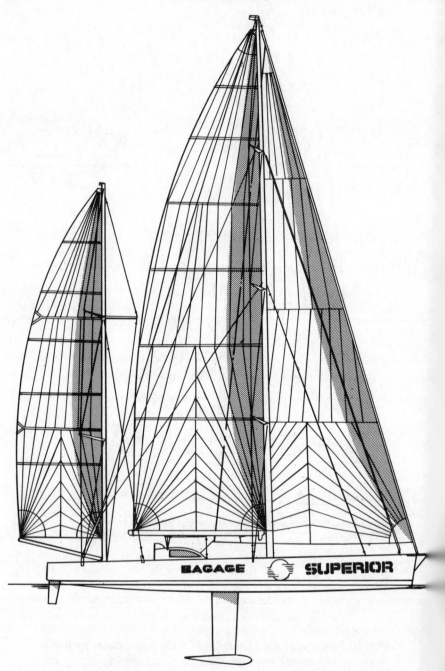

Fig 10.8 *The Open 60 class for single-handed ocean racing (especially the Vendée Globe round the world). The only rules are a limit on LOA and no outriggers allowed. But natural control is provided by the race course and lack of crew.*

SOME YACHT RATING RULES TODAY

TYPE OF RULE	CLASS	DATE OF ORIGIN	NUMBER CERTIFIED	AREA AND REMARKS
DESIGN FORMULA	International Measurement System (IMS)	1976	4500	USA and 23 countries
	International Rule	1906	150	6-metre, 8-metre, 12-metre
	International 5.5-metre	1946	50	
	International America's Cup Class (IACC)	1988	14	Cyclic
	Model Yacht 'A' and 10-rater			Long established for model yachts
	International Multihull Offshore Rule (IOMR)			Multihulls only
DESIGN RESISTANT	Dansk Handicap (DH)	1984	6000	Baltic
SECRET FORMULAE	Channel Handicap System (CHS)	1984	6000	UK, France and 30 countries
	Caribbean Yachting Association (CYA)	1960	550	Caribbean
RESTRICTED CLASSES	Whitbread 60 (W60)	1990	22	For WRTWR
	Mount Gay 30	1994		Derived from W60
	International 14 foot	1927		Centreboard dinghy UK, USA, Canada, Australia, New Zealand
PERFORMANCE	PHRF	1972	20,000	USA, Canada, Caribbean - VERY BIG
	LYS	1984	6,000	Baltic
	Portsmouth Yardstick (PY)	1947	12,000	UK (different numbers in USA)

Fig 10.9 *Yacht rating rules of the modern world. With apologies to a number not shown of varying status and in different countries and regions. (1997: USS was introducing Americap (national), evolved from both PHRF and IMS).*

Portsmouth works by obtaining annual returns from clubs of results in handicap racing. From these the RYA works out a national figure for every design. The actual rating is a *Portsmouth number*, defined as a measure of performance. It is a whole number representing a time over an unspecified distance. One can think of this as 'seconds per mile', but it is not! To obtain the corrected time for a race:

CT = (Elapsed time × 1000)/Portsmouth number

There are numbers of various grades which have been given fancy names. Primary yardstick means a very reliable Portsmouth number; secondary yardstick means published by RYA but less reliable; recorded numbers are even less reliable! Club numbers are locally derived; trial numbers are what they say, given to a boat whose performance is unknown.

As in all time-on-distance systems, the higher the number the 'slower' the boat. Thus among racing dinghies an International Fourteen is 884, a Europe (for women's Olympic Games) 1145 and an Optimist 1646. The corrected time for the Europe after a one hour race becomes 52 minutes 24 seconds.

Readers will see that if TCFs were used, which for some reason they are not, the TCF would be 1000 divided by the number. The Europe would have a TCF of 0.873.

Among 'cruisers' (racers?) the Sigma 38 is 841 and a Folkboat is 1172. Therefore Portsmouth issues its numbers as time-on-distance, yet recommends them to be used with time-on-time, which is most unusual.

But then Portsmouth is run by the bureaucracy of a sizeable yachting national authority, which is in direct line from the old YRA of our early chapters. Even one hundred years ago the YRA list of time allowances for ratings from 1 to 599 and fractions thereof, covered several pages of, yes, small type, though to look at, it was rather more elegant.[10]

11 Rating folly in the past: sailing fun for the future?

'So inch by inch, I tightened the winch, and chucked the sandbags out-
'I heard the nursery cannons pop, I heard the bookies shout:
' "The Meteor wins!" "No, Wooden Spoon!" "Check!" "Vantage!"
"Leg before!"
' "Last lap!" "Pass Nap!" At his saddle-flap I put up the helm and
wore'. – Sir Arthur Quiller-Couch, (1928), *The Famous Ballad of
the Jubilee Cup*.

'Be wary of forecasts, especially those involving the future' – anon

MUCH OF THIS BOOK has followed the rating rules
used for offshore racing and offshore or 'habitable'
boats. That was the track marked 'CCA and RORC to
IOR to IMS and others'.

One reason for such emphasis is that today the most active rating
rules are still among such boats and races. Inshore rating rules, if
not of a long past era (fascinating though they may be in our early
chapters), remain in small pockets outside the 'mainstream' of
racing, and among model yachts! This may be a bit hard on a class
like the 5.5-metre, which is active but select and confined to a few
places – while making such places even more attractive! The fact is
though that a newly introduced inshore class will invariably be a
one-design.

It is possible that what happened inshore before, say, 1950, will
happen offshore before 2000. In other words rated ocean racing
classes will no longer be seen in the main or popular events, but
will be confined to a few local enthusiasts. That is what we
suggested was about to happen when introducing three offshore
one-designs in the UK in 1977. Subsequently other offshore one-
designs have appeared and prospered. Yet they have remained as
minorities in ocean racing. The number of classes which have

proved popular has been quite limited: this is right, for if every proposed class is popular then none will be popular enough!

However twenty years later it looks as though offshore boats may well not go the same way as their inshore predecessors for the following reasons: (1) a number of the yachts are much bigger than any modern inshore boats and so have expensive variations which make one-design status physically difficult; (2) unlike many inshore classes which spend all season racing in one patch of water, offshore boats move further afield and race with differently based organizations; (3) genuine cruising potential means that offshore racers move in and out of racing under the same or changed ownership.

The vast number of production designs (which can change design and minor dimensions during production runs) and quite a few one-designs (where the owner wants to take his one-design on an offshore race which is not in the class programme), means there must be a time allowance system for different boats such as, at least, of PHRF or PY type.

If time allowances are required then they have to be obtained either from performance observations or measurement. So it looks like the need for ratings is to continue. Assuming this need to run rating rules, *how should they be run? who should run them? at what level should they be controlled? and, in broad terms, what type of rating rules should they be?*

The author has now presented a story of the achievements, the successes and the follies of yacht rating rules and those who sailed with them. Like any history, the resulting lessons may be utilized or may be rejected, but neither those in authority, nor sailors themselves, should ever be simply ignorant of them.

So *HOW? WHO? WHAT LEVEL? WHAT TYPE OF RULE?*

How to run a modern rule

Rules controlling racing yachts, be they one-design rules, restricted class rules or rating rules, invariably need to be changed from time to time. In long established local classes, this may be very infrequently, but even here the impact from 'outside' of new materials results in nice judgements having to be made. In more widely used rating rules, there will surely be changes every year; remember we listed such in IOR and in CHS.

The controlling authority has to accept at the outset that no change will please everybody. Indeed any change in respect of two rival yachts will please one and displease the other. Therefore declarations that changes are well received, fairer (more on *that* word shortly) and so on, never apply to all, or to state it more strongly, cannot apply to all.

In rating rules, changes are typically (1) to correct features that designers have invented that were not previously envisaged; (2) put heavier ratings on a design which has managed to reduce rating; (3) taxes new speed producing aspects that circumvent the rule.

When the rule makers announce their intention to change, controversy breaks out. Those who have just had yachts designed or recently built yachts incorporating these 'rule cheating' features are indignant. They say that they designed these boats to the rule and no sooner had they done this than the rule is changed. The ones with boats from a few years before are happy to see their old designs restored. Those about to build observe carefully the detail of this latest change.

If there is a weak authority, it caves in wholly or partly to the owners and designers of the latest boats, outdating all previous. A stronger body would insist on the changes, but then holds its breath as designers look at the rule change to see if it may have new undiscovered elements which can give an advantage to yet some further speed-against-rating innovation.

With luck they will not discover this for a year or so. If the new design comes sooner or comes later then the authority, must change the rule again. The complaints now come from that next batch of boat owners/designers! 'You are forever changing the rule.' Yes, they are, but in the interests of suitable ratings for all.

Amazingly suggestions are still heard that a rule should be 'frozen' in the interests of 'stability'. We saw that this was what happened to the IOR; it was a reason for its destruction. The 'freezers' are the 'just built', or modified, yacht owners; those who have installed the latest rule loopholes. It was to be heard again in IMS in 1996. It is madness: and an invitation for designers to exploit without fear of retribution.

When a boat is measured and rated it must be remembered that it is not a solitary act. Her rating is relative to all other boats that have been measured and rated – in effect her competitors. So it is no generosity to allow this loophole or give that benefit of the doubt. Sometimes an owner says that the measuring authority seems to be working against him, despite the big fee which he pays. In a sense the authority is; it is working in the interests of all its other rated yachts.

In truth any design rule will suffer from this cycle of loophole to correction to new possible design. Computers speed the process which one hundred years ago took a number of seasons to work to a conclusion. In the real world what rules does this include? The answer is IMS and IACC; the metre boat rules are at fixed size and so old and worked through as unlikely to result in a breakthrough. Anyway only a small number of owners (friends?) are involved with them and the controlling authorities are the same people.

Other rules (previous chapter) are secret, restricted or performance and the above stresses seldom apply.

But if the rating authority is going to jump immediately on rating advantage then it seems there will be no point in designing a new boat to race, no chance of improvement of the breed.

This is not true. There are many avenues of design improvement for racing: easier deck layout, faster handled rig, stiffer construction, room below for sail handling, incorporation of new gear such as winches and spars, or simply an experienced owner's preferences. None of these need concern reduced rating or increased speed against rating.

For one hundred and seventy years rule beating and rule cheating have brought to an end a succession of promising rated classes. Maybe now is 'the end of history' for such methods, or will some authority hail a revised or 'new' rule and plunge again into certain folly?

Who shall run a rule?
Rules, and indeed yacht racing classes in general, originated by institutions, have a bad record. The classic case was that of the cruiser racer metre boats of the 1950s, after which the IYRU kept well away from ratings of any sort. In 1947 the RYA held trials for a British 'national three man keel boat' and chose the Swallow. You may not have heard of it, but it still exists – as a local one-design in a sheltered English harbour. (Amazingly as late as 1993, the RYA took it upon itself to choose a youth dinghy, the '4-0-5': it flopped.)

Successful major classes are more likely to have been initiated by small groups, newspapers and magazines or even individuals. The Mirror dinghy, tens of thousands world wide, came from the mass circulation *Daily Mirror*. The Enterprise, a starter dinghy, from the defunct *News Chronicle*, the Cadet, GP14 and Merlin Rocket from *Yachting World*.

The International rule, longest lasting of all, was not originated by the IYRU, but was the result of work by Bookstall Smith and colleagues on the continent to put together a rating rule. The IYRU was formed *after these initiatives* to administer the rule. Similarly we have seen that the IOR was the result of the Bremen meeting, a private forum, and many conversations before that between people like John Illingworth, Olin J. Stephens II, Dick Carter and Buster de Guingand. When negotiations between the CCA and the RORC became intense, there was still only an Offshore Rules Co-ordinating Committee. The Offshore Rating (later Racing) Council (ORC) was formed *after* the two great club rules had been joined together.

The Bermuda race was the initiative of Thomas Fleming Day, editor of *The Rudder*. The Fastnet race was spurred on by Weston Martyr, yachting writer, and created by a small group of cruising men. *Afterwards* came the respective controlling clubs (CCA and 'ORC', later RORC). The Admiral's Cup was presented by private members (albeit senior ones of RORC including its Admiral) as a challenge to American yachtsmen before becoming officially club based. The first viable round the world ocean race was started by Anthony Churchill and Guy Pearse, who had magazine and PR interests, and subsequently, as the British armed services showed most interest, was handed over to the Royal Naval Sailing Association, who then obtained some sponsorship from a brewery, Whitbread. Now the event is the famous Whitbread race (WRTWR). One could go on and mention CHS and Jean Louis Fabry, PHRF and groups in Southern California, PY and Sinbad Milledge.

Sooner or later the expanded classes, events or rating rules are handed over to newly created or existing institutions. These may or may not run the system well, probably the former. Problems arise when these institutions (1) *age*, so that the original innovators are replaced by committee men and (2) *decide that they are empowered to create new rules and classes*.

Those who knew all these things watched with trepidation as the Offshore Racing Council, formed to run IOR, decided to adopt MHS and rename it IMS. Apart from the flaws and technical objections of the rule (Chapter 8), this imposition 'from the top' was potential folly. When the ORC then announced 'international' classes (we have seen there was some hesitancy on the sizes but they in due course became 'ILC 30, 40, 46' and others), the likelihood of a major misjudgement was compounded. *Institutions creating classes are on shaky ground, but international institutions are on quicksand!*

This was readily demonstrated by the lack of world wide interest in the ILC classes, despite a high level of promotion. By late 1996, they had got nowhere. As mentioned, the so-called world championship of the ILC 40 in 1996 in the Mediterranean raised nine boats, mostly Greek and Italian; the ILC 46 raised two and was dropped as an Admiral's Cup class (the latter reverted to time allowances for this approximate size of yacht); the ILC 30 was almost unseen! Maxis were built to the ILC70 rule, but maxis at any moment need an upper limit somewhere.

Regions and nations. These seem to have more success than international bodies. Many a country has its own performance or measured rule and sometimes links with countries close by or those with long association, even if distant. So we have discovered Dansk Handicap serving the countries whose shore lines are on the Baltic, PHRF throughout the USA, Canada and others, Channel Handicap System in use in western Europe, the Mediterranean and the Far East. However the type of rule (see below) may have more influence than who controls it.

United States Sailing Association. The influence of the USA upon all these matters is unique, owing to the size of the country, the numbers of racing yachts per head on top of such absolute size and the psychology of the users there.

Readers have seen the story unfold from 1883 onward, the year of the creation of the Seawanhaka rule. The strongly held opinions, often by a large number of wealthy people, in different parts of a huge country, a non-existent (until 1925), then a weak, national authority and a different attitude from Europe have caused major fault lines in attempts at international rules and classes. Enlightened racing men have compromised by simply adapting the respective US or European rule and using it for competition: examples are the J-class and MHS (American) and 6-metre, 5.5-metre and Whitbread 60 (European). The 'split-the-difference' IOR is gone and on IMS (ex-MHS) the jury is out (1996).

(There is no problem when sailors in one country adopt a one-design from another, as the boat comes 'take it or leave it'; probably an international class association is formed whose secretary does the work in the evenings.)

As for the psychology and attitudes, the historic evidence is there. Americans have favoured destroying (purposely or by default) rules which are 'not working': Universal rule, IOR. Europeans go for repair and evolution: RORC rule (from Seawanhaka and Universal), IOR from RORC, IOR 90 (rejected via US pressure), CHS (probably much revised IOR), International rule (operating quietly after ninety years).

There is also the characteristic American optimism which expects rules to be 'fair' or at least strive towards that, or even keep heading towards 'perfection'. Europeans accept that rules are never fair to all and perfection does not come in to it. They are just a practical mode of racing differing yachts on time allowances.

The European and Far East countries, and certainly the newer yachting nations, have national authorities whose word is followed and usually final! This simply does not apply in the USA. In America designers, sailmakers, rich owners and others shout loudly in a manner not found elsewhere. Lastly, the sheer size of the market makes it worth spending effort (and money) or propagating strong (and inevitably conflicting) views.

The 'American problem' is therefore endemic to international yachting bodies.

What level?

It looks as though international rating rules may be impossible, except in the sense of a class association recognized 'internationally' by, for instance, the ISAF. When IMS was introduced to the world by ORC, rather than remaining as an interesting concept for about 800 American yachts, it was envisaged that it would take over the all embracing role of IOR in the 1970s. This was never realized. **Fig 11.1** shows changes of rule from IOR for some well known races and regattas and, as recounted in Chapter 9, how they have diverged into different systems.

The unavoidable conclusion is that rating or rather actual *time allowances are best applied at the lowest possible level consistent with practicality and control.*

Event	1950s	1970s	1990s
ADMIRAL'S CUP	RORC	IOR	IMS
FASTNET	RORC	IOR	CHS
COWES WEEK	RORC	IOR	CHS
BERMUDA	CCA	IOR	IMS
SORC	CCA	IOR	PHRF/IMS/OD
WHITBREAD	—	IOR	W60
SYDNEY-HOBART	RORC	IOR	IMS
SKAW/GOTLAND	RORC	IOR	DH
ONE TON CUP	6-METRE	RORC/IOR	IOR/45ft
AMERICA'S CUP	12-METRE	12-METRE	IACC
HAWAII	—	IOR	IMS
BRIT-AM CUP	6-METRE	—	OD

Fig 11.1 *How some major events have shifted rating rules over about fifty years.*

That simply means that for a local club evening race, time allowances can well be handed out by the club handicapper who knows every boat and owner well. When several clubs get together, one of the national systems are applied; then for a region even with visitors from abroad the system controlled at that level is best used.

The necessity for elaborate 'world' rules, 'so that yachts can easily sail in each other's countries' is highly exaggerated. When European yachts (a handful) travel to the US, they receive a PHRF rating on which to race. American and German yachts in England's Cowes Week use CHS like the rest of the regatta; French, Italian and Hong Kong yachts have CHS already. For the Caribbean races all of us, who unfortunately do not keep our boats there, need to be measured CYA.

What does that leave? Why, a top racing class, sometimes known as 'grand prix', where the chosen game is to design and build a yacht under a rule of measurement and rating with a view to an event, or a succession of further events. Typically this would be: Admiral's Cup and Fastnet, Sardinia Cup, January Key West regatta, Rolex Long Island Sound series, some others. Here is your ILC yacht: yacht racing perfection, manned by rock stars, designed, tuned, expensive, a delight to watch on the race course. But, like any exclusive racing class, with its own set of rules and only indirectly related to other kinds of fixture.

The type of future rule: head for sailing fun
Our story has shown that no rule of measurement and rating continues to prosper indefinitely. Some end on a quick downward spiral; others, as emphasized, become a localized and small but select class. Therefore we are looking for a rule that will work this season and not unreasonably for the next few seasons. If it lasts longer, so be it. Nor is it expected to be 'fair', whatever that may mean, to every competitor or rule certificate holder.

A rating rule needs to be *PRACTICAL* and *ACCEPTABLE* in the widest sense. Almost all desirable qualities will be found to occur under one or both of these headings. The rule is not 'fair', nor is it trying to be 'perfect': such words mean nothing.

IMS. The rule currently (1996) promoted for active international use is the International Measurement System. There is a question whether this rule suffers from the customary difficulties of any rating rule under pressure from top competitors, or if it has particular problems of its own.

In Chapter 8 it was demonstrated that its creation was flawed. In outline terms it was a yacht laboratory research project prematurely pitched by rule politicians, wearing NAYRU hats, into use as a rule of measurement and rating. Much of the thinking was negative ('no point measurement', 'no time allowance tables' (not used outside the USA anyway!), 'quick correction to any exploitation of the rule').

It existed for a decade in the US, because relatively low level rules can be accepted and pulled around to fit. Then it was lifted from under its stone into the glare of international racing and, beyond belief, was made the international grand prix rule and on top of that with a range of level ratings. Expressions about Caligula making his horse a consul come to mind. Oscar Wilde might have said something about the unsuitable in pursuit of the unmanageable.

Underlying IMS is a concept of deducing the actual speed of the vessel; time allowances then follow. Somewhere in here is a search for perfection and fairness. So in there, with these admirable sentiments, is the American dream.

But the author says: in there with them lie impracticality and unacceptability. Added to this, those who run the ORC are those who destroyed the IOR. There is no reason why they should prove any less incompetent in running IMS. So we saw the rule reach a peak around 1992 and now its adherents diminish, its technical problems continue and the mistaken policy of employing its use for grand prix racing will destroy it.

In 1996 IMS boats that were being designed and built were largely to take advantage of an astonishingly crude percentage bonus on rating of 1 per cent for 'cruisers' The latter were stupidly defined with an elaborate set of written rules on bunks, accommodation, cockpit accessories and so on. Such pages could almost be considered 'written loopholes'! Readers of this book need not be told that this invited designers to jump in and design 'cruisers' that to anyone else looked like first class racing yachts! It was found they gained better corrected time than the few ILC40s which they encountered. (1997. The 1 per cent was abolished and a sliding scale attempted).

1996 was a bad year for IMS in other ways. Its complexity gave rise to a form of 'bumping', that horror which the founders of IMS had sworn to eliminate. Admittedly it was not a localized IOR bump, but a swelling and fairing of the afterbody to take advantage of the LPP (lines prediction program, mentioned in Chapter 8).

This was a rule cheating move made by several leading IMS yachts, but it was the subsequent actions of the Offshore Racing

Council that caused a sensation. An emergency announcement promised that in accordance with the principles of IMS for swift rule correction to loopholes, these bumps would be penalized by an amount to be published. However ILC boats (such as existed) when racing at level rating, could hold to their ratings – in other words they were 'frozen'. When racing on time allowance, they would incur the penalty.

Within seven days of these rulings in May 1996, the ORC rescinded the intended rule change. Seldom can a rule authority have caved in to pressure in quite such a pathetic manner. The reason (which sounded suspiciously like Weller-speak) was 'in order not to disrupt a significant number of race campaign programmes'. Obviously it was preferable for races to be sailed by badly rated yachts.

Further pressure from the age old lobby of owners of yachts just optimized to the rule actually caused the ORC to freeze the ILC40 at its level rating until November 1997 (that was after the pending Admiral's Cup event). In the 170 years covered in these pages few abdications of responsibility by a rating authority have sunk as low as this. The ORC chairman, John Dare, made 'rule stability' his reason; not only was this in direct contravention of the rule of which he was the trustee, but readers of these pages understand the dire consequences of a freeze. The ORC seemed to have learned nothing from its destructive freeze of the IOR.

Meanwhile at US Sailing, the authorities had decided to enforce the proposed rule amendment for the LPP and its associated formulae. The US IMS program was already out of line with that of ORC. *It was back to the old story of the US national authority breaking ranks when it suited. Yes, with tradition, even in time for the 1996 Bermuda race!*

Thus the ORC lost almost all credibility as a body able to deliver a rule of measurement and rating. The Royal Ocean Racing Club, up to then loyal as anyone to ORC, reacted by setting up in the summer of 1996 a small body under one of its flag officers to come up with practical ways of creating of a new rating rule, a revolutionary step. (It was already running its races on CHS, but this would be a new rule for the Admiral's Cup and first class racers).

CHS, CYA, DH, MOCRA, PHRF. These regional/national rules have almost unfair (that word again!) advantages over IMS. There is tight control at a level nearer to the owners and sailors, designers are not involved in running the rule, the numbers are up where racing is viable, measuring/registration is inexpensive (re-

member the list of '14 reasons for CHS success'!) and all five rules
have grown without promotion or edicts from on high.

Performance deduced rules, PHRF and PY and others, especially local, may be criticized, but if the users do not like them,
then they can invent a different set of numbers. So in effect they
can be from time to time renewed. In reality, the existing ones are
well run. A number of competitors mainly want a 'ticket to join in a
race' and, as in the Jubilee Cup (chapter head), sail hard while
being relaxed with technical terms.

Secret formulae and factors are the basis of CHS, CYA and
MOCRA, while design resistance is installed in DH. The author
can only say that time will tell on these while the motto about
forecasts, at chapter head, should be noted. CYA is relieved of
'pressure' because many top boats tend to visit the Caribbean for a
limited period, but are designed to race mainly in their home
waters using CHS, IMS and so on.

The author admits to have been closely associated with CHS,
but would predict the following. If CHS suddenly receives a body
blow because of a loophole or unexpected advantage for a boat or
boat type, then the British and French will have to go back into the
computer and alter their program and algorithms. They have no
one to answer to technically and changes they have already made
are not all announced. The innards of a rule can be as complicated
as the rating offices wish: the answer for the owners is still a TCF
which will correct his time accurately on a hand calculator and,
roughly, in his head! Another way of looking at this is: *if CHS did
not exist, then something like it would have to be invented*.

IACC, Whitbread 60. These two modern rating/restricted class,
respectively, rules serve their purpose admirably. As they are for
events on a four/five (or similar) year cycle for specific events, are
for craft bought by sponsors and in each case are for a single size/
speed/rating of boat, successive batches of boats are duly built to
them. They do not have to compromise towards cruising, or even
service in later life. Here the events created the rules. Some regular
series currently using IMS could well look at these concepts.

Time allowances. (Chapters 5 and 8). Even if modern rules (CHS,
CYA, MOCRA, IMS) produce the time allowance system as part
of the rule without showing a linear rating (length and sail area,
CCA, RORC, Universal), time allowances remain something apart
from measurement and rating. However for differing boats, racing
anywhere, time allowances are required and the logical mode of

thought is to find the best way of obtaining these. For instance, are they best deduced from performance figure or measurement? It is asking for trouble to invent a rating system, as in the case of IMS, and then subsequently search for a time allowance system to fit it. (Remember Newman's revealing lecture.)

Since 1830, in the struggle between designer and rulemaker, the latter has come off worst. He has seen freaks built to his laws, speed increase beyond his expectations, millions of dollars poured into those beautiful creatures called racing yachts to frustrate his intentions and in due course his rating rule destroyed before his eyes.

The rulemaker has not helped himself with indecision, appeasement and bureaucracy, but that is the human condition. Yet often the executioner, the yacht designer, finds his creations turn sour. So he moves to other vessels than rated yachts – to one-designs, to deep sea cruisers, to training ships, to fun day boats to a hundred other kinds of sail.

Even so in the confines of the rating rule have been discovered new techniques, unexpected useful hull shapes, rigs that were found to prove practical. Under the great rules, each in its heyday, the racing yachts inshore and offshore have provided unforgettable memories for the participants and history for those who were not there or who heard of such doings in later years.

Notes and references to text

These provide remarks and explanations, but sometimes simply a book, magazine or document reference for the facts given. Among magazines are as follows: USA: *Sail; Sailing World; Yachting;* British: *Yachting World* – *YW (abbreviation); Yachts and Yachting* – *Y&Y; Yachtsman* (ceased publication); *Seahorse*.

Introduction and definitions

1. *Ocean Racing* (1946) by Alf Loomis (Yachting Publishing, New York); chapter on Cruising Club of America rating rule by Herbert L. Stone, a founder of modern Newport-Bermuda race, for many years member of CCA and editor of *Yachting*, New York.

2. This was actually the spring 1974 meeting of the ORC (Offshore Rating (later Racing) Council), which controlled the IOR, with many US observers. The author was then chairman of the International Technical Committee. In the early 1970s, there were both spring and winter meetings.

3. Sailing and maritime dictionaries all fail to define rating and measurement terminology.

4. From the *Oxford English Dictionary*: this word dates from 1653.

Preface

1. X one-design inshore keel boat, wooden carvel design , LOA 21ft (6.40m) with regular racing at four English south coast ports. When some new boats were built to class rules and official drawings and passed by measurers, they were 'bigger and faster' than the existing boats, which had never in 85 years changed appreciable shape.

2. *The March of Folly – from Troy to Vietnam* (1984) by Barbara W. Tuchman, American historian. Fascinating insight into lack of judgement and worse by those in authority, including 'how the Trojans take the wooden horse into their city', 'how the British lose the American colonies', 'how America betrays herself in Vietnam'.

Chapter 1   Cutter cranks and tonnage tyranny

1. George Lennox Watson (1851-1904), leading Scottish yacht designer from 1872. Designed *Britannia* in 1893 for HRH Prince of Wales, America's Cup challengers *Valkyrie II, Thistle* (later *Meteor* owned by HIM Kaiser Wilhelm, who also had *Meteor II* designed by Watson) and some 500 other racing yachts, cruising yachts and steamers.

2. William P. Stephens (1854-1946) was an outstanding American histor-

ian and yacht designer of an age which bridged the early rating rules of
this book and ones to which boats sailed today were built. He was closely
involved with the evolution of rating rules and design. Of these subjects
he wrote very extensively (mostly from his house at Bayside, LI) and he is
a major source for these early chapters. He wrote 83 factual historic
articles for successive issues of the American magazine *Motor Boating*
between 1939 and 1946. These have been republished at least twice, most
recently as *Traditions and Memories of American Yachting* (1981), International Marine Publishing Co., Camden, Maine.
3. Looking further into the nineteenth century, this use of beam would
compensate a little in yacht tonnage rules for the use of B/2 as depth,
which, in turn, meant narrowness was needed for low rating. The disaster
of this ancient convention will unfold, but a tendency for narrow beam
did not finally leave British yachts until *around 1965* in the last years of the
RORC rule (Chapter 4).
4. Royal Thames Yacht Club, London. Founded in 1775 as the Cumber-
land Fleet; now has a modern club house and is an active organization for
racing and cruising.
5. Author has changed many initial capitals from upper to lower case,
which bespatter these old laws and quotations.
6. *Memorials of the Royal Yacht Squadron: origins to 1901* (1903) by
Montague Guest and William Bolton (John Murray, London).
7. The monarch presented a fresh cup each year for Cowes regatta from
1827 to 1939. In 1951 King George VI presented the Britannia Cup,
which is permanent and the major trophy in Cowes Week. It was sailed
under the main rating rule of the day, first the RORC rule, then the IOR
and now using CHS.
8. *Memorials* (as note 6).
9. It was George Holland Ackers (schooner *Brilliant*, 393 tons), who was
to lodge a protest against the schooner *America* for failing to leave the Nab
Light to starboard in the race of 22 August 1851. Once it was pointed out
that there were two sets of instructions, he quickly withdrew his case. He
was an innovator and devised a code of flag signals for the yachts of RYS
members.
10. W.P.Stephens (WPS).
11. *Memorials*.
12. *Beam* will be used throughout to mean maximum breadth of a yacht,
even though these old rules mentioned 'breadth'. Strictly 'maximum
beam' meant the breadth at the position of the actual biggest wooden or
steel beam across the vessel. Modern plastics yachts do not have such
beams, so 'beam' has come to mean the maximum breadth.
13. Badminton *Yachting*. See quote at chapter head.
14. *The King's Britannia* (1937) by John Irving (Seeley Service, London).
The author begins by showing the disastrous effect on British yachting of
the rating/tonnage rules prior to the appearance of *Britannia* in 1893.
15. *Ibid*. But WPS writes that *Sylvie* was second in her race around the
Nab at Cowes and was presented with a cup, which he says ended up at
the South Shore Yacht Club at Milwaukee. The point is, however, that
the British boats, with lessons learnt from *America*, were not inferior

16. Dixon Kemp (1839-1899), yacht designer, secretary of the YRA from its formation until 1898 at an unchanging salary of £100 per annum plus five shillings for each yacht measured, creator of rating rules and author of big classic works such as *Yacht and Boat Sailing* (1891) (Horace Cox/ The Field, 7th edition, 750 pages), and *Yacht Architecture*.

17. *Yachting: historical sketches of the sport* (1902) by Julius Gabe (John Macqueen, London). Gabe was a yachting writer at the turn of the century and probably editor of *Yachting World* in those days of anonymous journalism.

18. *Minute by Minute* (1983) by Gordon Fairley, foreword by HRH Prince Philip (published by Royal Yachting Association). The YRA changed the initials to RYA in 1953 when it took on responsibilities other than racing.

19. *Memorials*.

20. Badminton.

21. *The King's Britannia* (note 14)

22. Badminton: contribution by G.L. Blake.

23. Most of this history of American tonnage rating is from WPS and *The History of the New York Yacht Club* (1975) by John Parkinson Jr (Two volumes, published by NYYC, New York).

24. *Ibid.*

25. This difference in approach will be seen again with a vengeance in the 1980s. (Chapter 8) The Americans wanted to bring in IMS to replace IOR, though the British had a scheme to repair it.

26. *The History of the New York Yacht Club*.

27. Boston YC is where the ORC held important rating meetings a little over one hundred years later; see Introduction.

28. *Ibid.* The opening words appear extravagant; WPS was writing in the 1940s.

29. *Ibid.* Quoting Rev George G. Hepworth of New York, who had modified his boat for offshore cruising.

30. The River Itchen is by Southampton, a major yachting area then and now. The 'Itchen Ferry' type was popular as a small cruiser.

Chapter 2   Skimming dishes of the Belle Époque

1. Edward Fitzgerald sailed his yacht *Scandal* out of Woodbridge, Suffolk, then and now a fishing and yachting port of East Anglia. Lord Dunraven, twice challenger for the America's Cup and subsequently (1896) expelled from the New York Yacht Club, was hardly 'uncultured', if eccentric. This piece is heavy with irony as he taunts the rule makers.

2. Dixon Kemp.

3. WPS.

4. 'Classification' was almost equivalent to rating in differences of opinion. It may be that if the measurement and time allowances were dubious, then it was at least important to have similar yachts in the same class. See a little further on in this chapter.

5. The British in this period will be seen to speak of a figure without units: just 'rating' or 'rater', once 'tons' was seen as meaningless. See further on

in this chapter. Later on the Europeans will use rules in feet and metres.
6. WPS.
7. Say from 1883 to 1898. It will be suggested later in the book, that 15 years is often the effective life of any rule of measurement and rating.
8. But only just: Fairley says that the required two-thirds majority was only attained by the dubious recasting of one vote by one member.
9. All time allowances were on time (seconds) per distance (nautical miles). Other forms will appear later, in the next century.
10. Kemp, reproducing 'his' YRA rules.
11. *Scantlings* strictly meant the dimensions of the wooden components in the hull. Its meaning extended to strength and heaviness of construction and more particularly its specification in a design. It gradually came to mean the stength of any material used in a yacht. 'The scantlings are insufficient' is a refined way of saying 'she will fall apart in heavy weather or in a minor grounding or collision'.
12. This is the British scene, but rules were debated in France and Scandinavia. European countries had then much smaller yachting fleets than the UK and the senior club/national authority (usually the same thing then) was more authoritarian (as they remain today) than in the Anglo-Saxon nations. The British Empire (except Canada) followed Britain; the USA (whom Canada followed in yacht racing) is discussed in text.
13. And has been published from London ever since; as a weekly until September 1939, thereafter as a monthly. The author has written for the magazine over many years.
14. Badminton. Though 'Thalassa' more usually wrote on rating problems in *Yachting World*.
15. *Capt Nat Herreshoff, the Wizard of Bristol* (1953 reprinted Sheridan House, Dobbs Ferry, NY, 1990) by L. Francis Herreshoff.
　　Nathanael Greene Herreshoff (1848-1938). American yacht design genius of Bristol, Rhode Island. Designed six defenders of the America's Cup, hundreds of sailing and steam yachts, launches and dinghies. A number of his creations affected the evolution of international design. On his death, there were 18000 drawings in his files.
16. In other parts of Great Britain and Ireland mixed fleets of new raters and old tonnage boats including plank-on-edge sailed happily, all rated by the YRA rule. Apparently the last extreme plank on edge boats were simply not raced or bought. This is the equivalent of the scene in the 1990s, where IOR of varying ages race CHS, but the last extreme IOR designs are seldom seen.
17. *The Britannia and her Contemporaries* (1929) by Brooke Heckstall-Smith (Methuen, London).
18. *Ibid*.
19. *Ibid*. Figures for 'equivalent' ratings under successive rules, are given by Brooke Heckstall-Smith and shown in our Chapter 3.
20. Badminton. Chapter IX, Small Class Racing on the Solent by Thalassa.
21. *Yachting World*, 5 October 1894.
22. *Ibid*.

23. The Imperial and Royal Yacht Squadron of Austria-Hungary, aping the RYS at Cowes, was in a fine building at Pula, Croatia, until the collapse of the empire and monarchy in 1918. The Count who wrote the letter has been mentioned earlier.

24. The formula for the Union des Yachts Français was:

Rating $= ((L - P/4) \times P \times S^{1/2})/130$. L is LWL.

For the Yacht Club de France,

rating $= (L - B/2 \times (P/4)^{1/2})5.5$. Here L is LOA.

In both formulae, P is 'perimeter'. This extended from deck and around hull, thus giving an incentive to low freeboard. The French racing yachts were also skimming dishes. See later in chapter for more on rules in France.

25. But here it is worth remembering that there are today (1996) at least two 'rater' one-design classes regularly raced in Britain. They are 'frozen' versions of the raters of the 1890s: the Seabird ½-rater in North Wales and the Thames 'A' rater, a real skimming dish on the River Thames. See Chapter 6 for one-design pros and cons.

26. *Yachting World*, 21 June 1895.

27. *Ibid.*, 28 June 1895, article by Thalassa.

28. See account by the author on expulsion from New York YC of 4th Earl of Dunraven, *YW* September 1994, p. 86, *Landmarks 1896* by Peter Johnson.

29. *Ibid.*, letter from Paris, 17 January 1896.

30. *Ibid.*, 17 July 1896, letter from J. Orr Ewing, an experienced owner. However, as by now he had a boat to the new rule, at the YRA meeting in November he proposed the rule was kept for a fixed period.

31. Maybe the effect on known yachts by inserting these changes was checked and found desirable by the YRA. Today vast numbers of boats are run through a computer for the same purpose. The author will point out the snags in this procedure, as each designer looks at effects on this boat or that.

32. *The King's Britannia.*

33. *The Britannia and her Contemporaries.*

34. Major Brooke Heckstall-Smith TD (1869-1944). Secretary of the YRA 1897-1943 and of IYRU 1907-1943. Yachting Editor of *The Field* 1900-1928; Yachting Correspondent *Daily Telegraph* for many years; Editor *Yachting World* 1929-1934 and contributor until 1944. Author of six major works on yacht racing including *The Helmsman's Handbook, The Complete Yachtsman, Yacht Racing* (dedicated by permission to HM King George V, who is said to have coined the sobriquet 'Bookstall'), *All Hands on the Mainsheet, The Britannia and her Contemporaries*. His brother, Malden Heckstall-Smith, assisted in running the RORC rule in its early years. His son, the late Anthony Heckstall-Smith DSC, wrote *Sacred Cowes*, (1955) and *The Consort* (1962, republished in pb 1993) and some dozen other books and plays. Efforts by the author since about 1980 to track down any surviving members of the Heckstall-Smith family have met with no success. Brooke Heckstall-Smith's big part in rating matters will appear as chapters follow here.

35. WPS. See also on this failure: Fairley, who quotes a terse YRA

minute; *Room at the Mark* (1991) by Robert C. MacArthur, (Yacht Owners Register Inc, Boston).
36. Until 1925.
37. *The Yachtsman*, London, 17 February 1898; letter by Thalassa. This magazine complained a few weeks later that French yachts did not race in English waters, though the British went every year to the Riviera, because 'the difference of rule no doubt is chiefly to blame'.
38. *Ibid.*, 28 April 1898.
39. *Ibid.*
40. Information given by Jean Peytel of Cercle de la Voile de Paris to ORC in 1970 about origin of the One Ton Cup. Fuller information received by author from Daniel Charles, Belgian designer and historian, on visit by author to *Conservatoire International de Plaisance*, Bordeaux, August 1995. Rating rules in France were in as much trouble as elsewhere.
41. *British Yachts and Yachtsmen – sixteenth century to the present day* (1907), Yachtsman Publishing Co, London.
42. *Ibid.*
43. *Yachtsman*, London, 23 June 1898; report of Seawanhaka special committee on measurement rules. As always, unless otherwise stated, author's italics. D may mean various dimensions in rating formulae: draft, as here, displacement or depth of hull, whole or immersed. It will be made clear which, on each occasion or in the respective rule.
44. *The History of the New York Yacht Club*. The author is aware this simply repeats opinions of length and sail area rules, but the fact is that these strong words remain forever in the official history of this historic club.

Chapter 3   Ratings cross the Narrow Seas

1. *History of the Seawanhaka Corinthian Yacht Club, second volume, 1897-1940* (1965) by John Parkinson Jr (published by the club). Abbreviated below as *Seawanhaka*.
2. *Ibid.*
3. Not exceeded until plans emerged in Switzerland in 1994 to build commercially sponsored 80ft one-design around the world ocean racers.
4. *Seawanhaka*.
5. WPS.
6. The 90ft limit was never legally changed and this caused the ludicrous ill matched challenge of 1988 using no measurement rule, but only the limits of the deed document.
7. *The America's Cup 1851-1983* (1983) by John Rousmaniere (Pelham Books, London)
8. *The America's Cup Races* (1958 edition) by Herbert L. Stone (Van Nostrand Co., New York)
9. *The Lipton Story* (1950) by Alec Waugh (Cassell, London). Thomas Lipton, tea and grocery millionaire, was born in 1850 in a Glasgow slum of poor immigrant but hard working Irish Protestant parents. *Shamrock*

V raced at Cowes in August 1931; by then the world was in its worst financial crisis. He died in October 1931.

10. *Endeavour*, relaunched in 1989 after a rebuild and with her full size racing rig of 1934, now crosses the oceans without difficulty; this is because of the huge advances over 55 years in the materials and engineering of racing yacht rigs.

11. *The History of Yachting* (1974) by Douglas Phillips-Birt (Hamish Hamilton, London).

12. *Kongelig Dansk Yachtklub 1866-1966* (1966) by Eyvin Schiøttz (published by KDY, Kobenhavn).

13. *The Helmsman's Handbook* (1908) by Brooke Heckstall-Smith (Horace Cox, *The Field*, London). The title of this book is misleading.

14. *The Yacht Racing Calendar and Review of 1903* (1904) edited by Brooke Heckstall-Smith (Horace Cox, *The Field*, London).

15. As given in the original IYRU 1906 rule, as are all these data, reproduced fully in *The Helmsman's Handbook*.

16. In the Olympics, the 8-metre last raced in 1936 and the 6-metre last raced in 1952.

17. Variable time allowances will be discussed in Chapter 5, as they have re-occurred as a major controversy.

18. *Yacht Racing* (second edition, 1933) by Brooke Heckstall-Smith (The Field Press, London).

19. Paper received from Mr L.P.Cooper 1970 and in *The Yachtsman* 13 February 1913 and Spring 1945.

20. *Further Memorials of the Royal Yacht Squadron, 1901-1938* (1939) by J.B. Atkins (Geoffrey Bles, London).

21. The Scandinavian nations, which were all neutral in WWI, did notice that the rule had expired. So they amended it for their own use by changing all the constants in the basic formula. This was called the S rule. It is believed that only three yachts were ever built to this rule and after the war, the Norse sailors put their experience at the disposal of the IYRU.

22. Designed by Nat Herreshoff: no connection with S rule, above.

23. *Clinton Crane's Yachting Memories* (1952) by Clinton Crane (Van Nostrand, New York).

24. *Yachting World*, 1 January 1927, page 5.

25. WPS.

26. *Seawanhaka*.

27. In the USA only five 12-metres had ever been built; starting in 1935, two designed by Clinton Crane, one designed by L. Francis Herreshoff (son of Nat) and two, prior to *Vim*, designed by Olin J. Stephens of Sparkman and Stephens. One of the Crane designs was *Gleam* built for himself. In the 1937 New York YC cruise he had to increase her sail area and ballast because, despite the 1930 agreement the club was using the Universal rule!

12-metre yachts built in other countries between 1919 and 1939 were: United Kingdom, 30; Belgium, 1; Italy, 1. A number of other countries launched 12-metres before 1914 or after 1960.

Chapter 4.   The Coming of Ocean Racing
1. See Bibliography for books with accounts of ocean racing. Many of
these are based on earlier accounts such as *Ocean Racing* (first published
1935, Yachting, New York) by Alf Loomis, famous American ocean
racing journalist and *British Ocean Racing* (1969) by Douglas Phillips-
Birt, Adlard Coles, London. The sequence of events is given in *The
Encyclopedia of Yachting* (1989) by Peter Johnson, Dorling Kindersley,
London (and editions in other countries). The author has also written a
brief history of the Royal Ocean Racing Club, which appeared in that
club's membership and rule book issued in 1991, 1994, 1997 and maybe
subsequently.
2. Herbert L. Stone, chapter in Loomis, op cit., see Introduction note 1.
3. Closeness or separation of corrected times is no guide to the merit of a
rating or time allowance system. This is argued in Chapter 5.
4. Stone, *ibid*.
5. The Blue Water Medal of the Cruising Club of America is acknowledged as the world's senior trophy for yacht *long distance cruising
achievement*.
6. *Lake Michigan Yachting Association Year Book 1936*.
7. *Yachting World* 28 August 1931, *The Future of Ocean Racing* by
'Solent'. However one imagines no one would want a 'bad' vessel. As for
'healthy', the distinguished ocean racing sailor and author, Mary Pera (see
note 35 of Chapter 7), once asked what constituted a healthy or unhealthy
yacht, but no one answered, not even medical advisers.
8. *YW* 16 June 1933, *Ocean Racing Rules, A Comparison of American and
British Formulae* by J. Laurent Giles, a designer of crack ocean racers in
England until the 1960s. The yacht design firm he founded, Laurent
Giles and Partners, is still in business today at Lymington, England.
9. While Uffa Fox said more colourfully in his *Second Book* (1935)
'The American and British clubs that arrange these long distance races
are like naughty children and cannot agree over a common ocean racing
rule'.
10. Stone.
11. *Racing at Sea* (1959) (Van Nostrand, New York) Chapter on US rules
by H. Irving Pratt.
12. *Yachting*, March 1964, page 44, *The Cruising Club Measurement Rule*
by Gordon M. Curtis Jr. He also said that the CCA was intending to
experiment with multiple time allowances for varying conditions, but it is
not known what was done on this. It probably had to wait until the CCA
and NAYRU created MHS (Chapter 8).
13. Early history and rating rules of the RORC almost all according to
British Ocean Racing (1960) by Douglas Phillips-Birt (Adlard Coles,
London) and contemporary articles and reports in *Yachting World*,
London.
14. For modern sailors: in wooden yachts the beams ran across under the
deck at intervals and the floors were solid athwartships members which
held together the planking in way of the bilges. This measurement is
instantly obviously open to exploitation; but there simply were no boats
adjusted to the rule in 1926.
15. *British Ocean Racing*.

16. The form of the rule has survived (1995) in the International 5.5-metre class. (Chapter 8).
17. *The RORC rule of measurement and rating 1957, amended to to 31 December 1967.* RORC, London. 32 pages each measuring only 184mm × 124mm; compare with today's lengthy rule books.
18. *Deep Water Cruising* (1928, 2nd ed 1950) by E.G. Martin, foreword by Herbert L. Stone (Oxford University Press, London). See also head of this chapter. Commander E. George Martin OBE BA RNVR. 1881-1945. Main founder of (R)ORC after resigning from Royal Cruising Club committee in which he won both RCC and CCA awards. Won first two Fastnets in gaff cutter *Jolie Brise* and was 1st in Class A of Bermuda race 1926. Won One Ton (6-metre) in 1912. As well as cruising on the ocean was author of sea books, educated at Eton, graduate of New College, Oxford, county cricket player, served in both world wars, height 6ft 5in. Such was a main initiator of the RORC and, not least, its rule. After his death, his partner gave *Griffin*, his last yacht, to the RORC as race training ship. The name *Griffin* lives for RORC training schemes.
19. *Deep Sea Racing Craft* (1933) issued by Royal Corinthian Yacht Club, Burnham-on-Crouch (Day and Co., London). 116 pages of large format with gold edged paper.
20. The author sailed against the well maintained *Stormy Weather* in RORC races in 1988-1995.
21. *British Ocean Racing*. Written in about 1958. Today we would consider the dimensions as long keeled, heavy displacement etc.
22. Numerous accounts. For Illingworth's own story see *The Malham Story* (1942) by John H. Illingworth (Nautical Publishing, Lymington). It was edited by this author. Illingworth was a towering figure in ocean racing (commodore RORC and RNSA) and other yacht racing, yacht design and sail training in the 1940s, 50s and 60s.
23. *Ibid.*
24. *Offshore Racing Council Year Book 1995.*
25. *Ibid.*
26. *Offshore Racing Council Championship Rule for Offshore Classes 1995.*
27. *Yachting Monthly*, London, 'Reflections' column by Douglas Phillips-Birt, later published as *Reflections on Yachts* (Nautical Publishing, Lymington, 1968).
28. *Yachting World Annual 1972*: article *The Not-So-New-Rule* by Peter Johnson.

Chapter 5.   Giving and getting time
1. *Britannia and her Contemporaries.*
2. *Manual of Yacht and Boat Sailing.*
3. The potentially fastest yacht in 'American' races has the smallest rating; in Britain (time-on-time) the fastest yacht has the biggest rating.
4. In the USA the race entry or 'race card' (as known in England, borrowed from the Turf) is often known as the 'scratch sheet'. This is quite confusing as the word 'scratch' implies no handicaps, where this list

is the opposite! This term caused continuous bafflement outside the USA in attempts to introduce IMS from America (Chapter 8).

5. William Theodore Snaith (1908-1974), leading ocean racing owner, skipper, character and New York industrial (not yacht) designer.

6. *Captain Nat Herreshoff* (1953) by L. Francis Herreshoff.

7. H.Irving Pratt in *Racing at Sea* (1959), above. He was also a distinguished offshore racer with success in well known CCA class yachts.

8. John J. Collins (PHRF, Maine and New Hampshire) in article *The Rule America Uses* in *Channel Handicap 1995* annual (1994), published by the author.

9. *YW* 13 Dec 1935.

10. *YW* 20 Dec 1935. If reported accurately, these claims, we know, are exaggerated, which Malden Heckstall-Smith and others surely understood.

11. *The Helmsman's Handbook*.

12. *The Yacht Racing Association Rules 1936, incorporating the rules of the International Yacht Racing Union*. Secretary of both bodies: Major B. Heckstall-Smith.

13. *The Yachtsman's Annual 1948-49* edited by K. Adlard Coles. In the 1950s this same formula was also published in the RORC rule itself as an available time-on-distance system; it may have been used on occasions in the Mediterranean, where time-on-time is sometimes not favoured because of the prolonged calms.

14. Later it was reported (*Yachting World Annual 1951-52*) to have huge errors. They would have been better off with performance estimates. Anyway this was another reason for switching to proper RORC measurement, rating and time allowance.

15. *Yachting World Annual 1951-52* edited by E.F. Haylock.

16. *Whitbread Round the World 1973-1993* (1992) by Peter Johnson (published by Whitbread plc, an English brewing and catering company).

Chapter 6   Keen racing, but no rating

1. Quoted in *The Water Wags 1887-1987* (1987) by A.F. Delaney, 84 pages, published by the Water Wags Class, Dublin.

2. *The Sailing Boat* (1901) by Henry Coleman Folkard (Edward Stanford, London).

3. *The Encyclopedia of Yachting* (1989) by Peter Johnson (Dorling Kindersley, London).

4. *International Yacht Racing Union 1996 Year Book* (1996) IYRU, London. Of these 43 international classes over half have international headquarters based in UK (17) and USA (6).

5. *The Sailing Boat*.

6. *The Water Wags*, above, has this in detail, facsimile of the original leaflet, old photographs etc.

7. The main annual class trophy of the Water Wags is the Jubilee Commemoration Cup. This has been presented every year from 1887 (Queen Victoria's silver jubilee) until this year (1997), except for the war years 1915-1918. *Pansy's* name appears as winner in 1907, 1949, 1969, 1990 and other years!

8. The class is controlled by the Royal Yorkshire Yacht Club, 1 Windsor Terrace, Bridlington, Yorkshire (founded 1847). A number of boats have been built since 1945, but four of the original 1898 boats remain racing in the class.

9. More detail in *Yachts and Yachting* dated 17 January 1992, *And Sailors Created One-designs* by Peter Johnson; also *The Encyclopedia of Yachting* by Peter Johnson pages 168-169, Inshore One-Design Classes.

10. The term OOD is not generally accepted, but it will be used in this work. Uffa Fox wrote in the first line of the first chapter of his first book 'Seamen are made up of deepwater men and coasters . . .' (*Sailing, Seamanship and Yacht Construction*, 1934, Peter Davies, London).

11. The OOD34 was essentially for ocean racing with the RORC Fastnet race as its main event. The first full season was 1979, when the twelve OOD34s were struck by the Fastnet storm; two of them were lost at sea. In particular there was wide and continuing publicity over the rescue of the crew of the RORC's own club OOD34, *Griffin*, which had taken to the liferaft. This combined with a BBC television post mortem on the race which roasted the inarticulate boatbuilders, meant that the class reached a total of 40 boats, but then dispersed by about 1990: a ten year life. The boats have meanwhile sailed thousands of miles offshore with few incidents. One OOD34 in the Fastnet rescued the complete crew of an abandoned Contention 33 and brought them to port; this received virtually no notice. One potential customer once wrote to the builder (in about 1983) 'How can you build boats that drown people?' No one was lost or drowned from any OOD34 in the Fastnet of 1979.

12. *Yachting World*, May 1984, page 85. *OODs Six Years On* by Peter Johnson.

13. The author wrote about this in detail as *Ratings – Fact or Fiction?*, *Yachting World*, September 1979. At some yachting conference at the time or other a senior official of the Offshore Racing Council came up and accused him strongly of wrecking faith in the IOR, in terms which left him quite shaken. Probably the provocative title wording caused some of the trouble, as well as the picture of a measurer dipping a metre rule into the sea with a crew leaning down on the rail, as he read off the figure for an official freeboard. Two months later the international authority closed the gap with OOD ratings.

14. *OODs Six Years On*.

15. Mumm 36 class rules and detail: RORC, 20 St James's Place, London SW1A 1AA UK or Farr International, 613 Third Street #11, Annapolis, MD21403, USA.

16. *The International Fourteen Foot Dinghy – History and Handbook 1928 to* (latest edition year) by T.J. Vaughan, published by the class. First published 1964, revised editions 1971, 1989 (and further). There are also extensive references and descriptions of designing, building and racing the class in the books of Uffa Fox, published from 1934 on.

Chapter 7.   For two decades: a world rule

1. Famous British parliamentarian and also Secretary of State 1756-61.

2. *The Writings of L. Francis Herreshoff* (1946), Rudder Publishing Co, New York. He was the son of Nathanael Herreshoff.

3. *Paper to ORC and its committees* by the author in his capacity as chairman International Technical Committee, the executive rule making group of six persons, answerable to ORC. He succeeded Olin J. Stephens II in 1973 and resigned in 1976; Stephens then took the position again until 1979. Records show that Stephens sat in on every ITC meeting during the chairmanship of the author except for one.

4. In Britain the first year in which measurement and computation of IOR was no longer available was 1995.

5. *YW* December 1969, page 536. But in English speaking countries and others the rating remained in feet and decimal feet (e.g. 37.43ft) for the whole life of the IOR.

6. *YW* March 1970, page 113, *Ring in the New* by David Fayle, Chief Measurer RORC.

7. *Yachting World Annual 1970* (1970) Iliffe Books, London.

8. IOR Mark IIIA was instituted in November 1975, but this was a special retrospective section to help 'cruisers', partly in response to the CCA threat to modify IOR for their 1976 race, though in the event they failed to use it. 'Mark IV', which would have been a major revision in about 1990, was talked about, but (unfortunately say many) was never created.

9. For full graphs and tables of numbers of yachts in the life of IOR and other rating rules, see later pages.

10. Actually in 1987, the fleet became split into IOR (37) and IMS (22), then mostly IMS (10!) for the next year. The arrival of IMS will be described in Chapter 8, but it inevitably impinged on the closing years of each of these great IOR series.

11. Especially *Fastnet Force 10* (1980) by John Rousmaniere (W.W. Norton & Co, New York, and Nautical Publishing Co, Lymington, England, also paperback by Nautical (1987) and later in at least one standard paperback sailing classic reprint).

12. *The Guinness Book of Records* (annually) (Guinness Publishing Co, London)

13. *1979 Fastnet Race Inquiry*: Report by Sir Hugh Forbes (High Court Judge), Sir Maurice Laing and Lt Colonel James Myatt to the committee of the RORC and the council of the RYA assisted by a working party of nine persons (1979).

14. The author is tempted to rewrite this as 'We have nothing to say about the IOR. Therefore the body which controls it should read our report before doing nothing about it'.

15. Figures for number of IOR certificates (and in later years IMS certificates) supplied annually to the author by Offshore Racing Council Each country made an annual return and was charged a levy.

16. *Yachting* February 1972, page 46 in *Deep Water Racing*, a monthly column by Jeff Hammond.

17. Remember the tradition of beamy boats in the US was eroded in the latter years of the CCA rule: in comparison the last of the RORC boats were beamy ('the pregnant cow').

18. *Yachting*, August 1973, page 40: interview by Jeff Hammond with Jerry Milgram. Milgram in particular attacked Olin Stephens and Robin Glover for their alleged arbitrary interpretations of IOR in repect of his design.

19. *Yachts and Yachting*, 1973-74, articles on Gordon Trower design by Rob Humphreys and Jack Knights and readers' letters.

20. *Yachts and Yachting*, 5 April 1974, letter from Peter Johnson, as chairman ITC, also stating all discussions and visits to the designer and the builder, Eric White, at the boat by officials, national (Keith Ludlow, RORC) and international, had been been extremely amicable.

21. *White Sails, Black Clouds* (1967) by John J. McNamara Jr, Burdette & Co, Boston, MA. A 'one-off' mainly on recent yacht racing wins, losses and disputes, it made an impact in its time.

22. This not unknown avenue of thought about rating rule management will be looked at in a concluding chapter.

23. *Soundings* (east coast yachting paper), June 1974, piece by Keith Taylor.

24. Letter to NAYRU by Richard J. Kerry, CCA member, of Littleton, MA, 1 May 1974.

25. Letter to NAYRU by Richard Kelton, Beverly Hills, CA, 22 May 1974. In both cases there is no mention of name or type of boat owned.

26. Lynn Williams (1909-1985) of Winnetka, Illinois, leading CCA personality and experienced ocean racing sailor. Owned *Dora IV*, which later became *Tenacious* (owned by Ted Turner and winner of 1979 Fastnet), then *War Baby* (Warren Brown). The CCA had, as mentioned, wanted to get out of rating rules, but now those in charge appeared to regret that decision.

27. Report of the CCA technical committee to the board of governors. It did not seem very technical; it was rather repetitive and called for changes. In America 'Rule' was often given an initial capital, which is revealing.

28. Nothing to do with ocean racing; Canada was to run the 1976 Olympic Games, so the time had come for its own yachting authority.

29. *Yachting* July 1976, page 148. This last sentence is 'Weller-speak'. We will meet more of this as Ken Weller remained at USYRU, combining the job of international chief measurer from 1984 when he succeeded a British chief measurer of ORC. In 1994 he left the USYRU post, remained in the international one and moved to England.

30. *Yachting* November 1974, page 48. *Deep Water Racing* by Jeff Hammond. A long interview with David Edwards, covering all the well rehearsed American difficulties with IOR. On the first page were three 'mug shots' with the caption *The three powerful Englishmen who administer the IOR and sport of world ocean racing*: hardly likely to be well received across the vastness of the USA! The portraits by Hammond were of Edwards, Robin Glover and the author.

31. *Handicapping Systems for Ocean Racing Yachts* by J.N. Newman read at the meeting of the Royal Institution of Naval Architects, March 1975 at

Southampton University.

32. *Yachting* August 1975, *Ocean Racing: USYRU's Objectives* by Lynn A. Williams. Quotes of his over optimistic pushing of what was in effect a laboratory experiment into use as a rule will be made in the next chapter. This policy was to cause numerous difficulties in MHS/IMS in the years ahead.

33. Letter from Williams to Edwards, 8 December 1975, marked 'confidential'. His remark about variable time allowances shows he was no longer in touch with reality or scientific results, but was simply determined to have a new rating rule. In 1996 (!), the variable time allowances were still unsatisfactory in USA, Australia and elsewhere see Chapter 8.

34. Letter from Edwards to Williams, 23 December 1975.

35. Mary Pera (aka Maria Blewitt), of Colchester, England, experienced ocean racing sailor and especially navigator to John Illingworth and others. Author of books on navigation and on IYRU racing rules, served on ORC and its committees, Secretary of RORC 1972-1978, Vice-Commodore 1981-1982.

36. Anthony Heckstall-Smith, see note 34 of Chapter 2.

37. Figures for starters year by year in many big events are in *The Encyclopedia of Yachting*.

38. As at 1991, but the basic rule formula appeared the same from 1985 until its fading in the mid-1990s.

39. This measurement saga was a long one and inevitably damaged enthusiasm for IOR. A full account in *Yachting World* by Tim Jeffery, September 1982, page 44. The RORC report was by David Edwards, Brigadier Sir Frederick Coates Bt, a successful racing skipper and Commander Sir David Mackworth Bt, formerly a rating consultant and colleague of John Illingworth.

Chapter 8.   Scatter

1. *The March of Folly*, see note 2 of Preface, above: section *The British lose America*.

2. *Yachting World* August 1989, page 78: *Admiral's Cup Preview* by Andrew Preece, offshore correspondent of the magazine 1989 onward (and currently); offshore correspondent *Yachts and Yachting* 1984-87.

3. Yet at each November meeting of ORC, usually attended by the author as an observer, there seemed to be changes to IOR. The impression was that there was resistance to major change because of the 'freeze' policy, but clauses were trimmed here and there. The author could detect no firm line of approach; one might say the worst of both worlds.

4. The ORC states (verbal by Secretary Joan Matthewson to author 1996) that there have been no IOR rule changes proclaimed since 1993. Now there are no enquiries. Who runs the remaining 'IOR boats'? The British (RORC Rating Office) last ran a program for RORC measurement in 1994: from 1995 onwards it was not possible to obtain an IOR rating in Britain.

5. *Ocean Racing: USYRU's Objectives* by Lynn A. Williams, see note 32, Chapter 7, above.

6. *Handicapping Systems for Ocean Racing Yachts* by Professor (of Naval Architecture at MIT, Cambridge, MA) J.N. Newman MSc ScD, see note 31, Chapter 7, above. The author was present and read a short comment as chairman ITC. A number of short verbal and written commenting papers were read (including by C.A. Marchaj, Commander Sir David Mackworth Bt, Prof Ir. J. Gerritsma, Alan Payne, Bennett Fisher).

7. *The IMS, a description of the new international rating system* (1986) by Charles L. Poor, Washington DC, 55 page A4 booklet. The terms 'more' or 'most complete' are typical of the obscure expressions that the reader will find accompany IMS. Presumably they mean 'not complete' or 'incomplete'.

8. *International Measurement System 1992* (rule book), published by Offshore Racing Council, London (hereafter 'IMS rule').

9. *Ibid.* The author has trimmed some of the verbiage of the written rule.

10. *Y and Y*, January 1989, *Measuring Up* by Peter Johnson, quoting John Warren, a senior measurer and later RORC Director of Rating.

11. Conversation of author with E. Alan Green, Secretary RORC in his office at 20 St James's Place, October 1988.

12. Letter to author from Captain Dan Bradby RN, Secretary Cowes Week Regatta, 20 January 1993.

13. *Y and Y*, November 1988, *ORC Words*, report of that month's ORC meeting by Andrew Preece.

14. *Seahorse Magazine*, London. January 1992 page 37, *ORC annual conference in London* by Malcolm McKeag.

15. ORC press release: *action on extreme draft*, May 1992. This is Weller-speak. Possibly there were too many designers involved, thinking of their latest designs. But the council was meant to be the body which made decisions. Yet instead of nipping these boats in the bud, it skirted around the problem with phrases like 'Indications are that extreme designs this season will begin to appear in events throughout the world and so jeopardise confidence in IMS as has already happened in North America' (John Bourke to members of council, 3 April 1992).

16. Letter to author from John Bourke, chairman ORC, 19 May 1992. He also wrote the strange sentence 'What we cannot do is actually instruct a national authority as to what it can or cannot do in its own waters and this (*sic*) really must be done by persuasion and example' What did this statement mean? Surely the ORC regulates the IMS. Is he is saying the Americans did whatever they wanted or, perhaps, failed to do what was wanted in saving IMS? The author has never asked.

17. Writing in the column for the commodore RORC in *Seahorse* magazine, which was circulated free to all RORC members. John Dare, an American based in London, had owned a number of boats including an OOD34, which was hit by the IOR DLF penalty and *Roller Skate*, a Humphreys Three Quarter Tonner, which suffered a crippling IOR rating rise when he took it in 1984 to Kiel for the cup races. In 1989 he launched a new IMS cruiser racer designed by Humphreys, *Apriori*. He became honorary treasurer of IOR. He became RORC rear commodore 1988-89, vice commodore 1990, commodore 1991-93, chairman ORC from 1993. His enthusiasm for IMS was, then and now, unrelenting.

18. *Myth of Malham,* in both the first and second Admiral's Cup, was a flat out racer of her time; his history was adrift.

19. *Y and Y* 14 August 1992, *Comedy Cup* by David Pelly, then Yachting Correspondent *Sunday Telegraph*.

20. *Seahorse* magazine, October 1992.

21. Based on *Y and Y*, 20 November 1992, page 48, *ORC Up-date* by Peter Johnson and quoted from *official Minutes of ORC* 7 November, which include some Weller-speak, as well as tautology. 'Velocity' includes direction and speed. Repetitive words about VPP accuracy did not seem to improve it for in the corresponding *Minutes*, one year on in 1993, page 3, Bourke stated 'Some of the new elements introduced into the VPP had been more difficult and recalcitrant than expected'.

22. *ILC Rule* issued by Ken Weller at ORC, 30 April 1993. The sub-committee members were Nicola Sironi (It.) chairman ITC, Bruce Farr (US), Rob Humphreys (Brit.), Axel Mohnhaupt (Ger.) and Ken Weller (US), chief measurer ORC.

23. Surely the most uninspiring name ever chosen for a class of yacht.

24. And ran into serious measurement problems, because the ratings would not repeat on customary checking for a series.

25. *Yachting*, New York, March 1964. Gordon M. Curtis Jr later became a US delegate in the early years of IOR.

26. *Desirable and Undesirable Characteristics of Offshore Yachts* (1987) edited by John Rousmaniere, page 44, *Trends in Yacht Design 1920 to 1986* by Olin J. Stephens II.

27. *Grand Prix Sailor* newsletter, Newport, RI, 22 February 1996.

28. *Sail,* October 1991, page 108, offshore race report.

29. Another term (by Brian Saffery-Cooper, hugely experienced British ocean racer) was 'I am a mess'. Rating rules have often been blamed, but never given quite such sobriquets!

30. *Grand Prix Sailor* newsletter, 4 January 1996, report by Rob Mundle from Hobart, Tasmania.

31. *IMS Race Committee Guide 1994* by ORC, London.

32. During an international IMS regatta, the race officer with his lap top computer down below in the committee boat called out for speed and direction of tidal stream. The author and others looked over the side, one observer said "What do you reckon? Three-quarters of a knot? North-north-east". Author: "Maybe one knot". First observer to computer buff: "One Knot. $22\frac{1}{2}$ degrees magnetic". The data were duly entered to four decimal places. In any case the yachts were not near the committee boat.

33. But (late news) the ORC in November 1996 approved insertion of the RORC TCF on all IMS certificates.

34. The RORC called TCF when used with IMS a TMF (time multiplication factor); there is no difference.

35. E. Alan Green, Director of Racing RORC in conference with author, 6 February 1996.

36. Weller-speak. *Seahorse*, May 1995, page 27, *ORC* with Ken Weller.

Chapter 9. What sailors did

1. One of the founders of the Royal Ocean Racing Club, Vice Commodore RORC 1928-34, Commodore 1951-52, great grandson of the 8th Duke of Beaufort, father of the present (1996) 11th Duke. Died 1965 in attempting a rescue in a cruising yacht in the Mediterranean.

2. Letter from author, owner then of *Highwayman*, 38ft (11.5m) IOR One Ton Cup (21.7ft) design by Rob Humphreys, to Rating Secretary RORC, 20 April 1989.

3. UNCL, L'Union Nationale pour la Course au Large, Face au 36 quai Alphonse Le Gallo, 92100 Boulogne (near Paris), France. Established as an association 1915, as a club 1982. The leading offshore organization in France for ocean races, long distance short handed races, national teams and now the administration of the CHS for France and allocated countries.

4. *Yachting World*, February 1984, page 33, editorial news.

5. *YW*, February 1994, page 62, *How did he rate you?* by Peter Johnson. Account of Ashmead's work at the RORC Rating Office.

6. *Channel Handicap 1996-year 13* (1995) edited by Peter Johnson with technical support of RORC Rating Office. This annual publication comprises CHS rules, guidance, addresses of outstations, racing news and other CHS material for English speaking users (not issued from Paris office). First produced May 1989, then December 1990 and every December following. Hereafter to imply any edition referred to as *CH*.

7. *Ibid*.

8. Titles for the same job became more pompous. In 1925, there was a 'measurer'; then a chief measurer. For many years the RORC had a Rating Secretary in charge, but in 1989 he was titled 'Director of Measurement and Rating'.

9. *Minutes of CHS User Group*, item 3, of 11 January 1990 at RORC, London.

10. *CH*

11. A crew number per yacht was inserted after noisy complaints and requests, yet at the end of the season it was found to have been barely invoked by any race committee.

12. *Y and Y*, 10 April 1992, page 47, *Channel Nine* by Peter Johnson. Review of nine years of the rule.

13. John Bourke, see Chapter 7, also its note 16. This was in regular commodore comment in *Seahorse*.

14. Written comment to author, October 1993, from Mike Richards, skipper of *Bounder*. Intended for *CH94*, but left unpublished. He probably refers to being beaten by old boats with low IMS ratings. His last sentence expresses the already stale topic of the IMS time allowance system.

15. Letters from Jonathan Bradbeer, commodore RORC, to author dated 20 October 1989 and 18 January 1990 (the former but not the latter copied to John Dare).

16. *The Daily Telegraph*, 4 May 1990, report by Tim Jeffery, yachting correspondent.

17. *RORC Rating Policy*, 6 November 1992, press information signed by E. Alan Green, Director of Racing and Special Events, RORC, 20 St James's Place, London.

18. *Yachting World*, April 1996, page 23, letter to the editor by David Walters, chairman RORC IMS committee. Same letter sent to other yachting press and published in *Seahorse* and *Y and Y*.

19. *Limiting the damage*, paper by the author presented at RORC seminar, London, 23 September 1995. Afternoon session on ratings.

20. *Minutes of RORC CHS committee* (formerly 'User Group'), 22 September 1995 at Southampton, item 4.

21. *United States Sailing Association Directory*.

22. Stated by John J. Collins, Marblehead, Massachusetts, chairman US Sailing PHRF Committee and of PHRF New England, in fax to author, 6 April 1996.

23. John J. Collins information.

24. *Sail*, May 1987, page 72, *PHRF: Grass Roots Giant* by Tom Linskey and Gail E. Anderson.

25. Collins, February 1994, letter to author.

26. *Ibid*. A paper entitled *New Boat: What's the Handicap?*

Chapter 10.   Take your pick

1. *Yachting World*, December 1946, page 433, editorial news.

2. *1995 International Six Metre class rating rule and measurement instructions*, (June 1995), IYRU, London.

3. A fascinating and virtually unknown story appears in a back page of *Yachting*, New York, October 1932, page 193. During the British-American Cup races of 1932, Olin J. Stephens II spent two days ashore in Cowes with Malden Heckstall-Smith, devising a rule for a new 'British racing class to fit between the 14ft International and the 6-metre'. Stephens's suggested rule was published as

$$(L \times (S)^{1/2}/2 \times (D)^{1/3}) + 1/2 \, (S)^{1/2}$$

This is actually the 5.5 rule without different constants and no length in the second term. The first term is of course the Universal rule; so Stephens was saying in a way 'why not return to Herreshoff?'. Aluminium and all alloys were to be prohibited (that must have been currently some controversy). However no figure was given for the rating, but it must have been about 4.5-metres (15ft). Nothing more was heard of this project. Remember a proposed 4.5 was rejected by IYRU in 1950 and only the 5.5 announced.

4. *The Daily Telegraph*, London, April 1989, published letter from the author, in reply to one by Major Ranulf Rayner.

5. *Caribbean Yachting Association Handbook 1995*, English Harbour, Antigua.

6. *Dansk Handicap* published by Dansk Sejlunion, 2605 Brondby.

7. Opinion of Simon Forbes, Technical Officer at ISAF, who control the rule (letter to author May 1996); Forbes also coordinates other multihull ratings and classes.

8. Surprisingly there an organization, the ISAF Model Yacht Racing Division with chairman, secretary and technical committee chairman (c/o ISAF).

9. *Portsmouth Yardstick Scheme*, booklet YR2/96, RYA Yacht Racing Division.

10. *Manual of Yacht and Boat Sailing* (1891) by Dixon Kemp, page 716, YRA time allowances.

Appendix I

THE INTERNATIONAL RATING CONFERENCE 1906

(Photograph page iv)

On Thursday 18 January, at a fourth sitting, in the Langham Hotel, London, the formula for the first international rule was carried unanimously 'after prolonged debate'.

Each country had come with its knowledgable delegates and armed with its current formula.

However the British rule and the German/Scandinavian (Danish led) rule already had a close resemblance. In the event the agreed International Rule 1906 had all the same factors ((L, B, G, S, F and d) as the German/Scandinavian rule, but with different coefficients (multipliers on some of the letters); the British rule also had these letters, with the exception of F (freeboard). The delegates and their rules were:

Denmark. F. Hegel (26, designer, sailing experience in USA); Alfred Benzon (authority on rating, inventor of d, designer, former member Danish parliament, convener first Scandinavian yacht race conference). Rule, as above, created 1899, due to expire 1907.

Germany. Admiral Burmester (DSV); Professor Busley (authority on rating, designer, yachting adviser to the Kaiser). Same rule as Denmark.

Norway. Johan Anker (racer, designer, KNS); Finn Knudson (yacht builder). Same rule as Denmark.

Sweden. Rear Admiral Jacob Hägg (commodore KSSS); Theodore Alpen (GKSS). KSSS (east coast), using since 1877 old British length and sail area rule with limits. GKSS (west coast) used variation of this until 1905, but recently changed to German/Scandinavian rule.

Austria-Hungary. Lieut Baron von Preuschen (Imperial and Royal YS, on Adriatic). Using British rule and will follow any European agreement.

Italy. Count Eugene Brunetta d'Usseaux. Will follow any European agreement.

Belgium and Holland. Hon Jonker W. Six; M. von Bernuth (Royal Netherlands, Royal Antwerp YCs). Using an old length and sail area rule which is not satisfactory and will follow any approved European agreement.

France. Louis Dyévre (designer); M. Blanchy (racing sailor).

Switzerland. Jean Miraband (racing sailor, banker). Both countries using different perimeter/girth/sail area rules, but are sympathetic to suitable European rule, though changes will be major for them.

Great Britain. HRH The Prince of Wales, President of the conference – not present. HM King Edward VII sent a message to delegates. Augustus

338

Manning (chairman of conference). William Fife, C.E. Nicholson, J.M.
Soper (designers), W. Baden-Powell (sailor). Brooke Heckstall-Smith
(secretary of the conference). Using YRA rule of 1901, needing revision
and, as above, was already close to Danish rule.

'Mr Augustus Manning is an ideal chairman never obtruding his
personal views except to elicit the franker impression of foreign views on
difficult points. He assists with something of a fine old courtliness that is
rare in these days of heated opinion and hurried thoughtlessness'.
(all above from extensive reports in Yachting World *of 18 and 25 January
1906)*.

Appendix II

KEY OFFICIALS OF THE (INTERNATIONAL*) OFFSHORE RACING COUNCIL
(ORC) (controlling IOR, then IMS)
* *Though delegates are from many nations with boats to these rules the
IYRU/ISAF has never allowed use of this word in the title.*

CHAIRMAN OF ORC
Buster de Guingand (UK) 1969-1970
David Edwards (UK) 1970-78
John Roome (UK) 1978-87
John Bourke (Ireland) 1987-1993
John Dare (USA) 1993-

CHAIRMAN OF INTERNATIONAL TECHNICAL
COMMITTEE (ITC)
Olin J. Stephens II (USA) 1969-73
Peter Johnson (UK) 1973-76
Olin J. Stephens II (USA) 1976-79
Gary Mull (USA) 1979-87
Nicola Sironi (Italy) 1987-1996
David Pedrick (USA) 1996-

CHIEF MEASURER ORC
Brigadier David Fayle CBE DSO MIMechE (UK) 1969-72
Major Robin Glover MC (UK) 1972-84
Kenneth B. Weller (USA) 1984-1996
Nicola Sironi (Italy) 1996-

**ROYAL OCEAN RACING CLUB, LONDON, CHIEF
MEASURER/RATING SECRETARY/DIRECTOR OF RATING**
(changing title)
Ray Barrett MC 1925-1956
Brigadier David Fayle CBE DSO MIMechE 1956-1972
Ron Matthews 1972-76
Keith Ludlow 1976-83
Mal MacDougall 1983-85
Commander Tony Ashmead MSc MIMechE RN 1986-1993
John Warren 1993-

USYRU/US SAILING, OFFSHORE DIRECTOR
Theodore A. Jones 1973-76
Kenneth B. Weller 1976-1994 (combined with ORC post above)
John W. Wright 1994-

Appendix III

RATING RULES USED FOR THE AMERICA'S CUP
Time allowances applied
1870 Waterline area rule
1871 Displacement rule
1876-81 Cubic contents rule
1885-1903 Seawanhaka (length and sail area) rule
1920 Universal rule

Level rating, no time allowance
1930-37 Universal rule, J-class
1958-87 International rule, 12-metre class
1988 No rule used
1992- IACC rule (International America's Cup class)

RATING RULES USED FOR THE ADMIRAL'S CUP
Time allowance applied
1957-69 RORC rule (Royal Ocean Racing Club)
1971-89 IOR (International Offshore rule)

Level rating, no time allowance
1991-1993 IOR

One level class and one time allowance applied
1995-1997 IMS (International Measurement System) and a one-design
class

Sources and Bibliography

Argonaut. *The Yacht Racing Calendar 1866*. The Field, London 1866.

Atkins, J.B. *Further Memorials of the Royal Yacht Squadron 1902-1936*. Geoffrey Bles, London 1939.

Beaufort, Duke of (Patron) *Yachting, the Badminton Library, 2 volumes*. Longman, London 1894.

Bonnor, George. *The Yachting Season of 1845*. Nautical, Lymington 1971 (reprint)

Bryer, Robin. *Jolie Brise*. Secker & Warburg, London 1982.

Conner, Dennis. *Comeback*. Bloomsbury, London 1987.

Cotter, Edward F. *The Offshore Course: Today's Ocean Races*. Crown, New York 1977.

Crane, C. *Clinton Crane's Yachting Memories*. Van Nostrand, New York 1952.

Dear, Ian. *Champagne Mumm Book of Ocean Racing*. Severn House, London 1985

---- *Enterprise to Endeavour*. Inkspot, London 1986.

---- *Fastnet; story of a great race*. Batsford, London 1981.

Delaney, A.F. *The Water Wags 1887-1987*. Class Association, Dublin 1987

Esterly, Diana E. *Early One-Design Sailboats*. Charles Scribners' Sons, New York 1979.

Finot, J.M. *La Jauge IOR*. Arthaud, Paris 1977.

Folkard, H.C. *The Sailing Boat*. Edward Stanford, London 1901.

Fox, Uffa. *Sailing, Seamanship and Yacht Construction; Uffa Fox's Second Book; Sail and Power; Racing, Cruising and Design; Thoughts on Yachts and Yachting 1930-1938*. Peter Davies, London 1930-38.

---- *The Crest of the Wave*. Peter Davies. London 1939.

Freer, Chris. *12-metre Yacht, The*. Nautical, London 1986.

Gabe, Julius. *Yachting*. MacQueen, London 1902.

Guest and Bolton. *Memorials of the Royal Yacht Squadron 1815-1901*. John Murray, London 1903.

Heckstall-Smith, Anthony. *The Consort*. Robert Clark, London 1962/93.

---- *Sacred Cowes*. Allan Wingate, London, London 1955.

Heckstall-Smith, B. *Britannia and her Contemporaries*. Methuen, London 1929.

---- *Helmsman's Handbook, The*. The Field, London 1908.
---- *YRA Annual and Rules*. YRA, London 1920-1938 (various)
---- *Yacht Racing*. The Field, London 1923/1933.
---- *Yacht Racing Calendar and Review 1903*. The Field, London 1903.
Herreshoff, L. Francis. *Captain Nat Herreshoff*. Sheridan House, New York 1953.
---- *The Writings of L. Francis Herreshoff*. The Rudder, New York 1946.
Holmes, Noel. *Go, Rainbow Go!* Hodder, London and Auckland 1970.
Illingworth, John. *Offshore*. Adlard Coles, London 1949/1963
Irving, John. *King's Britannia, The*. Seeley Service, London 1937.
---- *Yachtsman's Weekend Book, The*. Seeley Service, London 1938.
Jeffery, Timothy. *Champagne Mumm Admiral's Cup*. Bloomsbury, London 1994.
Johnson, Peter. *Channel Handicap (annual) 1989-1997*. Johnson, Lymington 1989-97.
---- *Encyclopedia of Yachting*. Dorling Kindersley, London 1989.
---- *Guinness Book of Yachting Facts and Feats, The*. Guinness Publishing, Enfield 1974.
---- *Ocean Racing and Offshore Yachts*. Nautical, Lymington 1970.
---- *Offshore Manual International*. Nautical Lymington 1977
---- *Whitbread Round the World*. Whitbread, Southampton 1993.
---- *Yachtsman's Guide to the Rating Rule*. Nautical, Lymington 1971.
Kemp, Dixon. *Manual of Yacht and Boat Sailing, A*. The Field, London 1891.
Kenny, Dick. *To Win the Admiral's Cup*. Nautical, Lymington 1974.
Larsen, Paul C. *To the Third Power*. Tilbury House, Gardiner, Maine 1995.
Loomis, Alfred. *Ocean Racing*. Yachting, New York 1935/46.
Lloyd's *Maritime Atlas*. Lloyds Register, London 1989
MacArthur, Robert C. *Room at the Mark*. Yacht Owners' Register, Boston 1991.
Lake Michigan YA. *Handbook 1936*. Lake Michigan YA, Chicago 1936.
Marchaj, C.A. *Sailing Theory and Practice*. Adlard Coles, Southampton 1964.
---- *Seaworthiness the Forgotten Factor*. Adlard Coles, London 1986

Martin, E.G. (and others) *Cruising and Ocean Racing*. Lonsdale Library, Seeley Service, London 1938.

---- *Deep Water Cruising*. Oxford University Press, London 1928

Morris, Everitt B., (and others) *Racing at Sea*. Van Nostrand, New York 1959.

Parkinson, John. *History of the New York Yacht Club, 1844-1973* (2 volumes). NYYC, New York, 1976.

Phillips-Birt, Douglas. *British Ocean Racing*. Adlard Coles, Southampton, 1960.

---- *History of Yachting, The*. Elm Tree Books, London 1974.

---- *Sailing Yacht Design*. Adlard Coles, Southampton 1966.

Plym, Gustav. *Yacht and Sea*. Adlard Coles, London 1961.

Rousmaniere, John. *America's Cup* (to 1983). Pelham Books, London 1984.

---- *Desirable and Undesirable Offshore Yachts (CCA)*. W.W. Norton, New York 1987.

---- *Fastnet Force 10*. Nautical, Lymington and W.W. Norton, New York 1980.

Royal Corinthian Yacht Club. *Designs of Deep Sea Racing Craft (to RORC rule)*. Ernest Day, London 1932.

Sherwood, Richard. *A Field Guide to Sailboats*. Houghton Mifflin, New York 1984.

Stephens, W.P. *American Yachting*. Macmillan, New York 1904.

---- *Seawanhaka Corinthian Yacht Club 1871-1940* (2 volume history). Seawanhaka, Oyster Bay 1941.

---- *Traditions and Memories of American Yachting*. Motor Boating, New York 1942/International Marine Publishing, Camden, Maine 1987.

Sciarelli, Carlo. *Lo Yacht*. Mursia, Milan 1979.

Spedding, Spud. *Sod's History of Yachting*. I am sailing, Plymouth 1996.

Stone, Herbert L. *America's Cup Races, The*. Werner Laurie, New York 1920.

---- and Taylor. *America's Cup Races, The*. Van Nostrand, New York 1958.

Talbot-Booth, E.C. *Yachts, Yachting and Sailing*. Sampson Low, London 1938.

Thornton, A.T. *The Offshore Yacht*. Adlard Coles, London 1984.

Tuchman, Barbara. *March of Folly, The*. Michael Joseph, London 1984

Vaughan, T.J. *International Fourteen Foot Dinghy 1928-1989, The*. International Fourteen Foot Dinghy Class Association of Great Britain, Emsworth 1989.

Viner, Alan. *A History of Rating Rules for Yachts 1854-1931*. National Maritime Museum, London 1979.

Whitaker, H.E. *British and International Yacht Racing Classes*. Ward Lock, London 1954.

Yachtsman, Editor of. *British Yachts and Yachtsmen*. The Yachtsman, London 1907.

Annuals.

1938-39 Yachtsman's Annual and Who's Who. Edited by: K. Adlard Coles. Witherby, London.

1946, 1947 Yachting Year, The. Eric Hiscock. Robert Ross, London.

1948, 1949, 1950-51 Yachtsman's Annual, The. K. Adlard Coles. Robert Ross, London.

1952 to 1971, 1973 Yachting World Annual. E.F. Haylock, Douglas Phillips-Birt, Bernard Hayman. Iliffe, London.

1978 to 1982 World of Yachting. Gerald Asaria, Patrick Teboul. Editions de Messine, Paris.

1987 Sailing Year. Timothy Jeffery. Hazleton, London.

Monthly, fortnightly and weekly periodicals.
(those covering rules of rating and related subjects).

Sail, Boston from January 1970.

Seahorse, London from October 1970.

Yachting, New York from January 1907.

Yachting World, London from 20 April 1894.

Yachts and Yachting, London from January 1947.

Yachtsman, London from 25 April 1891.
(ceased publication 1962)

Acknowledgements

After all these words and pictures, heartfelt thanks are owing to all those whose references are in the numbered notes, whether by their own names or those of their organizations. Much use has been made of extracts from magazines, but particularly from over 100 years of *Yachting World*, so thanks to its present editor, Andrew Bray.

The story of rating would not exist without yacht designers around the world and I am grateful to so many talented designers past and present, drawings of whose racing boats are here, including in more recent years John Corby, Ed Dubois, Bruce Farr, Jean Marie Finot, Rob Humphreys, Sparkman and Stephens, David Thomas, Bill Tripp. A number of institutions featured heavily in these pages. Therefore I wish to thank for both direct help and also meetings, formal and informal, over the years, the International Sailing Federation (ex-IYRU) (especially Simon Forbes), the Junior Offshore Group (Brian Goulder), the Royal Ocean Racing Club (Alan Green, Janet Grosvenor and many members), the Royal Yachting Association (ex-YRA), the Offshore Racing Council (Joan Matthewson and members), the Union Nationale pour la Course au Large (Jean-Louis Fabry), and the United States Sailing Association (John Wright). But I also thank scores of other associations, clubs, members and officials.

To the rating office of the Royal Ocean Racing Club, I give particular thanks for technical cooperation, specifically on rules of rating over a period of many years; among its officers past and present are the late Keith Ludlow, Tony Ashmead, John Moon, John Warren, Mike Urwin and Jenny Howells.

On the editorial side of this work, Carole Abbott trawled through my early print outs, David Pelly polished them and Tim Davison guided the project towards the public. As in many of my previous writings, Ray Harvey has translated my ideas into superb drawings of technical standing and clarity.

Without the unique yachting library of the Cruising Association, London, in its handsome new building, I would have had a near impossible task. Another major source was provided by Mrs Gerald Sambrooke Sturgess, who sold me a selected part of the book collection of her late husband, the famous racing rules expert. The time allowance table and TCF calculation graph (Figs 5.3 and 5.5) are from Sailing Theory and Practice by C.A. Marchaj (Adlard Coles Ltd 1964).

All those sailors who have crewed for me in races or with whom I have crewed under other skippers, I thank for their observations, queries, sometimes bafflement and not infrequently stimulating ideas on varied aspects of speed and rating. What they have said out on the water and back ashore have been important sources in attaining purpose and balance in this book.

Index

Covers preface, introduction, all chapters and captions, but not reference notes,
bibliography, acknowledgements nor letters within reproduced formulae.
YC = Yacht Club; i to xvi refer to photograph pages

Ackers, George H. 20, 126
Admiral's Cup (later Champagne
    Mumm Admiral's Cup, CMAC)
    118, 162, 179, 183 et seq, 203,
    206, 215, 240, 311
Ailsa 52
Alarm i
Allenby, John 230
America schooner 24, 38
American reservations on IOR 189 et
    seq
America's Cup 24, 32 48 et seq, 57
    63, 287, vii; rules of 73
Annapolis 213
Aphrodite 101 class 157
Apriori 238
Arcadia 206
Argenteuil 62
Asta (ocean racer) 132
Astra (23-metre) 77
Atlantic schooner 95
Atlantic YC 41
Australia 105, 168, 182, 184, 192,
    213, 243, 179, xvi
Austria 54, 78, 79, 184
Autissier, Isabelle xvi

Baltic ports 79, 220
Baltic rule 60
Bar Harbor 30 class 69
Barratt, Ray 132; resigns over rule
    changes 117
Base boat system 98, 297
Batthany-Strattman, Count 54
Bavier, Bob 71
Baxter, Mark 199
Belle Époque, explanation of 45
Bembridge Redwing class 150
Benzon, Alfred 60, 63, 77 et seq

Berlin 57, 60
Bermuda race 71, 177, 181, 186, 200,
    206, 311; early 95 et seq
'Big' class of cutters in 1893 47
'Big' class in 1906 84
Bloopers 177, 197
Boat Racing Association (BRA) rule
    84, 105
'Bookstall' (see Heckstall-Smith)
Boston YC 69, 130
Bourke, John 204, 233, 235, 267, v
Britannia 47 et seq, 58, 77, iv
British-American Cup 88, 89, 284,
    vii
Brynhild 84
Builder's Old Measurement (BOM)
    17, 22
Bulb keel (see Fin keel)
Bureau Veritas 81
Burgess, Edward 39
Burgess, W. Starling 74, 92
Burke, Edmund (quoted) 214
Burton, Sir William 90
Buzzard's Bay 30 class 69

Caillebotte, Gustave, and his rule 62
Cal 40 class 103
Calluna 48
Cambria 95
Camper and Nicholsons 153
Canada, yachts from 65, 88, 199,
    227, 278,
Canada Cup 284
Capsizes 35
Caribbean Yachting Association
    (CYA) rule 295
Carter, Dick 121, 168, 202
Cary Smith, A. 36
Cascade 193
Castro, Tony 211

Centre of gravity factor (CGF) 169, 171
Centreboard 322, 44; 'bugs' 33
Cercle de la Voile de Paris 61, 119
Certificate of rating: CHS 257; IMS 225
Cervantes IV 179
CCA rule 98, 100, 101 et seq, 278; gives way to IOR 166 et seq
Chain girth 56, 61
Channel Handicap System (CHS) 137, 205. 233, 316; (chapter largely on) 248; growth of 251, 269; reasons for success 269; replies to criticism of 264; rule changes 260 et seq; TCF compared with IOR 252; and compared with IMS 271
Channel race (of RORC) 118, xii
Chief Measurer IOR 195
Christian Science Monitor (rule policy stated) 89
Cintra vi
Clyde (estuary) 49, 87
Clyde half raters iii
Clyde 20-ton one-design 147
CMAC (*see* Admiral's Cup)
Colonia 48
Columbia 50
Commodores' Cup 235
Common British-US rule: early attempts at 89, 101, 102; in ocean racing 118 et seq; views on imminence of 121
Comparison of 6 rating rules 282; of 15 rules 305
Constitution 50
Contention 33 class 189
Continental mind 119
Corby, John 275
Corsair 22
Corum xv
Cowes 155, 235, vi
Cowes Week regatta 19, 85, 112, 118, 147, 159; and IMS 230
Crane, Clinton 74, 89, 90
Creole 40-rater ii
Crew, rules about 63, 263
Cruising Club of America (CCA) 9, 221; concerns with IOR 198 et seq; stages in forming a rule 96 et seq
Cruising Yacht Club of Australia (CYA) 112, 243
Cubic Contents rule 34, 40
Curtis, Gordon M. Jr 104, 201, 241
Custom House Tonnage 30
Cygnet (Brit) 23
Cygnet (US) 30

Danish Handicap (DH) rule 296, 312
Dare, John 235, 267, 316
Daring class 153, 155
Dauntless 95
Day, Thomas Fleming 311
Decimal Three dinghy 163
Defender 42, 50
Definitions (*not individually indexed*) 12 et seq
Denmark, rating in 60, 77
Depth measurements: beaten by *Myth* 116; cause of error 206; quarter beam in Universal rule 68; repaired in IOR 176
Designers of yachts (*see* under names)
Diamond 27
Dorade 101, 109
Doris 27
Dreyfus affair 196
Dubois, Ed 191, 213, 236
Dun Laoghaire, Ireland, 55, 148
Dunraven, Earl of 38, 42, 48, 57

Eastern YC 9, 59, 88
Edlu 98
Edward I, King 16
Edward VII, King (earlier Prince of Wales) 48, 65, 70, 84, iv
Edwards, David 192, 198 et seq; declines to negotiate with CCA 201; heads rating inquiry 213; last appeal to ORC 230
Eight/8 metre class (*see* International Rule)
Endeavour (I) 75, 111
Endeavour II 67
England (*see* United Kingdom)
Ethelwynn 64
Europe class 153

Fabry, Jean-Louis 250 311
'Fair' 34
Falcon xv
Family tree of major rating rules 175
Farr, Bruce 162, 213, 214, ix
Fastnet race 95, 101, 105, 183 et seq, 215, 217, 314; 1979 fatal storm in 183 et seq
Fay, Sir Michael 292
Fayle, David 118, 121, 168
Fife, William ii, vi
Fifth Avenue Hotel, meeting at 58
Fifty/50ft IOR class 210, xiv
Figaro 123
Fin keels, early 52, 62
Fitzgerald, Hon Edward 38 (quoted)
Firefly class 153

Five/5.5-metre class 146, 153, 154, 290, 291, 307, xvi
Fixed rating (*see* Level rating)
Formula 1 one-design 162
Fortuna 208
Fox, Uffa 164
Foxhound 111
France, rating in 30, 54, 57, 60 et seq, 105, 168, 180, 258
France, Yacht Club de 62, 79
Franklyn, Benjamin 15
Freaks: *Cascade* cat ketch 193; capsizes by 35; *Fortuna* ketch 208; *Trirumph* in Berlin 60; *Warbird* Quarter Tonner 195
Freeboard 33, 52, 80, 195, 213
Froude, R.E., rule of 55, 59, 77

Gaucho 238, xiv
George IV, King 19
George V, King (also as Duke of York, later as Prince of Wales) 58, 65, 77, 84, 85
Germania, captured 85
Germany, rating in 62, 77 et seq, 105, 168, 179, 192, 227; by KR rule 118, 254
Giles, Laurent 109, 111, 112, viii
Giles, Morgan 164
Girth measurements 56, 61, 77, 82, vi; in ocean racers 97
Glover, Major Robin 121, 168, 192, 195, 204
Godinet *formule* (rule) 62
Grand prix rule proposed 234
Gray, Alan 213, 214
Great Lakes 58, 65, 223
Green, E. Alan 247, 267
Guingand, E.P. 'Buster' de 119, 311

Hajo 132
Half Ton Cup (*see* Ton Cups)
Hammond, Jeff 199
Hatcher, Dan i
Hawaii (Kenwood Cup) 217
Hayman, Bernard 171
Heckstall-Smith, Anthony 202
Heckstall-Smith, Major Brooke ('Bookstall') 58 et seq, 63, 77, 90 et seq, 101, iv; compares ratings under successive rules 81; name used in IOR controversy 202; views on ocean racing 78
Heckstall-Smith, Malden 101, 105, 109, 118, 132, 202, 285, 290
Heligoland, race to 63, 106, 132
Herreshoff, L. Francis 74, 166

Herreshoff, Nathanael 42, 46, 50 et seq, 59, 65, 67 et seq, 106, 107; length measurement for CCA 95; rule inventiveness 59
Howth 17 class 150
Hoyt, Sherman 101
Hull length measurement 97
Humphreys, Rob 232

ILC (*see* Level rating)
Illingworth, John 114, 311
Impulse 236
IMX 38 class 144
Independence 50
Inflation of rules 205, 207
International Measurement System (IMS) 128, 137, 205, 223 et seq, 235 et seq, xiv-xvi; age of 221; named 223; time allowances in 241 et seq; use in USA 221, 316; versus IOR 233
International Offshore Rule (IOR) 9, 127, 137, 284, 285, ix-xv; American attitude to 200; (chapter largely on) 166 et seq; end of 217; final form of 205; latter use of 215; mark II 170; mark III 171; mark IIIA 177, 201; page of rule book 174
International Rule 112, 144, iv, v, vi, vii; agreement to split sizes with Universal 90; creation of 78 et seq; formula today 286; loses One Ton Cup to RORC rule 119; seaworthiness noted by Americans 92; versus Universal rule 89
International Sailing Federation (ISAF) 79, 313
International Technical Committee (ITC) 204
International Yacht Racing Union 142; attitude to ocean racing 92; begins 79; 1933 conference 92; 1938 and 1946 conferences 285; creates IYRU cruiser-racer classes 119, 288; requests CCA and RORC to combine rules 119
Ireland (*see* under club, organization, place, rule etc)
Irish chairman of ORC 204
Irish Mist 186
Irish Times 141, 147
Iskareen 93

Jamarella 213
J-class (Universal rule) 69, 72 et seq, 90, viii
Jiminy Cricket ix
Jocasta ix

Johnstone, Robert 203
Jones, Stephen 210
Jones, Theodore A. 197
Josephine 35
Jubilee 48
Judel-Vrolik xvi
Junior Offshore Group (JOG) 219
Justine IV 211

Katrina 41
K-class (Universal rule) 74, 90
Kemp, Dixon 26, 39 et seq, 53, 127, 163, 300
Kershaw, Ken 251
King's Cup i
Knights, Jack 156
Key West regatta 159, 236, 314

Langham Hotel, London (conferences in) 53, 55, iv
Larchmont YC 41
L-class (Universal rule) 69, 90
Length and sail area rules 43 et seq
Leonore plank-on-edge ii
Level rating 80, 311; in IMS 239
Linear rating rules begin 55
Linear rule, second 58
Linear rule, last British 63
Lipton, Sir Thomas, Bt 50, 65, 72 et seq
Lloyds Register of Yachts and its scantling rules 25, 38, 74, 81, 117, 290
Long Island Sound 39, 88, 284, 314; YRA of 67
Louisa 19
Louisiana Crude 206
Ludlow, Keith 204, 213
Lulworth 19

McGruer, James 288, 289
McKeag, Malcolm 233
McNamara, John J., Jr 196
Magic 32
Maid of Malham 111
Maitenes II 109
Mallory, Clifford D. 88
Marblehead, Massachusetts 9, 17, 72
Marshall, John 242
Martin, Commander E.G. 101, 108 et seq
Martyr, Weston 105, 311
Massachusetts Institute of Technology 195, 200, 221, 222
Masts, hollow 82
Maximum number of boats under each rule 273
M-class (Universal rule) 69, 90

Measurement Handicap System (MHS) 201 et seq, 221
Measurement of one-designs 142
Megalopolis 232
Memory 71, 95
Meteor 51
Meteor II 58, 85
Metre boat classes, 23-metre, 15, 12, 8, 7, 6 etc (*see* International Rule)
Michael, James 168, 198
Midget Ocean Racing Club (MORC) rule 297
Milgram, Prof. Jerry 193 et seq, 221, 222
Miranda 32
Model yacht rating rules 300
Modern rating rule, how to run a 308
Mohawk 35
'Motherhood' 221
Moon, John 251
Mount Gay 30 class 301, 303
Mustang Sally 275
Mull, Gary 204, 205
Multihull Offshore Cruising and Racing Association (MOCRA) 297
Mumm 36 class 157, 160, 162
Muran *formule* (rule) 62
Mylne, Alfred 90
Myth of Malham 49, 170, viii; arrival and effect of 114 et seq

Nargie 80
National authority, first British attempt at 26
National 12ft class 153, 300
Nautor Swan rule (NSR) 298
Newman, Prof. Nick 201, 222, 318
Nicholls, George (commodore NYYC) 90
Nicholson, Charles A. 109
Nicholson, Charles E. 73, 74 et seq, 84, 93, 109, 285
New York (city or harbor) 17, 33, 35, 39, 58, 62, 95
New York Yacht Club (NYYC) 9, 30 et seq, 40 et seq, 59, 65, 66 et seq, 79, 88, 89; club cruise 195
New York YC 30 class 69
New York YC 40 class (old) 71; (new) 156
New York YC 50 class 71
New Zealand 105, 177, 182, xiii
Nina 109
Norfolk dinghy 163
North American Yacht Racing Union (NAYRU) 58, 92; formed at last 88; joins IYRU 118; time allowance tables of 129

Noyra 146
Numbers (yacht name) 238
Numbers of yachts existing 9, 78

Ocean Racing Club of America
    (ORCA) 199
Ocean Racing Fleet of Southern
    California 200
Ocean racing ratings 94 et seq
Oddjob 196
Offshore Racing (previously Rating)
    Council 192 et seq, 311, 315, v
Offshore one-design 34 class, 51, xi;
    concept 153 et seq; conference 156
Offshore Rules Co-ordinating
    Committee 119, 311
Off Soundings Club 102
Olympic games 89, 119, 146, 285
One-design classes 65 (chapter
    largely about) 141 et seq; numbers
    of 159
One Ton Cup (for various classes,
    also see Ton Cups) 62, 89, 119,
    180, 216, 284, xi
One Ton rating 61
Oona 28, 30
Open 60 class 302, 304, xvi
Orr-Ewing, J. 62, 63, iii
Ortac 111

Paine, Frank C. 74
Pansy 149
P-class (Universal rule) 69, 70; in
    Great South Bay 72
Pelly, David 238
Pera, Mary 202
Performance Curve Scoring in IMS
    244
Performance Handicap Racing Fleet
    (PHRF) 132, 143, 249, 312, 316,
    317; (chapter largely about) 277 et
    seq; rapid expansion of 203
Perimeter, rule factor in France 61
Peterson, Doug 156, 189
Peytal, Jean 119
Phillips-Birt, Douglas 109, 121
Pilgrim 48
Pitt, William (quoted) 166, 200
Plank-on-edge 27 et seq, 39, 89
Plym, Gustav 121
Port Huron to Mackinac race 243
Portsmouth Yardstick rule 143, 277,
    302
Pratt, Irving 131, 221
PRB (yacht name) xvi
Preece, Andrew 215
Pregnant cow: of RORC rule 170; of
    IOR 186
Prelude 112

Promotion xiv
Propaganda xiii
Propeller rating 104, 171, 280
Pursuit race 139

Q-class (Universal rule) 69, 70
Quarter Ton Cup (*see* Ton Cups)
Quiller-Couch, Sir Arthur (quoted)

Ragamuffin 179
Rainbow 75
Ranger 67, 75
Raters, 10, 5, 2½ etc 20, 40, 52, 56;
    still existing 150
Rating rule aspects: beating/cheating
    of 23, 67; complications of 65;
    using displacement 33
R-class (Universal rule) 69, 89, 98;
    lines of 91
Reliance 50, 63, iv
Restricted classes 162, 300
Resolute 67, 73
Richard II, King 16
Rigs: Bermudian just arrived on 6-
    metre 87; gaff v. Bermudian 74,
    109; in CHS 255; in IOR 172; in
    PHRF 280; measurement in IMS
    225; ocean racing rules for 117;
    weakness of in J-class 75
Roome, John 203
Royal Corinthian YC 1932 design
    competition 109, 111
Royal Cruising Club 96
Royal Irish YC 72
Royal London YC 24
Royal Naval Sailing Association 139,
    182 (*see* also Whitbread)
Royal Ocean Racing Club (RORC)
    98, 104 et seq, 132, 199, 219, 235;
    efforts to promote IMS 264 et
    seq; expansion of 111; IOR 90
    proposal 230; new club house
    after bombing 111; successive
    time allowances of 134; 1996 looks
    into possible new rating rule 316
Royal Western YC 106
Royal Victoria YC 26
Royal Yacht Squadron 19, 20 et seq,
    89, 203
Royal Yachting Association (RYA)
    168, 251, 298
Royal Yorkshire YC offshore one-
    design class 156
RORC Rating Secretary (or Director
    of Rating) 248; Ashmead on IMS
    239; Fayle appointed 118; resigns
    117

RORC rule 105, 106 et seq, viii, ix; 1968 view of 117; gives way to IOR 166 et seq; wide adoption 111

RORC/RYA Sports Boat rule (SBR) 298; compared to CHS 299

Rudder, The 95, 311

Rule beaters and cheaters (*see* Freaks)

Rumours (yacht name) 243

S&S 34 class 275

Safir class 153

Sail area: old arguments on 59

Sakuntala iii

San Diego, California 204

Satanita and fatal collision 48

Satquote British Defender 209

Savary, Peter de 213

Sayrona 243

'Scandals' in rating 206

Scandicap rule 297

Scandinavian Gold Cup 89

Scandinavia, rating in 7, 30, 61, 62, 77 et seq, 83, 86, 118, 168, 192, 285

S-class (Universal rule) 69

Schimdt, Rolf 119

Seabird Half-Rater class 150

Seawanhaka Corinthian YC 34, 39, 64, 65,88; time allowances of 127

Seawanhaka Cup 43

Seawanhaka Gold Cup (distinct) 89

Seawanhaka rule 40 et seq, 61; end of 63; good English opinion of 54; other rules based upon 98, 105, 205, 290, 291

Secrecy in rating rules 252

Shakespeare, William (quoted from) 66, 123, 214

Shamrock II 62

Shamrock IV 67, 73

Shamrock V 74

Sigma 33 offshore one-design class 144, 157

Sigma 38 offshore one-design class 157

Sironi, Nicola 204, v

SJ 35 class 210

Skimming dish 44 et seq, 57

Skin girth 56, 61

Snaith, William 123, 130

Solent One-Design class 55, 149, ii

Somerset, Robert 248

Soper, J.M. 45, 47

Sopwith, T.O.M. (later Sir Thomas) 75

South African war 62

South America, CCA rule in 102, 105

South Coast one-design class 156

Southampton University 201

Southern California, yachts in 279

Southern Ocean Racing Conference (SORC) 180, 206, 234, 259

Southern Cross Cup 177, 183

Sparkman & Stephens 179

Spi-Ouest regatta 159

Sports Boat rule 298

Star class 144

Starflash 191

Stephens, Olin J., II 75, 76, 93, 101, 109, 121, 311, v; and IOR 168, 199; becomes chairman ITC 121; backs IMS v. IOR 230; comment on IMS time allowances 242; defends IOR 191; involvement in MHS 201

Stephens, Rod 75

Stephens, W.P. 16

St Francis YC 176

Stock market crashes 74, 91

Stone, Herbert L. 95

Storm Trysail Club rule 102, 200, 240, 297

Stormy Weather 109

Svenska Havskryssar rule 118

Sydney to Hobart race 112, 182, 213, 243

Sylvie schooner 24

Szechwan 213

Telegraph, The Daily 202

Ten/10-metre class, batch built for US owners 92

Tenacious 185

Thirty/30-square metre class 118, 285

Thistle 51

Thomas, David 157

Thower, Gordon 195

Three Quarter Ton Cup (*see* Ton Cups)

Time allowances: (chapter about) 123 et seq; changes in 215; defect of 124; earliest 19, 125; first TCF with IOR 170; for Universal rule 69; four sources of 124; in Bermuda race 96 et seq 104; in CHS 256; in IMS 241 et seq; in International rule 83; NAYRU tables of 129; on IMS certificate 225; schemes for multiple TCF invented 133

Time-on-distance 131 et seq

Time-on-time 132 et seq; in CYA rule 296; in IMS 244; in SBR 299

Tomahawk 93
Ton Cups 2, 1, $\frac{1}{2}$, $\frac{1}{4}$ etc 180, 195, 217, 270, xiii
Tonnage rules 15 et seq; collapse of 28; Custom House 30; displacement 31; Thames 24 et seq
Tornado class 153
Transatlantic races 95
Trenchmer 111
Tripp, Bill 231, xv
Tripp 36 IMS design 231, 279
Trirumph (freak) 60
Tuchman, Barbara 7, 8, 214 (quoted)
Tuns (*see* tonnage)
Turner, Ted 185
Twelve/12-metre class (*see* International rule)
Twenty-three/23-metre class (International rule) 84
Two Ton Cup (*see* Ton Cups)

Union des Yachts Français (UYF) 57
Union Nationale pour la Course au Large (UNCL) 159, 205, 249
Universal rule 67 et seq, 89, 111, 144, viii; agreement to split classes with International rule 90; among ocean racers 95; declared 'dead' 92; other rules based upon 100, 105, 106, 205, 290, 291
United Kingdom (*see* under club, organization, place, rule etc)
United States of America (*see* under club, organization, place, rule etc)
United States Sailing Association (USSA or USS) 312
United States Yacht Racing Union (USYRU): objectives with MHS 221; takes over from NAYRU 199

Valkyrie II 48
Valkyrie III 42, 57
Vanessa i
Van de Stadt, E.G. 121, 168
Vanderbilt, Cornelius 73
Vanderbilt, Harold 75, 93; right-of-way rules of 118
Vaughan, T.J. 163
Velocity Prediction program (VPP) 222, 240
Velsheda 75
Vendée Globe race 302
Venetta 57

Victoria, Queen, death of 62
Victory of Burnham 206, xii
Vigilant 48
Vim 93

Wai-Aniwa and blooper 177, x
Warbird 195, x
Watson, George L. 15, 23, 46, 58
Wales, Prince of (later Edward VII, which *see*) 48
Wales, Prince of (later George V, which *see*)
Water Wag one-design class 55, 147
Weetamoe 74
Wee Win $\frac{1}{2}$ rater 52, ii
Weight in CHS 259
Weller, Kenneth B. v; appointed to ORC 204; appointed to USYRU 199; starts work on MHS 202
Wenohah 52
Whirlwind 74
Whitbread round the world race 39, 182, 209, 311
Whitbread 60 restricted class 162, 301, 317
White Heather 84
Wilhelm II, Kaiser (Emperor) of Germany 51, 57, 63, 65, 85, iv
William III, King 16
William IV, King 18
Williams, Lynn 198 et seq
Williwaw 206
'Wings' on hulls 195
WWI (World War I) 71, 85, 94, 112, 149, 163, 286
WWII (World War II) 93, 105, 111, 118

X class one-design 7

Yacht Racing Association (British YRA) 26 et seq, 39, 43 et seq, 55, 58, 59, 77, 138; new Secretary 58; rule castigated 58; tries to return to handicapping 112
Yacht Racing Association (YRA) of Long Island Sound 67
Yachting World 127, 168; begins 45; H35 class 277
Yankee 74
Yorkshire One-Design class 150

Zeearend 111